The Design of Social Research

The Design of Social Research

BY RUSSELL L. ACKOFF

THE UNIVERSITY OF CHICAGO PRESS

CHICAGO & LONDON

H
62
.A4

International Standard Book Number: 0–266–00255–1
Library of Congress Catalog Card Number: 53–12546

The University of Chicago Press, Chicago 60637
The University of Chicago Press, Ltd., London

To Alec

whose tolerance and typing made this possible

Preface

This book will hardly make easy or relaxing reading. This is due in part to the imperfections of style, but to a large extent it is due to the technical nature of the work. The social sciences are out of their infancy; hence books dealing with these sciences are no longer necessarily restricted to either journalistic or philosophical speculation or to the reorganization of familiar social facts.

An important step in the maturation of a science is the development of its research techniques and methods. The social sciences are already well advanced technically, but they are not so well advanced methodologically. This uneven development is due (in part) to a failure to distinguish between research techniques and methods. Since there is no generally accepted formulation of this distinction, I take the liberty of offering one. Techniques refer to the behavior and instruments used in performing research operations; for example, making observations, recording data, treating the data, etc. Methods, on the other hand, refer to behavior and instruments used in selecting and constructing research techniques. Thus methods are more general than techniques and lie behind them.

In the past the study of research methods, in the sense defined above, has taken place primarily in the realm of the philosophy of science. In this realm the approach has been speculative, reflective, and (in some cases) crudely empirical. Recently, however, research methods have themselves been subjected to scientific study. As a result, a new area of science has emerged, *methodology*.

In this book I have made an effort to provide *a* (not *the*) methodology of social research. That is, I have tried to raise to consciousness each type of decision that can arise in the course of research and to suggest methods by which these decisions can be made and criteria by which these decisions can be evaluated. Wherever possible, the methods and criteria suggested are based on methodological research; where not, they are so formulated that they are susceptible to scientific evaluation. My hope is that social researchers will make such evaluations and improve on the procedures and criteria suggested.

Like many authors, I feel that this work is unfinished as it goes to press. I have found that, with each of the reworkings through which it has gone, major as well as minor modifications were necessary. I have no doubt that another revision would result in further major modifications. But I have learned that the most constructive modifications have been based on the criticism and suggestions which have come from others who have read the manuscript and particularly from those who have tried out the methods suggested. I feel now that it is time to enlarge the group which can provoke further changes, and this can best be done by publication. I hope some social researchers, professionals and students, will accept the invitation to make suggestions for further changes and revisions. More important, I hope they will make efforts of their own to advance the methodology of social research and will offer the results of their efforts in print.

Since this book is a difficult one, it may help the reader to have the following outline of the book's organization:

    I. Introduction (chap. i)
   II. Formulating the Problem (chap. ii)
  III. The Idealized Research Design (chap. iii)
  IV. The Practical Research Design
        A. Statistical Phase (chaps. iv, v, vi, vii, and viii)
        B. Observational Phase (chap. ix)
        C. Operational Phase (chap. x)

References are made in the body of the text. In general, they are inclosed in parentheses; e.g., "(4:15)." When they are already included within a parenthetical remark, they are inclosed in brackets; e.g., "[7:xiv]." In either case the number to the left of the colon refers to the book so numbered in the "References and Bibliography" given at the end of the chapter. The numbers after the colon are page references when Arabic and chapter references when Roman. The figures and tables in the body of the text are designated by Arabic numerals; those in Appendix V, by Roman numerals.

At the end of each chapter are "Discussion Topics," "Exercises," and "Suggested Readings." These are designed to facilitate use of the book in the classroom. I would like to suggest that the "Exercises" be done by teams of students working together. This will give students practice in doing research co-operatively, as they will eventually have to do it. It will also be helpful (but not necessary) to students if computing machines can be made available to them for the exercises at the end of chapters vi, vii, and viii.

Many of the examples and problems used in the statistical sections are fictitious; they were deliberately constructed to simplify the mathematics. The figures used in these examples should not be interpreted or used as social data.

Appendix III provides a list of definitions of the more commonly used mathematical and statistical symbols.

This book is not the work of one author; no book ever is. Many others were involved in its preparation. Most of the thinking that went into this work is a result of extended and intensive co-operation with Professor C. West Churchman. It is accidental rather than essential that I have performed the mechanics involved in putting our thought into book form. But even in this respect his contribution has been considerable.

Leon Pritzker, of the United States Bureau of the Census, has stirred the manuscript since its inception. He has been able to raise problems more quickly than I have been able to solve them. Fortunately, I was successful in persuading him to help answer some of his own questions. His influence is pervasive, but in particular he has co-authored the last chapter.

That I undertook this work in the first place is due to a large extent to the exciting period I spent at the Bureau of the Census. It was a privilege to work with and learn from such people as Morris H. Hansen, William N. Hurwitz, Joseph F. Daly, Benjamin J. Tepping, Harold Nisselson, Eli S. Marks, and W. Parker Mauldin. My contacts during this period with W. Edwards Deming were equally stimulating. I am also indebted to Max Bershad of the Bureau for his help on the chapter dealing with sampling. I alone am responsible, however, for any errors this chapter may contain.

Many others have been very kind in giving their time and talents to the work. I should like to single out Harvey V. Roberts, Martin J. Klein, Chester Topp, Fred Leone, and Thomas Baker, all of whom critically reviewed part or all of the manuscript at various stages of its development. To the many students whose creative imagination and keen critical abilities provided the background against which the writing was done, I am greatly indebted; in particular, to J. S. Minas and James Bates.

Finally, I am indebted to the following publishers, publications, and persons for permission to use material from their publications: The American Marketing Association (*Journal of Marketing*); American Psychological Association, Inc. (*Psychological Review*); The American Public Health Association (*American Journal of Public Health*); American Sociological Society (*American Sociological Review*); American Statistical Association (*Journal of the American Statistical Association*); *The Annals of Mathematical Statistics* and C. Eisenhart, F. Swed, C. O. Ferris, F. E. Grubbs, and C. L. Weaver; *Biometrika;* Columbia University Press; Mrs. Earle E. Eubank; The Free Press; Charles Griffin & Co., Ltd.; Harper & Brothers; Harvard University Press; Henry Holt and Company, Inc.; Houghton Mifflin Company; McGraw-Hill Book Company, Inc.; The Macmillan Company; Professor R. A. Fisher, Cambridge, and to Messrs. Oliver and Boyd, Ltd., Edinburgh (for permission to reprint Tables V and VIII from their book, *Statistical Methods for Research Workers*); Philosophical Library, Inc.;

Princeton University Press; *Public Opinion Quarterly;* Rinehart and Company, Inc.; Royal Statistical Society (*Journal of the Royal Statistical Society*); Routledge and Kegan Paul, Ltd.; The University of Chicago Press; The University of North Carolina Press; University of Pennsylvania Press; Warwick and York, Inc. (*Journal of Educational Psychology*); and John Wiley & Sons, Inc.

R. L. A.

CLEVELAND, OHIO
March 16, 1953

Table of Contents

CHAPTER I

The Meaning of Methodologically Designed
Research and Experiments

1. Introduction

Not too long ago (less than one hundred years) scientists and philosophers argued that a science of mind and society was impossible or at least that an experimental science of mind and society was impossible. They claimed that the human mind and society were inherently incapable of being subjected to scientific and especially experimental inquiry. But the history of science has repeatedly demonstrated that an area which one age takes to be incapable of scientific treatment is treated scientifically by a succeeding age. There are still philosophers who echo the past and claim that mind and society, or at least important aspects of them, are incapable of being scientifically investigated. But the psychologist and social scientist go right ahead and scientifically inquire into mind and society despite the philosopher. To those who assert that a science of mind and society is inconceivable, we can address the question (as did Lewis Carroll in a similar situation): "Have you tried it?"

Scientific inquiry into mind and society can be conducted both badly and well. Here we want to find out how to conduct it in the best way we can. Our purpose is neither to summarize current practices nor to consider what most scientists actually do. Many such summaries are already available. Our purpose is rather to show how the best possible investigation can be conducted in the social sciences by using the latest developments in scientific method. In effect, we want to make explicit how research *should* be conducted, not necessarily how it is conducted. In actual practice the social scientist may find it impossible to meet all the conditions we will set down; but there is a great advantage to his knowing where he falls short of the optimum procedure. Only when a scientist is aware of these shortcomings (whether imposed from without or within) can he efficiently improve his methods.

Since our primary concern in this book is with *methodologically designed experiments* and *research*, we should begin by clarifying the meaning of "experiment," "research," "design," and "methodology." Clarifying the meaning of these concepts will not only provide a "preview of coming attractions" but is essential for an understanding of *why* research should be methodologically designed.

2. The Meaning of "Experiment" and "Research"

First, let us consider the meaning of "experiment." We begin by making some rather obvious but important observations: (1) experimentation is an activity, and (2) it is the kind of activity we call "inquiry." Not all inquiries, however, are experiments; but all experiments are inquiries. What we must do, then, is determine what differentiates experiments from other types of inquiries. To facilitate this discussion, let us give nonexperimental inquiry a name; let us call it "common-sense inquiry." Common-sense inquiry is that kind of inquiry we conduct every day with respect to both important and trivial issues. We set out to determine how best to get from home to work, where to store articles of clothing, how to invest savings, etc. Such inquiries are generally nonexperimental. To convert common sense into science, we must know what makes an inquiry scientific and what turns an experience into an experiment.

Experimental inquiry has historically been distinguished from common-sense inquiry in two different ways: on the basis of (1) what problems are investigated, that is, *subject matter;* and (2) how problems are investigated, that is, *method.*

It is sometimes said that experimentation deals with less immediate or less practical problems than does common sense; that is, science and experimentation are said to be concerned only with long-run problems. But a moment's reflection will show that this assertion does not conform to the facts. Science continually deals with all kinds of problems of immediate and practical importance; it tells us how to cure a disease, how to build a bridge, how to improve a crop, etc. We also realize that common sense very frequently inquires into long-run problems of a very general nature. Historic inquiries into ethical and philosophical problems, for example, have used common sense rather than experimentation. One of the characteristics of our age is the prevalent conviction that any problem which can be fruitfully investigated by nonscientific means is at least potentially capable of being more fruitfully investigated by scientific means.

It seems advisable to look for the difference between common sense and experimental inquiry in method rather than in subject matter. Once we decide to look in this direction, common sense itself provides a clue to this difference: it asserts that experimentation is *controlled* inquiry. This does not tell us what the difference between common sense and experimental inquiry is, but it does give the difference a name and indicates where to look for an explanation of this difference. Let us use an analogy to start us on our way.

We say that some instructors "control" their classes and that others do not. What is meant by this distinction? The instructor who does not control his class cannot do with it what he wants. To have something under control is to be able to *direct* it in a *desired* direction. If the class can lead the instructor where it wills, then it has him under control. Now it is seldom, if ever, that an instructor has a class under either absolutely complete or incomplete control. That is, it seems as though control can be represented by a scale, and instructors can be said to vary in the amount of control they have over their classes.

What does this mean when applied to our problem? If experiment is controlled inquiry, it is inquiry in which the scientist directs events so that they move toward his desired objective—the solution of a problem. A person whose actions are completely determined from without cannot control his experience and hence cannot experiment. Freedom of choice is necessary to control and hence to experimentation.

What does it mean to say that experience is directed toward a desired objective? It means that the activity engaged in is *efficient* relative to that objective. Controlled inquiry is efficient inquiry. Thus experimentation is a more efficient way of inquiring than is common sense. This does not mean that common sense cannot find solutions to problems; it does mean that it is not so likely to do so as experimentation is.

Common sense and experimental inquiry represent ranges along the scale of efficiency in conducting inquiry. It is difficult to say at what precise point on the scale we pass from common sense to experimentation; in fact, the problem should not even be posed this way. It is better to recognize that all inquiry involves some common sense and some experimentation. Our goal in science is to rely more and more on experiment and less and less on common sense.

Control, though necessary, is not sufficient to distinguish *scientific* experimentation from common-sense inquiry. As we indicated, to control is to direct, and we must consider what an experiment is directed toward before we can call it scientific. At one time science was taken to have the function of "finding more efficient means for pursuing any end." From this point of view it follows that science could inquire into more and more efficient ways of destroying (as well as preserving) civilization. Science was said to be completely "impartial." But a contradiction in this definition of science has become apparent, and it requires a revision of our notions of what objectives science can serve. The contradiction is this: according to this conception of science, a scientist could deliberately try to determine how to destroy science itself. For example, he could attempt to determine how to fashion a society in which all scientific activity would be prohibited. Now such activity is clearly antiscientific. Even if we call such activity "experimentation," it is certainly not "scientific experimentation." We would say of such an effort that it employs scientific means in order to obtain nonscientific objectives.

Science is an ongoing historical institution which pursues a long-run objective, an *ideal*. Science's ideal is to provide more efficient means not only now but in the future as well. Hence its objective is to produce *continuously* more and more efficient means, to increase our knowledge *without limit*. It never expects to attain perfect knowledge, but it seeks to pursue this ideal without end.

The term "experiment" is sometimes used in a more restricted sense than we have used it here. The restriction is to inquiry conducted in situations in which the objects and events involved can be deliberately manipulated by the investigator; that is, where the investigator can intervene to influence the events to be observed. Many of those who make this restriction mistakenly assume that manipulation is the only method of control, but this is not so. The astronomer cannot manipulate stars and planets, but he can conduct controlled inquiries into their movements and relationships. Though he cannot manipulate the variables, he can *know* their values, and this knowledge enables him to use the results of his inquiries efficiently in pursuing his objectives. Similarly, the social scientist may not be able to manipulate the group of people he studies, but, if he can determine what the important properties of the group are, he can investigate the group in a controlled manner.

There is a historic reason why manipulation is sometimes identified with control. At one time the methods of mathematical and statistical analysis used in science could handle only two changing variables at one time. Consequently, the physical sciences (which were the only sciences at the time) developed a concept of the "ideal" experiment—one in which all variables are supposed to be held constant except two. One of these, called the "independent" variable, is manipulated so that it takes on various values desired by the experimenter. Observations are then made on how the other "dependent" variable changes. The environment in which such manipulation is carried out is called a "laboratory." But today—as we shall see in some detail in later chapters—the dependence of a variable on any number of independent variables can be determined by using modern statistical analysis. Consequently, though manipulation was once necessary to reduce the number of changing variables to the two which could be dealt with mathematically, it no longer is. The development of methods of "multivariate analysis" has removed the necessity of manipulation and the laboratory, and it permits the scientist to go out into the world and tackle increasingly complex problems in their natural habitat.

Though control is not synonymous with manipulation, some scientists consider it useful to make a distinction between the general class of controlled inquiries and the special class of inquiries in which control is obtained by manipulation. The general class they call "research"; the special class they call "experimentation." This practice has had the unfortunate consequence of giving non-manipulative inquiry a lower status than manipulative inquiry. It would be preferable to call all controlled inquiry "experimentation." Then the emphasis would not be on manipulation but on control, where it belongs. But, in order to avoid doing too much violence to scientific usage, we shall employ the term "research" to designate the general class of controlled inquiries. Our concern, henceforth, will be with methodologically designed research.

3. The Meaning of "Design"

The problem we want to consider now is how the various phases of inquiry can be brought under control. It can be done by *designing* the research. Again let us approach the meaning of "design" by analogy. We say an architect "designs" a building; for example, a house. In designing a house, the architect considers each decision that will have to be made in constructing the building. He decides how large it will be, how many rooms it will have, what materials will be used, etc. He does all this *before* the actual construction begins. He proceeds in this way because he wants a picture of the whole before starting construction of any part. By means of this "picture" he can correct mistakes and make improvements before construction starts. To design is to plan; that is, design is the process of making decisions before the situation arises in which the decision has to be carried out. It is a process of deliberate anticipation directed toward bringing an expected situation under control.

The application of these remarks to research is obvious. If, before we conduct an inquiry, we anticipate each research problem and decide what to do beforehand, then we increase our chances for controlling the research procedure.

The architect cannot hold all his decisions in his head. Even if he could, he would have difficulty in seeing how they are all interrelated. Consequently, he records his decisions by using symbols in drawings, specifications, etc.; that is, he records and interrelates his decisions in either a verbal, graphic, or sculptural *model*. An architectural model is a symbolic representation of all the decisions made in designing a building—a representation which shows the interrelationships between all the decisions which have been made. Thus the model makes possible an over-all evaluation of the over-all plan.

Similarly, in science, the designer can record, by use of symbols, the various research decisions he has made. Such a symbolic construction, composed of concepts and images, is called the "research" or "experimental" model.

4. The Meaning of "Methodological"

It is one thing to make a decision beforehand and another to evaluate the basis for making that decision. We make numerous decisions without knowing how good the grounds are on which they are based. In these cases we either are not conscious of or do not intend to investigate the *method* by which the decisions are reached. In so far as we investigate or make investigatable the method of making design decisions, we are methodologically designing that research.

Whereas design *exposes* research decisions to evaluation before they are carried out, methodology actually makes the evaluation and exposes the method used in arriving at these design decisions so that it too can be evaluated beforehand. The better the method, the better the resulting decisions are likely to be.

No inquiry is ever completely methodological or completely unmethodological. Inquiries vary between these extremes. Even common-sense inquiry may have some degree of methodological self-consciousness. A completely methodological design is another scientific ideal which we can never attain but which we may constantly approach.

Summarizing, then, research is methodologically designed (*a*) to the extent to which it is planned and evaluated beforehand and (*b*) to the extent to which the method for making research decisions is evaluated or is made susceptible to evaluation. The symbolic representation of this design is the research model.

5. Why We Should Methodologically Design Research

Expositions on the nature of scientific inquiry usually emphasize the primacy of observations in scientific method. The emphasis is frequently accomplished by asserting that observations "come first" and that the data are then classified and subsequently analyzed. Such a description of the method of science is deceptive because we cannot make observations before deciding what, when, where, how, and why to observe. Making observations can never be a completely unplanned process, though it may be unconsciously planned. It is highly desirable to raise this planning to consciousness so that it can be evaluated before observations are made.

There is considerable variation in the amount of planning or design engaged in by different researchers. We are urged by some to get to observations as quickly as possible and to keep to a minimum of preobservational design. We are told that a plan for analysis of the data can be developed after they are collected, when we can see "what the data are like." The advocates of "minimum design" feel that the time required to design research is not well spent. They argue something like this: "The extensive design of research is costly and time-consuming. The accuracy required for most research can be obtained without going through all the rigmarole of constructing methodologically designed research models." This argument may be true for some emergency situations, but it certainly is not true for the vast majority of research situations. The argument fails to consider several very important points.

1. In many inquiries the researcher does not know how accurate his results ought to be in order to be useful. Where this is the case, he has to determine how much inaccuracy can be tolerated. In many cases he may not even know how much inaccuracy his method of research will produce. In either of these cases he should design his research if he wants to assure himself of useful results. Design is insurance against failure; it is economical in the long run because it is less likely to result in fruitless inquiry.

A scientist gets into trouble not only when he fails to obtain results which are accurate enough but also when he gets "too accurate" results. In some cases the required accuracy can be obtained with little trouble; greater accuracy can be obtained only with difficulty. If the scientist works for the greater accuracy, then he is wasting time, effort, and research funds.

2. In many research projects the time consumed in trying to find out what the data mean after they have been collected is much greater than the time required to design an inquiry which yields data the meaning of which is known when collected. Present research suffers a great deal from a lust for "fresh" data; researchers rush off to collect data and postpone worrying about what the data mean until they are collected, when it is usually too late to improve them. It is true that in some cases the delay produced by research planning may result in obtaining "stale" data. But the failure to plan research may produce more inaccuracy than would a designed research project run later. For example, suppose we rush to make observations before we have developed adequate instruments (e.g., tests or questionnaires). The error produced by our inferior instruments may be greater than the inaccuracy we would have obtained had we waited to develop better instruments and allowed our data to get a bit stale.

3. This third point is less "practical" than the preceding two, but it is probably more important. As we indicated earlier, a scientist has certain obligations to science (and hence to society); his right to the title "scientist" rests in part on his ability to develop better and better ways of inquiring. This is true of all the sciences, but it is particularly true of the social sciences today. The hope for *any* future for society and for science, let alone a progressive one, may well depend on the extent to which the social scientists demonstrate how important social problems can be effectively solved in a peaceful and scientific way.

The scientist must never be content with his methods; if he is, he is no longer a scientist. As a scientist, he is obliged to question every phase of his method and to open up the possibility of continuous improvement. We cannot wait for a lucky discovery to improve our methods; we must improve them systematically and take what luck has to offer as a bonus.

6. The Meaning of "Inquiry"

Many fruitful analyses of the process of inquiry have been made and are still being made. Our understanding of inquiry is ever expanding. Not only is such understanding important to scientists who want to conduct their research more efficiently but it is particularly important to the social scientist who wishes to study social inquiry as a cultural phenomenon. Those who have analyzed inquiry from the point of view of science in general have tended to conceptualize inquiry as a *problem-solving* process. Social scientists have been interested in the process from the point of view of interactions between individuals and environments; that is, they have tended to conceptualize inquiry as a *communicative* process. Both approaches have been very fruitful, and they become even more so when they are combined.

A simplified diagrammatic model of the process of inquiry can be constructed, one which shows both the problem-solving and the communicative phases (see Fig. 1).

First let us consider the communicative aspects of this model. There are four communicants: (1) the consumer(s); (2) the scientist(s); (3) the observer(s); and (4) the observed. These do not necessarily represent four distinct individuals; they represent communicative *roles*. Several or all of the roles may be filled by a single person. For example, the scientist is frequently his own observer; he may also be the research consumer. On the other hand, each role may be filled by a social group. For example, a governing body of a civic group may sponsor research by a large agency into some aspect of a city's entire population. The important thing to note is that regardless of the number of people involved, whether one or one million, these communicative roles are present in every inquiry.

The communicative operations are (1) transmission of the problem; (2) training and supervision of observers; (3) stimulation of the observed; (4) response of the observed; (5) recording and transmitting of responses; and (6) reporting on the recommended solution to the problem. In social research the "observed" are usually animate communicative beings and are referred to as subjects or respondents. In some social research the observers need produce no stimulation; they need only observe the subjects' responses to existing stimuli. This is the case, for example, where "participant" or "mass" observational techniques are used. In these cases the observer's identity is unknown to the subjects, who are observed under "natural" circumstances.

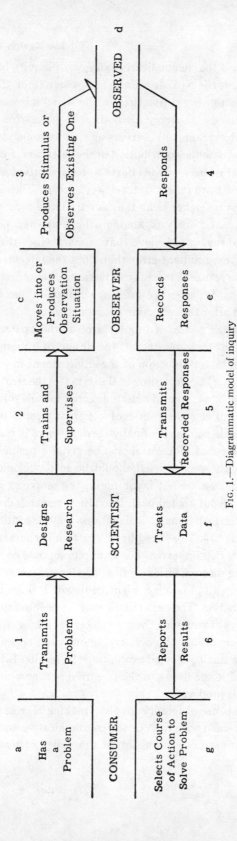

Fig. 1.—Diagrammatic model of inquiry

CONSUMER	SCIENTIST		OBSERVER		OBSERVED

a — Has a Problem

1 — Transmits Problem

b — Designs Research

2 — Trains and Supervises

c — Moves into or Produces Observation Situation

3 — Produces Stimulus or Observes Existing One

d — OBSERVED

4 — Responds

e — Records Responses

5 — Transmits Recorded Responses

f — Treats Data

6 — Reports Results

g — Selects Course of Action to Solve Problem

The formulation of the communicative aspects of inquiry has one very useful purpose: it points out the possible sources of research error. This has particular significance relative to present practices in the social sciences where many research projects make use of survey methods. The survey frequently requires a large number of interviewers or observers as well as respondents. The present tendency is to emphasize the contribution of the interviewer to the error arising in the inquiry. That is, most of the efforts to reduce survey errors are directed toward reducing what are called "interviewer" errors. The communicative interpretation of inquiry makes clear the fact that the consumer, research designers, respondents, and analysts, among others, are also possible sources of error. There is good reason to believe that in many cases these communicants contribute more to the resultant error than does the interviewer.

It is important to realize that error can be carried *into* observations as well as arise in observations. We shall see later how various types of error can arise before, during, and after the collection of data.

The problem-solving phases of inquiry are (*a*) the existence of a problem; (*b*) the formulation of the problem and the design of a method for solving it; (*c*) the movement into or production of the environment in which the observations are to be made; (*d*) the recording of the data; (*e*) the treatment of the data; and (*f*) the selection of a course of action directed toward solving the problem. In many research projects the course of action suggested by the research is tested on a small scale before it is finally used. If there is reason to doubt the adequacy of the proposed solution, it will be given a preliminary tryout in a small-scale *pretest*. The pretest itself should be methodologically designed. If the results of the pretest are not favorable to the proposed solution, the data obtained from this tryout are fed back into a new research design, and another circuit of the research loop is made. This process may be continued until a satisfactory solution is found. This "feed-back" pattern is characteristic of what is commonly called "action" research. For example, suppose one is faced with the problem of reducing discrimination against a religious group in a certain community. The first circuit of inquiry might be devoted to finding out what produces this discrimination. The next circuit may be devoted to finding out what are the possible ways of removing these producers and how efficient the alternatives are. Another circuit may involve trying out what appears to be the most efficient action on a small scale and evaluating the results. If the results are not so good as expected, these data can then be used in a new circuit, etc., until a satisfactory result is produced.

Since the design phase of inquiry involves making all research decisions beforehand, it is concerned with each of the communicative and problem-solving phases. Consequently, in our discussion of the design of research, each phase will be considered in turn. These phases can be conveniently grouped under three major headings: (1) the formulation of the problem; (2) the idealized research design; and (3) the practical research design.

The formulation of the problem is concerned with specifying exactly what the research problem is. The idealized research design is concerned with specifying the optimum research procedure that could be followed were there no practical restrictions. The practical research design deals with the translation of the idealized design into a realizable working procedure. The practical design will itself be considered in four phases: (1) the sampling design, which deals with the method of selecting the subjects to be observed; (2) the statistical design, which deals with how many are to be observed and how the observations are to be analyzed; (3) the observational design, which deals with the conditions under which the observations are to be made; and (4) the operational design, which deals with the specific techniques by which the procedures specified in the sampling, statistical, and observational designs can be carried out.

None of these designs and their resultant models is independent; a decision in any phase of the design may affect a decision in any other phase. Consequently, the design phases generally overlap. Unfortunately, they cannot be presented in an overlapping way. Here we shall consider the design phases in the order in which they are listed above. This order is convenient for exposition, and it is also an efficient order to follow in designing most research projects.

Before we turn to a detailed study of the design phases, several warnings should be given. We are going to study one particular design procedure in great detail. This is *not* the only possible design procedure. This particular design procedure is one which has proved fruitful in the past but is still subject to considerable improvement. The study of scientific method is itself a new and expanding science. Its results must also be subject to the scientific demand for continuous improvement. This caution does not mean, however, that a researcher should take the liberty of changing the design procedure on the basis of a hunch or even common sense. The advantage of this procedure lies in the fact that it is more explicitly formulated than are its alternatives. Departures from it should be based only on controlled inquiry.

DISCUSSION TOPICS

1. What would constitute a *proof* that a certain subject matter (say, "mind" or "culture") could *not* be investigated scientifically?

2. Is the following assertion true? "Common sense of today is the science of yesterday."

3. Are there any common-sense examples of control without manipulation?

4. What is the difference between a scientific method and a scientific technique?

5. In what respects do you think the following quotations are correct or incorrect?

"Science we shall define as a series of concepts or conceptual schemes arising out of experiment and new observations" (6:4).

"Scientific method, although in its more refined forms it may seem complicated, is in essence remarkably simple. It consists in observing such facts as will enable the observer to discover general laws governing facts of the kind in question. The two stages, first of observation, and second of inference to law, are both essential, and each is susceptible of almost indefinite refinement" (13:13).

"Whenever one has a choice of alternative ways of trying to solve a problem, decides on one, and then says in essence 'let's try it and see,' he is getting ready to perform an experiment. Framing various possibilities as to what is wrong with an automobile engine when the car is stalled is usually a preliminary to carrying out an actual trial, an experiment" (6:7).

"In scientific experimentation we control everything that happens. We determine when it shall occur and where. We arrange circumstances and surroundings, atmospheres and temperatures; possible ways of getting in and possible ways of getting out. We take out something that has been in, or put in something that has been out, and see what happens" (9:55).

"Brearley classifies legislation, social reform and utopian communities in one category and calls them *uncontrolled experiments*. Giddings also regards social legislation and reform as examples of experiments. Although he adds that they are not of a strictly scientific sort. . . . At times he refers to them as uncontrolled experiments . . ." (10:11).

EXERCISE

Select a relatively complete report of a social research project which either you or someone else has conducted. Break it down into the various problem-solving and communicative phases and identify the participants.

SUGGESTED READINGS

The literature on scientific method and the nature of inquiry is abundant. Here are a few books which can serve as an introduction to the subject: Churchman and Ackoff (4), Dewey (7), and Columbia Associates (5) presuppose no knowledge of science or philosophy. Churchman (3) and Dewey (8) are more advanced introductions.

A background in the history of science is an essential part of any scientist's training. Here are a few histories which emphasize the development of methods: Butterfield (2), Jaffe (11), and Randall (12).

Every social scientist should be familiar with the history of psychology, particularly experimental psychology. Boring (1) is suggested.

REFERENCES AND BIBLIOGRAPHY

1. BORING, E. G. *A History of Experimental Psychology.* New York: D. Appleton–Century Co., 1929.
2. BUTTERFIELD, HERBERT. *The Origins of Modern Science.* New York: Macmillan Co., 1951.
3. CHURCHMAN, C. W. *Theory of Experimental Inference.* New York: Macmillan Co., 1948.
4. CHURCHMAN, C. W., and ACKOFF, R. L. *Methods of Inquiry.* St. Louis: Educational Publishers, 1950.
5. COLUMBIA ASSOCIATES. *An Introduction to Reflective Thinking.* Boston: Houghton Mifflin Co., 1923.
6. CONANT, J. B. *Robert Boyle's Experiments in Pneumatics.* "Harvard Case Histories in Experimental Science," Case 1. Cambridge: Harvard University Press, 1950.
7. DEWEY, JOHN. *How We Think.* Boston: D. C. Heath & Co., 1933.
8. ———. *Logic: The Theory of Inquiry.* New York: Henry Holt & Co., 1938.
9. GIDDINGS, F. H. *The Scientific Study of Human Society.* Chapel Hill: University of North Carolina Press, 1924.
10. GREENWOOD, ERNEST. *Experimental Sociology.* New York: King's Crown Press, 1945.
11. JAFFE, HAYM. "The Development of the Experimental Method," in *Philosophical Essays in Honor of Edgar Arthur Singer, Jr.,* ed. F. P. CLARKE and M. C. NAHM. Philadelphia: University of Pennsylvania Press, 1942.
12. RANDALL, J. H., JR. *The Making of the Modern Mind.* Boston: Houghton Mifflin Co., 1940.
13. RUSSELL, BERTRAND. *The Scientific Outlook.* Glencoe, Ill.: Free Press, 1951.

CHAPTER II

Formulating the Problem

1. The Nature of the Problem

It is an old and wise saying that "a problem well put is half-solved." In scientific research we must abandon the idea that we can phrase our problems in the form of simple common-sense questions; we have to put a great deal of thought into the formulation of our questions if we hope to get anything out of an effort to answer them. For example, suppose that in the course of an ordinary conversation you ask a friend, "How many people live in your house?" He probably would have no trouble in answering, and you would probably be willing to accept his answer without further questioning. But now suppose you are conducting an important housing survey. Would you be willing to ask your respondents the simple question, "How many people live in your house?" Chances are that you would not. A moment's consideration shows that you would be concerned with such questions as these: Should a son who is away at college most of the year be included among those living in the house? Should a boarder who travels during the week and is in his room only on week ends be included? Or the maid who sleeps in three or four nights and spends the others at her family's home? It becomes clear that, the more important it is to solve a problem, the more carefully the problem must be formulated. The more carefully the problem is formulated, the more assurance we gain in obtaining a satisfactory solution.

In order to learn how to provide an optimum formulation of a problem, we must first determine what a "problem" is. We can begin by identifying the five components of a problem.

1. There must be an individual or group which has the problem. If this individual or group uses research to solve the problem, he or it becomes the research-consumer to whom we referred earlier. For most problems there are also other "participants." The researcher, if different from the research-consumer, is a participant in the problem. So are all individuals or groups who may be affected by a decision on the part of the research-consumer.

2. The research-consumer must have something he wants, some objectives or ends he desires. Obviously, a person who wants nothing cannot have a problem.

3. The research-consumer must have available alternative means for obtaining the objectives he desires. "Means" are courses of action which have at least some efficiency for obtaining the objective(s). A course of action may involve the use of objects; for example, the use of a yardstick in measuring the length of a table. Objects so used are *instruments*. A yardstick is an instrument, but the *use* of a yardstick is a means. It is important to keep in mind that *means are patterns of behavior* usable in the pursuit of objectives. Instruments, on the other hand, need not be objects; they may be concepts or ideas. For example, a mathematical formula, a scientific definition, a language, and a mental image are also instruments. An instrument is any object, concept, idea, or image which can be efficiently incorporated into pursuit of an objective.

There must be at least two means available to the research-consumer. If he has no choice of means, he can have no problem. His problem, however, may consist of how to make alternative means available. Then (risking the confusion of redundancy) he must have alternative means available for making alternative means available.

4. The existence of alternative courses of action is not enough to have a problem; the research-consumer must have some doubt as to which alternative to select. Without this doubt there can be no problem. The research-consumer must desire to dispel his doubt with regard to the efficiencies of the alternative means; in effect, he must have a question concerning the efficiencies of the alternative means, and he must want to answer it.

All problems ultimately reduce to the evaluation of the efficiency of alternative means for a designated set of objectives. It may not be clear that this is the case, particularly with regards to research which is directed toward obtaining pure "information." We will discuss this point in some detail below, but it is worth pointing out here that information is an instrument and its use is a means. Hence an inquiry directed toward obtaining correct or true information is directed toward obtaining efficient instruments. Since instruments cannot be considered independent of their use, such inquiry also reduces to determination of efficiency of alternative means.

5. There must be one or more environments to which the problem pertains. A change in environment may produce or remove a problem. A research-consumer may have doubts as to which is the most efficient means in one environment but have no such doubt in another. For example, an individual may have a problem involving a decision as to which topcoat to wear on a clear cool day. But, should it rain, he may have no doubt that he should wear his one raincoat.

The range of environments over which a problem may be said to exist may vary from one to many. Some problems are specific to only one environment; others are quite general.

The five components of a problem, then, are: (1) the research-consumer and other participants; (2) the objective(s); (3) alternative means for obtaining the objective(s); (4) a state of doubt in the research-consumer concerning the efficiency of the alternatives; and (5) the environments to which the problem pertains.

It is apparent that the seriousness of the problem depends on the importance of the objectives and the efficiency of the alternative means. The seriousness of possible mistakes (i.e., selecting less than the most efficient available means) also depends on the efficiency of the alternative means and the importance of the objectives.

The formulation of the problem consists in making the various components of the problem explicit and in determining the seriousness of any possible mistakes which might be made. The various aspects of a problem cannot be formulated separately, but they must be discussed separately. We shall consider the participants and their objectives in one section. Then we shall consider the alternative means and the questions to be asked about them in a second section. In a third section we will consider the efficiencies of the alternative means and the seriousness of the possible mistakes. Finally, we will consider the problem environments.

2. Participants and Objectives

It was noted earlier that a problem can exist only where there is one or more desired objectives. We shall consider, then, how to make explicit just what the objectives are. That is, we must become as clear as possible about *why* we are conducting the research—what we are trying to get out of it.

Many researchers claim that a good deal of research is directed only toward obtaining information for its own sake. They assert that in such cases the researcher should not be concerned with the uses to which such information may be put. This lack of concern with applications they take to be the essence of "pure" as opposed to "applied" research. Is it true that informational research does not involve any objective other than the desire to obtain information?

Consider, for example, a scientist who is studying voting behavior presumably *just* to find out why some who have the right to vote do not actually vote. This scientist asserts that he intends to take no action whatsoever to affect voting behavior; he *just* wants to understand it. What happens when his inquiry is completed? One of two things: he either does or does not communicate his results to others. If he does not communicate the results to anyone, the inquiry is not scientific, because science is a social institution and could not exist if all inquirers refused to communicate results. Science is necessarily public. This is hardly a typical case. The researcher is more likely either to publish his results or to incorporate them into his own subsequent research. In either case he is making information available for subsequent research. This, as a matter of fact, is an objective of informational research. In addition, in so far as the researcher is a scientist, he wants to provide *accurate* information (i.e., an efficient instrument) for future research. His problem, then, is to select the most efficient of alternative instruments to be made available for solving a certain *class* of problems. The objective is to facilitate the solution of this class of problems. Informational research, then, like all other research, is objective-oriented. Its objective is scientific in nature, but this does not affect the fact that it is objective-oriented. Research is pure not to the extent to which it is free of concern with applications but to the extent to which the applications with which it is concerned are scientific.

Where do we look for the objectives and how do we go about formulating them? In general, there are three sources to take into account: (1) the research-consumer; (2) the researcher(s); and (3) those who will be affected by use of the research results. Let us consider each of these in turn.

2.1. The Research-Consumer's Objectives

In this discussion we shall proceed as though the research-consumer were distinct from the research agent or agency. The discussion, however, is equally applicable to situations in which the research-consumer(s) and the researcher(s) are the same person or group.

The task of getting at the research-consumer's objectives does not usually consist of persuading a reluctant research-consumer to reveal his interests. Rather, in most cases, it involves helping a willing research-consumer to formulate objectives which he may not have systematically formulated in his own mind. If he has formulated his objectives, he will usually make them known. If he has not, it is necessary to help him formulate his objectives as completely as possible. It is futile merely to ask, "What are your objectives?" More sophisticated and fruitful techniques can and should be used.

Once the researcher has even a vague idea of the problem, he can quickly formulate guesses as to the nature of the research and the possible alternative results it might yield. He can use this rough-and-ready formulation to probe for the research-consumer's objectives. He can do this by employing depth-interviewing methods and by asking the research-consumer questions of the following type: "If the research demonstrates that such-and-such is the case, what will you do?" When the research-consumer replies by outlining a course of action, the researcher can then ask, "Why would you do this? That is, what would you hope to accomplish by doing this?" Such probing is likely to yield information on both the possible courses of action (means) and the research-consumer's motivation. For example, suppose a political organization asks a research agency to find out why so many eligible voters fail to vote in local elections. If the researcher were to ask, "Why do you want this information?" the answer is likely to be unenlightening. But if the researcher were to ask, "If the research were to show that the principal reason for not voting is the inaccessibility of voting booths, what would you do?" The answer might be: "We will pressure the city for an increase in the number and accessibility of these booths." Such an answer already reveals motivation which can be probed further. From such beginnings as these we can begin to get at the research-consumer's specific objectives. In the voting-behavior example we would have to probe much further, for the illustrative answers are just a beginning.

Consider, for example, the case where the research-consumer sponsors the research (i.e., finances it). Then, in order to conduct the research, we must also determine how much the sponsoring agency is willing to spend, how soon it wants results, how much it desires itself identified with the research, etc. That is, we have to find out just what limitations the sponsoring organization imposes on the research, and these limitations spring from objectives of the research-consumer.

Verbal probing of the research-consumer should be supplemented by similar probing of others who are familiar with the research-consumer and his problems. For example, suppose a research project is sponsored by a city planning commission, and the director of that commission lists the agency's objectives. Other related public and private agencies can be asked to comment on the list. If one of the other agencies feels that the list is not accurate and can defend that feeling, further investigation is indicated. In some cases it may be possible to determine the research-consumer's interests by reviewing his past behavior. For example, the past actions of a city agency such as a planning commission may clearly show whether or not it really desires to obtain, say, a slum-clearance program. If it claims this objective but has never introduced or supported legislation to that effect, the objective should not be ascribed to the agency unless there is good reason for this inconsistency. In brief, all the techniques for determining interests are applicable here, and they should be part of the stock and trade of the social researcher.

It is quite possible that some of the research-consumer's objectives will conflict; in fact, this will usually be the case. For example, he may wish to have the study performed very economically and also want very accurate results. If the designer is convinced that he cannot obtain the desired accuracy for the allotted amount, then, with the help of the research-consumer, he should determine the relative importance of the conflicting objectives so that he can determine what sacrifices should be made.

If the research-consumer should refuse or be unable to give anything more than a "curiosity formulation" of his objectives, then the designer should formulate as best he can what he takes the research-consumer's objectives to be. In such cases the assistance of personality and group analysts is highly desirable. These experts may be able to unearth the objectives of which the research-consumer may himself be unaware. It is only by measures such as these that the researcher can provide himself with the best criteria for subsequent design decisions.

The researcher will also have to define the objectives in cases where the research-consumer cannot be clearly identified. Such is the case, for example, for some of the research conducted by data-gathering agencies (e.g., the United States Bureau of the Census). In such circumstances it is advisable not only to formulate the objectives explicitly but to publish them along with the data, thereby increasing the chances subsequently of determining who the consumers are by their response to the publication. In addition, subsequent research may disclose the identity of the consumers and their objectives. We would then want to know if the correct objectives were assumed, and this can be determined only if the assumptions were explicitly formulated in the first place.

If there are several research-consumers, they may have conflicting objectives. Since conflicting objectives cannot simultaneously be served, the relative importance of the conflicting objectives must be determined so that the researcher can decide which to try to attain. Since at the present time there is no completely *scientific* way of determining the importance of objectives, we must resort to common-sense or semiscientific methods. Whatever method is used, it should be made explicit so that it is subject to subsequent evaluation; only by encouraging such evaluation can the development of scientific methods for evaluating objectives be encouraged. Common sense need not proceed blindly, however; it has the history of culture and ethics to go on. (In Sec. 2.6 we will consider a semiscientific method of evaluating objectives.)

The research-consumer's objectives (or, for that matter, those of the researcher) will seldom be completely formulated before any other phase of the design is begun. Usually the objectives will undergo progressive reformulations as the design proceeds. The design process makes such design progress possible; but, it should be noted, it requires the continuous participation of the research-consumer(s) in the design process. If possible, the research-consumer should be involved in *continuous* consultation and discussion, for, as he sees how the research project begins to take shape, he may discover how he can and should clarify his objectives. That is, if the research-consumer sees how decisions in the design of the research depend on his interests, he is likely to provide more adequate formulations of his objectives, and the designer can address more and more pointed questions at the research-consumer with respect to his objectives. The availability of the research-consumer for consultation is essential for maximum design efficiency.

One caution: the consumers of research are not only those who sponsor the research; there are other users of the research results. For example, if the results are to be published in a scientific journal, the readers of the journal are potential consumers. It is not always possible to know what objectives these readers have, but, if we publish research results in order to serve the interests of other professionals, then their interests should be taken into account. If we do not know what these interests are, we should make explicit assumptions concerning them and publish these assumptions along with the results. This is necessary to assure proper use of the research results by those to whom these results are to be made available.

Those who do not use but are affected by the research are also consumers of the research. We shall, however, consider them separately.

2.2. The Researcher's Objectives

It is frequently argued that the researcher should be completely impartial; that is, he should not permit his personal interests to influence his research decisions. Taken literally, such advice is nonsense. Most researchers, for example, would not deliberately select an observational method which would involve risking their lives. The researcher's desire for prestige, profit, self-education, etc., is generally operative in design decisions, even if he is not conscious of this fact. Some of the researcher's own interests are involved in most design decisions. Consequently, the researcher should explicitly formulate his own interests. If, for example, a researcher selects a method because it will require less of his time than an alternative method, even though it may be less accurate, he should make it clear that the desire to save his own time is operative in the selection of the method. Only by so doing can the decision be completely understood and evaluated subsequently by the researcher and others.

It is often difficult for a person to understand his own motives and to recognize his interests as they operate in decision-making. For this reason it is desirable to have others (particularly psychologists) co-operate in this phase of the design procedure. It is helpful to have others review one's own decisions and the reasons one gives for making them, for only in this way can interests of which the researcher is unaware be raised to consciousness. When we are unaware of our interests, we frequently construct elaborate rationalizations for our decisions—rationalizations which can be penetrated only by others. Such appraisal by others may be embarrassing to the researcher, but, if he is interested in improving his methods, such self-understanding as can be promoted by frank criticism is essential.

The researcher is not only a person; he is a scientist, and hence science's objectives should be taken into account. The objective of science, as we indicated earlier, is not only to increase knowledge but to increase our chances of *continuing* to increase knowledge. Science, by its very nature, is obliged to improve itself. If a researcher presumes to the title of "scientist," he should conduct each investigation so that each research venture improves his method of conducting subsequent research. The researcher as scientist should seek to do more than solve the problem on hand; he should learn about inquiry itself in the process. That is, he should seek to produce more efficient instruments and means for conducting subsequent research.

This self-improvement objective of science has serious implications for the researcher. If he believes or has evidence that the results of his research will be used only in such a way as to be detrimental to the future progress of science, he is under obligation *as a scientist* not to make those results available to potential misusers. This responsibility relates to the use of research results, and we will discuss it later in that context. It is brought up here to show the reason for taking the objectives of science into account. It is true that many deny that the researcher has any moral responsibility for the uses to which his research results are put. But, if we conceive (as history has done) of science as an ongoing institution, the scientist has at least moral responsibility for science's "going on."

2.3. Objectives of Those Who Will Be Affected by the Research

Suppose a scientist were given a project by a producer of consumer goods in which the objective of this producer involved doing harm to the consumers of his goods. Should the producer's objectives be accepted uncritically because he is willing to finance the research? It is foolish to assert that the researcher should not concern himself with the interests of those who will be affected adversely by the use of his research results. Suppose, for example, the researcher himself is one of those who will be so affected. Should he automatically sacrifice his own interests in such a situation? No scientist would expect another to do so *automatically;* the scientist is expected to weigh the situation and evaluate the alternatives. The same procedure should be followed even if the researcher is not included among those who will be affected adversely by use of the research results.

The objectives of the research-consumer and of those who will be affected by the use of the research results may be compatible. But even in this case the objectives of both parties should be taken into account. We shall see later how these objectives regulate subsequent design decisions.

The individual (or group) who has the problem (referred to above as the "research-consumer") is not the only consumer of the research; he (or it) is only the *immediate* consumer of the research. Those who carry out the immediate consumer's decisions are *intermediate* consumers of the research, and those who are ultimately affected by these decisions are the *ultimate* consumers. Suppose, for example, that a city's board of education sponsors research into ways of treating backward students. The board of education is the immediate consumer (and decision-maker). Any decision it makes will be carried out by the teachers, who are the intermediate consumers. The students are the ones ultimately affected, and hence they are the ultimate consumers.

The failure to take into account the interests of those who will be affected by the use of the research results is frequently very costly. One case in point is that of a large manufacturer who asked industrial psychologists and sociologists and engineers to determine what kind of factory should be built to manufacture a high-precision instrument. One of the recommendations resulting from the study was that the building, or at least the work space, should be windowless and that an even, artificial light be provided, thus producing more precise work. The factory was built, and though the quality of the product was high, the rate at which it was produced was much lower than that desired. Researchers were again called in. They found, among other things, that an unreasonable amount of time was being spent by the workers in the washrooms. They discovered that the frequent and prolonged visits to the washrooms were made because the washrooms had windows, and the workers wanted to look out and see what the weather was like and relieve their claustrophobic feelings. The result was that holes were punched through the windowless walls of the work space, and windows were inserted.

If the problem under consideration is one whose solution will affect people, it is always important to take into account their possible responses to the solution. This point was dramatically illustrated during the war when the possible responses of our own troops (intermediate consumer) and the enemy (ultimate consumer) to a new tactic or strategy always had to be considered. A good deal of applied social research has the same problem. But even in so-called "pure" research, where the only ones directly affected are other scientists, the interests of the other scientists should be taken into account. In such research the results are intended to be useful to other scientists, and "usefulness" has no significance independent of "interests."

2.4. Methods of Determining Objectives

Reference has already been made to several ways of determining what the objectives of the various participants are. It may be useful, however, to gather them together and list them.

1. *Questionnaire.*—Questionnaires may be effective where the participants can be assumed to know what their pertinent interests are and are willing to communicate their interests.

2. *Probing and depth interviewing.*—This method may be useful where the participants are not aware of any or only some of their pertinent interests.

3. *Conference method.*—If the immediate consumer is a group, its collective interests may not be a simple sum of its total interests. In this case the individuals should be questioned as a group to determine what they would do as a group and why. The method is also applicable to other groups of participants.

4. *Behavioral method.*—If the participants have been in similar problem situations in the past, an examination of their past actions may reveal their interests. In some cases preference tests can be constructed to determine participants' interests.

5. *Informants.*—Those who are familiar with the participants may be able to yield valuable information and insights into the participants' interests. One set of participants may be able to reveal interests of other participants; for example, workers and employers.

2.5. Check List of Participants and Their Objectives

It is always advisable to record the results obtained in each phase of the research design. This not only prevents oversights but exposes the results to subsequent evaluation. In this case, it is desirable to record the identity of the problem's participants, their objectives, and the evidence for asserting that a set of objectives is desired by the participants. This can be done in tabular form as shown on the following page.

Even if the same individual(s) fills several participant roles, his (or their) objectives should be entered separately for each role. This will tend to prevent pertinent objectives from being overlooked.

2.6. Importance of Objectives

It will be rare if ever that all pertinent objectives are compatible. Some conflict of interests is always to be expected. Consequently, it is necessary to know which objectives are the most important in order to know how to evaluate any potential solution to the problem.

Our purpose here is not to go into philosophical problems concerning ultimate values or even to suggest possible scientific measures of value. This has been done in another place (1). Rather, our purpose is to suggest a practical method by which the researcher and the consumers can self-consciously assign weights to the objectives involved in the research. It would be premature at this stage of the development of science to require measures of importance of objectives

Participants	Identity	Pertinent Objectives	Evidence of Identity and Objectives (If Not Obvious)
Immediate consumer			
Intermediate consumer			
Ultimate consumer			
Research staff			

along a well-defined scale; but we can rank a set of objectives in a nonarbitrary way.* A concept of importance on which the ranking can be based is the following:

> Given two objectives, O_1 and O_2, O_1 is more important than O_2 in a given environment if, granted that *only* one of these two objectives could be pursued, O_1 rather than O_2 would be pursued.

That is, if O_2 would be sacrificed (if necessary) in order to pursue O_1, then O_1 is more important than O_2. This does not tell us how much more important O_1 is than O_2 but merely that O_1 is *more* important.

The following method of ranking will yield a measure of *relative* importance of objectives: We start with a set of objectives $(O_1, O_2, \ldots, O_n)$. For illustrative purposes let us start with four objectives.

(1) Rank the four objectives in the order of their importance. Let O_1 represent the most important objective, O_2 the next in importance, then O_3 and O_4.

(2) Assign the value "1" to the most important objective, O_1. Call this value R_1 (i.e., $R_1 = 1$).

(3) Tentatively assign numbers between zero and one to O_2, O_3, and O_4, so that these numbers roughly approximate their relative importance. Call the assigned values R_2, R_3, and R_4.

* The possibility of ranking objectives in economics was recognized by Pareto (10). One mathematical model for such ranking is provided by von Neumann and Morgenstern (8).

(4) Compare the most important objective, O_1, with all the others combined; i.e., O_1 versus $O_2 + O_3 + O_4$. (If you could obtain either O_1 alone or O_2, O_3, and O_4 in combination, which would you prefer?)

    (4.1) If O_1 is more important than the combination of O_2, O_3, and O_4, adjust the number assigned to O_1, R_1, if necessary, so that it is greater than the sum of the numbers assigned to the other objectives (i.e., $R_1 > R_2 + R_3 + R_4$). Proceed to step (5).

    (4.2) If O_1 is less important than the combination of O_2, O_3, and O_4, adjust R_1, if necessary, so that $R_1 < R_2 + R_3 + R_4$.

        (4.2.1) Compare O_1 with $O_2 + O_3$. If O_1 is more important than $O_2 + O_3$, adjust R_1, if necessary, so that $R_1 > R_2 + R_3$, and proceed to step (5). If O_1 is less important than $O_2 + O_3$, adjust R_1, if necessary, so that $R_1 < R_2 + R_3$.

        (4.2.2) Repeat (4.2.1) for O_1 versus $O_2 + O_4$.

        (4.2.3) Repeat (4.2.1) for O_1 versus $O_3 + O_4$.

(5) Compare the second most important objective, O_2, with the combination of O_3 and O_4. If O_2 is more important than $O_3 + O_4$, adjust R_2, if necessary, so that $R_2 > R_3 + R_4$. If O_2 is less important than $O_3 + O_4$, adjust R_2, if necessary, so that $R_2 < R_3 + R_4$. Make sure that R_2 is not changed in such a way as to contradict any previous comparisons.

(6) Total the resulting rank values, $R_1 + R_2 + R_3 + R_4$.

(7) Assign to O_1 the value $R_1 / (R_1 + R_2 + R_3 + R_4)$,

        to O_2 the value $R_2 / (R_1 + R_2 + R_3 + R_4)$,

        to O_3 the value $R_3 / (R_1 + R_2 + R_3 + R_4)$,

        to O_4 the value $R_4 / (R_1 + R_2 + R_3 + R_4)$.

The sum of these values should be equal to 1.*

In the case of four objectives this process would now be complete. The method is applicable, however, to any number of objectives. The more objectives involved, the larger the number of comparisons required by the procedure.

For purposes of illustration, let us consider a housing problem and see how this procedure can be applied to weighting housing objectives. We shall oversimplify the example by considering only the following four objectives:

---

* This method of obtaining measures of relative importance makes the following assumptions:

    a) *Additivity:* if one objective O_a is more important than the combination of objectives, $O_b, O_c, \ldots, O_n$, then O_a is more important than any subset of $O_b, O_c, \ldots, O_n$.

    b) *Transitivity:* if one objective O_a is more important than another, O_b, and O_b is more important than O_c, then O_a is more important than O_c.

    The following precaution can be taken to assure the validity of (*a*). In listing the objectives to be ranked, make sure that no two separately listed objectives, O_i and O_j, are related so that *either* O_i or O_j is desired, but not both. If two objectives are related in this way (i.e., disjunctively), they should be listed as a single objective: "O_i or O_j."

O_1 = To replace inadequate housing facilities by adequate ones.

O_2 = To create community interest in neighborhood rehabilitation projects.

O_3 = To achieve economy of time, money, and effort.

O_4 = To maintain respect for and prestige of the city planning commission.

The steps might go as follows:

(1) The objectives in order of importance are O_1, O_2, O_3, and O_4.

(2) $R_1 = 1.0$.

(3) $R_2 = 0.5$, $R_3 = 0.3$, and $R_4 = 0.2$.

(4) O_1 is less important than $O_2 + O_3 + O_4$.

    (4.2) Change R_1 so that $R_1 = 0.9$, then $R_1 < R_2 + R_3 + R_4$: $0.9 < (0.5 + 0.3 + 0.2)$.

        (4.2.1) O_1 is more important than $O_2 + O_3$; no adjustment is required, since $R_1 > R_2 + R_3$: $0.9 > (0.5 + 0.3)$.

(5) O_2 is more important than $O_3 + O_4$. Since $R_2 = R_3 + R_4$, adjust R_2 so that $R_2 = 0.6$. Then $R_2 > R_3 + R_4$: $0.6 > (0.3 + 0.2)$. Step (4.2) still holds, since $0.9 < (0.6 + 0.3 + 0.2)$, but step (4.2.1) does not, since $0.9 = (0.6 + 0.3)$. Then change R_1 back to 1.0. Now all conditions are satisfied: (4.2), $1.0 < (0.6 + 0.3 + 0.2)$; (4.2.1), $1.0 > (0.6 + 0.3)$; and (5), $0.6 > (0.3 + 0.2)$.

(6) $R_1 + R_2 + R_3 + R_4 = 1.0 + 0.6 + 0.3 + 0.2 = 2.1$.

(7) Assign to O_1 the value $1.0/2.1 = 0.48$

          to O_2 the value $0.6/2.1 = 0.29$

          to O_3 the value $0.3/2.1 = 0.14$

          to O_4 the value $0.2/2.1 = 0.09$

$$\text{Total} = 1.00$$

In cases where a large number of objectives (say, more than eight) are involved, the procedure described becomes very cumbersome. This is due to the large number of complex comparisons which are required. In such situations the alternative procedure given in Appendix I can be used.

It should be clear that, in order to best perform this weighting, it is necessary to obtain the co-operation of the participants in the problem. In so-called "practical" research the researcher seldom knows enough about the possible consequences or the participants' evaluation of the objectives to take sole responsibility for the weighting. It is also a good idea to have the weighting done independently by as many different informed and involved persons as possible. If there is no consistency in the weights given by the different persons, then the basis for the differences should be uncovered and resolved by collective evaluation where possible. That is, in cases where disagreement is marked, the researcher should seek to bring the disagreeing participants together to arbitrate the differences. If this fails to produce agreement, an arbitrator acceptable to the conflicting parties can be used to settle the disagreement.

In any case, the researcher should consult others who are familiar with the weighters' past actions to judge the accuracy of the weights. For example, a city planning commission may rank "adequate housing" as its most important objective, but people familiar with their actions may know that "maintaining prestige" is actually more important to the commission.

If evaluations are made independently by several weighters, and there are only slight differences in the standardized weights obtained, the average of the weights for each objective can be used as the final value. The averages will also total to 1.0.

This method of assigning weights to objectives is based on subjective evaluations. The evaluations, however, could be checked by behavioristic tests. Ideally we would like to place the weighters in real sacrifice situations and observe their choices. The accuracy of their assertions as to what they would do in such situations could then be checked. But on the basis of behavior in less-than-ideal situations good inferences may be drawn as to what they would do in the ideal situation.

The method described has an important practical advantage: it enables the researcher to locate the specific points of disagreement among different weighters, if such differences exist. If two or more weighters were merely asked to list items in order of importance, and their results disagreed, there would be little basis for arbitration. But in any explicit method of weighting, such as the one presented, the specific points of agreement and disagreement are exposed. Subsequent discussion can then be directed to these points of disagreement, and hence ultimate agreement is more likely to be attained.

3. Alternative Means and Hypotheses

It was pointed out earlier that all research problems reduce to the question: Which of a set of alternative means is the most efficient? In formulating the problem, then, it is necessary to make explicit the alternative means which are involved. Once these alternatives are formulated, we should ask of each, "What would constitute evidence that this means is the most efficient of the alternatives?" The answer to this question constitutes a formulation of the conditions under which the means ought to be accepted as the most efficient of the alternatives. A set of acceptance conditions should be formulated for each alternative means. The statements of these conditions are called "hypotheses." We do not know which of the alternative hypotheses is true; this is precisely what the research should be designed to determine. Consequently, the formulation of the problem requires that the alternative means be specified and that a hypothesis be associated with each alternative.

3.1. The Pertinent Alternative Means

There may be two or more alternative means in any given problem situation. But the immediate consumer's problem may not involve all the alternatives. For example, there may be three alternatives, one of which he already knows to be less efficient than either of the other two. His problem, then, does not involve the means known to be least efficient. If the immediate consumer is wrong about the inefficiency of this means, he may not find the best solution to his problem. Such an error must be prevented if possible.

The researcher should attempt to determine all the alternative courses of action available in the problem environment(s). The immediate consumer may not be aware of all of these. In this case, the researcher will have to deal with informed sources to make sure he has taken into account all the available alternatives. This *resources survey* is very important, since in some cases a problem is dispelled by the "appearance" of a means previously not known to be available. In informational research, for example, the information sought may already be available, in which case unnecessary duplication can be avoided. The resources survey should be as extensive as possible both within science and, if the problem is a practical one, within the field of application.

It should be clear that we cannot decide what the alternative means are unless we have a clear idea of the objectives. Furthermore, we clarify our notion of the pertinent objectives by deciding what courses of action constitute means for these objectives.

Once the list of alternative means is prepared, it can be examined to see if any of the alternatives can be eliminated. If previous research or past experience leaves no doubt about the inefficiency of one alternative relative to the others, it should be removed from the list. It is the researcher's responsibility critically to evaluate the evidence of inefficiency. If reasonable doubt remains after such evaluation, the alternative should be retained for such evaluation.

In some cases the researcher will have little or no assurance that he has included all possible alternatives. In the course of the research a new alternative may become apparent. In this case the formulation of the problem should be modified so as to permit the research to evaluate this new alternative.

3.2. The Alternative Hypotheses

The research will attempt to determine which of the alternative courses of action is the most efficient. The task in formulating the alternative hypotheses is to state for each alternative means the conditions under which it can be said to be the most efficient. This obviously requires (*a*) that the researcher have measures of efficiency available and (*b*) that he can determine the conditions under which that measure would be greatest for each alternative. We will consider both these problems. First, let us see what measures of efficiency are available to the researcher.

3.2.1. Measures of Efficiency

There are a number of different measures of efficiency in use today. The six most common measures are the following:

1. Hold *time* constant. Measure percentage of task completed.
2. Hold *cost* constant. Measure percentage of task completed.
3. Hold *effort* constant. Measure percentage of task completed.
4. Specify task to be completed. Measure time required to complete specified task.
5. Specify task to be completed. Measure cost required to complete specified task.
6. Specify task to be completed. Measure effort required to complete specified task.

For example, a worker's efficiency in doing a certain job is sometimes measured in terms of how long it takes him (No. 4). The measure of efficiency of two systems producing the same item may be based on the cost of producing each item (No. 5). On the other hand, two workers can be compared in terms of how much of a job they complete in a specified period of time (No. 1). The reader can readily find examples of the use of the other measures.

Each of these measures, though useful in many circumstances, is restricted. For example, suppose a person's objective is to get exercise. Then we would hardly measure efficiency of alternative means of exercising in terms of how little effort is expended. Or, again, a person may want to find ways of spending money. Then we could hardly measure efficiency in terms of how small the monetary cost. Finally, a person may engage in an activity precisely because it absorbs his time. Then we could hardly measure the efficiency of the activity in terms of how little time it takes. In these cases the measure must be reversed.

The restrictions illustrated do not imply that these measures should not be used. They point up, however, the desirability of a completely general measure of efficiency, one which can be applied in any situation. One such general measure is the following:

The efficiency of a course of action for an objective in a specified environment is the probability that the action will result in the attainment of the objective.

For purposes of illustration, let M_1 represent the course of action, O_1 the objective, and N the environment. It follows from the definition that, if we have two courses of action in an environment, the one which has the greatest probability of yielding the objective is the most efficient. The measure of efficiency lies between 0 (the minimum) and 1 (the maximum), since it is a probability measure. The measure of *in*efficiency of M_1 for O_1 in N is 1 minus the degree of efficiency. If the efficiency of M_1 for O_1 in N is (for example) 0.6, its inefficiency for O_1 is $(1.0 - 0.6)$, or 0.4.

Consider the case where we want to determine which of the two means is the most efficient for an objective. Suppose the objective is "to add correctly a column of twenty five-digit numbers in one minute." Suppose, further, that M_1 is "using the pencil-and-paper method" and M_2 is "using an automatic computer." Let us say that this test is to be made relative to a specific individual, A. Suppose now that A is given ten columns to add each way. Suppose he computes one total correctly in the allotted time using the paper-and-pencil method and eight correctly using the machine. Then the efficiency of the paper-and-pencil method (as estimated from this data) would be 0.1. The efficiency of the use of the computer would be 0.8. The efficiencies of the alternatives need not total to 1.

The measures of efficiency discussed in this section by no means exhaust all the possibilities. In different situations variations of the measures given here will suggest themselves. For example, suppose we want to determine which of two textbooks in a specified subject is the better. We might decide that it is the one which enables students to get the higher scores on a standard test in the subject. Here we would be using test scores as a measure of efficiency. The test score is a modified measure of the percentage of the job completed in a specified time.

The researcher should make explicit the measure of efficiency he will use, and he should demonstrate its suitability to the problem at hand.

3.2.2. Formulating the Hypotheses

Once the researcher has selected the measure of efficiency which is most suitable to his problem, he is in a position to specify the acceptance conditions for the alternative courses of action. Suppose, for example, he has the problem mentioned above: to select one of a pair of alternative textbooks to be used by students in a specified course. Suppose further that he decides to use test scores as a measure of efficiency. Then for each text the acceptance condition would be something like "the average test scores produced by the use of this text is greater than that obtained by the use of any of the alternative texts." Since there are only two texts involved, the acceptance conditions can be translated into the following hypotheses (H):

Select text A if, H_1: the average test score produced by text A is greater than the average test score produced by text B.

Select text B if, H_2: the average test score produced by text B is greater than the average test score produced by text A.

It is apparent that one possible outcome has not been taken into account—the case where the average test scores are equal. If we should permit the hypotheses to remain as they are, and if the average test scores turn out to be equal, we would have no specified course of action to select. Consequently, we must either add another course of action or change one of the hypotheses. Suppose text A happens to be the one currently in use. We might then decide to change to text B *only* if it turns out to be better than text A. The first hypothesis can now be reformulated as follows:

H_1: the average test score produced by text A is equal to or greater than the average test score produced by text B.

The hypotheses now exhaust all the possibilities.

The textbook illustration serves to introduce the steps involved in the formulation of alternative hypotheses:

(1) Select a measure of efficiency which is applicable to all the alternative courses of action.

(2) Assign to each alternative course of action a unique set of acceptance conditions based on the selected measure of efficiency.

(3) Reformulate the acceptance conditions as hypotheses; that is, as statements which cover all the possible outcomes of the research and which do not overlap.

(4) Make explicit the assumptions involved in the use of the selected measure of efficiency. (These are the points of agreement among the hypotheses.)

The pairing of acceptance conditions and courses of action and of hypotheses and acceptance conditions is necessary, even in theoretical research, if we want the best possible design. In such research, efficiency may be defined in terms of predictability, conformity to theory, and other similar measures. For example, suppose one theory can be used to predict events more accurately than another. The first theory would then be the more efficient to use in problems whose solution depends on such predictions. As we indicated earlier, theoretical or pure research is always used as a basis for subsequent research. In all such research the alternative courses of (scientific) action, acceptance conditions, and hypotheses should be made explicit. In fact, if the acceptance of one alternative hypothesis rather than another would make no difference whatsoever in subsequent scientific behavior, then the problem or its formulation is scientifically meaningless.

In cases where more than one objective is involved, a generalization of the procedure just described is required. The need for generalization can be made clear by a simple example. Suppose that only two objectives, O_1 and O_2, and two courses of action (means), C_1 and C_2, are involved. Then there are four possible efficiency determinations, not merely two. They are the efficiency of (1) C_1 for O_1; (2) C_1 for O_2; (3) C_2 for O_1; and (4) C_2 for O_2. Suppose further that these efficiencies are determined to have the values shown in the following matrix:

	O_1	O_2
C_1	0.7	0.3
C_2	0.2	0.8

Which is the more efficient means? To answer this question, the importance (weight) of O_1 and O_2 must be taken into account. Suppose O_1 were very important and O_2 were very unimportant. Then C_1 would obviously be the better means to select. If the importance were reversed, C_2 would be the better means to select. These considerations suggest the necessity of weighting the efficiencies by the importance of the objectives. As before, let R_1 represent the weight of O_1 and R_2 represent the weight of O_2. Also let E_{11} represent the efficiency of C_1 for O_1 and E_{12} represent the efficiency of C_1 for O_2. Then the over-all weighted efficiency of C_1, $WE(C_1)$, can be expressed as follows:

$$WE(C_1) = R_1E_{11} + R_2E_{12}.$$

Similarly, for C_2,

$$WE(C_2) = R_1E_{21} + R_2E_{22}.$$

For example, let R_1 equal 0.6 and R_2 equal 0.4. Then

$$WE(C_1) = (0.6)(0.7) + (0.4)(0.3) = 0.54.$$
$$WE(C_2) = (0.6)(0.2) + (0.4)(0.8) = 0.44.$$

Under these circumstances, then, C_1 would be the more efficient course of action.

Suppose the following two assertions were the ones we wanted to convert into hypotheses:

(1) $WE(C_1) > WE(C_2)$.
(2) $WE(C_1) \leq WE(C_2)$.

By substitution in (1) we can obtain

$$H_1: R_1E_{11} + R_2E_{12} > R_1E_{21} + R_2E_{22}.$$

Since R_1 and R_2 can be determined before the research is conducted, their values may be substituted in H_1. For example, if R_1 is equal to 0.6, and R_2 is equal to 0.4, then

$$H_1: 0.6E_{11} + 0.4E_{12} > 0.6E_{21} + 0.4E_{22}.$$

Simplifying, we get

$$H_1: 1.5E_{11} + E_{12} > 1.5E_{21} + E_{22}.$$

Similarly, we can obtain the alternative:

$$H_2: 1.5E_{11} + E_{12} \leq 1.5E_{21} + E_{22}.$$

This formulation of the hypotheses makes it clear that four efficiency determinations are involved. In general, if there are N_o objectives and N_c courses of action, there are N_oN_c efficiency-determinations required to compare the over-all weighted efficiencies of the alternative courses of action.

Another complication may arise if more than one objective is involved. It may be desirable to use different measures of efficiency relative to the different objectives, and these measures may not be commensurate. For example, suppose that in the textbook problem there are two objectives: O_1 is to provide the best possible training and O_2 is to minimize the cost of the text to the student. "Average test score" may be used as a measure of efficiency relative to O_1, and "sales price" as a measure of efficiency relative to O_2. It is meaningless to add two measures, one from each of these scales. Either one scale must be equated to the other or both must be converted into a common scale. The latter is generally the easier to accomplish.

The general measure of efficiency given above—probability of producing a given objective—provides a convenient common scale. The following transformation procedure can be used:

The average test score, say, can take on values from 0 to 100. The probability scale can take on values from 0 to 1.0. A graphic transformation can be prepared by using "test scores" as the abscissa and "probability of production" as the ordinate of a graph (see Fig. 2).

Decide what average test score is equivalent to maximum efficiency. In this case the decision is obvious: an average test score of 100 is optimum. Therefore, equate 100 on the abscissa to 1.0 on the ordinate; that is, plot the point (100, 1.0) as is done in Figure 2. Now select that average test score which is equivalent to absolute inefficiency. This is not so obvious. The researcher may decide, for example, that a text which yields an average test score below a passing grade

(60) has no efficiency. If this is the case, plot the point (60, 0), and connect the points (100, 1.0) and (60, 0) by a straight line. By use of this line any value on the abscissa can be translated into a value on the ordinate. For example, consider the average test score of 90. Draw a vertical line up from 90 on the abscissa to the transformation line and then a horizontal from the intersection on that line to the ordinate. The value on the ordinate at which this horizontal line intersects (0.75) is the transformed value of 90.

The transformation line need not be a straight line; it may be curved. The

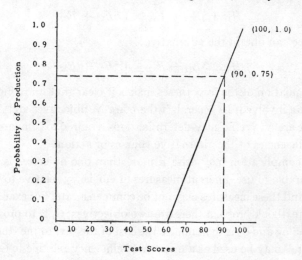

Fig. 2.—Transformation of test scores into probability of production

determination of the shape of the line depends on conditions which are specific to the problem. At present there is no systematic way of making this determination. It depends on the researcher's judgment.

The second scale of efficiency—sales price—can be similarly transformed to the probability-of-production scale. Once this is done, the transformed values of the two original scales can be added as is required in the formulation given above. For example, suppose we use the transformation shown in Figure 3 for the second efficiency scale. Suppose further that a given text produces an average test score of 90 and that its cost to the student is $5.00. The transformed measures of efficiency are 0.75 and 0.50, respectively. Let the weight of the training objective be equal to 0.9, and the weight of the minimization-of-cost objective be equal to 0.1. Then the over-all weighted efficiency of the text is given by the following:

$$(0.9)(0.75) + (0.1)(0.50) = 0.725.$$

Let us see what these considerations mean in the formulation of hypotheses in the following case. A new introductory text in sociology has become available. We want to teach the introductory course as efficiently as possible (O_1), and we want to keep the cost of the text to the students as low as possible (O_2). The scale of efficiency to be used for O_1 is the average test score (T); that is, the average test score of a class using the old text (T_1) and the average test score of a class using the new text (T_2) will be compared. Let T_1' and T_2' represent the transformed values of these scores. The scale of efficiency to be used for O_2 is the cost of the texts (K); that is, let K_1 represent the cost of the old text and K_2 the

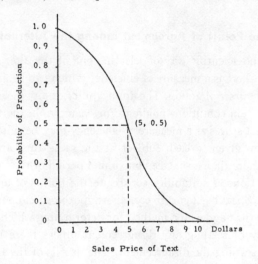

Fig. 3.—Transformation of sales price of text into probability of production

cost of the new text. Also let K_1' and K_2' represent the transformed cost measures. R_1 and R_2 continue to represent the weights of O_1 and O_2, respectively. A preliminary formulation of the courses of action and their corresponding hypotheses can be made as follows:

Continue to use the old text if

$$H_1: R_1T_1' + R_2K_1' \geq R_1T_2' + R_2K_2'.$$

Select the new text if

$$H_2: R_1T_1' + R_2K_1' < R_1T_2' + R_2K_2'.$$

R_1 and R_2, and K_1' and K_2' can be determined before the research is conducted. Suppose $R_1 = 0.9$, $R_2 = 0.1$, $K_1' = 0.4$, and $K_2' = 0.6$. Then, substituting in H_1 and H_2 and simplifying, we obtain

$$H_1: T_1' \geq T_2' + 0.022.$$
$$H_2: T_1' < T_2' + 0.022.$$

The multiobjective hypotheses formulation just described, or other procedures designed to do the same thing, are seldom used in actual practice. The research designer is generally inclined to eliminate all but the most important objective and solve the problem relative to it. This procedure, however, does not yield a solution to the consumers' complete problem. It can only solve an abstracted problem, and the solution obtained may be inefficient in an over-all sense. This should be kept in mind when so-called "complicating objectives" are eliminated during the formulation of the problem.

3.2.2.1. The Points of Agreement among the Alternative Hypotheses

There is no scientific way of selecting one of the alternative hypotheses as valid unless there is a measure of efficiency which can be applied to each of the alternative courses of action. The applicability of any measure of efficiency depends on certain conditions holding. For example, in the textbook illustration the use of test scores as a measure of efficiency may be suitable only if the same test has been given to each subject at the same time and if each subject is allowed no more than a specified maximum period of time to complete the test. These conditions of suitability constitute the points of agreement among the hypotheses. Speaking figuratively, the hypotheses cannot agree on which is valid unless they agree on a method for determining which is valid. There is no rational way of settling any disagreement unless there is agreement on the method for settling the disagreement. The details of the method of validation are the points of agreement common to the alternative hypotheses.

The points of agreement among the alternative hypotheses may be either known or assumed to be valid. The validity of at least some of the points of agreement will have to be assumed, since all that we "know" is based on some assumptions. Any assumption may itself be investigated and "proved," but not without making other assumptions. Whatever the assumptions made, they should be made explicit. It may turn out that one or more are unjustified. In this case we can frequently make compensating adjustments in the data if they have already been obtained and thereby avoid having to collect new data.

Suppose, for example, that in the textbook study we assume (in a later design stage) that the effect of the texts on test scores is independent of the sex of the students. Suppose that we learn by examining equal numbers of both sexes that the average score of text-*A*-students is 10 points higher than that of text-*B*-students. Suppose further that subsequent inquiry shows that the effect of text *A* is not independent of sex, though the effect of text *B* is independent of sex. Text *A* yields an average male student score 5 points higher than that of female students. Since we assumed no difference between sexes, we can adjust the findings of the first study. The result would be that the average test score of text-A-male-students was 12.5 points higher than the over-all average test score of text-B-students. The average test score of text-A-female-students was 7.5 points higher. Then we see that the text is more efficient when used on male students than when used on female students.

All assumptions common to the hypotheses cannot be formulated at this, the problem-formulation stage of the research. As the design of the research proceeds, more and more assumptions are made. We shall consider these assumptions in subsequent phases of the research design. But even at this stage we can make explicit the assumptions involved in the use of a common measure of efficiency.

3.2.2.2. Exclusive and Exhaustive Hypotheses

If we have two hypotheses, they must have at least one point of agreement (say, a) and one point of disagreement (say, b and b'). Then we can represent the hypotheses symbolically as follows:

H_1: ab (asserts a and b to be true),

H_2: ab' (asserts a to be true but denies b).

In this formulation b and b' represent contradictory assertions, and hence one and only one of the hypotheses can be true, and one must be true.

There may be more than two hypotheses involved in a research problem. Suppose, for example, that we want to evaluate three alternative textbooks. Then there would be three alternative hypotheses which might be represented symbolically as follows:

H_1: ab_1

H_2: ab_2

H_3: ab_3

There should be one hypothesis for each alternative course of action, no matter how large the number of alternatives. The alternative hypotheses, on the other hand, should cover all possible outcomes of the research; that is, they should be *exhaustive* with respect to the points of disagreement which will be tested. Furthermore, the alternative hypotheses should not overlap and hence should be *exclusive*. This means that no two of them should be able to be accepted simultaneously as the result of any research. Otherwise the research might not indicate which *one* course of action should be selected.

The alternative courses of action should also be exclusive. For example, returning to the two-textbook illustration, we might have three courses of action:

(1) Use only text A.

(2) Use only text B.

(3) Use an equal number of text A and text B.

These courses of action are exclusive; the instruments involved are not. That is, text A will be used in either (1) or (3), but (1) and (3) cannot both be selected at the same time. Notice, however, that the courses of action (unlike the hypotheses) need not be exhaustive; an *un*equal number of text A and text B may be selected.

One convenient way of assuring ourselves that the hypotheses are exclusive and exhaustive is to use a logical technique called the "Boolean expansion." Suppose, for example, we have two points of agreement, a and b, and two points of disagreement, c and d. Then we can construct the following list of alternative hypotheses:

H_1: $abcd$
H_2: $abcd'$
H_3: $abc'd$
H_4: $abc'd'$

Note that a and b remain unchanged throughout. If there were three points of disagreement, there would be eight possible alternatives:

H_1: $abcde$	H_5: $abcd'e'$
H_2: $abcde'$	H_6: $abc'de'$
H_3: $abcd'e$	H_7: $abc'd'e$
H_4: $abc'de$	H_8: $abc'd'e'$

In general, if there are n points of disagreement, then there are 2^n alternative hypotheses in an exclusive and exhaustive classification.

As we have already indicated, a point of disagreement may involve more than just two possibilities. We might have, for example, a situation in which c can take on three values:

c_1: A is greater than B.
c_2: A is equal to B.
c_3: A is less than B.

If c were the only point of disagreement, there would be three alternative hypotheses.

If the research involves more than two hypotheses, it is advisable to formulate the points of disagreement symbolically to facilitate the construction of the hypotheses. Intuition is not a satisfactory guide to exclusiveness and exhaustiveness. For example, suppose we are going to evaluate three textbooks by use of test scores. To facilitate the discussion, let T_1, T_2, and T_3 represent the average test scores obtained by students using texts 1, 2, and 3, respectively. The possible relations between any two of these three test scores can be represented as follows:

$$T_1 = T_2 \qquad\qquad T_2 = T_3 \qquad\qquad T_1 = T_3$$
$$T_1 > T_2 \qquad\qquad T_2 > T_3 \qquad\qquad T_1 > T_3$$
$$T_1 < T_2 \qquad\qquad T_2 < T_3 \qquad\qquad T_1 < T_3$$

Now there are twenty-seven ways we can combine one assertion from each column. By writing these out, we would find that fourteen of these combinations are impossible; for example, $(T_1 = T_2)\,(T_2 > T_3)\,(T_1 < T_3)$. The thirteen consistent combinations which remain have to be combined into three exclusive and exhaustive hypotheses. One such set of hypotheses is the following:

$$H_1\colon\; T_1 \geq T_2 \text{ and } T_1 \geq T_3$$
$$H_2\colon\; T_1 < T_2 \text{ and } T_2 \geq T_3$$
$$H_3\colon\; T_1 < T_3 \text{ and } T_2 < T_3$$

That is, the first text will be selected if the average score obtained by students using it is equal to or greater than the corresponding score of those using the second and third texts. The second text will be accepted if it yields a better average than the first and one equal to or greater than that yielded by the third. The third text will be accepted only if it yields better results than both the first and the second texts.

The advantage of the symbolic approach to hypothesis formulation should be apparent from this illustration.

3.2.2.3. Problems of Estimation

In some problems we may find that there are a very large number of possible courses of action. For example, if our problem is to solve a housing shortage, the alternative courses of action may be to build one dwelling unit, two units, or any specifiable number. Thus there are a large number of courses of action, each distinguishable by the number of dwelling units to be built. Then, if we could determine how many dwelling units are needed, the most efficient course of action could be selected. Such a problem is one of *estimation*, since the selection of the most efficient course of action depends on an estimate of the value of a critical variable. In such cases it is not necessary to formulate explicitly each alternative course of action and to associate a hypothesis with each. We can use a shorthand formulation. For example, the alternative courses of action in the illustration can be designated as: "to build N dwelling units." The acceptance conditions can be formulated as: "to build N_i dwelling units if N_i dwelling units are needed." Then the alternative hypotheses can be simply stated as: "N houses are needed," and the research problem is to estimate N.

If the relationship between possible estimates and the possible courses of action cannot be expressed as a mathematical function (as it is in the dwelling-unit example), this is a good indication that estimation procedure is not proper. If a function is established which provides for the same course of action to follow a range of estimated values, the ranges should be specified in the form of hypotheses.

An estimate of the value of any variable is always subject to error. This error is usually taken into account by expressing estimates as a range of values rather than a single value. We might say, for example, that the number of dwelling units required is equal to "1,000 $\pm$ 100," or, equivalently, it lies between 900 and 1,100. The size of the range given in the estimate depends not only on the data but also on the risk of making a mistake we are willing to take. That is, the smaller the risk of making a mistake we are willing to run, the larger will be the range, and conversely. We will not go into the statistical aspects of estimation procedure here, but we will consider several nonstatistical aspects which are very important. It should be noted, however, that it is important to specify whether or not the problem is one of estimation, since the statistical methods of analyzing the data in an estimation problem are different from those used in a hypothesis-testing problem. On the other hand, it is equally important to realize that the logic underlying estimation procedure is identical with that underlying hypothesis testing.

In research involving estimation we should still indicate the courses of action associated with each possible outcome of the research, even though we do so in an abbreviated form. In most applied research which involves estimation it is apparent that the courses of action can be expressed as a function of the value to be estimated. In informational research, however, the only course of action immediately involved may be the publication of the research results. It is true that the material included in the published report is a function of the research results, but this relationship is obvious and hardly need be made explicit. It is important to remember, however, that the results (whether published or not) are presumably to be used in subsequent research, perhaps by the researcher himself. At least some subsequent research actions depend on the estimate. Various properties of the estimate affect the uses which it may have: the conditions under which it was obtained, its accuracy, reliability, etc. To use properly the information provided by estimation procedures, all such properties of the estimate should be known.

We have already noted that research directed toward producing information should take into account the possible uses of such information. This involves not only knowing what the information is to be used for but also *how* it is to be used; that is, the courses of action into which it may be incorporated. This point can be illustrated by an analogy. An automobile, like information, is an instrument. To develop an efficient automobile, the designer must know not only what it will be used for but also the different ways it will be used; for example, the driving habits and abilities of operators. In a sense, then, the pure researcher should take into account the driving habits and abilities of his fellow-scientists. He can do this by formulating the various types of actions into which he believes his estimate can be incorporated.

4. The Possible Mistakes

In every scientific research project we should take into account the possibility of reaching an erroneous conclusion. Observations and assumptions are always subject to a certain error, and this error leads to the possibility that a conclusion we reach is not a correct one. If we are to face this situation realistically, we must evaluate the mistakes that might occur in order to know which ones to try to avoid. Obviously we want to avoid the more serious mistakes.

One of the most important developments in modern statistics consists of a method which enables us to select a statistical procedure which minimizes the chance of our making a serious mistake. These methods will be considered in chapter v. But research decisions other than those involving statistical procedures should also be designed to avoid serious mistakes. For example, suppose we are developing a method for distinguishing between normal and subnormal school children for the purpose of providing separate instruction for the latter. Suppose we agree that treating a normal student as though he were subnormal is more serious a mistake than treating a subnormal student as though he were normal. This would mean that we should devise a criterion of subnormality such that it is less likely to include a normal child in the subnormal group than to include a subnormal child in the normal group.

To take such precautions as these, we must determine first what are the possible mistakes and how serious they may be. The possible mistakes and their seriousness are aspects of the problem; their definition depends on the formulation of the aspects of the problem which we have considered up to this point.

The number of mistakes a researcher can make is a function of the number of hypotheses he is testing. If there are two hypotheses, there are two mistakes which can be made:

(1) Accept H_2 when H_1 is true.
(2) Accept H_1 when H_2 is true.

If there are three hypotheses, there are six mistakes which can be made:

(1) Accept H_1 when H_2 is true.
(2) Accept H_1 when H_3 is true.

    (3) Accept H_2 when H_1 is true.

    (4) Accept H_2 when H_3 is true.

    (5) Accept H_3 when H_1 is true.

    (6) Accept H_3 when H_2 is true.

In general, if there are n hypotheses, the number of mistakes which can be made is equal to $n(n-1)$. If, for example, there are four hypotheses, the number of possible mistakes is equal to $4(4-1)$, or 12.

The nature of possible mistakes becomes clearer when we consider an example. In the following example not only are the possible mistakes listed but the possible consequences of each mistake are indicated.

PURPOSE OF THE RESEARCH: To determine whether a need for a change in housing conditions exists in a neighborhood, and whether such a change can be carried out immediately, for the sake of preparing plans and providing housing where it is needed and can be provided.

Hypothesis	Course of Action	Possible Mistakes	Possible Consequences
H_1: the need exists, and change can be carried out immediately	City planning commission prepares plans and construction of housing	Accept H_1 when H_2 is true	Community interest is aroused and becomes annoyed at lack of foresight; produces unrest in neighborhood and jeopardizes other projects
		Accept H_1 when H_3 is true	Loss of time and funds for getting housing in other places where it is needed; loss of prestige of planning commission through public criticism
H_2: the need exists, but neighborhood has to be convinced first	Delay steps to create plans and use education and political action to overcome resistance	Accept H_2 when H_1 is true	Unnecessary delay in execution of plan, additional costs; loss of prestige of planners
		Accept H_2 when H_3 is true	Loss of time and funds in providing housing in other places where it is needed; loss of prestige of planners, but possibility of learning about mistake before too late
H_3: the need does not exist	Do not make plans for this neighborhood but conduct same research for another neighborhood	Accept H_3 when H_1 is true	Indefinitely prolongs suffering that can be alleviated at once; loss of prestige, etc.
		Accept H_3 when H_2 is true	Prolongs suffering that could eventually be alleviated if steps were taken to overcome resistance

The formulation of the possible consequences enables us to understand the nature of the mistakes and prepares the ground for determining how serious the mistakes are.

4.1. The Seriousness of Mistakes

At present there is no generally accepted scientific procedure for weighting possible mistakes. Nevertheless, the best conduct of research requires that the possible mistakes be weighted. We cannot solve a problem by ignoring it and keeping ourselves unaware of its existence. Here we will describe *one* method of assigning weights. No claim is made for its being the best method; the only claim to uniqueness is that it is explicit. Some aspects of the proposed procedure are defensible; others are arbitrary, because at this stage of scientific development we do not know enough to make these choices on better grounds. But, since the procedure is explicit, it is subject to eventual evaluation and improvement.

We can define a mistake as the selection of less than the most efficient means available for a desired objective. Research is purposive activity, and purposive activity consists of the choice of means for desired objectives. If the means selected on the basis of the research are not the most efficient available, the research is responsible for a mistake.

The two factors which are used to evaluate a course of action are (1) the efficiency of the action relative to an objective and (2) the importance of the objective. For example, if the objective of the research is trivial, then the seriousness of selecting almost any means for that objective will not be great. On the other hand, if the objective involved is very important, even the selection of a means only slightly less efficient than the most efficient available would be serious; the smaller the relative efficiency of the means selected, the more serious the mistake committed.

First let us consider the procedure of weighting the seriousness of a mistake relative to one objective, O_1. Let us say that the mistake consists of accepting H_i when H_j is true; that is, of selecting course of action C_i when C_j is the most efficient.

(1) Estimate or determine the efficiency of C_j for O_1, when H_j is true.

(2) Estimate or determine the efficiency of C_i for O_1, when H_j is true.

(3) Subtract the result of (2) from the result of (1). This is the *relative inefficiency* of C_i; that is, the loss of efficiency due to the mistake. This measure has 1 as a maximum and -1 as a minimum.

(4) Estimate the importance of O_1. (This will have been done at an earlier stage of formulating the problem.) This measure also has a maximum value of 1, but its minimum value is 0.

(5) The seriousness of this mistake, S_{ij}, is then equal to the product of the result of step (3) and the result of step (4). The maximum and minimum values of this measure are 1 and -1, respectively. A negative

value indicates that a mistake has not been made. This is not a contradiction, as we shall see in a moment. Since (3) gives a value on a probability scale (i.e., efficiency) and (4) gives a value on a preference scale, their product (5) is a measure of what can be called the "expected preferential loss."

Suppose, for example, we obtain the following values:
(1) The efficiency of C_j for O_1 is equal to 0.8 (when H_j is true).
(2) The efficiency of C_i for O_1 is equal to 0.3 (when H_j is true).
(3) The relative inefficiency of C_i is equal to $(0.8 - 0.3)$, or 0.5.
(4) The importance of O_1 is equal to 0.6.
(5) The seriousness of the mistake S_{ij} is equal to (0.5×0.6), or 0.3.

To obtain a measure of the seriousness of a mistake relative to a set of objectives $(O_1, O_2, \ldots, O_n)$, the following procedure can be used:
(1) Determine the seriousness of the mistake relative to O_1 using the method described above. Let S_1 represent this measure.
(2) Determine the seriousness of the mistake relative to O_2 using the same method; that is, S_2. Repeat this process for each objective up to and including O_n.
(3) Compute the sum of these measures:

$$S_1 + S_2 + \ldots + S_n.$$

(4) Compute the average $\bar{S}$, where

$$\bar{S} = \frac{S_1 + S_2 + \ldots + S_n}{n}.$$

$\bar{S}$ is the average seriousness of the mistake which consists of accepting H_i when H_j is true, relative to all the objectives. Any individual, S, may have a negative value, but the total of the S's cannot. If the total were negative, it would mean that C_i is more efficient than C_j when H_j is true. This would indicate that the hypotheses are improperly formulated and should therefore be reformulated.

Each possible mistake should be weighted in the manner described.

Consider, for example, the two-textbook problem described on page 35. The essentials of that problem can be summarized as follows:
C_1: continue to use the old text.
C_2: select the new text.
T_1': the transformed average test score produced by the old text.
T_2': the transformed average test score produced by the new text.
H_1: $T_1' \geq T_2' + 0.022$.
H_2: $T_1' < T_2' + 0.022$.

O_1: teach the introductory sociology course as efficiently as possible.

O_2: minimize the cost of the text to the students.

R_1 (the importance of O_1) = 0.9.

R_2 (the importance of O_2) = 0.1.

K_1' (the transformed efficiency of C_1 for O_2) = 0.4.

K_2' (the transformed efficiency of C_2 for O_2) = 0.6.

Let us weight the mistake which consists of selecting C_1 when H_2 is true. First consider this mistake relative to O_1. On the basis of past experience, say, we are fairly certain that the difference in average test scores will be no greater than 10, and both averages will be greater than 60. Then we can assume that, if H_2 is true, the inefficiency of C_1 for O_1 will be no greater than a difference in average test scores of 10, which, if transformed by use of Figure 2, is equal to 0.25. Since R_1 is equal to 0.9, the seriousness of this mistake (the most serious that has a chance of occurring) is equal to (0.25) (0.9), or 0.225.

The seriousness of the mistake relative to O_2 can also be computed. The efficiency of C_1 and C_2 in this case is independent of whether H_1 or H_2 is true. The inefficiency of C_1 for O_2 is equal to (0.4 − 0.6), or −0.2; that is, C_1 is less efficient for O_2 even if H_1 is true. Hence, since R_2 is equal to 0.1, the seriousness of this mistake is equal to (−0.2) (0.1), or −0.02.

Then the total seriousness of the mistake—selecting C_1 when H_2 is true—is equal to (0.225) + (−0.02), or 0.205. The seriousness of the other mistake—selecting C_2 when H_1 is true—can be similarly computed. In this case it turns out to be equal to 0.245. Hence, the selection of C_2 when H_1 is true is slightly more serious than selecting C_1 when H_2 is true.

In weighting the mistake relative to O_1, we made a number of assumptions in order to estimate the efficiency of C_1 when H_2 is true. The necessity for such assumptions arises out of the fact that "H_2 is true" is ambiguous. H_2 is the assertion that T_2' is greater than T_1'. This is ambiguous because we do not specify "how much greater." The efficiency of C_1 obviously depends on how much greater T_2 is than T_1. Since we do not know this amount beforehand, we could get a more complete understanding of the mistake if we considered the efficiency of C_1 for each amount by which T_2 can be greater than T_1. In chapter v we shall see how we can make this and other refinements in weighting the seriousness of mistakes.

5. The Environment(s)

The discussion up to this point has assumed that the problem involves only one environment. We want to see now how the involvement of several environments affects the problem and its formulation. How can a change of environment affect the problem? It may affect any of its aspects: participants, objectives, their importance, available means, their efficiency, etc. A change in any one of these would mean, in effect, that there is a separate problem for each environment. In this case a separate formulation would be required for each environment. The various formulations, however, would have a great deal in common. Similarities in formulation will, of course, be reflected in similarity of research design and procedure.

If a change in environment does not affect any aspect of the problem, then, in effect, there is *no* change in the environment relative to the problem.

In some cases where separate environments are involved, it may not be desired to find a separate solution for each environment. Rather, one course of action may be sought which will have maximum over-all efficiency, even if it does not have maximum efficiency in each environment. In such a case the problem environments can be considered to be a group, and the efficiency of the alternative means can be taken to be the average efficiency (or some other suitable statistic) over each of the "subenvironments." Otherwise, the formulation would not be affected. The design and execution of the research will be affected because of the generality of the environment. But this is a matter for later discussion (chap. ix).

6. Summary

We have now considered each aspect of formulating the problem. The decisions made in each phase should be recorded so that they can be continuously re-evaluated and modified if necessary. The record should include at least the following information:

1. *The participants.*—They should be identified and their identification should be justified if it is not obvious.

2. *The pertinent objectives of all the participants.*—The evidence in support of those which are not obvious should be included.

3. *The weighting of the objectives.*—The method used and those using it should be recorded. A complete record of the weighting procedure should be included.

4. *The alternative courses of action.*—The method by which they were uncovered should be recorded. If any were excluded, justification for having done so should be included.

5. *The acceptance conditions.*—These should be justified by making explicit the measure(s) of efficiency adopted and the assumptions involved.

6. *The alternative hypotheses.*—A demonstration of their exhaustiveness and exclusiveness should be provided if these properties are not obvious.

7. *The possible mistakes and their consequences.*

8. *The seriousness of the possible mistakes.*—A record should be included of the procedure by which these were computed.

DISCUSSION TOPICS

1. Who are the various participants in an election poll? What are their respective interests?

2. What measures of efficiency would be applicable to the following:

   a) Alternative slum-clearance programs?

   b) Magazine advertising campaigns?

   c) Graduate training in sociology?

   d) Explanations of a race riot?

3. What are the objectives of social science? Weight them by use of the procedures described in this chapter.

4. To what uses might the following information be put, and how?

   a) A measure of religious segregation in public housing.

   b) The number of people living in a city.

   c) The number of people holding various opinions toward religion.

5. Is the following statement by the eminent sociologist, Louis Wirth, relevant to the physical sciences? To the social sciences?

"We cannot afford to disregard the values and goals of acts without missing the significance of many of the facts involved. In our choice of areas of research, in our selection of data, in our method of investigation, in our organization of materials, not to speak of the formulation of our hypotheses and conclusions, there is always manifest some more or less clear, explicit or implicit assumption or scheme of evaluation" (14:xxii).

6. Is the following evaluation of social science by one of its eminent practitioners, S. A. Stouffer, justified?

"Quick plausible 'answers' in sociology and social psychology are rewarded in our culture: tedious modest experimental design is not in demand, and hence our discipline is not accumulative.

"In a society which rewards quick and confident answers and does not worry about how the answers are arrived at, the social scientist is hardly to be blamed if he conforms to the norms. Hence, much social science is merely rather dull and obscure journalism: a few data and a lot of interpretation" (12:355).

EXERCISES

1. Select a problem on which to work throughout this book, a *course project*. Formulate this problem in accordance with the procedure described in this chapter.

2. Read "Studies of the Postwar Plans of Soldiers: A Problem in Prediction" (13: xv and xvi) and formulate the problem discussed in the manner considered in this chapter. (If this volume is not available, select some other relatively comprehensive research report.)

SUGGESTED READINGS

There is very little written on the formulation of research problems. This aspect of research design is usually dismissed with a sentence or is ignored. Some of the aspects of formulating the problem are discussed in other contexts. For example, the measurement of utility in economics is related to the weighting of objectives. For some discussion of this aspect see (2), (3), (8:i), and (11:v).

For discussion of the social responsibility of the social scientist, see (6) and (7). In (12) will be found a provocative discussion of the influence of the social scientist's interests on his own work. A general consideration of the problem of the scientist's responsibility for the use of his results can be found in (4:Postscript), (5:xvi), and (9:v).

REFERENCES AND BIBLIOGRAPHY

1. ACKOFF, R. L. "On a Science of Ethics," *Philosophical and Phenomenological Research*, IX (1949), 663–72.
2. ARROW, K. J. "Mathematical Models in the Social Sciences," in *The Policy Sciences*, ed. DANIEL LERNER and H. D. LASSWELL, Stanford University: Stanford University Press, 1951.
3. ———. *Social Choice and Individual Values.* New York: John Wiley & Sons, 1951.
4. BORN, MAX. *The Restless Universe.* 2d rev. ed. New York: Dover Publications, Inc., 1951.
5. CHURCHMAN, C. W. *Theory of Experimental Inference.* New York: Macmillan Co., 1948.
6. DANIELS, FARRINGTON. "Science as a Social Influence," in *Science and Civilization*, ed. R. C. STAUFFER. Madison: University of Wisconsin Press, 1949.
7. MERTON, R. K.; BAIN, READ; BARKIN, SOLOMON; CORTWRIGHT, DORWIN; HAUSER, P. M.; SHILS, E. A.; and ULRICH, D. N. "Symposium: Social Research with Respect to Policy Formation," *Philosophy of Science*, XVI (1949), 161–249.
8. NEUMANN, J. VON, and MORGENSTERN, OSKAR. *Theory of Games and Economic Behavior.* 2d ed. Princeton: Princeton University Press, 1947.
9. OTTO, MAX. *Science and the Moral Life.* New York: New American Library (Mentor Books), 1949.
10. PARETO, VILFREDO. *Manuel d'économie politique.* 2d ed. Paris: M. Giard, 1927.
11. SAMUELSON, P. A. *Foundations of Economic Analysis.* Cambridge: Harvard University Press, 1947.
12. STOUFFER, S. A. "Some Observations on Study Design," *American Journal of Sociology*, LV (1950), 355–61.
13. STOUFFER, S. A., *et al. Measurement and Prediction.* Princeton: Princeton University Press, 1950.
14. WIRTH, LOUIS. "Preface" to KARL MANNHEIM's *Ideology and Utopia.* London: Routledge & Kegan Paul, Ltd., 1936.

CHAPTER III

The Idealized Research Model

1. The Research Procedure

In the process of formulating the immediate consumer's problem the researcher also defines the research problem: to determine which alternative hypothesis is valid or to estimate the value of a variable. On the basis of the solution to the research problem a solution to the immediate consumer's problem will be selected.

Once the research problem is formulated, the researcher is in a position to consider how he will solve it. The first step toward obtaining a solution should be the design of an *ideal* research procedure; that is, the researcher should specify how he would like to go about solving the problem if he were completely unrestricted. At first glance such a step might seem like a very impractical one. Why bother with procedures we cannot carry out? Why dream idly or engage in wishful thinking? The answer is that concern with *ideal* (or *optimum*) research conditions and procedures is neither idle dreaming nor wishful thinking; it is quite important if we want to know how good the results are we eventually obtain. The ideal conditions and procedures act as a *standard* by means of which we can evaluate the practical research conditions and determine their short-comings. If these shortcomings are made explicit, in many cases it is possible to determine their effects on the observed results and hence to adjust the results so as to eliminate the effects of the shortcomings.

The use of an ideal research model (research standard) for the adjustment of actual data is pervasive throughout all the sciences. Consider a familiar physical example: the determination of the acceleration of freely falling bodies. The ideal model for determining such acceleration requires (among other things) a perfect vacuum in which the bodies could fall with complete freedom. Actually, the physicist can never create a perfect vacuum, but he can conduct his experiment so that he can determine how a body *would* fall if it were in a perfect vacuum. He determines how acceleration is affected by variations in atmospheric pressure. He uses mathematical functions to relate changes in atmospheric pressure to changes in acceleration. Then by extrapolation he determines what would occur in a complete vacuum and thereby infers the acceleration of a freely falling body.

The idealized research design should consist of specifications of the most efficient conceivable conditions and procedures for conducting the research. This involves asking: (1) What shall I do? (2) To whom? (3) Under what conditions? (4) For what shall I look? More specifically, an idealized formulation of the following aspects of the research is required:

1. *X: The subject(s) to be observed.*—In social research the subjects are usually human beings taken separately or in groups. In some cases, however, houses, farms, newspapers, or other objects are observed. The collection of all the elements to be observed is called the "population." The population may consist of one, several, or many individuals, groups, etc.

2. *N: The environment(s) to be observed.*—The environment consists of the background conditions against which the subjects are to be observed. These conditions are ones which actually or potentially affect the subject's behavior, but these effects are not of central interest in the research.

3. *S: The stimulus (or stimuli) to be observed.*—The stimulus consists of the foreground conditions whose effects on behavior are of central interest. The stimulus can be conceived as being something either added to, subtracted from, or changed in the environment. The research is concerned with the effect, or lack of it, of this addition, subtraction, or change on the subject's behavior.

4. *R: The response(s) to be observed.*—The response(s) consists of the changes in the subjects produced by the stimulus.

The properties of the responses to be observed are the dependent variables, whereas other pertinent properties of the subjects and the pertinent properties of the environment and stimulus constitute the independent variables.

Observations of the responses provide the data on the basis of which one of the alternative hypotheses will be accepted. For example, if a hypothesis asserts that the average test score of a certain population is equal to some specified quantity, then the pertinent responses are those made to the test. From these responses the researcher could compute a test score and determine the average over the population. In general, then, the researcher should specify how the data obtained from observing the specified responses should be used to select one of the alternative hypotheses. To give a brief and oversimplified illustration, suppose we have two alternative hypotheses:

H_1: An individual X_1 prefers using black ink to using blue ink for writing letters.

H_2: X_1 does not prefer using black ink to using blue ink for writing letters.

The idealized research conditions and procedures might be specified as follows: Place or observe X_1 in an environment in which he has a strong desire to write letters and has no conflicting desires (N). Make available only blue ink and black ink and a clean fountain pen which requires filling (S). Observe the color of ink which X_1 selects (R).

Now we can specify the property of R required to accept each of the two hypotheses involved.

(*a*) If the frequency with which X_1 selects black ink is greater than the frequency with which X_1 selects blue ink, accept H_1.

(*b*) If the frequency with which X_1 selects black ink is not greater (i.e., is equal to or less) than the frequency with which X_1 selects blue ink, accept H_2.

Such a formulation may be quite ambiguous (even if considerable care is taken), since the meaning of the concepts involved may not be too clear. For example, what is meant (in the illustration above) by "selects," "desire," "prefers," and "conflicting"? Should we use only one brand of black ink? What kind of letters ought to be considered, personal or business? In sum, how can we determine whether or not the procedure specified is efficient and suitable? The answering of such questions as these is the subject of this chapter.

First we will consider the problem of determining which properties, objects, and events should be used in formulating the idealized research model and the type of definition they should be given. We shall subsequently consider the problem of how these variables should be used to specify the idealized research conditions and procedures.

2. Selecting Pertinent Concepts

A research model is a symbolic construct, one in which all phases of the research are conceptualized. Concepts are needed to formulate the problem and to design ways of solving it. In research, as in any other type of behavior, we deal with objects, events, and their properties. In the design of research we have to decide *beforehand* what objects, events, and properties we need to conceptualize. That is, we should decide which concepts are *pertinent* or *relevant* to the problem. Once these concepts are identified, they should be defined. Consequently, we need (1) criteria of pertinence to aid in the selection of concepts and (2) guiding principles for constructing scientific definitions.

2.1. Criteria of Pertinence

The decision to include a concept of an object, event, or property in the research model should depend on two related considerations: (1) Does the object, event, or property have any effect on the efficiency of any of the possible solutions to the problem? (2) If it does, is its effect significantly large relative to the research objectives? Suppose, for example, we want to determine which of a set of alternative textbooks is best suited for teaching a certain subject. Should the teacher be taken into account? We know that the efficiency of a text depends on the teacher who uses it and, furthermore, that this effect can be considerable. The concept of "teacher," therefore, would be pertinent in this study. For similar reasons, the kind of students is also relevant. Is the sex of a student pertinent? We may not know how much this property affects the efficiency of the text. In this case it is better to "play safe" and *assume* that sex has a significant effect. If this and similar assumptions are explicitly formulated, the research can be designed to test them. If testing the assumptions involves more time, money, or effort than can be expended, at least subsequent research can examine their validity. Thus we should make decisions regarding pertinence of concepts either on the basis of prevous knowledge or on the basis of doubts which we convert into assumptions capable of being tested.

One critical problem lies in the question, "How can we be sure that we have taken into account all pertinent aspects of the problem?" Or, in other words, how can we be certain we are using all the available pertinent information? No research ever breaks completely new ground. Previous research has always been concerned with at least part of each so-called "new" problem. All research, therefore, is part of a continuous and cumulative scientific development. It is a platitude to say that we have much to learn from the history of science. But the way that we can most effectively benefit from the history of science is not common knowledge.

We all know that general and specialized histories of science have been written. In addition, we know that there are journals devoted to almost every branch of science. In most fields periodicals are available which contain abstracts of articles appearing in many other journals. There are also bibliographies which list important contributions to general and specific scientific problems. The average scientist is familiar with at least some of these; he recognizes that a library is almost indispensable in research design.

These facilities are so numerous, however, that the researcher does not have time to become familiar with all of them. At best he can only cover the publications in his own field. But frequently there is information in other fields which would prove useful if it were readily accessible. It is difficult, for example, for the psychologist to know if there have been any developments in physics which throw light on measurement of visual sensitivity. As scientific knowledge increases and research grows more and more extensive, it becomes impossible for any one scientist to keep up with all the aspects of science which may be pertinent to his problems. Even the extensive use of abstracts from other fields is not satisfactory simply because most scientists cannot determine from the abstracts whether or not the results can be applied to their own work.

The consequence is that today no one scientist can be aware of all the facts, laws, and theories that are potentially useful to him in selecting pertinent concepts. There are usually so many things of which we are not aware but which nevertheless significantly affect research results. Too often scientists take on the responsibility for decisions which they as individuals are not qualified to make. The only assurance we can have that we have taken account of all or most of the pertinent available knowledge lies in *co-operative* scientific effort. Too often it is only after the research has been conducted and published that one learns from critics about important concepts which were neglected. It would be much better to get such criticism at the design stage, so that criticism becomes an effective tool in preparing the research and not merely a way for scientific hecklers to gain prestige.

A group of scientists from the same field are frequently not in a position to think of all that is pertinent to a problem. Hence, interdisciplinary, as well as intradisciplinary, co-operation is necessary. For best selection of pertinent concepts, therefore, we should consult with representatives from as many diverse fields as possible.

It is one thing to agree verbally to this principle of interdisciplinary co-operation but another to act accordingly. Interdisciplinary and intradisciplinary co-operation should be made an *institutionalized* aspect of the design procedure.

There is one way of getting interdisciplinary and intradisciplinary co-operation which has worked out very successfully to date. It consists of setting up a co-operative group from all the scientific and nonscientific fields that are even faintly suspected of being able to contribute to the problem at hand. When such groups work informally around a table or in a seminar, the interrelationship between the disciplines grows more and more apparent, and the applicability of knowledge from these diverse fields to the problem at hand becomes evident as well. Even if it turns out that scientists from other fields cannot help solve the problem at hand, it is only by such a procedure that a researcher can assure himself that he has exhausted all available relevant information.

During World War II teams of scientists were attached to military staff units to provide efficient information in a ready-to-use form for critical problems as they arose. These "operations research" groups were made up of scientists from many diverse fields. For example, one such group consisted of a mathematician, a physicist, a psychologist, and a lawyer. Such operations research groups were found to be highly efficient. They were and are being used extensively in both Britain and in this country in nonmilitary as well as military research.

In large research organizations and universities there is ample opportunity for the formation of co-operative interdisciplinary research groups. It is regrettable that our modern universities are not taking full advantage of the facilities at their disposal. In some instances such groups have been temporarily set up to attack specific problems (14), but as yet few such groups have been organized on any permanent and institutionalized basis. Often there is the fear that a scientist will lose his individuality in such co-operative efforts, though quite the opposite is the case. The expert in a field is no less an expert in his field because he can find help from others.

It may seem a bit puzzling that interdisciplinary co-operation should be effective in highly restricted problems; that is, in problems which seem clearly to lie in only one area of science. Yet there is no mystery involved. The explanation lies in the fact that most research is concerned with processes, that is, systems of behavior. We have become increasingly aware that analogous systems are operative in all scientific areas. Consider one dramatic case in point— the development of cybernetics ([19], [33], and [45]). Cybernetics is the science of control and communication in man and machines. The general components of the cybernetic model of control and communication processes can be found in electronic devices, in an animal's nervous system, in an industrial plant, in a department store, or in a relationship between any two individuals or two nations. Representatives of many different sciences were involved in the development of cybernetics itself, as Norbert Wiener acknowledges in the Preface to his book *Cybernetics*. Their objective was to develop "a team of scientists, each a specialist in his own field, but each possessing a thoroughly sound and trained acquaintance with the fields of his neighbors; all in the habit of working together, of knowing one another's intellectual customs, and of recognizing the significance of a colleague's new suggestion before it had taken on full formal expression. The mathematician need not have the skill to conduct a physiological experiment, but he must have the skill to understand one, and to suggest one. The physiologist need not be able to prove a certain mathematical theorem, but he must be able to grasp its physiological significance and to tell the mathematician for what he should look" (45:9). It was only through such co-operation that so general and comprehensive a picture of communicative processes could be developed. All this has helped emphasize the fact that most processes and problems which appear to apply to only one science have their counterpart in all other sciences. In many cases, several fields have worked out different techniques for studying the same process. Hence there is considerable potential aid which can be derived from other disciplines by virtue of the difference in their attack on these general processes and problems.

The mere gathering of a group of experts from different fields is no guaranty that such a group will be productive. The success of such groups depends in part on the psychological and social characteristics of the members. The psychological and social characteristics which make for efficient research groups are by no means "intangibles." As yet, however, they have been little investigated. There has been a good deal of study of small groups by such organizations as the Research Center for Group Dynamics at the University of Michigan and the Office of Naval Research. Few of the results thus far obtained are applicable to the formulation of co-operative research groups. Columbia University's Center for Studies of Research Administration in its "Team Research Project" is making a frontal attack on the problem. But as yet we are forced to rely mainly on past experience and common sense in forming such groups.

Summarizing, then, in the search for pertinent available information the researcher has several means available to him:

1. He obviously has his own knowledge, experience, and intuition from which to draw.

2. By personal contact he can draw on the knowledge, experience, and intuition of others (nonscientists as well as scientists) either separately or in co-operative research or consulting teams.

3. He can use the literature dealing directly or indirectly with the problem he is considering. Familiarity with "the literature" is indispensable. In the "Suggested Readings" at the end of this chapter are listed some useful guides to conducting an examination of the literature in the psychological and social sciences.

In whatever way the pertinent available information is gathered, it is important that the scientist record what assumptions he makes and what information he uses and how it is obtained. The explicit statement of these aspects of the research will facilitate subsequent inquiry into available information for related problems.

2.2. Criteria of Defining

It is not enough to decide that a concept is pertinent. We must make explicit (1) the conditions under which and (2) the operations by which the pertinence can be investigated. For example, if we select "educational attainment" as a pertinent property, then we must show how we can determine its influence on the process under consideration. Even if we eventually decide that we want to "cancel out" the effect of this property in the research, we must know how to determine whether or not its effect has been canceled out. The function of a scientific definition of a concept, then, is *to make explicit the conditions under which and the operations by which we can answer questions about that which is conceptualized.*

Scientific definitions should be *directive;* they should tell us *how* to investigate that which is conceptualized. It is not enough to require definitions which "clarify" a concept; we must say what clarification means relative to research. Since the purpose of research is to answer questions, clarification can only mean "making explicit the process of answering questions." Thus, scientific definitions should not be *merely* directive; they should be research-directive; they should indicate how we can conduct controlled investigations into questions involving the concept.

For purposes of discussion, we shall consider the content and form of scientific definitions separately, even though they are inseparable in practice.

2.2.1. Content of Definitions

By "content" of definitions we refer to the meaning of the concept defined. In many cases we deal with concepts whose meanings already have been well formulated. Here we want to discuss the procedure required if an adequate formulation is not available. The lack of clarity of meaning of many psychological and social concepts is considerable. (Though not generally recognized, this is also the case in the physical sciences.) For some concepts there are as many different meanings as there are scientists who have tried to define the concept.

When we compare definitions of a concept offered at different times in the history of science, or different definitions offered at the same time, we generally find that there is a common core of meaning which runs through all the definitions. That is, if we "line up" the definitions, we frequently find that they point in one direction. That meaning toward which definitions of a concept evolve may be said to constitute the "true" meaning of the concept. We can never *know* what the limit of the evolutionary process is, but we can make better and better successive approximations to it on the basis of accumulative efforts of scientific defining. Some scientists advocate looking for a definition with which most contemporary scientists would agree. If this became a general rule, there would be little if any progress in defining. We should seek to improve, not accept, prevalent definitions. But improvement can be made only by taking present and past definitions into account.

Describing the procedure in these general terms is not of much help in specific situations, but the analysis of concepts is not an easy task. Here we suggest one procedure for defining concepts which has proved fruitful:

    (1) Examine as many definitions of the concept, past and present, as possible. Seek the help of others in locating them. Keep the chronology of the definitions in mind.

(2) Try to get at the core of meaning toward which most of the definitions seem to point.

(3) Formulate a tentative definition based on the "core."

(4) See if the tentative definition covers all the cases you think it should, relative to your research objectives. Where it does not, make necessary revisions.

(5) Submit the definition to as wide a critical appraisal as possible. Include nonscientists as well as scientists from various fields among the critics.

(6) Make final revisions on the basis of the legitimate criticism you receive.

In Appendix II we have illustratively used these rules to analyze the concept "social group."

The research objectives should play an important role in determining the content of a definition. To understand this role, it is necessary to make a distinction which historically and currently causes considerable difficulty in obtaining efficient definitions—the distinction between *structural* and *functional* properties. A structural property is one which refers to the *matter* of which a thing is composed and to changes in this matter. For example, one dictionary offers the following definition of "book": "a collection of tablets, as of wood, ivory, or paper, strung or bound together." Note that all the properties referred to in this definition deal with structural properties. On the other hand, the same dictionary offers an alternative definition: "a written or printed narrative or record, or series of such." In this definition reference is made to how the object is produced (written or printed) and to its use (to narrate or record). These are functional properties. Functional properties deal with what produces the thing defined, what are its products, and/or its uses. For a detailed technical distinction between these types of properties see (10) and (11).

Before defining a concept we should decide whether to consider it structurally and/or functionally. This decision should be based on the research objectives. For example, suppose we are conducting research to determine the standard of living of families in a community. We might decide that one measure of standard of living is the number of persons per room in a dwelling unit. To conduct the study we would have to define a room. A "room" might be defined structurally, as one dictionary does: "a space inclosed or set apart by a partition." The researcher should ask himself if the *use* of this definition in the research will produce the results he ideally wants. In this case it is obvious that it would not. According to this definition, a carton, a box, a closet, a drawer, etc., would all be rooms, and these should not be included. The researcher could try a more sophisticated structural definition: an inclosed space large enough for human occupancy. But again many closets, automobiles, telephone booths, etc., would satisfy these conditions. When the researcher stops to think about the research objectives, he realizes that he is interested in spaces that can be lived in; that is, spaces which can be *used* for certain purposes. It is the *function* of the room, and the efficiency with which it performs this function, that is of primary concern. It is true, of course, that the function of the space is dependent on its structural characteristics, but it is also true that rooms with different structural properties can function equally well.

It may seem obvious that, if the research is concerned with functional properties, the researcher should deal with them. There are, however, great temptations to the contrary. It is generally assumed that structural properties can be observed more accurately and precisely than can functional properties. The temptation, then, is to define in terms of structural properties in order to gain "accuracy and precision" in observation. But such "accuracy and precision" may yield useless data. It is true that in some cases practical demands may subsequently require at least a partial translation of functional properties into structural properties, but in the idealized research design we should not take such limitations into account. We should define the pertinent concepts in terms of properties which ideally make it most useful for the research objectives.*

Some scientists feel that all this concern with the content of definitions is not justified. They argue that a scientist can define a concept however he wants (i.e., arbitrarily) as long as he makes his meaning clear. They argue that one definition is as good as another, provided only that the definitions are equally explicit.

Even the most ardent proponent of arbitrary definitions would not like to be taken literally. If he were, then one could define intelligence as "the number of legs a chair has" with complete justification. The proponents of arbitrary defining mean arbitrary *within certain limits;* but they fail to make explicit what these limits should be.

The defense of arbitrary defining suffers from a critical weakness which the specification of limits will not remove: it fails to recognize that scientific concepts are symbols of scientific problems which have a history of their own.

---

* The inclination to structural definitions in psychology and social science is sometimes defended by reference to the theory of conceptual *reductionism*. The reductionist attitude appears in the psychological sciences in the form of molecular behaviorism (44) and in the social sciences among what Sorokin calls "social mechanists" and "social physicists" (36). This attitude is based on the conviction that there are ultimately simple data, concepts, and operations and that these are physical (i.e., structural) in nature. The reductionists attempt to reduce all psychological and social concepts to those of physics (18). The effect has been to minimize the significance of those psychological and social concepts the physical translation of which is not apparent. For example, at one time or another reductionists have suggested eliminating such concepts as "mind," "consciousness," "disposition," "social group," and "society." The opponents of reductionism point to the persistence of these concepts as evidence of the existence of psychological and social problems which are not reducible to purely physical problems. A detailed discussion of this issue can be found in (13). Efforts to disprove reductionism experimentally are reported by Ames and his associates ([3], [7], and [24]).

Scientific concepts have acquired a social and scientific significance which is independent of any particular scientist. Even where individual scientists disagree on the meaning of a concept, there is some cohesiveness relating their definitions, some common core of meaning which each scientist is obliged to try to capture in his definition.

The matter can be put in another way. Since definitions are research instruments, the progress of research and science depends in part on the development of better and better definitions; that is, definitions which accelerate the development of methods for solving both old and new problems. The concepts we use symbolize these problems; if the concepts are poorly defined, so are the problems. But the lack of good definitions does not make the problem any less persistent or important. If we ignore the fact that a concept's meaning lies in human problems, we prevent science from progressing in its development of solutions to these problems. In short, the use of arbitrary definitions not only makes progress in defining a matter of luck but imposes serious restrictions on progress in other aspects of science.

One particularly harmful form of arbitrary defining arises when a test is developed to "measure" a poorly defined property. Then the property is defined as "that which the test measures." Aside from the circularity of such a procedure, it prevents us from improving our methods of measuring the property. That is, if a property is that which the test measures, then there is no better way of measuring the property. Whatever else this may be, it is *not* a scientific definition, since improvement is made impossible.

2.2.2. Form of Definitions

The dictionary type of definition is wholly inadequate for research purposes. Consider, for example, a typical dictionary definition of the psychological concept "trait": "a distinguishing characteristic." Such a definition does not help us at all in determining what traits any specific individual has. The professional psychologist is more sophisticated than the dictionary in his defining, but frequently he is not much more helpful in *directing* us how to find out about traits. Here are two examples of the psychologist's definitions of traits:

An individual is said to possess, or to be characterized by, a certain personality trait when he exhibits a generalized and consistent form, mode, or type of reactivity (behavior), and differs (deviates) sufficiently from other members of his social environment, both in the frequency and intensity of this behavior, for his atypicality to be noticed by relatively normal and impartial observers, themselves members of the same environment . . . [43:542].

[A trait is] a generalized and focalized neuropsychic system (peculiar to the individual), with the capacity to render many stimuli functionally equivalent, and to initiate and guide consistent (equivalent) forms of adoptive and expressive behavior [1:295].

Such definitions may give us some insight into the meaning (content) of a trait, but they are of little help in designing research to answer questions about traits. They do not tell us what to do in order to determine if a trait is present and the degree to which it is present.

Definitions can be made directive by imposing a certain form on them. The form imposed depends on whether a property, object, or event is being defined. We will consider each of these in turn.

A scientific definition of a property should in general take the following form:

X has the property p if, when X is in an environment N and is under stimulus S, X exhibits (or has a certain probability of exhibiting) a property q or behavior b.

This means that, in providing a scientific definition of a property, we would specify the following:

X: the class of things (subjects) to which the property can be attributed.

N: the kind of environment in which X should be observed.

S: the kind of stimulus to which X should be subjected in the specified environment N.

R: response of the subject (X) to the stimulus (S) in the specified environment (N).

It will be noted that the components of a scientific definition of a concept are the same as the components of the idealized research model. A scientific definition should be, in effect, an idealized research model for answering questions concerning the concept defined.

Let us apply these formal requirements of scientific defining to what is generally considered to be a "simple" physical property, "redness." To say that an object (X) is red (p), we should specify somewhat as follows: if an object is placed in a spectroscope (N) and is illuminated by white light (S), the spectroscope will record for the reflected light a wave length within a specified range (R).

Pertinent psychological and social concepts should be similarly treated. But, since this is not an easy task, it is avoided more often than not. If it is avoided, we can have no assurance that the data eventually collected pertain to the pertinent property. Remembering for the moment that our concern is with the *form* of scientific definitions (and not with their content), let us return to the concept of a trait and see what form a definition of this concept should take. In defining any particular trait, we will have to specify (1) subjects, (2) environment, (3) stimuli, and (4) responses to be observed. Hence, in defining the general concept "trait," we should make explicit the general restrictions to be imposed on these four aspects.

"A trait of personality," writes Allport, "is a characteristic form of behavior more generalized than a single reaction or simple habit" (1:119). Furthermore, "traits have no . . . definite reference to objects," "traits may only be general," and traits do not signify "the acceptance or rejection of the object or concept of value to which it is related" (1:293–94). Traits are necessary for clarifying "the repeated occurrence of actions having the *same significance* (equivalence of response), following upon a definable range of stimuli having the same personal significance (equivalence of stimuli)."

From these selected passages one begins to grasp the intended meaning of "trait." The problem is to cast these intentions into an operational form. We might proceed as follows:

1. *X: Subjects.*—Any psychological individual can display traits, hence the population to which traits can be attributed consists of the class of individuals to whom we can attribute "mind."

2. *N: Environment.*—A trait is a *typical* or *habitual* type of response to various classes of stimuli. Traits involve habits where the efficiency of behavior is not a factor; that is, choices of behavior which are independent of efficiency. Then we want to know how an individual characteristically responds in situations where his choice is not influenced by the efficiency of the alternative courses of action available to him. Consequently, we can specify N as an environment in which the subject desires an objective for which there is available a set of equally efficient means.

3. *S: Stimulus.*—In traits we are not concerned with how an individual responds to structurally defined stimuli such as redness, hardness, weight, etc. Such responses refer to an individual's sensibilities, not traits. In studying traits, we are concerned with functionally defined stimuli such as "aggression," "co-operation," and "instruction." That is, traits involve typical responses (sensitivity) to functionally defined stimuli.

4. *R: Response.*—We are concerned with characteristic responses, but characteristic in a functional, not a structural, sense. For example, we might be interested in "the extent to which the subject tends to co-operate with others" or "the extent to which he seeks revenge from those who have wronged him." In a sense, then, traits are habitual functional responses to functional stimulation.

These content decisions can be brought together into an operational definition of "trait." That is, one which specifies the general conditions and operations by which the presence of specific traits can be determined. An individual can be said to have a specific trait, T, if (*a*) when he is in an environment in which he desires an objective, for which equally efficient means are available, and (*b*) when he is subjected to a specific functionally defined stimulus, (*c*) he has a greater probability of selecting one specific type of functionally defined means than another.

This definition is quite general, but it directs the formulation of specific trait definitions. Specific trait definitions will differ only in the way the stimuli and responses are functionally classified. Consider, for example, the trait *aggressiveness*. On the common-sense level we say that a person is aggressive if he enters into conflict with others without provocation. This definition can be molded into the form of a scientific definition of a trait as follows:

An individual, X_1, is aggressive if

(1) X_1 shares an environment with another individual or individuals, X_2.
(2) X_2's behavior has no effect on the efficiency with which X_1 can pursue his desired objective O_1.
(3) X_1 has equally efficient alternative means each of which falls into one of two classes: (*a*) means for O_1 the use of which reduces X_2's efficiency in pursuit of his objective O_2 and (*b*) means which do not reduce X_2's efficiency.

Then, X_1 is aggressive to the extent that he chooses means falling into class (*a*), and he is nonaggressive to the extent that he selects means falling into class (*b*). X_1's degree of aggressiveness can be defined as the probability that he chooses a means of type (*a*). His degree of nonaggressiveness is equal to the probability that he chooses a means of type (*b*).

A definition such as this one immediately suggests behavioristic and verbal test situations, and it provides criteria for the pertinence of data obtained from any suggested situation. It is in this sense that such definitions are directive. In chapter ix we shall see in detail how a trait test can be constructed on the basis of a definition such as this.

So much for the form of definitions of properties; let us turn now to objects and events.

Definitions of objects and events should have a different form from that specified for definitions of properties. Let us first consider the definition of a class of objects. A collection of objects constitute a class if they have one or more properties in common. Consequently, one form a definition of such a class can take is:

An object x is a member of class X if it has properties $p_1, p_2, \ldots, p_n$.

The properties specified must be necessary and sufficient to distinguish members of the class defined from nonmembers of the class. That is, an object which does not have these properties should not be a member of the class, and every object which has these properties should be a member.

The properties defining the class can either be properties of the individual members or properties of the collection; that is, *distributive* or *collective* properties. For example, a person is a member of the class of males or females by virtue of properties of the person himself or herself. Thus sex is a distributive property. On the other hand, a man is a husband not only because of his own properties but because of the properties of the social group which includes his wife; that is, there can be no husband without a wife. Consequently, in defining a class characterized by a collective property, collective as well as distributive properties must be used. For example, a husband is a male (distributive property) who is married (collective property).

A class can also be defined either.*denotatively* or *connotatively*. Connotative definitions are the kind we have been considering thus far: ones which specify the necessary and sufficient properties of class membership.

A class may also be defined by enumerating the members (i.e., denotatively). For example, in defining the faculty of a specified school, we can either specify the necessary and sufficient condition for faculty membership (i.e., a connotative definition) or list the faculty members' names (i.e., a denotative definition). Denotative definitions identify each member of the class separately, as by name, number, or location.

Before the individual members of a class can be identified, we must know what properties identify them as class members. Consequently, a connotative definition is a prerequisite for constructing a denotative definition. Once the members of a class have been identified by the use of a connotative definition, repetition of the identification process can sometimes be avoided by enumerating the class members, that is, defining the class denotatively. It must be remembered, however, that the membership of a class may change; members come and go, are built or destroyed, are born or die. The necessary and sufficient conditions for class membership are generally more stable than lists. Hence a connotative definition is always necessary as an instrument for checking the adequacy and pertinence of a denotative definition.

In defining an event, we should remember that an event always happens *to* something (X) and consists of a change in one or more of X's properties. Thus, the general form of a definition of an event is as follows:

Event E occurs if the properties $p_1, p_2, \ldots, p_n$ of object(s) X change to other properties, $q_1, q_2, \ldots, q_n$.

For example, a crowd "disperses" when the group of people making it up (X) change from being "close together" (p) to being "far apart" (q). Or a person "moves" when he changes his location from one place (p_1) to another (q_1). In many cases we are concerned with the failure of an event to occur, such as the failure of an individual to respond to a stimulus. Such a *non*event can be defined as the negative of an event.

A sequence of events which *together* yield a specified product or state is called a *process*. Maturation, education, the manufacture of a product, and preparation for retiring at night are all processes. A process can be defined as a series of events which collectively have a specified function (e.g., to produce an automobile, to learn how to make a living).

Summarizing this discussion of the form of definitions, it is important to realize that the *formal* requirements discussed are designed to produce definitions which direct research procedures. That is, by constructing definitions in the specified forms, the definitions are made more than merely suggestive; they are made *directive*. And directive they should be.

3. Fixing or Changing Variable-Values

Once the pertinent variables (i.e., objects, events, and properties) have been defined, it is necessary to decide whether their values ought to be kept constant (fixed) or changed during the idealized research procedure. In some research projects we may want to observe changes in responses for a single change in environment, subject, or stimulus. For example, we may want to observe the difference in an individual's response to the same physical environment (1) when no one is present and (2) when one or more people are present. Here only the stimulus would be changed. Or we may want to observe the difference in response between two individuals in the same environment under the same stimulation. The changes in the stimulus may be specified by a change in only one property or by a change in many. Any one or more of the variables which specify the stimulus, subject, and environment may be changed. Consequently, two decisions need to be made: (1) whether to fix or change the value of a variable relative to the idealized research procedure and (2), if the value is to be changed, to what values it should be changed. The answers to both these questions depend on the hypotheses being tested and the research objectives. Suppose the hypotheses require the determination of the value of a property, p_1. Suppose further we know that values of another property, p_2, affect the values of p_1. Then there are two kinds of decisions we can make with regard to p_2 in the idealized model:

(1) We may want to determine the value of p_1 for a fixed value of p_2. In such a case the results obtained would hold only in situations characterized by the fixed value of p_2. For example, we may know that a person's income (p_1) is affected by his education (p_2); yet in some projects we may want to determine p_1 only for college graduates with a

B.A. degree and no more. Then we fix the value of p_2, and our results will be applicable only to this group.

(2) We may want to determine how p_2 and p_1 are related; that is, we might want to express p_1 as a mathematical function of p_2. In this case we would want to use various assignable values of p_2. For example, if we wanted to know how education and income are related, we would want to specify the values of educational attainment for which observations on income are to be made.

Whether or not we change a variable and how we fix or change it depend on the range of situations relative to which the problem is formulated. If the problem were to be solved for one specific unchanging situation, then all the variables would be held constant at a specific set of variable-values. The more general the problem, the more variables are changed and the wider is the range of values over which they should be changed. At this extreme we would want to observe responses for all possible combinations of all possible values of all the variables. It should be apparent that a clear formulation of the problem situations is the essential basis for deciding how to treat a variable.

Before we can consider the effect of the "relationship" of p_1 and p_2 on the design of the ideal model, we should first consider the ways in which p_1 and p_2 may be related.

3.1. Cause-Effect, Producer-Product, and Correlation

There are three types of relationships between properties with which science is concerned: cause-effect, producer-product, and correlation.

Unfortunately, cause-effect has been treated ambiguously in science, and hence an important distinction between cause-effect and producer-product relationships is seldom made. Let us see what the distinction is.

An X may be said to be the cause of a Y if the occurrence of X is *sufficient* for the subsequent occurrence of Y. This means that, whenever X occurs, Y follows. Thus cause-effect may be taken as a strictly deterministic relationship, since X determines the occurrence of Y. It is clear that in this strict sense of cause-effect, no object, event, or property can by itself be said to be the cause of another object, event, or property. The effect that an object, event, or property has on another always *depends* on its environment, and hence the object, event, or property is never sufficient for the effect. Striking a bell does not cause the subsequent sound, because, if the bell is struck in a vacuum, no sound will result. Hence the act of striking the bell is not sufficient for the sound; its effect depends on the values of other variables. Actually cause-effect in this strict deterministic sense is a relationship which holds only between comprehensive cross-sections of nature. It is a relationship studied primarily in "mechanical systems."

On the other hand, there are $\bar{X}$'s the occurrence of which is _necessary_ but _not sufficient_ for the subsequent occurrence of Y. For example, in some situations the striking of the bell is necessary for making it sound, for the sound would not occur unless the bell were struck—but the blow is not sufficient. This type of relationship we call "producer-product." The psychological and social sciences are concerned with producer-product rather than cause-effect relationships.

Under what ideal conditions could an object, event, or property $\bar{X}$ be said to be the producer of another object, event, or property Y? Two conditions should be satisfied:

(1) There must be an environment (X) such that, when X is placed in it, Y follows. For example, there must be an environment in which an increase in education is followed by an increase in income, for education to be said to be a producer of higher income.

(2) The environment X must be such that if X does _not_ occur in it, then Y will _not_ follow. Thus, there must be an environment not only in which an increase in education is followed by an increase in income but in which, if there is no increase in education, there will be no increase in income.

If these two conditions hold, then X is a producer of Y _in the environment $\bar{X}$_. Note that an increase in education may produce an increase in income in some environments but not in others.

Now the question arises as to how one can determine if an X is, as a matter of fact, a producer of Y in any given environment. An idealized model for such an inquiry was formulated in the last century by John Stuart Mill (29), one he called the "Method of Difference." What he said, in effect, is the following: Characterize an environment which contains X, in terms of all its pertinent variables, $A, B, \ldots, X$. Now see if Y follows. If it does, observe an environment in which all the properties are the same except that X is absent. If Y does not follow, then X is a producer of Y in that environment. Several variations of this model have been advocated in the psychological and social sciences. One of the most common goes as follows: Suppose we want to determine if X produces a change (Y) in an individual or group of type Z. Then construct two environments which are exactly alike in all their properties except that X is present in one and is absent in the other. Place a group of type Z in each environment. The group placed in the environment in which X is absent is called the "control" group. Then if change (Y) follows in the environment in which X is present and does not in the situation in which it is absent, X is said to be the producer of the change Y in Z.

If, under the circumstances described, Y *always* occurs, then X is certain to produce Y, that is, its probability of producing Y is equal to 1. There are many cases, however, where X is not always followed by Y but is followed only by Y part of the time. *The relative frequency* (proportion) *of the times that Y follows X is the probability that X will produce Y.* This probability can range from 0 to 1. Where this probability equals 0, X never produces Y and hence is not a producer of Y.

The use of a probability scale to characterize the producer-product relationship has advantages over the use of a simple two-way classification of producer and nonproducer. Most X's and Y's with which we are concerned will have a probability of production less than 1 and more than 0. For example, an increase in education will not be followed by an increase in income for every person but only for a certain proportion of people. This proportion is the probability that an increase in education produces an increase in income over the population of persons considered.

One possible source of confusion should be removed. The model described for determining producer-product is an *ideal* one. In psychology and social research, however, it is frequently impossible even to "come close" to the ideal. We can seldom, if ever, match environments and individuals in the manner required by the ideal model. The important thing to remember, however, is that it is not necessary to be able to produce this ideal research situation to determine what would happen if it were produced. As we have indicated earlier, modern statistical techniques are available which enable us to determine what would happen under these circumstances, even though we cannot produce them.

Two variables may be related and yet be neither causally connected nor connected as producer-product. Consider, for example, a person who usually brushes his teeth once a day, just before going to sleep at night. Brushing his teeth is neither sufficient nor necessary for his going to sleep and hence is neither the cause nor the producer of his retiring for the night. And yet the two events usually occur together. To take another example, in one large city it was discovered that people who live in neighborhoods in which there is a heavy soot-fall are more likely to get tuberculosis than people who live in neighborhoods with less soot-fall. Yet medical research has shown that soot-fall is neither necessary nor sufficient for the occurrence of tuberculosis. Hence, the values of two variables may tend to change together, and yet the variables may be neither causally nor productively connected.

The knowledge that two things tend or do not tend to change together can, nevertheless, be very useful. For example, when we see the person in the above illustration brush his teeth, we can predict with some assurance that he is about to retire. That is, we can use our knowledge of one variable as a basis of predicting the value of the other.

Suppose, for example, that we learn that tall men tend to make better interviewers than short men. Height may or may not have any productive connection with interviewing ability. Yet if we have to make an emergency selection of an interviewer, we know we are more likely to get a good one if we pick a tall man than if we pick a short one. We may not know why this is so, but we can use the fact that it is so.

Correlation analysis enables us to measure the tendency of variables to change or not to change their values together. We shall discuss the technical aspects of such analysis in chapter vi. But it is important to post a warning here —a warning which shall be posted again, since failure to heed it leads to one of the most prevalent errors in the social sciences. To establish that two things tend to change or occur together is not to establish that they are related directly or even indirectly by a producer-product relationship. We cannot infer production from correlation alone. On the basis of the correlation between soot-fall and tuberculosis one researcher concluded that soot-fall was a producer of tuberculosis. Subsequent research revealed that this was not the case: it showed that dietary deficiencies are among the producers of tuberculosis. Further, it revealed that dietary deficiencies are likely to occur most frequently among low-income groups. Low-income groups are likely to live in low-rent districts. Districts become low-rent, among other things, because of heavy soot-fall. Thus soot-fall and tuberculosis are *accidentally*, not essentially, connected.

Summarizing, then, social research may deal with variables which are related as producer-product and/or with correlated variables. If the research involves determining whether or not one variable is the producer of another, or if two variables are correlated, the values of these variables will have to be varied in the research. If all we are concerned with is to determine whether one value of one variable, V_1, is the producer of one value of another variable, V_2, then at least two values of V_1 are required, since we must determine whether or not a change in V_1 is followed by the nonoccurrence of V_2. In many cases, however, we want to determine what changes in V_2 are produced by changes in V_1. That is, we want to determine how sensitive V_2 is to V_1. In such cases a number of different values of V_1 will be required.

4. Quantified and Qualified Variables

Once we have decided whether we ideally want to change or fix the value of a variable, we should next determine the values of the variable to be used. If we fix the value of the variable, only one value need be specified. If we decide that the variable should be changed, we need to specify the different values which we would ideally like to use. The values we specify depend on whether we conceive of the variable in quantitative or qualitative terms. Qualitative variables are called "attributes" and will be referred to as such henceforth. The term "variable" will be reserved only for quantitative variables.

On a common-sense level the distinction between an attribute and a variable is clear; the latter involves numbers and the former does not. If we refer to a person as "tall," "medium," or "short," we treat the property "height" qualitatively. If we refer to the person's height as "5 feet 11 inches," we treat height quantitatively.

The distinction between quantification and qualification, however, is not so simple. Arbitrary assignment of numbers to variations in a property is not scientific quantification. For example, we could assign a number to the length of an object by selecting a number "out of a hat." This would not be scientific quantification. Scientific quantification requires a logic behind the system of assigning the numbers and a utility for the results. In most general terms, scientific quantification is a way of assigning numbers to properties, objects, and events so as to yield useful information. For example, knowing that a table is "long" is good enough for some purposes, but it is not good enough for others, such as covering the table with a plate-glass top or building a nook into which it will fit snugly. If we know that the table is between 68 and 69 inches long, this information is efficient in a much wider range of circumstances than is the information that the table is "long." If we know the table is between 68.4 and 68.5 inches long, this information is even more useful than the information that the table is between 68 and 69 inches long. If such a thing as an absolutely accurate determination of length were possible, and we knew that length, then this information would be perfectly efficient in *any* situation in which the table's length was of any importance. Thus "efficiency in use" is the key to scientific quantification, and "accuracy" of quantification refers to this efficiency.

The more critical a problem is, the more inclined we are to quantify accurately the various aspects of it. That is, the more costly the use of *in*efficient information is, the more we need efficient (i.e., accurately quantified) information. In some cases, however, the cost of quantifying may be greater than the savings produced by using more efficient information. For example, in determining the adequacy of housing, we can either count the number of rooms in a dwelling unit or determine the number of square feet of available floor space. The latter may be more efficient information relative to our purposes, but the cost of obtaining it may be disproportionate to the gain in accuracy. That is, the errors resulting from counting the number of rooms may cost less than measuring the floor space. To take a homely example, a tailor measuring the length of an arm does so to the nearest quarter-inch. He does not make finer measurements, because they would be more costly and would yield results which are not any better relative to his and his customer's objectives.

Ideally the decision to qualify or quantify, and how to quantify or qualify, should be based on a systematic comparison of costs. For each method of making measurements two costs are pertinent: (1) the cost of actually making the measurements and (2) the cost one can expect to incur due to error produced by the method. From these two costs a total expected cost could be computed, and alternative methods of quantification and qualification could be compared. The one yielding the minimum total expected cost would be the best choice.

Unfortunately, we do not know enough about any method of qualifying or quantifying in the social sciences to make such a determination. Until we do, we can use this method and estimate the required values as best we can. By so doing, we will encourage research directed toward determining these values. In a sense it is a sad commentary on the social sciences that such research has not yet been conducted, but this is not nearly so unfortunate as would be the continued failure to conduct such research. In any case, the researcher should formulate as best he can a justification for the method of qualifying or quantifying which he selects.

4.1. Types of Quantification

What are the general methods for quantifying a variable?

First, there is *counting*. Counting is frequently and mistakenly thought to be a very simple type of quantification. But counting requires that the units to be counted be identified, and such identification can be very complex. We have already referred to one such case: counting those who "live in a house." Once "living in a house" or "usual residence" is unambiguously defined, the counting may not be so complex; but identifying the unit to be counted is an integral part of the counting operation.

In the counting process we must match the units to be counted with elements of the real number system. There are two types of errors which can arise in this matching process—errors which can be guarded against only by proper design: *underenumeration* and *overenumeration*. Underenumeration consists in failing to count an element which should be counted, and overenumeration consists in counting the same element more than once or counting elements which should not be counted.

We have all experienced the difficulty of trying to count the people milling about in a crowded room. For one thing, we may have trouble in counting each person once and only once. We know that the process can be simplified by organizing the people in the room so that they can be counted systematically. For example, we can close off all the entrances except one and have the occupants of the room file out the one exit in single file. Or we can line the people up in some kind of formation. Numerous well-known techniques for counting are available. The point here is that in the idealized research model, if a quantified variable requires counting to determine its value, then an idealized process for the counting procedure should be specified.

A variable that is quantified by counting can be called an "enumeration variable." Such a variable will always take the form: the number of a's in A; for example, "the number of people present," "the number of children in the family," and "the number of dollars (amount of money) earned." An enumeration variable—as can be seen from these examples—is always a collective property; that is, it is always a sum of elements.

Suppose now we are concerned with an individual unit rather than a collection of units. (Any units dealt with in the social sciences can be broken down into a collection of smaller units. But here we are concerned with the unit and not its parts.) The unit may vary with respect to any one or more of its properties which are pertinent to the research. How can we quantify such properties? One semiarbitrary method is to rank the elements. For example, if object a is approximately twice as long as object b, we can refer to the length of object a as 1 and the length of b as 2. We can do the same for two other objects c and d; say, assign c's length the number 1 and d the number 3. But now suppose we want to compare a's and c's lengths. A new comparison is required; the numbers we have assigned their respective lengths have no meaning out of the context of the original comparison. If a and b, and then c and d, are compared with a common *standard* of length, then a and c can be compared indirectly. The use of a standard in this way yields a *measurement*. If the standard consists of an ordered set of units (among other things), it is called a "metric scale." A metric scale of length, for example, consists of an ordered set of inches, or centimeters, or some multiple or fraction thereof.

Standards and metric scales enable us to compare things "by proxy." We can determine, for example, which of two tables is the longer even though the tables are in different quarters of the world. Scales can be manipulated even where the objects scaled cannot.

A metric scale permits efficient comparisons to the extent to which the units are small enough to distinguish significant differences in the property measured. A yardstick cannot be used efficiently to measure the difference in the diameter of two microbes. On the other hand, it may be inefficient to use a micrometer to measure a person's height. As science progresses, however, smaller and smaller units become more and more important. The smaller the unit, the greater the accuracy of measurement tends to become. Hence, from the point of view of the long-run objectives of science, the development of more discriminating scales is a necessary aspect of the progress of science.

There are many properties which an efficient scale should have, but our purpose here is not to enumerate all of them (see [9], [15], [16], [37], [38], and [39]). But there are some important properties which affect the usefulness of psychological and social scales which should be considered here.

How do we know that a yardstick can be used to measure length? We know it can be so used because length is a well-defined concept, and we can demonstrate that the numbers yielded by a prescribed use of the yardstick yield information concerning the length of objects which is useful in problems concerning length. If we are not clear as to what length means, we have no assurance that a scale does or does not measure it. That is, the usefulness of a scale is dependent on our ability to define the property scaled. The use of a scale in situations where we do not have a clear definition of the property involved may yield quantities but not necessarily measures. Such is the case in many psychological and social scales. Many psychological and social scales consist of a set of questions, or problems, and a scoring system which enables a number to be assigned to the subject's answers or performance. The score on a true-false test, for example, may be determined by subtracting the number of incorrect answers from the number of correct answers. Such a score is not necessarily a measure. It is a measure to the extent that (a) the property involved can be defined and that (b) the process of assigning a score can be shown to provide information concerning the property in question which is useful in solving problems involving the property. For many psychological and social tests the property is not well defined, and the connection between the test and the property remains intuitive rather than demonstrable.

It is common practice in psychology and social science to construct a scale with only a vague idea as to the property that is being quantified. After the scale is constructed, the researcher tries to determine what property it measures. In many cases he finds no answer; if he does, it is more a matter of luck than of intelligent research design. The procedure should be reversed: the property should first be defined and then a scale constructed which will yield (what can be demonstrated to be) measures of the property defined. If the property is defined in the manner we have described above, the definition itself will suggest measures and methods of obtaining measurements. In the definition of aggressiveness, for example, the formulation itself specified that the measure of aggressiveness is the probability of a specified kind of behavior being selected. We can then construct a method for determining this probability and hence measure the property defined.

Since scales deal with numbers, it has been found that their usefulness is dependent on their having certain mathematical properties. There has been a good deal of mathematical analysis of scales. This has resulted in some psychologists and sociologists becoming more interested in the mathematical properties of a scale than in its usefulness. It makes no difference what mathematical specifications are imposed on scale construction; the satisfaction of these requirements provides no guaranty that a scale which satisfies these demands measures the property in question. The meaning of the property, not the mathematics of scale construction, should be the starting point in the development of a measure for that property.

Many psychologists and sociologists are aware of the shortcomings of their scales but point out that these scales are, after all, useful in predicting certain kinds of behavior. It is cited, for example, that an I.Q. is a good predictor of classroom performance in school. This may be so, but its being so is no assurance that I.Q. is a measure of intelligence. As a matter of fact, intelligence is not clearly enough defined to determine whether or not I.Q. does measure it. An I.Q. test may very well measure something, but knowing this much helps us little; we need to know what it measures.

Such scaling techniques as have recently been developed by Thurstone (42), Guttman (41), and Lazarsfeld (41) do provide some assurance that their scales measure something, but their methods themselves provide no controlled basis for deciding what that something is.

The basic methodological principle in scale construction, then, is that the development of a scale should start with meaning, not with mathematics. In chapter ix we will develop a scale for measuring the trait "ascendance-submissiveness." We shall see there how the meaning of the trait provides a basis for "building into" the scale its subsequent pertinence and usefulness.

Suppose we are concerned with a comparison of the height of a group of seven people, A, B, C, D, E, F, and G. If we have no way of measuring height, we can line the people up from the tallest to the shortest, using our eye as best we can. We thereby *rank* these individuals according to their height. We can select the middle person and assign his height the value "0." To the next tallest person we assign "1," to the next "2," etc. To the next shortest person we assign the value "−1," to the next "−2," etc. Eventually we might have an ordered array as follows:

A	B	C	D	E	F	G
3	2	1	0	−1	−2	−3

We have, in effect, constructed a rank scale of height. It could be used in many ways, but it has some serious limitations. We do not know how much difference in height there is between any two members of the group. We simply know whether one is taller or shorter than another. We do not even know whether the differences are equal. It is quite possible that "3" is 6 inches taller than "2" but that "2" is only an inch taller than "1." Nevertheless, we can classify any individuals with respect to their relationship to the standard rank order. In the height illustration we can construct eight ranked classes. The first would consist of those who are taller than A, the second of those who are taller than B but not taller than A, etc., until we reach the last class—those who are not so tall as G.

Many psychological and social scales are rank scales of this type. In a good number of these, however, the property with respect to which the ranking is made is poorly defined, if defined at all. The usefulness of a ranking scale, like that of a metric scale, is a function of its relation to the property in question. The procedure in developing a rank scale should be no different from that in developing a metric scale: the development should begin with definition.

In the example of ranking used above, the initial comparisons were not quantitative; they were qualitative. Ranking, however, may be based on quantitative comparisons. For example, where all that is required is a ranking of height, we may still measure the height of each individual and rank them on the basis of these measurements. Even where only a ranking is required by the research design, it is sometimes desirable to base the ranking on measurements rather than qualitative comparisons. Such ranking is likely to be more accurate, and we have an efficient method for checking its accuracy. Modern statistical theory enables us to express the error of measurement, and we are thus provided with a basis for improving the method of measurement as well as the method of observing. This is not to say either that qualitative judgments cannot be made more accurate or that the accuracy of qualitative judgments cannot be measured. It is simply to say that in most cases quantification makes possible more accurate and reliable observations.

4.2. Qualification

Attributes, as we said, are qualitative aspects of the research problem; numbers are not involved in their description (but, as we shall see, this does not mean that quantification may not be involved in their determination). For example, a sociologist may refer to a group as "organized," or "disorganized" or to "competitive," "co-operative," and "conflicting" situations. A psychologist may refer to an individual as "selfish," "aggressive," "honest," etc. For the purposes of some inquiries such descriptions may be efficient.

Any property which is capable of quantification can also be treated qualitatively. A quality can simply be defined as a range along the scale in terms of which the property can be measured. For example, a person can be said to be "tall" if he is over 5 feet 10 inches, "medium" if he is between 5 feet 6 inches and 5 feet 10 inches, and "short" if he is under 5 feet 6 inches.

It is also true that any qualified property is potentially capable of being expressed in terms of such a range along a scale. We will never be able to translate all qualities to such measures, but, as science progresses, it converts more and more qualities into equivalent quantitative expressions. But this is not a one-sided development. As science develops more and more measures, it also requires new kinds of qualitative judgments. For example, height can be measured as a vertical distance; but this requires our ability to determine verticality. We can convert verticality into a measure in terms of the angle between a straight line and a radius projected from the earth's center of gravity. This requires our ability to determine straightness, etc. Quantification at any stage depends on qualification. What is qualified at one stage may be quantified at another; but at any stage some qualitative judgments are required. Consequently, progress in science is a function not only of an increased capacity to quantify efficiently (i.e., to measure) but also of an increased capacity to qualify efficiently.

Once we have decided to treat an aspect of the problem qualitatively, then we must specify the alternative qualities any of the objects or events to be observed may be said to have. For example, if we are going to qualify the property "yearly income," we can classify income as high, medium, and low. We may want more classes than these three. Thus qualification becomes a problem of classification, and in the idealized research model we should specify the classification desired for characterizing each qualitative property. If the classes are based on intervals along some scale running from lower to higher, the resulting classification is called "stratification." Thus stratification involves a ranking of qualities along a scale.

Classification and stratification, like definition, can be structural or functional in content; and, consequently, our earlier remarks with respect to definitions are pertinent here. For example, in some public opinion surveys the "environment" is critical. The usual procedure is to treat the environment in physical or structural terms; that is, in terms of geographic regions, in terms of density of population, etc. In one case, for example, communities were classified as (*a*) large cities (population greater than 250,000); (*b*) small cities (population between 10,000 and 250,000); and (*c*) towns, villages, etc. (population less than

10,000). It may be, however, that relative to the influence on opinion such a classification is quite inefficient. A large industrial city and a distant small industrial town may be more alike in their influence on public opinion than are two near-by large cities, one industrial, the other governmental. Classification should (where possible) be based on the characteristics of environments which *produce* the opinion, *not* on characteristics which are *merely* correlated with or unrelated to opinion. We should therefore take a functional approach to classification by centering our attention on those characteristics which produce the behavior we intend to observe.

When we classify the values of a property and examine its relationship to what we are examining, what we are frequently trying to do is to determine whether or not the various attributes (defined by the classification) have an effect on the response observed. We pointed out earlier that if one property is correlated (even highly) with another property, it by no means follows that changes in one of these properties produce changes in the other.

Consider, for example, the way "time" is sometimes classified in social surveys. We use a clock to break the day into periods of time: 9:00 A.M.–11:00 A.M., 11:00 A.M.–1:00 P.M., etc. Yet these hours may mean entirely different things to different people. Conducting interviews in the morning will be effective for some families in some areas but not in others, depending on what activity is interrupted by the interview. It is the activity indulged in during the time of interview that influences the responses, not the readings on the clock. It is only when we look for this productive relationship and construct functional classifications that we get the most efficient breakdown of attributes.

5. Summary

In the formulation of the problem, alternative hypotheses are constructed. These hypotheses consist of an explicit statement of the conditions under which each of the acceptable alternative courses would be selected; that is, the conditions under which each would be accepted as being the most efficient means for obtaining the research objective. The acceptance conditions, as formulated in the hypotheses, represent the outcomes of possible research. In the idealized research model we attempt to make explicit what we consider to be the optimum research conditions and procedures that could be conducted to determine which of the acceptance conditions, and hence which hypothesis, is true. The specification of a research procedure consists of determining what is to be done to whom, where and what is to be observed. The "what is to be done" is the required stimulation. The "to whom" is the population or subjects to be observed. The "where" is the environment in which the subjects are to be subjected to the stimuli. The "what is to be observed" is the response in which we are interested.

The stimuli, subjects, environment, and responses are composites of objects, events, and/or properties. We must decide which objects, events, and properties are necessary for their specification. This involves deciding what are the pertinent concepts. The decision as to whether or not a concept is pertinent depends on whether or not the object, event, or property specified would have some effect on the responses to be observed. The determination as to whether or not any specific object, event, or property would affect the response depends on available knowledge or assumptions which the researcher is willing to make. The most efficient way of making such determinations involves the maximum use of available information. This requires an exhaustive search of the literature and maximum use of the assistance that other scientists and nonscientists can provide.

Once the pertinent concepts are selected, they should be defined in such a way as to indicate how questions concerning them can be answered by controlled research. The content of such definitions depends on two things: the historical use of the concept and the research objectives. The content should be such as to be useful in the specific research conducted and also contribute to the general historical development of the concept in science. The form in which the content is cast should make explicit the conditions under which and operations by which questions about the concept can be answered.

Once the pertinent concepts are defined, we must decide whether they should be held constant at one value during the research or whether their value should be changed. This decision should be based on the range of situations over which the research conclusions ought to be valid.

Whether we decide to change or fix any pertinent aspect of the research situation, we must decide how to treat each aspect, quantitatively or qualitatively. This decision should be based on a comparison of costs associated with alternative treatments of the variable or attribute. The required accuracy of either the quantitative or the qualitative determinations should be established by a similar procedure.

With the specification of the various pertinent values of the variables and attributes, the idealized research model is completed. But, like all other design phases, it is subject to subsequent modification. It may subsequently become apparent, for example, that a pertinent variable was omitted or that an attribute should be quantified.

The procedures and conditions specified in the idealized research model can seldom, if ever, be met in practice. The next design job, then, is to translate the ideal model into a practical one. The remainder of this book will be devoted to this practical translation. Before beginning it, however, let us consider some of the factors which prevent our meeting the idealized conditions.

We begin by considering the case where it is possible for the researcher to manipulate all the variables and attributes which are involved in the ideal model. Even in this case practicality may impose many restrictions on what the researcher can do. The number of subjects or events that he wants to study may be larger than he has time, money, or energy to study. In such a case he will only be able to observe a portion of the whole. Once this restriction is imposed, the use of statistics and sampling becomes necessary. Hence the translation of the ideal model into a statistical model is a necessary aspect of carrying out the research.

Even in the case where there is only one subject, event, or property to be observed, the researcher is aware of the fact that his observations are always subject to error. Hence he will need more than one observation for each set of variable-values. He would like to take an infinite number of observations of even a single subject. This is obviously impossible, so he must deal with a sample of the possible observations also. Sampling possible observations also requires a translation of the idealized model into a practical statistical model.

Even if situations existed in which the researcher could take an infinite number of observations on each subject, it might be wasteful for him to do so. He may not need so much accuracy as so large a number of observations would yield. Therefore, if he wants only to do as much work as is necessary to get the amount of accuracy he requires, he will again want to use only a sample of the possible observations and make a statistical translation of his idealized research model.

In many psychological and social research situations, manipulation of all the variables is not possible. Hence research must be conducted in situations which differ from the idealized one. Then we must determine how we can infer from the results observed in some real situation to what we would observe if we produced the ideal situation. This requires that we make explicit what kind of real situation we will look for, how we will characterize it, and how we will adjust the results observed so that we can make assertions about the idealized situation. This will also require a statistical translation of the idealized research model and a formulation of the research operations to be actually performed.

DISCUSSION TOPICS

1. Evaluate the following definitions. How would you improve them, if at all?

a) *Adjustment:* "that which leads toward a state of adjustment, i.e., some relatively stable and mutually acceptable relationship among the participants" (17:286).

b) Attitude: "a tendency and will to act which emerges when the several desires have been balanced against each other" (17:200).

c) Communication: "all of the procedures by which one mind may affect another" (33:95).

d) Folkways: "behavior patterns of everyday life, which generally arise unconsciously in a group. . . . They seem to individuals, when the latter think of them at all, merely to be handy solutions of immediate problems" (20:134).

e) Social institution: "a functional configuration of cultural patterns (including actions, ideas, attitudes, and cultural equipment) which possesses a certain permanence and which is intended to satisfy fundamental social needs" (20:318).

f) Competition: "that social process in which rival individuals or groups seek advantages through the favor and preference of a public (individual or group), and use an appeal to the interests or prejudices of that individual or group rather than violence or the fear of it to secure their ends" (20:608).

g) Group institution: "such official, impersonally patterned functions and statuses of members of any organized social group who act and are reacted to as if through them the group as a whole were acting" (46:211).

2. How adequate a characterization of "empirical research" do you take the following quotation to be?

"With a few conspicuous exceptions, recent sociological discussions have assigned but one major function to empirical research: 'testing' or 'verification' of hypotheses. The model for the proper way of performing this function is as familiar as it is clear. The investigator begins with a hunch or hypothesis, from this he draws various inferences and these, in turn are subjected to empirical test which confirms or refutes the hypothesis" (28:505-6).

3. What are some social variables which are usually treated qualitatively? Is there any way of treating them quantitatively?

4. What are some social variables which are usually treated quantitatively? Under what conditions could and should they be treated qualitatively?

5. Using the definition of production provided in the chapter, how would you define (a) reproduction and (b) coproduction?

6. When we refer to a group as "organized," do we refer to structural, functional, or both types of properties?

EXERCISES

1. Prepare an idealized research model for the course project.

2. Using the instructions provided in this chapter, construct a scientific definition of one of the following: (a) community; (b) exploitation; (c) culture; (d) property; (e) employed.

3. Define the trait "tolerant" and construct a scale for measuring it.

4. Design an ideal research procedure for determining whether or not a particular newspaper's editorial is a producer of a particular person's opinion on the subject discussed in the editorial.

5. (a) Select a metric scale used in the social sciences. Determine what it measures, if possible. If not possible, why? (b) Do the same for a rank scale. (c) Determine how a physicist would ideally measure the length of an object.

SUGGESTED READINGS

The following are some useful guides in conducting surveys of literature. The researcher should familiarize himself with them.

Book Review Digest, The. New York: H. W. Wilson Co.
Bulletin of the Public Affairs Information Service. New York: Public Affairs Information Service.
Catalogue of Economic and Social Projects. Lake Success, N.Y.: United Nations Department of Public Information, 1949 and 1950.
Education Index, The. New York: H. W. Wilson Co.
Encyclopaedia of the Social Sciences. New York: Macmillan Co., 1931.
Encyclopedia of Psychology. New York: Philosophical Library, 1946.
Historical Statistics of the United States, 1789–1945. Washington, D.C.: United States Department of Commerce, Bureau of the Census, 1949.
Index to Labor Articles. New York: Rand School of Social Science.
International Index to Periodicals. New York: H. W. Wilson Co.
Monthly Catalogue, United States Government Publications, and *Annual Index.* Washington, D.C.: Superintendent of Documents.
Poole's Index to Periodical Literature. Boston: Houghton Mifflin Co.
Psychological Abstracts. Washington, D.C.: American Psychological Association, Inc.
Readers' Guide to Periodical Literature. New York: H. W. Wilson Co.
Review of Educational Research. Washington, D.C.: American Educational Research Association.
Science Abstracts. London: Institution of Electrical Engineers.
Social Science Abstracts. Menasha, Wis.: Social Science Research Council.
Statistical Abstracts of the United States. Washington, D.C.: United States Department of Commerce, Bureau of the Census, 1951.
Statistical Yearbook, 1949–50. Lake Success, N.Y.: United Nations Department of Public Information, 1951.
Technical Book Review Index. Pittsburgh, Pa.: Special Libraries Association.
Ulrich's Periodical Index. 6th ed. New York: R. R. Bowker Co., 1951.
United Nations Publications. Lake Success, N.Y.: United Nations Department of Public Information, 1950.
United States Quarterly Book Review, The. Washington, D.C.: Superintendent of Documents.

For an extensive bibliography on a special aspect of social research see

EATON, A., and HARRISON, S. M. *A Bibliography of Social Surveys.* New York: Russell Sage Foundation, 1930.
PARTEN, M. *Surveys, Polls and Samples.* New York: Harper & Bros., 1950.
SMITH, B. L.; LASSWELL, H. D.; and CASEY, R. D. *Propaganda, Communication and Public Opinion.* Princeton: Princeton University Press, 1946.

The following are articles and books which deal with some of the basic research problems discussed in this chapter. They are not suggested because they agree with the author; many are suggested precisely because they differ with the position taken here.

a) *Conceptualization:* Eubank (17) and Singer (34).

b) *General research procedure:* Burgess (5), Chapin (8), Greenwood (21), and Lundberg (27).

c) *Quantification and measurement:* Arrow (4), Campbell (6), Churchman (9), Coombs (15) and (16), Lazarsfeld and Barton (26), Reese (32), Stevens (37), (38), and (39), and Stouffer (41).

REFERENCES AND BIBLIOGRAPHY

1. ALLPORT, G. W. *Personality: A Psychological Interpretation.* New York: Henry Holt & Co., 1937.
2. ———. "A Test for Ascendance-Submission," *Journal of Abnormal and Social Psychology,* XXIII (1928), 118–36.
3. AMES, A., JR. *Some Demonstrations Concerned with the Origin and Nature of Our Sensations: A Laboratory Manual.* Preliminary draft. Hanover, N.H.: Hanover Institute, 1946.
4. ARROW, K. J. "Mathematical Models in the Social Sciences," in *The Policy Sciences,* ed. DANIEL LERNER and H. D. LASSWELL. Stanford University: Stanford University Press, 1951.
5. BURGESS, E. W. "Research Methods in Sociology," in *Twentieth Century Sociology,* ed. GEORGES GURVITCH and W. E. MOORE. New York: Philosophical Library, 1945.
6. CAMPBELL, N. R. *An Account of the Principles of Measurements and Calculations.* New York: Longmans, Green & Co., 1928.
7. CANTRIL, HADLEY. *The "Why" of Man's Experience.* New York: Macmillan Co., 1950.
8. CHAPIN, F. S. *Experimental Designs in Social Research.* New York: Harper & Bros., 1947.
9. CHURCHMAN, C. W. "A Materialist Theory of Measurement," in *Philosophy for the Future,* ed. R. W. SELLARS, V. J. MCGILL, and MARVIN FARBER. New York: Macmillan Co., 1949.
10. CHURCHMAN, C. W., and ACKOFF, R. L. "An Experimental Definition of Personality," *Philosophy of Science,* XIV (1947), 304–32.
11. ———. "Purposive Behavior and Cybernetics," *Social Forces,* XXIX (1950), 32–39.
12. ———. "Psychologistics." Philadelphia: University of Pennsylvania Faculty Research Fund, 1946. (Mimeographed.)
13. ———. *Methods of Inquiry.* St. Louis: Educational Publishers, 1950.
14. CHURCHMAN, C. W.; ACKOFF, R. L.; and WAX, M. (eds). *Measurement of Consumer Interest.* Philadelphia: University of Pennsylvania Press, 1947.
15. COOMBS, C. H. "Mathematical Models in Psychological Scaling," *Journal of the American Statistical Association,* XLVI (1951), 480–89.
16. ———. "Psychological Scaling without a Unit of Measurement," *Psychological Review,* LVII (1950), 145–58.
17. EUBANK, E. E. *The Concepts of Sociology.* Boston: D. C. Heath & Co., 1932.
18. FEIGL, HERBERT. "Logical Empiricism," in *Twentieth Century Philosophy,* ed. DAGOBERT RUNES. New York: Philosophical Library, 1943.

19. FRANK, L. K., *et al.* "Teleological Mechanisms," *Annals of the New York Academy of Sciences*, L (1948), 187–278.
20. GILLIN, J. L. and J. P. *An Introduction to Sociology.* New York: Macmillan Co., 1943.
21. GREENWOOD, ERNEST. *Experimental Sociology.* New York: King's Crown Press, 1945.
22. GUILFORD, J. P. *Psychometric Methods.* New York: McGraw-Hill Book Co., 1936.
23. HEBB, D. O. *Organization of Behavior: A Neuropsychological Theory.* New York: John Wiley & Sons, 1949.
24. ITTELSON, W. H., and KILPATRICK, F. P. "Perception," *Scientific American*, CLXXXV (1951), 50–55.
25. KITTEL, CHARLES. "The Nature and Development of Operations Research," *Science*, CV (1947), 150–53.
26. LAZARSFELD, P. F., and BARTON, A. H. "Qualitative Measurement in the Social Sciences: Classification, Typologies, and Indices," in *The Policy Sciences.* See (4).
27. LUNDBERG, G. A. *Social Research.* New York: Longmans, Green & Co., 1946.
28. MERTON, R. K. "The Bearing of Empirical Research upon the Development of Social Theory," *American Sociological Review*, XIII (1948), 505–15.
29. MILL, J. S. *A System of Logic.* 5th ed. London: Parker, Son & Bourn, 1862.
30. PAYNE, S. L. "The Ideal Model for Controlled Experiments," *Public Opinion Quarterly*, XV (1951), 557–62.
31. *Proceedings of the First Seminar in Operations Research, November 8–10, 1951.* Cleveland: Case Institute of Technology, 1952.
32. REESE, T. W. *The Application of the Theory of Physical Measurement of Psychological Magnitudes.* "Psychological Monographs," Vol. LV, No. 251. New York, 1943.
33. SHANNON, CLAUDE, and WEAVER, WARREN. *The Mathematical Theory of Communication.* Urbana: University of Illinois Press, 1949.
34. SINGER, E. A. *Mind as Behavior.* Columbus, Ohio: R. G. Adams Co., 1924.
35. SOLOW, HERBERT. "Operations Research," *Fortune*, XVIII (1951), 105 ff.
36. SOROKIN, PITIRIM. *Contemporary Sociological Theories.* New York: Harper & Bros., 1928.
37. STEVENS, S. S. "On the Problem of Scales for the Measurement of Psychological Magnitudes," *Journal of Unified Science*, IX (1939), 94–99.
38. ———. "On the Theory of Scales of Measurement," *Science*, CIII (1946), 677–80.
39. ———. "Mathematics, Measurement, and Psychophysics," in *Handbook of Experimental Psychology*, ed. S. S. STEVENS. New York: John Wiley & Sons, 1951.
40. STOUFFER, S. A. "Some Observations on Study Design," *American Journal of Sociology*, LV (1950), 355–61.
41. STOUFFER, S. A., *et al. Measurement and Prediction.* Princeton: Princeton University Press, 1950.
42. THURSTONE, L. L. *The Vectors of Mind.* Chicago: University of Chicago Press, 1935.
43. VERNON, P. E. "The Biosocial Nature of a Personality Trait," *Psychological Review*, XL (1933), 533–48.
44. WATSON, J. B. *Behaviorism.* New York: Peoples Institute Publication Co., 1934.
45. WIENER, NORBERT. *Cybernetics.* New York: John Wiley & Sons, 1948.
46. ZNANIECKI, FLORIAN. "Social Organizations and Institutions," in *Twentieth Century Sociology.* See (5).

CHAPTER IV

The Practical Research Design: Sampling

1. Introduction

The first problem we shall consider with respect to the practical formulation of research involves the various methods of selecting a portion of the population to be observed. This selection procedure is called *sampling*.

The statistical aspects of sampling have received considerable attention on both the theoretical and the applied levels. A copious literature is available, some of which is noted at the end of this chapter. The subject of sampling has been developed to such an extent that many statisticians devote themselves almost exclusively to it. Because of this extensive development, it has become increasingly difficult to be an expert in sampling and in some other area of statistics, let alone social science. Consequently, the purpose of this discussion is not to produce experts in sampling but to provide a basis for efficient co-operation between the social scientist and the sampling expert.

Throughout the chapter we shall emphasize sampling from populations of individuals rather than from populations of observations on a single individual. We do this for a reason already discussed: in social research repeated observations on the same subject may increase rather than decrease error. This is not to say that repeated observations always increase error and therefore should be avoided. To the contrary, repeated observations should be made wherever the observations can be adjusted or require no adjustment; that is, wherever the effect of repeating observations on the value of the characteristic being observed is known and hence can be canceled out or wherever repeating the observation does not affect this value. It should be emphasized, however, that the basic principles and the logic of sampling methods are identical in sampling populations of individuals and populations of observations on a single individual.

2. Errors in Sampling and Estimating

By way of getting into the problem of sampling, let us consider a simple "toy" population which consists of six members. Assume the members are

2, 3, 4, 6, 9, and 12 years old, respectively. Now, if we want to determine the average age of the population (which is 6 years), we must first determine the age of each member. But suppose practical considerations prevent us from determining every member's age, and therefore we must estimate the average age of the population on the basis of data obtained from only a sample of the population. It is apparent that there are various ways of selecting samples from the population and various sizes of sample which can be selected. The problem of sampling design, then, is to determine how to select the sample and how large a sample to select. In actual practice these design problems cannot be considered independently of the method of deriving an estimate from the data obtained from the sample; that is, the estimating procedure. For purposes of exposition, however, only the sampling design will be stressed in this chapter. Estimating procedures will be considered in chapters v and viii. The expression "sampling-estimating procedure" will be used to refer to a combination of a sampling and estimating procedure.

The design of a sampling-estimating procedure is directed toward yielding a "good" estimate of a population characteristic. The meaning of "good," of course, is critical. Also critical is the requirement that the criteria of "goodness" in this context be such as to permit quantitative evaluation of the procedure designed. A design which can be evaluated in this way is called a "measurable" design. A measurable design is not necessarily a good one, but it is desirable because we can know, rather than merely judge, how good it is and because progressive improvement in the design is made possible where explicit and measurable criteria are available.

Measurable criteria which are used in evaluating sampling-estimating designs are generally based on costs of two types: the cost of carrying out the design and the cost that can be expected to be incurred as a result of errors which might be made. In general, we will consider the best design to be that one which minimizes the sum of these costs. The operating costs are not difficult to understand. To understand costs due to error, some notion of sampling and estimating errors is necessary. It is important to note that errors must be measurable if they are to be used in evaluating a design. Let us consider the types of error that can be incurred in the use of a sampling-estimating procedure and how these errors can be measured.

2.1. Accuracy

To simplify the discussion of sampling error for the moment, let us assume that we have decided on practical grounds to select a sample of two members from the "toy" population. In addition, let us agree to use the average age of the sample as an estimate of the average age of the population. Then if we select two members whose ages are 2 and 4 years, we would estimate the average age of the population to be $(2 + 4)/2$, or 3 years. Actually, the average age of the population is 6 years, and hence the estimate is inaccurate. If we had selected the two members whose ages are 3 and 9 years, we would have obtained a perfectly accurate estimate. Accuracy and inaccuracy of an estimate can be defined more precisely as follows: let T represent the true value of the characteristic of the population being estimated and let e represent the estimated value of that characteristic. Then, if e and T are equal, the estimate is perfectly accurate. If e and T are not equal, then the estimate is inaccurate by the amount $(e - T)$. If this value is positive, e is an *overestimate;* if it is negative, e is an *underestimate.*

2.2. Bias

Now let us consider all the possible samples of two members which can conceivably be selected from the "toy" population. Before we list these possible samples, we must decide whether the same individual can be selected more than

TABLE 1

POSSIBLE SAMPLES OF TWO ELEMENTS FROM THE
POPULATION: 2, 3, 4, 6, 9, AND 12

Sample	Sample Average	Sample	Sample Average
2, 3	2.5	3, 12	7.5
2, 4	3.0	4, 6	5.0
2, 6	4.0	4, 9	6.5
2, 9	5.5	4, 12	8.0
2, 12	7.0	6, 9	7.5
3, 4	3.5	6, 12	9.0
3, 6	4.5	9, 12	10.5
3, 9	6.0		

once in the same sample. If each individual can only be selected once in any sample, the procedure is sampling *without replacement.* If an individual can be selected more than once in any sample, then the procedure is sampling *with replacement.* In social research, sampling without replacement is perhaps the more common procedure. Consequently, our emphasis will be on this type of procedure, although almost all the discussion to follow is applicable to either type of sampling.

All the possible samples of two which can be drawn without replacement from the "toy" population are shown in Table 1, together with the average of each sample. Note that only one of the samples (3, 9) yields a perfectly accurate estimate of the population's average age.

Now suppose we have a method of sampling such that there is an equal chance of selecting each of the fifteen samples shown in Table 1. Then we would have an equal chance of obtaining each of the fifteen sample averages shown as an estimate of the population average. In the long run, then, we would expect each sample average to be obtained 1/15th of the time. If each of the sample estimates were actually obtained 1/15th of the time, the average of the estimates would be

$$1/15(2.5 + 3.0 + \ldots + 10.5) = 90/15 = 6.0.$$

This value (6.0) is called the *expected value* of the estimate yielded by the sampling-estimating procedure used. The expected value of an estimate yielded by a sampling-estimating procedure is the average of the estimates we would expect to obtain in the long run by use of the procedure.*

TABLE 2

POSSIBLE SAMPLES OF TWO ELEMENTS FROM THE
POPULATION: 2, 3, 4, 6, 9, AND 12, WHERE 2 AND
12 CANNOT BE SELECTED

Sample	Sample Average	Sample	Sample Average
3, 4	3.5	4, 6	5.0
3, 6	4.5	4, 9	6.5
3, 9	6.0	6, 9	7.5

Note that in the illustration the expected value is equal to the true population average. Consequently, the procedure used would be said to yield *unbiased* estimates. A procedure would be said to yield *biased* estimates if the expected value of the estimate, $E(e)$, deviates from the true value of the characteristic being estimated, T. Thus, bias is equal to $[E(e) - T]$. The bias of an estimate, strictly speaking, is due to the combination of sampling and estimating procedures. A change in either may affect bias. For example, let us combine the estimating procedure used above with a different sampling procedure. Suppose the new sampling procedure is such that the youngest and the oldest members of the population cannot be selected in the sample. Then the possible samples and their averages are shown in Table 2.

Now, if we have an equal chance of obtaining each of these sample averages

* The expected value of a statistical variable can be defined more rigorously as follows: Let T represent the true value being estimated and $E(e)$ represent the expected value of the estimate yielded by the procedure. Let $e_1, e_2, \ldots, e_n$ represent all the possible estimates of T, and p_1 represent the probability that e_1 will be obtained by the procedure, p_2 represent the corresponding probability for e_2, etc. Then

$$E(e) = p_1 e_1 + p_2 e_2 + \ldots + p_n e_n.$$

for an estimate, the expected value of the estimate yielded by this procedure would be

$$1/6(3.5 + 4.5 + 6.0 + 5.0 + 6.5 + 7.5) = 33/6 = 5.5.$$

Then the bias introduced by changing the sampling procedure and not changing the estimating procedure is equal to $(5.5 - 6.0)$, or (-0.5).

Note that a sampling-estimating procedure which yields a biased estimate can nevertheless yield an accurate estimate. It is also true, as Table 1 shows, that a procedure which yields an unbiased estimate can yield an inaccurate estimate. It should be remembered that accuracy refers to the deviation of a specific estimate from the true value being estimated, whereas bias refers to the deviation of the expected value of the estimate from the true value.

Measuring bias appears to involve measuring a deviation from the true value of the characteristic being estimated. The true value, of course, is not known where an estimate is being made. Then how can bias be measured? By use of mathematical methods it is possible to show that various procedures are unbiased or biased and what extent. That is, it is possible to demonstrate that a given procedure does or does not yield an expected value equal to the true value, whatever that true value is. Hence, statistical and sampling theory provides measures of bias inherent in a sampling-estimating procedure.

2.3. Variability and Precision

Measuring accuracy also seems to involve knowledge of the true value of the characteristic being estimated. There is no way of directly measuring the

TABLE 3

POSSIBLE SAMPLES OF FOUR ELEMENTS FROM THE
POPULATION: 2, 3, 4, 6, 9, AND 12

Sample	Sample Average	Sample	Sample Average
2, 3, 4, 6	3.75	2, 4, 9, 12	6.75
2, 3, 4, 9	4.50	2, 6, 9, 12	7.25
2, 3, 4, 12	5.25	3, 4, 6, 9	5.50
2, 3, 6, 9	5.00	3, 4, 6, 12	6.25
2, 3, 6, 12	5.75	3, 4, 9, 12	7.00
2, 3, 9, 12	6.50	3, 6, 9, 12	7.50
2, 4, 6, 9	5.25	4, 6, 9, 12	7.75
2, 4, 6, 12	7.25		

accuracy of a specific estimate by the use of sampling theory alone. Various ways of checking the accuracy of a specific estimate will be considered in chapter ix. But sampling theory can provide a measure of the probability that a procedure will yield an estimate of any specified accuracy or inaccuracy. This determination depends on the *variability* of the estimates yielded by the procedure.

To grasp the meaning of variability, let us consider possible samples of four elements drawn from the "toy" population. These are shown in Table 3.

Now let us compare the results shown in Table 3 with those in Table 1. Note that the estimates (sample averages) shown in Table 1 range between 2.5 and 10.5, while those in Table 3 range between 3.75 and 7.75. The estimates based on samples of four have less variability (or less dispersion or spread) than estimates based on samples of two. There are many ways of measuring this variability, but the most commonly used measure is called the *standard error* of the estimate. This measure will be discussed in detail in the next chapter. For the time being it is important only to realize that the standard error is a measure of variability of estimates yielded by a sampling-estimating procedure.

We have already seen how the use of one sampling-estimating procedure on

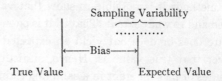

METHOD A: Large Bias; Large Sampling Variability (Imprecise)

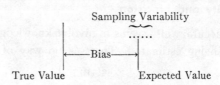

METHOD B: Large Bias; Small Sampling Variability (Precise)

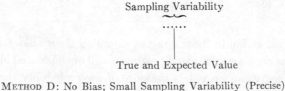

METHOD C: No Bias; Large Sampling Variability (Imprecise)

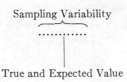

METHOD D: No Bias; Small Sampling Variability (Precise)

FIG. 4.—Bias and variability

the same population can yield estimates of different variability; that is, by changing the sample size. There are also differences between sampling methods, even relative to equal sample sizes from the same population. The less variability there is among possible estimates yielded by a procedure, the more *precise* the procedure is said to be. "Precise" is used here in much the same way as it is used to refer to a scale which yields the same reading on repeated weighings of the same object. The more varied the weight readings on the same object, the less precise the scale. Absolute or perfect precision would be obtained only if all readings (in the case of the scale) or all estimates (in the case of a sampling-estimating procedure) yield exactly the same values.

A sampling-estimating procedure which yields an unbiased estimate may be very imprecise, and a procedure which yields a biased estimate may be very precise. This can be illustrated by use of a target analogue.* Suppose we consider each sample estimate of a population characteristic to be a "shot" at the true value of that characteristic. If we take several such shots, we get a shot pattern. Four types of patterns that might result from using different sampling methods are shown in Figure 4.

By combining measures of bias and variability of a procedure a measure of confidence can be obtained for an estimate obtained by that procedure. This measure will be discussed in chapter viii.

2.4. The Cost of Sampling Error

In Section 2 the "best" sampling-estimating procedure was defined as one which yields a "minimum" sum of (a) the cost of taking the sample and obtaining an estimate and (b) the cost of error. The concepts "cost of error" and "minimum" are not simple, but they can be made more explicit now that sampling errors have been considered.

Consider a population of five elements whose values along some scale are 2, 3, 6, 9, and 10, respectively. The average value for the population is 6. Now suppose we do not know this value but want to estimate it on the basis of data obtained from a sample drawn from the population. It would be possible to select samples of 1, 2, 3, or 4 elements. How many should be selected? Let us see what is involved in getting a rational answer to this question (see Table 4).

First, all the possible samples of each size are listed in column *B*. Let us assume that we are using a sampling procedure in which each sample of a specified size has the same chance of being selected as any other sample of the same size. Suppose, further, that we use the average of the sample as an estimate of the average of the population. The resulting estimates are shown in column *C*. The

* This analogue is due to Deming (8:19–21). Figure 4 is adapted from his diagram.

TABLE 4

TOTAL EXPECTED COST OF POSSIBLE SAMPLES SELECTED FROM THE
POPULATION: 2, 3, 6, 9, AND 10

(A) Sample Size	(B) Sample	(C) Estimate	(D) Error	(E) Cost of Error	(F) Expected Cost of Error
1	2	2	−4	$24.00	$ 4.80
	3	3	−3	18.00	3.60
	6	6	0		
	9	9	3	9.00	1.80
	10	10	4	12.00	2.40
Total expected cost of error					$12.60
Cost of one observation					3.00
Total expected cost of procedure					$15.60
2	2, 3	2.5	−3.5	$21.00	$ 2.10
	2, 6	4.0	−2.0	12.00	1.20
	2, 9	5.5	−0.5	3.00	0.30
	2, 10	6.0	0		
	3, 6	4.5	−1.5	9.00	0.90
	3, 9	6.0	0		
	3, 10	6.5	0.5	1.50	0.15
	6, 9	7.5	1.5	4.50	0.45
	6, 10	8.0	2.0	6.00	0.60
	9, 10	9.5	3.5	10.50	1.05
Total expected cost of error					$ 6.75
Cost of two observations					6.00
Total expected cost of procedure					$12.75
3	2, 3, 6	3.67	−2.33	$14.00	$ 1.40
	2, 3, 9	4.67	−1.33	8.00	0.80
	2, 3, 10	5.00	−1.00	6.00	0.60
	2, 6, 9	5.67	−0.33	2.00	0.20
	2, 6, 10	6.00	0		
	2, 9, 10	7.00	1.00	3.00	0.30
	3, 6, 9	6.00	0		
	3, 6, 10	6.33	0.33	1.00	0.10
	3, 9, 10	7.33	1.33	4.00	0.40
	6, 9, 10	8.33	2.33	7.00	0.70
Total expected cost of error					$ 4.50
Cost of three observations					9.00
Total expected cost of procedure					$13.50
4	2, 3, 6, 9	5.00	−1.00	$ 6.00	$ 1.20
	2, 3, 6, 10	5.25	−0.75	4.50	0.90
	2, 3, 9, 10	6.00	0		
	2, 6, 9, 10	6.75	0.75	2.25	0.45
	3, 6, 9, 10	7.00	1.00	3.00	0.60
Total expected cost of error					$ 3.15
Cost of four observations					12.00
Total expected cost of procedure					$15.15

inaccuracy of each estimate can be determined by subtracting the true population average (6) from each estimated value. The results are shown in column D.

Now let us suppose that each error of overestimation costs $3.00 per unit of error and that each error of underestimation costs $6.00 per unit of error. The resulting costs associated with each error (under the specified conditions) are shown in column E. But we do not know beforehand which error will be made. Nevertheless, we do know what the chances are that each error will be made. For example, there are five possible samples of one element, and—according to the method we are using—each sample has an equal chance $(1/5)$ of being selected. Therefore, each error has the same chance of being incurred. Then, the first error listed is -4, and its cost, $24.00, will be incurred $1/5$th of the time in the long run. On the average this error will cost $1/5$ (24.00), or $4.80, per estimate. This is the expected cost of this particular error. The expected cost of each error can be computed similarly. The results are shown in column F.

The total of these costs for each sample size is the total expected cost of error; that is, the average cost of error that will be incurred if the procedure is used repeatedly.

Now suppose each observation costs $3.00. Then, the cost of observations for the various samples is $3.00, $6.00, $9.00, and $12.00, respectively. If this sum is added to the total expected cost of error, we obtain the total expected cost of the procedure. In the illustration samples of two elements are the most economical in the long run relative to the specified sampling-estimating procedure. Note that the cost of a complete count would be $15.00.

Similar computations could be made for other sampling-estimating procedures which might be applied to this population. That method should be selected which would yield the lowest total expected cost.

The procedure just described can be expressed in a general form. Let e_i represent an error of estimation, let $C(e_i)$ represent the cost of that error, and let $P(e_i)$ represent the probability of making that error. Then the expected cost of that error is $C(e_i)P(e_i)$, the product of the cost and the probability. The total expected cost of error can then be expressed as the following sum:

$$C(e_1)P(e_1) + C(e_2)P(e_2) + \ldots + C(e_n)P(e_n).$$

If the cost of taking the observations is added to this sum, the result is the total expected cost of the procedure.

In order to be able to perform this type of cost evaluation of sampling-estimating procedures, it is necessary to obtain estimates of the probability that any specified error will occur. In the simple illustration given above this caused no difficulty, because we had knowledge of the value assigned to each member of the population. In the real situation it is precisely the lack of this knowledge which requires that a sampling-estimating procedure be used. But, even without knowing the value of each member of the population, it is possible to obtain estimates of the probability that each possible error will be made by the use of statistical theory. We will see how this probability can be estimated, and, in the next chapter, there will also be further discussion of the errors and cost involved in evaluating a procedure. In Appendix IV a method is given for determining that size of sample for a particular procedure which minimizes the total expected cost of the procedure. Even without the use of advanced techniques for comparing alternative sampling designs, however, it is frequently possible to make a reasonable selection of a plan by considering the various costs associated with its preparation, operation, and analysis. But this, in turn, requires a familiarity with the operational phases of each sampling method. These vary from plan to plan. It is virtually impossible, therefore, for anyone with little sampling experience to make reasonable estimates of the costs associated with the alternative methods of sampling. Those with little sampling experience would do well to enlist the aid of those who have had the required experience.

3. Simple Random Sampling

In the illustrations used in Section 2 (Tables 1 and 3) we assumed that every possible combination of two (or four) elements had an equal chance of being selected. A sampling procedure for which this condition holds is called *simple random sampling*. In general, a simple random sampling procedure of *n* elements is one for which every possible combination of *n* elements from the population has an equal and greater than zero chance of being selected. From this definition it follows that in simple random sampling every member of the population has an equal and some chance of being selected.

Simple random sampling is, in a sense, the basic theme of all scientific sampling. All other methods of scientific sampling are variations on this theme— variations which have been designed, in the main, to increase sampling efficiency (i.e., to reduce costs and/or errors). An understanding of any of the refined variations presupposes an understanding of simple random sampling. If social researchers would come to know how to select and use simple random samples, many sampling experts would feel that the "big" job in sampling education of social researchers had been accomplished.

In the illustrations used above (Tables 1 and 3) it was observed that simple random samples can—when combined with a suitable estimating procedure— yield unbiased estimates. A number of estimating procedures can be combined with simple random sampling to yield unbiased estimates of a variety of population characteristics. Some of these will be presented in chapter viii. As indicated above, this lack of bias can be demonstrated mathematically.

Simple random sampling has an important property relative to variability: the variability of estimates obtained from such samples decreases as the sample size increases. This property can be illustrated by returning to the "toy" population and comparing the estimates obtained from samples of various sizes. All the possible samples and their corresponding estimates are shown in Table 5. Each estimate which differs from the true population average (6 years) by no more than 1 unit (year) is marked with an asterisk. At the bottom of each col-

TABLE 5

POSSIBLE SAMPLES OF ONE, TWO, THREE, FOUR, AND FIVE ELEMENTS
FROM THE POPULATION: 2, 3, 4, 6, 9, AND 12

	1		2		3		4		5
Sample	Average	Sample	Average	Sample	Average	Sample	Average	Sample	Average
2	2	2, 3	2.5	2, 3, 4	3.0	2, 3, 4, 6	3.8	2, 3, 4, 6, 9	4.8
3	3	2, 4	3.0	2, 3, 6	3.7	2, 3, 4, 9	4.5	2, 3, 4, 6, 12	5.4*
4	4	2, 6	4.0	2, 3, 9	4.7	2, 3, 4, 12	5.2*	2, 3, 4, 9, 12	6.0*
6	6*	2, 9	5.5*	2, 3, 12	5.3*	2, 3, 6, 9	5.0*	2, 3, 6, 9, 12	6.4*
9	9	2, 12	7.0*	2, 4, 6	4.0	2, 3, 6, 12	5.8*	2, 4, 6, 9, 12	6.6*
12	12	3, 4	3.5	2, 4, 9	5.0*	2, 3, 9, 12	6.5*	3, 4, 6, 9, 12	6.8*
		3, 6	4.5	2, 4, 12	6.0*	2, 4, 6, 9	5.2*		
		3, 9	6.0*	2, 6, 9	5.7*	2, 4, 6, 12	6.0*		
		3, 12	7.5	2, 6, 12	6.7*	2, 4, 9, 12	6.8*		
		4, 6	5.0*	2, 9, 12	7.7	2, 6, 9, 12	7.2		
		4, 9	6.5*	3, 4, 6	4.3	3, 4, 6, 9	5.5*		
		4, 12	8.0	3, 4, 9	5.7*	3, 4, 6, 12	6.2*		
		6, 9	7.5	3, 4, 12	6.3*	3, 4, 9, 12	7.0*		
		6, 12	9.0	3, 6, 9	6.0*	3, 6, 9, 12	7.5		
		9, 12	10.5	3, 6, 12	7.0*	4, 6, 9, 12	7.8		
				3, 9, 12	8.0				
				4, 6, 9	6.3*				
				4, 6, 12	7.3				
				4, 9, 12	8.3				
				6, 9, 12	9.0				
	17%†		33%†		50%†		67%†		83%†

* Deviates by no more than 1 unit (year) from the population average.
† Percentage of sample averages which deviate by no more than 1 unit from the population average.

umn of sample averages, the percentage of the averages in the column marked with an asterisk is given.* As the sample size increases, so does the percentage of estimates that deviate by no more than 1 unit from the population average.

3.1. Random Numbers

How can a simple random sample be selected? Let us permit our imaginations to run wild for a moment. Suppose we place all the members of a population into

* This measure of variability is not a common one. It is used here because of its simplicity for expository purposes.

a large bowl and mix them up thoroughly; then we dip in and pick one out. We identify the person, make the necessary observations, replace him in the bowl, and repeat the operation. Then it would appear that the probability of selecting any one member is equal to the probability of selecting any other member. That is, if we were to mix the members between each drawing, we would expect that in the long run we would select each member with equal frequency. But this expectation is not justified unless we devise an ingenious mixing system, because (among other things) the heavier people would tend to settle on the bottom and at the sides of the mixing bowl, and we would not be as likely to draw one of them as a lighter person who would tend to be pushed up and into the center of the bowl. If we mixed marbles of different weights, for example, the heavier marbles would tend to go to the bottom and sides of the bowl owing to their greater centrifugal force. Consequently, we can conceive of a more efficient procedure: (1) assign to each member of the population a unique number (i.e., no two members have the same number); (2) place each number on a chip, where each chip is the same as all the others with respect to weight, size, shape, etc.; (3) place the chips in a bowl and mix them thoroughly; and (4) have a blind-folded person select a chip from the bowl. Under these circumstances (where the chips are all "identical" and the mixing is "thorough"), the probability of drawing any one chip can be expected to be the same as the probability of drawing any other chip. Since each chip represents a member of the population, the probability of selecting each would be exactly the same. If, after selecting a chip, it were replaced in the bowl and the contents again thoroughly mixed, each chip would have an equal probability of being selected on the second drawing, etc. Such a procedure would yield a simple random sample.

In actual practice we can never actually know whether or not a population is thoroughly mixed and, hence, whether or not a selection is perfectly random. To know this, we would have to know a great deal more about the population than we ordinarily know. The practical question, then, is: Under what conditions can we *assume* that a population is thoroughly mixed and that the selection procedure is such that each member of the population has an equal and some chance of being selected?

On the basis of mathematical theory it is possible to make explicit statements about the characteristics that randomly selected observations would have. That is, we can say what properties the observations would be likely to have *if* we had a perfect mixing and selecting procedure. Suppose, then, that we design an apparatus for mixing chips, or a machine for generating a sequence of numbers. We can "test"* the apparatus or machine by determining whether the numbers they yield are like those that would be expected to occur according to the theory. For example, according to the theory we would expect an equal

*A more complete discussion is to be found in (29:147-66).

number of odd and even numbers; we would expect each digit to occur an equal number of times. If the generated numbers do not satisfy these and other expectations which follow from the theory, the method of mixing and selecting is not assumed to be adequate; if the numbers generated satisfy these expectations, the method is accepted provisionally, and the numbers yielded are called "random numbers."

Long lists of random numbers have been prepared by using very complex methods. In fact, the methods are usually so complex that no one has worked out the physical theory of their origin. These numbers are generally listed in columns on consecutive pages.* For example, the following is a portion of a set of random numbers:

42827	70203	78569	60281	20145
41519	84612	30877	37989	58210
38273	91905	33891	31641	84041
48225	65290	85998	11528	28896
56506	27841	56560	28947	49788
29280	51213	96336	79288	88449
73184	26689	05928	65869	32256
52677	23027	51511	87251	04495
48663	02427	30909	27370	02050
22635	58903	53662	11169	42025

These lists of random numbers can be used in the following way: each member of the population is assigned a unique number in any manner at all. For example, one person may have the number "72" assigned to him, another "89," etc. The number of digits in the largest number assigned is determined. Then we open the text to any page of the tables and begin at any place in any column, paying attention to the number of digits with which we are concerned. For example, if we have two hundred elements in a population, we note any combination of three columns, or sets of three consecutive digits, or three rows, etc. Suppose we use the last three digits in each set of five. As we proceed down the column (starting with 827), we note each number less than 201. We continue until we have as many numbers as items we want in the sample. The sample would then be taken to consist of the elements of the population with numbers corresponding to those chosen. For example, using the numbers above, we would obtain the following sequence:

$$184, \ 027, \ 169, \ 145, \ 041, \ 050, \ 025, \ldots$$

This means that persons with numbers 184, 27, 169, etc., are selected for the sample,† and this would be a simple random sample.

* For tables of random numbers see, e.g., (11), (27), (30), and (52).

† The original numbers need not be assigned consecutively. If they are not, one skips all nonassigned numbers in the random-number table.

3.2. Systematic Sampling

Systematic sampling is a variation of simple random sampling. It requires that the population or a list of its members be *ordered* in such a way that each element of the population can be uniquely identified by its order. A membership list, a city directory, a card-index system, and a waiting line of people would all generally satisfy this condition. Usually we deal with an identification list of members rather than the population itself. Any symbolic system which uniquely identifies each member of the population is called a *frame* of that population.

Consider a frame consisting of a card-index system in which there is one and only one card for each member of the population. Suppose there are 1,000 cards (and, hence, 1,000 members of the population), and we want a sample of 100. We can select a number between (and including) 1 and 10 at random, say, 6. Then we can select the members whose cards are in the following positions: 6, 16, 26, 36, . . . , 986, 996. This would be a *systematic random sample*, or what is more commonly called a *systematic sample*.

In general, a systematic selection can be used as follows: If the population contains N elements, and the desired sample size is n, compute the value of the ratio: N/n. If this ratio is not a whole number, round it off to the nearest whole number. Let m represent this whole number, which is called the *sampling interval*. Select at random* a number from 1 to m; call this number x. Then sample the elements identified by the numbers:

$$x, x + m, x + 2m, \ldots, x + (n - 1)m.$$

It should be clear that, if N/n is an integer, this procedure is such that each individual has an equal chance of being selected.† For example, if we want to sample 5 out of 25 cards, then $N/n = 25/5 = 5$. Now we must select a number from 1 to 5 at random. Once this number is selected, we can specify the rest of the sample. There are, then, five possible samples which can be drawn, each with equal probability:

$$
\begin{array}{llllll}
(1) & 1, & 6, & 11, & 16, & 21 \\
(2) & 2, & 7, & 12, & 17, & 22 \\
(3) & 3, & 8, & 13, & 18, & 23 \\
(4) & 4, & 9, & 14, & 19, & 24 \\
(5) & 5, & 10, & 15, & 20, & 25
\end{array}
$$

Each individual appears in one and only one of these possible samples, and, since the samples have an equal probability of being selected, so do the individuals.

One advantage of such a procedure is that it can be used to assure a sample's

---

* Only by so doing will each number from 1 to m have an equal probability of being selected.
† If N/n is not an integer, this will not be true unless the sample size is permitted to vary.

being representative, or close to it, with respect to a pertinent property. Suppose, for example, that we want to determine the average weight of a group of students. Suppose, further, that we know that weight and sex are related. Then we would like to select a sample which is representative with respect to sex. We can do this with a list in which the females and males are grouped together. For example, suppose that the population of 25 contains 10 females and that these are listed first (from 1 to 10). The 15 males would then be listed from 11 to 25. Then each possible sample of 5 members would contain two-fifths females and three-fifths males, the same proportions that occur in the population as a whole. Proportional representation relative to a pertinent property tends to reduce the variability of the estimates.

Reduction or increase in the variability of estimates yielded by systematic sampling depends on the way the population is ordered.* It may be costly to order the population in such a way as to reduce the variability of the estimates. Very frequently lists are available which are ordered on the basis of a property that is known or can be assumed to be uncorrelated with the characteristic being investigated. For example, the list of names may be alphabetically ordered, and this order may be uncorrelated with the characteristic investigated, say, income. Then the population can be assumed to be "thoroughly mixed" with respect to income. A systematic sample under these conditions would yield the equivalent of a simple random sample.

If the population is not thoroughly mixed with respect to the characteristic under study, the variability of the estimates will be affected. This fact can be illustrated by use of the "toy" population. Suppose this population to be ordered so that the ages occur in the following order: 2, 3, 4, 6, 9, and 12. Now suppose we want to obtain a sample of three by systematic selection. The two possible samples are (*a*) 2, 4, 9 (with an average of 5 years) and (*b*) 3, 6, 12 (with an average of 7 years). Both (and hence 100 per cent) of these samples deviate from the population average (6 years) by no more than a year. A comparison of this result with that obtained from simple random sampling for samples of the same size (see Table 5, where only 50 per cent of the sample averages deviate by no more than a year) shows that variability has been reduced.

But now suppose the population to be ordered in the following way: 2, 6, 3, 9, 4, and 12. The two possible systematic samples in this case are (*a*) 2, 3, 4 (with an average of 3 years) and (*b*) 6, 9, 12 (with an average of 9 years). Neither (and hence 0 per cent) of these averages deviates from the population average by a year or less. Hence, in this case the variability has been increased over that yielded by simple random sampling.

* Strictly speaking, it depends on what is called the "serial correlation" in the pertinent ordering.

Note that in either case of systematic sampling, however, the estimates are unbiased.

For a detailed discussion of systematic sampling see (31) and (32). Systematic selection procedures which differ from those considered here are discussed in (41:266–70).

4. Variations of Simple Random and Systematic Sampling

In some situations it is impractical to take either a simple random or a systematic sample. Difficulty may arise from the fact that a complete listing of the members of the population cannot be obtained in any practical way. Simple random sampling, which requires no information concerning the characteristics of the members of the population, may lead the researcher to ignore such information when it is available and pertinent. In such cases, it is frequently desirable to divide (or use available divisions of) the population into subgroups or classes and to use these divisions in the development of a sampling design.

Suppose, for example, that we have a population of sixteen items. These may be divided into four groups of four items each (see Fig. 5). Each item of the

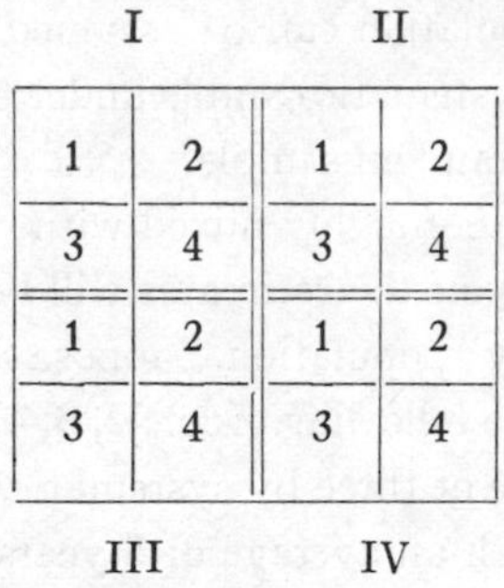

I		II	
1	2	1	2
3	4	3	4
1	2	1	2
3	4	3	4
III		IV	

Fig. 5.—Division of a population of sixteen elements into four classes of equal size

population can be identified by a combination of two numbers: the group number (I, II, III, or IV) and the box number (1, 2, 3, or 4). Now a sample can be selected from this population in two *stages:* (1) select one or more group numbers and (2) select one or more box numbers from those groups which have been selected in the first stage. In the first and second stages either a complete count may be made (i.e., each possible number is selected) or a simple random or systematic sample may be selected. If a complete count is made in each stage, then it is obvious that a complete count of the population has been made. There are three possible ways of selecting a sample in two stages from this subdivided population (see Table 6).

Any sampling plan which involves more than one sampling stage is a *multi-*

stage sampling plan. There may, of course, be any number of stages of sampling; the more stages, the more possible combinations of complete counts and samples. In general, if the population or any subgroup of the population is divided into exclusive and exhaustive classes, and if a sample is selected from each class, the sample is said to be *stratified*. If the last stage of any number of stages involves a complete count, the procedure is that of *cluster* sampling. Finally, in sampling which involves more than two stages, stratified and cluster sampling can be combined into a *stratified cluster sample*.

TABLE 6

TYPES OF TWO-STAGE SAMPLES

First Stage (Selecting Groups)	Second Stage (Selecting Items)	Name of Sampling Plan
Sample*	Sample*	Two-Stage Random Sampling
Complete Count	Sample*	Stratified Sampling
Sample*	Complete Count	Cluster Sampling

* Simple random sampling or a variation thereof.

If simple random sampling or one of its variations is used in one-stage sampling, or if either these procedures or complete counts are used at each stage of a multistage procedure, the resulting sample is called a *probability*, or simply a *random*, sample. In such sampling the probability of selecting any member of the population can be computed, and hence errors can be measured. Samples in which this probability cannot be computed but must be left to one's judgment are called *judgment* samples. We shall consider several types of judgment samples after we have considered each of the common types of probability samples.

4.1. Grouping and Subgrouping the Population

The population consists of a set of items some of which we intend eventually to observe. These items are called *ultimate* or *elementary units* of the population. (The population is also sometimes referred to as a *universe*.) In two-stage sampling, the ultimate units should be grouped in such a way that each and every ultimate unit is in one and only one of these groups or *sampling units*. A sampling unit may contain any number of ultimate units, including none; but the sampling units collectively should exhaust the population. The sampling units may be defined in terms of any property or properties which permit each ultimate unit to be assigned to one and only one such unit. For example, the ultimate units may be grouped by age, sex, place of residence, occupation, income, place of birth, marital status, and innumerable other properties.

If we sample in three stages, the ultimate units in each sampling unit must be subgrouped twice. The more inclusive groups are then called *primary sampling units;* the subgroups are called *secondary sampling units.* If more than two stages are involved, each ultimate unit should be capable of being assigned to one and only one sampling unit at each stage. Therefore, each ultimate unit should be included in $(n - 1)$ sampling units, where n represents the number of sampling stages.

Suppose we want to sample the employees of a company which operates two factories. Factory A and Factory B could serve as primary sampling units. We could then divide the employees of each factory into their departments; these would be secondary sampling units. There is no restriction on the possible number of primary or secondary sampling units, except those of convenience and efficiency. Considerations of convenience, efficiency, and cost have resulted in an increased usage of geographically defined sampling units (e.g., city blocks, wards, precincts, tracts, counties, etc.). In the course of our discussion we shall consider some of the advantages of such geographic grouping, particularly where survey research is involved.

Whatever property serves as a basis of grouping or classifying the population, it should be defined operationally in the sense discussed in the last chapter. That is, the definition of the sampling units should provide operational directives which make possible accurate and unique allocation of each ultimate unit to the proper sampling unit(s). Probability sampling presupposes such allocation; without it, estimates yielded by such samples may be in serious error.

The property which forms the basis of subgrouping the population may or may not be related to the property or properties under study. Suppose, for example, that we are going to observe the political attitudes of the members of a population. If we classified the population members by income, we would expect that income and political attitudes were correlated. On the other hand, if we grouped the population members by the month of their birth, we would not expect income and month of birth to be correlated. We shall see that in stratified sampling in particular it is advantageous to use classifications based on properties which are correlated with those under investigation.

4.2. Sampling with Varying Probabilities

There is an important type of random sampling that can and should be applied to multistage selection where two conditions hold: (1) the property being investigated is correlated with some function of the size of the population and (2) the size of each sampling unit is known. The first condition should be clarified. Suppose we want to investigate the total income of a certain population. In general, we expect that the total income of a population increases as the size of the population increases; then total income of the population is correlated with the size of the population. This will be true in general for any population characteristic that is equal or proportionate to the sum of properties of the members of the population. If we deal with a property which is correlated with some function of the size of the population, then it is desirable to set up the sampling procedure so that the probability of selecting any sampling unit is proportionate to that function of its size. That is, we should set up the sampling procedure so that we have more chance of selecting a large sampling unit than a small one. This procedure tends to reduce the variability of estimates of population characteristics which are correlated with the size of the population (see [19]).

Suppose we want to estimate the total income of members of all branches of the American Legion in a certain city. We can obtain lists of the membership of each branch and determine the number of members in each. For illustrative purposes let us assume some convenient figures. Assume the four branches have memberships of 100, 200, 300, and 400, respectively. Now suppose we want to sample within only two of these branches. We could select two numbers from 1 to 4 at random, but such a selection would not be made with probability proportionate to size. We want the probability of selecting the first group to be equal to

$$\frac{\text{Size of Class}}{\text{Size of Population}} = \frac{100}{100 + 200 + 300 + 400} = \frac{1}{10} = 0.10 \, .$$

Correspondingly, the probability of selecting the second, third, and fourth groups should be 0.20, 0.30, and 0.40, respectively. This can be done by using a table of random numbers as follows: if we draw a number from 1 to 100, the first group falls into the sample; if we draw a number from 101 to 300, the second group falls into the sample; if we draw a number from 301 to 600, the third group falls into the sample; and, if we draw a number from 601 to 1,000, the fourth group falls into the sample. Such a procedure would give the desired probability of selecting each group. The method can be easily generalized to cover any number of groups and any probabilities.

The probability of selecting a sampling unit may be made proportionate to other properties of the sampling unit. The ideal property of the sampling unit for this purpose is the dispersion or spread of the values of the characteristic under investigation, within the sampling unit. That is, there is an advantage to increasing the chances of selecting those groups whose members differ a good deal among themselves. The reasons for this are quite technical and need not be considered here (see [17] and [19]). The point here is that, if a good deal is known about the properties of the sampling units, this information can be used effectively in selecting a random sample. The error of such sampling can be considerably reduced by using what we know about the sampling units. It is particularly desirable, in such cases, to consult a sampling expert.

5. Multistage Random Sampling

Multistage random sampling involves the use of a type of random sampling at each of its stages. Consider the case where both simple and systematic random sampling are used. Suppose we want to sample the population of public schoolteachers in a certain city. The board of education provides us with a mimeographed list of names. The list consists of, say, 100 pages with approximately 20 names per page. The pages are numbered and constitute the sampling units. The names are not numbered but are arranged alphabetically; they constitute the ultimate sampling units. Let us suppose we want a sample of 50 teachers. Then the sample might be selected as follows. We might decide to select 5 teachers from each of 10 pages. Select a number from 1 to 10 at random, say, 8. Select pages 8, 18, 28, 38, 48, 58, 68, 78, 88, and 98. On each of these pages enter a unique number beside each name listed. Then by use of a table of random numbers select 5 names from each of the 10 pages. This procedure is a combination of systematic and simple random sampling. We could, of course, reverse the procedure and take a simple random sample of pages and a systematic sample of names on the pages selected. In sum, we could use any combination of simple and systematic random sampling.

The variability of estimates yielded by multistage random sampling may be greater than that of estimates yielded by simple random sampling for equal sample size. This can be demonstrated by returning to the "toy" population. Suppose this population is divided into three primary sampling units: (a) 2, 12; (b) 3, 9; and (c) 4, 6. Let us consider samples of two drawn from two primary sampling units. These are shown in Table 7.

Note that only 17 per cent of the estimates deviates by no more than one year from the population average, whereas in the case of simple random sampling 33 per cent was the corresponding figure (see Table 5).

The variability of estimates obtained from multistage random sampling depends on the composition of primary sampling units. For example, see Table 8, where results are obtained for a different subdivision of the same "toy" population, using the same procedure as was used to obtain the results shown in Table 7. The results obtained in Table 8 are no more variable than those obtained by simple random sampling. The variability obtained by multistage random sampling can never be less than that obtained from simple random sampling for corresponding sample sizes, but it can be greater. For estimation procedures which yield unbiased estimates when used with multistage random sampling see (8:v). Note also that the procedure used in Tables 7 and 8 is unbiased.

TABLE 7

POSSIBLE TWO-STAGE RANDOM SAMPLES OF TWO ELEMENTS
FROM TWO OF THREE PRIMARY SAMPLING
UNITS: 2, 12; 3, 9; AND 4, 6

Sample	Sample Average	Sample	Sample Average
2, 3	2.5	12, 4	8.0
2, 9	5.5*	12, 6	9.0
2, 4	3.0	3, 4	3.5
2, 6	4.0	3, 6	4.5
12, 3	7.5	9, 4	6.5*
12, 9	10.5	9, 6	7.5
			17%†

* Deviates by no more than 1 unit (year) from the population average.
† Percentage of sample averages that deviate by no more than 1 unit from the population average.

TABLE 8

POSSIBLE TWO-STAGE RANDOM SAMPLES OF TWO ELEMENTS
FROM TWO OF THREE PRIMARY SAMPLING
UNITS: 2, 3; 4, 6; AND 9, 12

Sample	Sample Average	Sample	Sample Average
2, 4	3.0	3, 9	6.0*
2, 6	4.0	3, 12	7.5
2, 9	5.5*	4, 9	6.5*
2, 12	7.0*	4, 12	8.0
3, 4	3.5	6, 9	7.5
3, 6	4.5	6, 12	9.0
			33%†

* See Table 7.
† See Table 7.

One advantage of multistage random sampling is that a complete listing of the population is not required. Suppose, for example, that we select two out of four primary sampling units in the first stage of the procedure. Then lists of ultimate units need only be prepared for the two primary sampling units selected.

From the point of view of minimizing the variability of the estimates it is desirable to sample from all the sampling units. From a practical point of view, however, the cost of preparing the lists increases as the number of sampling units selected increases. If the sampling units are defined geographically, then, the more units used, the more travel is required, since the ultimate units will be more widely dispersed and fewer observations will be made at any one place. Such dispersion also makes supervision and operational control in the field more difficult. The problem, then, in designing a multistage random sample is to balance the expected cost of sampling errors and other errors resulting from the use of the procedure against the operating cost of the procedure.

This problem can be better understood by examining what is involved in the operating costs of multistage random sampling. Let

m = number of sampling units selected

n_j = number of elements selected from the jth sampling unit

c_1 = overhead cost of preparing and obtaining sample from one sampling unit

c_2 = additional cost of obtaining an observation on one element

C = total operating cost

Then the total operating cost of the procedure can be expressed as follows:

$$C = c_1 m + c_2(n_1 + n_2 + \ldots + n_m).$$

From this equation it is apparent that the cost of taking the sample increases as the number of sampling units selected (m) increases and as the number of elements selected from sampling units (n_j) increases. It is also true, however, that as m and n_j increase, the error decreases. The problem of designing a multistage random sample, then, is to get an optimum balance between the operating and error costs.

Methods for minimizing the cost of taking the sample for fixed error or minimizing the error for fixed costs are discussed in (8:v).

6. Stratified Sampling

In stratified sampling a sample is selected from every subgroup of the population in at least one stage of the procedure. The basis for constructing the subgroups or *strata* may be one or several properties. We may have two simple strata such as "male" and "female" or a large number such as "age at last birthday." If more than one property is used to define the strata, a classification matrix is required. For example, if we combine native-born and foreign-born with male and female, we obtain four strata: native-born male, native-born female, foreign-born male, and foreign-born female.

The properties used as a basis of stratification may or may not be correlated with the population characteristic under investigation. Ideally there is an advantage in having such a correlation. For example, consider the case in which the population of professional workers is divided into two groups, male and female. Suppose we want to determine what percentage of this population practices each of a set of professions. It is clear that a person's sex influences his or her choice of a profession. Suppose further that we know what percentage of the total population is male and what percentage is female. Then we can select from each group a random sample which is proportionate in size to the male and female subgroups. Such a procedure would assure us that our sample is representative with respect to sex. For example, if 70 per cent of the total population is male and 30 per cent female, and if 70 per cent of the sample is male and 30 per cent female, we are sure that the sample represents the sex distribution in the population. Such a sample is called a *proportionate stratified sample.*

6.1. Proportionate Stratified Sampling

If we can divide a population by means of several pertinent properties, then we can stratify with respect to each. The larger the percentage of the pertinent properties with respect to which we can stratify and from which we can draw proportionate samples, the less error we can expect.

There is one practical difficulty in drawing from each stratum a sample proportionate to its size. To use this method, we must know what proportion of the population falls into each stratum. In some cases such information may not be available. But, even if such information is available, it may be "dated" and hence no longer be applicable. Some population characteristics change very quickly; for example, income. If we base a proportionate stratified sample on incorrect proportions, the variability of the estimates is higher than would be the case if correct proportions were used. For this reason caution should be used in the selection of classificatory properties and data regarding their distribution in the population.

It may take considerable time, effort, and money to stratify a population in ways other than those in which we already find them stratified. Hence, "extensive additional stratification, beyond introducing some of the fairly obvious criteria that may be readily available, is not likely to produce a substantial increase in precision in the estimates of general population characteristics, such as distributions by age, sex, and other classes" (21:664).

Stratified sampling enables the researcher to make a comparison of the properties of the strata as well as to estimate a population characteristic. The research objectives are frequently such that a comparison of the properties of subgroups in the population is essential or at least advantageous. For example, we may want not only to determine the average I.Q. of students in a university but also to compare average I.Q.'s of the various colleges within the university.

By stratification separate estimates can be obtained for each college, as well as an estimate for the total population (see [49]).

Regardless of the nature of the strata, it is usually convenient and economical to draw a sample from strata which are well defined and for which identification lists are available, particularly if the population is not dispersed and travel costs are not significant.

The cost of preparing and obtaining a stratified sample (C) includes the cost of preparing the sample (c_1) and the cost of an observation (c_2) and depends on the number of observations per stratum (n_j) and the number of strata (m). Thus,

$$C = c_1 + c_2(n_1 + n_2 + \ldots + n_m) .$$

If a stratified list of the population is available, the cost c_1 is reduced. It may be desirable, however, to prepare a new list, since the additional cost may be more than offset by the decrease in error cost. At any rate, it is possible to combine knowledge of the population with a cost analysis to establish an optimum stratification procedure.

To see how stratification can affect the variability of estimates, let us return to the "toy" population. For purposes of illustration, suppose the population is divided into two strata: (2, 3) and (4, 6, 9, 12). Let us confine our attention to samples of three elements that may be obtained by combining random selections from each stratum. Under this plan we draw at random either one or two elements from each stratum so as to obtain a total of three elements. This is a stratified but not a proportionate stratified sampling procedure (e.g., disproportionate stratified sampling). The possible samples together with sample averages are shown in Table 9.

TABLE 9

POSSIBLE STRATIFIED SAMPLES OF THREE ELEMENTS
FROM THE STRATA: (2, 3) AND (4, 6, 9, 12)

Sample	Estimated Average†	Sample	Estimated Average†
2, 3, 4	3.5	2, 6, 12	6.7*
2, 3, 6	4.8*	2, 9, 12	7.7
2, 3, 9	6.8*	3, 4, 6	4.3
2, 3, 12	8.8	3, 4, 9	5.3*
2, 4, 6	4.0	3, 4, 12	6.3*
2, 4, 9	5.0*	3, 6, 9	6.0*
2, 4, 12	6.0*	3, 6, 12	7.0*
2, 6, 9	5.7*	3, 9, 12	8.0

* Deviates by no more than 1 unit (year) from the population average.

† To obtain an unbiased estimate of the population average in disproportionate stratified sampling, the sample average cannot be used. An unbiased estimate can be obtained by taking the average of the sample from each stratum, multiplying it by the size of the stratum, and dividing the sum of these values by the size of the population. For example, in the first sample listed (2, 3, 4) the estimate is computed as

$$1/6\left[2\left(\frac{2+3}{2}\right) + 4\left(\frac{4}{1}\right)\right] = 3.5 .$$

We observe that 9 out of 16, or 56 per cent, of the estimates deviate by no more than one year from the population average. By comparing this result with simple random samples of three elements from the same population (Table 5), we see that in simple random sampling only 50 per cent of the sample averages is within one year of the population average. Hence, there is less variability in this stratified sampling procedure than in simple random sampling relative to the same sample size. Similar results would be found for other stratification procedures but not for all, as we shall see.

To see the effect of proportionate selection on sampling variability, let us use the same strata and sample size as were used in Table 9. But now, since the stratum (2, 3) contains 2/6 or 1/3 of the population, we will select only 1/3 of 3, or 1 item from this stratum, and 2/3 of 3, or 2 items from the second stratum. The possible samples together with the estimates (which are sample averages) are shown in Table 10.

In Table 10, 8 out of 12, or 67 per cent, of the sample averages deviate by no

TABLE 10

POSSIBLE PROPORTIONATE STRATIFIED SAMPLES OF THREE
ELEMENTS FROM THE STRATA: (2, 3) AND (4, 6, 9, 12)

Sample	Estimated Average	Sample	Estimated Average
2, 4, 6	4.0	3, 4, 6	4.3
2, 4, 9	5.0*	3, 4, 9	5.3*
2, 4, 12	6.0*	3, 4, 12	6.3*
2, 6, 9	5.7*	3, 6, 9	6.0*
2, 6, 12	6.7*	3, 6, 12	7.0*
2, 9, 12	7.7	3, 9, 12	8.0

* Deviates by no more than 1 unit (year) from the population average.

more than one year from the population average. By comparing this result with those obtained in Tables 5 and 9, we note that the variability of the proportionate stratified sampling results is less than that of simple random or disproportionate stratified sampling. Only 50 per cent of the simple random samples of three elements and 56 per cent of the disproportionate stratified samples were within the one-year range.

Now let us divide the population into different strata of the same size—(2, 12) and (3, 4, 6, 9)—and again select a proportionate stratified sample of three elements. The possible samples together with the estimated averages are shown in Table 11.

We observe that 4 out of 12, or only 33 per cent, of the sample averages fall within the one-year range. Hence, variability here is greater than in Tables 5, 9, and 10. This shows that proportionate stratified sampling is not necessarily better with respect to variability than the methods previously considered. The difference between the two illustrations of proportionate stratified sampling is important. It demonstrates the fact that the variability of results obtained by this procedure depends on the degree of *homogeneity* of the strata. That is, the more widely dispersed the values are in a stratum, the more sampling error; and, conversely, as this dispersion is decreased, so is the variability. In the illustrations, for example, use of the stratum (2, 3) produced less variable results than did use of the stratum (2, 12). The former is more homogeneous than the latter. Since the results shown in Table 11 are even more variable than those for simple random samples of the same size (Table 5), it is also clear that, though proportionate stratified sampling can yield less variability than simple random sampling, it does not necessarily do so. Hence, wherever possible, stratification should be designed to yield as homogeneous strata as possible.

TABLE 11

PROPORTIONATE STRATIFIED SAMPLES OF THREE ELEMENTS
FROM THE STRATA: (2, 12) AND (3, 4, 6, 9)

Sample	Estimated Average	Sample	Estimated Average
2, 3, 4	3.0	12, 3, 4	6.3*
2, 3, 6	3.7	12, 3, 6	7.0*
2, 3, 9	4.7	12, 3, 9	8.0
2, 4, 6	4.0	12, 4, 6	7.3
2, 4, 9	5.0*	12, 4, 9	8.3
2, 6, 9	5.7*	12, 6, 9	9.0

* Deviates by no more than 1 unit (year) from the population average.

6.2. Optimum Allocation

The proportion of a sample drawn from a stratum can be made proportionate to properties of the stratum other than its size or to a combination of properties including size. The discussion of the results obtained in Table 11 suggests that the dispersion of values in a stratum affects the variability of estimates. It is natural, therefore, to use this property as a basis for determining the size of sample to be drawn from the stratum. *Optimum allocation* is a procedure which does so. In this procedure the size of the sample drawn from each stratum is proportionate to both the size and the spread of values within the stratum. A precise use of this method involves some statistical concepts which have not yet been introduced. An approximation to this method, however, can be used to illustrate the way it works.

One way of measuring the dispersion of values in a stratum is by use of the *range* of the values. The range is simply the difference between the smallest and greatest value in the stratum. The basic idea involved in the approximate method of optimum allocation is "the weighted range of a stratum." The weighted range is the product of the number of items in the stratum and the range. The proportion of a given sample allocated to a particular stratum is made equal to the ratio of this weighted range of the stratum to the sum of the weighted ranges of all the strata. For example, if we have two strata containing n_1 and n_2 items, respectively, with ranges R_1 and R_2, respectively, the proportion of the sample allocated to the first stratum is

$$\frac{n_1 R_1}{n_1 R_1 + n_2 R_2}.$$

Correspondingly, the proportion of the sample allocated to the second stratum is

$$\frac{n_2 R_2}{n_1 R_1 + n_2 R_2}.$$

Let us now return to the "toy" population and apply this method to determine what proportion of a sample of four elements should be taken from the strata: (2, 3, 4) and (6, 9, 12). For this case it is apparent that both n_1 and n_2 are equal to 3 and that $R_1 = (4 - 2) = 2$, and $R_2 = (12 - 6) = 6$. Then the proportion of the sample to be allocated to the first stratum is

$$\frac{(3)(2)}{(3)(2) + (3)(6)} = \frac{1}{4}.$$

The proportion of the sample allocated to the second stratum is

$$\frac{(3)(6)}{(3)(2) + (3)(6)} = \frac{3}{4}.$$

A sample of four elements is to be selected. Hence, the number of elements to be selected from the first stratum is $(1/4)(4)$, or 1, and the number of items to be selected from the second stratum is $(3/4)(4)$, or 3. Table 12 shows the results

TABLE 12

OPTIMUM ALLOCATION (APPROXIMATE) OF A
SAMPLE OF FOUR ELEMENTS FROM THE
STRATA: (2, 3, 4) AND (6, 9, 12)

Sample	Estimated Average
2, 6, 9, 12	5.5*
3, 6, 9, 12	6.0*
4, 6, 9, 12	6.5*

* Deviates by no more than 0.5 unit (year) from the population average.

obtained from using this method.

Let us now compare the results obtained in Table 12 with those obtained by use of proportionate stratified sampling, keeping all the conditions the same. Since both strata are the same size, samples of two elements will be selected from each. The results are shown in Table 13.

The advantage of optimum allocation is clear from a comparison of Tables 12 and 13. In the case of optimum allocation 100 per cent of the estimates deviate by no more than 0.5 unit from the population average, whereas the corresponding figure for proportionate stratified sampling is 56 per cent. If this same accuracy limit (0.5 unit) is applied to samples of four elements in Table 5, it is observed that only 33 per cent of the simple random samples yield estimates within this range.

Though optimum allocation can reduce the variability of estimates, it requires either prior knowledge or preliminary investigation of the dispersion of values in each stratum. This knowledge is frequently not available and may be more costly to obtain than the reduction in error warrants. For further details see (5), (8), (19), and (55).

TABLE 13

PROPORTIONATE STRATIFIED SAMPLES OF FOUR ELEMENTS
FROM THE STRATA: (2, 3, 4) AND (6, 9, 12)

Sample	Estimated Average	Sample	Estimated Average
2, 3, 6, 9	5.00	2, 4, 9, 12	6.75
2, 3, 6, 12	5.75*	3, 4, 6, 9	5.50*
2, 3, 9, 12	6.50*	3, 4, 6, 12	6.25*
2, 4, 6, 9	5.25	3, 4, 9, 12	7.00
2, 4, 6, 12	6.00*		

* Deviates by no more than 0.5 unit (year) from the population average.

6.3. Disproportionate Stratified Sampling

The procedure used in Table 9 was that of disproportionate stratified sampling. This procedure has advantages where a comparison of strata is an important aspect of the research. Such a comparison is most efficiently accomplished where the same size sample is drawn from each stratum. Except in the case where the strata are of the same size, samples of equal size would yield a disproportionate stratified sample. The precision of comparisons between strata is limited by the smallest sample taken from any of the strata. Consequently, when a comparison between strata is critical, equal size samples enable a more precise comparison to be made.

In general, a stratified sample in which the number of elements drawn from the strata is independent of their size is a disproportionate stratified sample. Thus, samples of equal size from all strata is only one type of disproportionate procedure. The sizes of samples used may be determined for analytical or tabulational purposes independently of the size of the strata. A good illustration of such a procedure is provided by Parten:

Stratification by states is necessar
college system makes the candidate's sta
the determining vote. Certain states are
relatively small samples will give a satisfact
on the other hand, require relatively large num
the direction of the vote. If the forecaster makes
tion of states by certainty, he can distribute his
centrating it in states where he most needs precision
guess about the characteristics of the strata is incorrect
unless last minute adjustments can be made and the contr

7. Cluster Sampling

As was indicated in an earlier section, for some population
difficult or impossible to identify uniquely each member of the
it may be possible to identify certain subgroups with relative ease.
a sample of these subgroups may be drawn as in multistage random
but a complete count can be taken of the selected subgroups or "cluste
cluster is a geographical or social unit, though it may be defined by
properties. Typical clusters are city blocks, households, families, organizatic
agencies, dwelling units, buildings, farms, etc.

Thus, for example, in a survey of a city's population, no up-to-date list of the
residents may be available, but a map showing each block may be. Then a
sample of blocks may be drawn, and a complete count taken of all those who
live in that block. Let us consider an illustration of cluster sampling provided
by Hansen and Hurwitz:

To obtain a random sample of dwellings or persons one need only take a random
sample of blocks and then take a census of the selected blocks. The steps are:

1. Number the blocks serially. The blocks may be numbered in any convenient
sequence throughout the city, although there will be some advantage in numbering
them in a geographic sequence in order to achieve some geographic "stratification" in
the selection of the sample.

2. Determine the size of the sample required. Of course, the size of the sample
needed will depend on the accuracy required as well as on the method of sampling.
The expected accuracy of results with a given method of sampling and size of sample
can be approximated in advance of drawing the sample. Let us assume for simplicity
that it has been determined that for the design under consideration a sample of 500
blocks will yield estimates of the various desired characteristics of the population
with the required reliability.

3. Draw a sample of blocks. If there are, say, 5,200 blocks in the city a sample of
500 blocks can be obtained by including in the sample 1 block in 10.4. To do this
choose from a table of random numbers a number between 1 and 104, and divide the
number obtained by 10. Record this number, and successively add 10.4 to it, recording each result. Then round the resulting series of numbers to the nearest whole numbers, and include in the sample the blocks having these numbers. Thus, if 17 is the

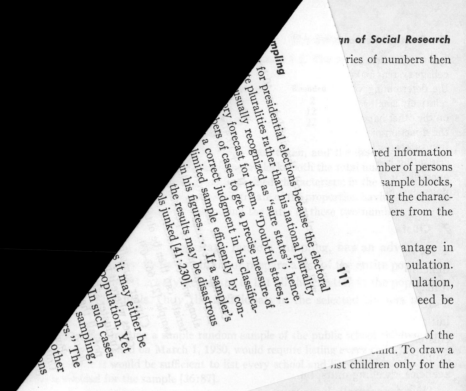

...ries of numbers then

...red information
...mber of persons
...sample blocks,
...ng the charac-
...ers from the

...antage in
...pulation.
...ulation,
...eed be

...of the
...d. To draw a
...st children only for the

...erved are widely dispersed, if geographically ...ted, considerable savings can be effected. The subjects ...ouped together so that travel is reduced. If, for example, the ...er is a city block, the observer or interviewer has a number of calls near each other. If the same number of calls are selected at random, they are likely to be widely dispersed and therefore require more travel and time between calls. Though cluster samples reduce field costs, they tend to yield more variable estimates than the other types of sampling presented.

Cluster sampling is also advantageous where we desire to estimate properties of population subgroups. For example, in a sample census we may desire not only to estimate the entire population of a city but also to estimate the average population per dwelling unit. A cluster sample in which the dwelling units (or groups of them) form sampling units would provide data on which the additional desired estimate could be based.

Another important advantage of a cluster sample is that in certain circumstances it may be used over and over again. In many research projects it is necessary to observe changes in a population over time. If the time interval is long, some of the individuals used in the first sample may move from the location with which they are identified in the sample. If the dwelling unit in which they live is treated as a cluster, the new occupants can be substituted for the old as part of the sample. The occupants of a designated set of clusters thus become a "panel." In fact, changes in the occupancy of the cluster in some cases can be used as a basis for estimating corresponding changes in the total population. This would be the case, for example, in a study of migration or any other population characteristic which changes in the period between observations or interviews.

In numerous periodic surveys cluster samples are selected. In some a portion of the designated clusters are changed each time. Eventually, then, the original clusters are all or nearly all replaced.

The efficiency of the cluster samples can be increased in many situations by any one of the following three methods or by various combinations of them.

1. *Stratifying the clusters.*—The individuals falling into the various clusters may have varied pertinent characteristics. In such a case classifying the clusters with respect to these characteristics and selecting clusters from each class will reduce the effect of these differences on the sampling error. If, for example, we use city blocks as clusters, and we know that the pertinent population characteristics vary from neighborhood to neighborhood, the following procedure could be used. Number the blocks in each neighborhood consecutively. If, for example, neighborhood A has 25 blocks in it, assign numbers from 1 to 25 to these blocks; if neighborhood B has 35 blocks in it, assign numbers from 26 to 60 to these blocks; etc. Now, if a systematic selection of blocks is made and the sampling interval is no greater than the least number of blocks contained in any neighborhood, the resulting sample will be stratified. That is, a selection will have been made from each neighborhood.

The clusters may, alternatively or in addition, be stratified with respect to size, that is, the number of individuals they contain. If, for example, the clusters are city blocks, we need to identify

in advance of drawing the sample, those blocks that have very large aggregate populations, say, blocks having more than approximately 50 dwelling units. It is particularly important to identify large blocks with unusual characteristics, such as those with large hotels, lodging houses, hospitals, jails, military establishments, etc. The large blocks can then be sampled separately from the other blocks of the city. . . . It is not necessary to obtain an accurate identification of this group of large blocks in accordance with some rigid definition of "large" blocks. If we fail to include certain large blocks in the group, the sample of the remaining blocks will still reflect their contribution to the average or total, but the reliability of the sample result will be lower than if they were all correctly classified beforehand [21:663].

The larger the cluster, the greater the variability of the resulting estimates relative to a fixed sample size. Therefore, stratification, which reduces this variability, becomes more important with increasing size of clusters.

2. *Decreasing the size of the cluster.*—If, for example, the cluster used is a half,

a quarter, or some other segment of a block, more clusters can be selected without changing the total sample size. Thus, the clusters will be more widely scattered throughout the population and are likely to provide better representation of the total population. The determination of the optimum number of blocks to select depends

on the relative costs of various operations, and on the amount of variability in the characteristics being observed from block to block (which is spoken of as "between-block variation") and from one listing unit to another within blocks ("within-block variation"). If there is a relatively large variation between blocks in the characteristics being estimated, then, as one might expect intuitively, the theory points to the use of a larger proportion of blocks and a smaller subsampling ratio than would be needed if the variation between blocks is relatively small [21:664–65].

Some statistical theory is available to aid in determining the optimum size for segments of a cluster (see [8:191 ff.] and [33]). Considerable savings can be brought about by using these methods.

In cluster sampling the cost of preparing and obtaining the sample is a function of the number of clusters selected and the size of the clusters. It also depends on the overhead cost per cluster (i.e., preparing lists and/or maps, and getting to and from the cluster) and the cost per observation. Let

c_1 = overhead cost per cluster

c_2 = additional cost per observation

m = number of clusters in sample

$\bar{n}$ = average number of observations per cluster

C = cost of preparing and obtaining the sample

Then,

$$C = m(c_1 + c_2\bar{n}).$$

It is clear from this last equation that the cost increases as the number of clusters and/or the average number of observations per cluster increases. With such increases, however, the sampling error and its cost decrease. But the best way to decrease the cost of error depends on whether there is more between-cluster variation or more within-cluster variation. The design problem, then, is to get the best balance between the operating and error costs.

It is helpful, in general, to select clusters so that they are as close to the same size as possible.

Where the cluster is a segment of an easily identifiable unit (such as a city block), the unsegmented units may be used in drawing the sample; then only those units selected need be segmented. Such a procedure is considerably more economical than segmenting each unit before the units are drawn.

3. *Subsampling.*—Instead of segmenting a large but convenient cluster (such as a city block), a sample may be selected from within the cluster. This would

reduce the average number of observations per sampling unit. For example, if every other (rather than every) dwelling unit is selected, it may be possible to select a larger number of blocks without increasing the operating costs. That is, a systematic or simple random sample of units (such as buildings, dwelling units, or families) can be drawn from each of the blocks selected. In this case, the building, dwelling unit, or family becomes a new and smaller cluster.

It is frequently possible to combine stratification and subsampling to obtain a very efficient sample. Hansen and Hurwitz suggest the following approximation to the optimum sampling ratios (ratio of sample size to population size) which can be used in these cases.

a) using a uniform overall sampling ratio in all strata;

b) determining the block sampling ratio and the subsampling ratio in the stratum of "small-blocks" as follows: for problems in which homogeneity within blocks is not high, take a subsampling ratio such that on the average about 5 families will be included per sample block; if there is great homogeneity within blocks, take somewhat fewer families—say 1 to 3—per sample block; and

c) making the proportion of blocks to be drawn from the "large-block" stratum equal to

$$P_s \sqrt{\bar{N}_i / \bar{N}_s}$$

where P_s is the proportion of blocks to be drawn from the "small-block" stratum, $\bar{N}_i$ is an estimate of the average number of families per block in the "large-block" stratum, and $\bar{N}_s$ is an estimate of the average number of families per block in the "small-block" stratum.

As an illustration, assume that a sample of 5 per cent of the households of the city is to be taken, and that the estimated average number of families per block in the "small-block" stratum is approximately 25, and in the "large-block" stratum, approximately 100. Assume that there is not too much homogeneity within blocks. To obtain an average of about 5 families per block from the "small-block" stratum the subsampling ratio would be $5/25 = 20$ per cent. Since the final per cent of dwelling units to be included in the sample is to be the same in both strata and equal to 5 per cent, the proportion of blocks to be drawn from the "small-block" group must be 25 per cent (because 20 per cent of the dwelling units in 25 per cent of the blocks gives the desired overall sampling ratio of 5 per cent). The proportion of blocks to be drawn from the "large-block" stratum would then be

$$25 \sqrt{100/25} = 50 \text{ per cent},$$

if we follow the rule just given; and the subsampling ratio for the "large-block" stratum would be 10 per cent (because 10 per cent of the dwelling units in 50 per cent of the blocks are needed to give the desired overall sampling ratio of 5 per cent). . . .

The introduction of subsampling may make it possible to attain, with perhaps a 3 per cent sample of families, the same accuracy that would result from a 10 per cent sample if the blocks were completely enumerated. Such a decrease in sample size for equivalent reliability is not unusual when one uses a reasonably close approximation to the optimum design, and may save considerably in time and cost [21:665–66].*

* For the cost assumptions implicit in this method see (19:428).

The principal difficulty in the use of cluster sampling arises out of the fact that each individual in the population must be capable of being uniquely assigned to one and only one cluster. This requires effective identification of individuals and clusters and the relationship between them. The assignment of individuals to clusters need not be done beforehand; in fact, it is usually done in the field by the observers. But this is by no means an easy task. For example, in the recent Bureau of the Census Post Enumeration Survey each individual in the population of the United States had to be potentially assignable to some living quarters as of April 1, 1950. This was extremely difficult to do, for it involved the complex concept of "usual place of residence." For example, it is frequently hard to assign a person who travels in his business to a "usual place of residence." Yet this transient portion of the population is important and must be assignable to some one cluster. To avoid errors in this assignment, the concept of "usual place of residence" and related notions had to be carefully defined in accordance with the principles given in the last chapter.

Determination of population characteristics from data obtained by a cluster sample is not a simple statistical procedure. Various types of adjustments of the data are required. To make such adjustments, expert statistical assistance is required. A discussion of these technicalities can be found in (8:189 ff.), (17), and (34).

8. Repetitive (or Multiple) Sampling

Up to this point in the discussion of sampling by stages, the decision as to how to draw the sample at any stage is completed before any stage of the sampling is performed. It is also possible, however, to draw one sample from a population, analyze it, and use the resulting information in designing a second sample from the same population. Such a procedure is called *double sampling*. In double sampling the data obtained from the second sample may be used in connection with the data obtained from the first sample to improve the efficiency of estimates of population characteristics. An illustration of double sampling is given in the following quotation from Hauser and Hansen:

This method was applied in the 1936 Consumer Purchases Study. A brief schedule was used to survey a large sample of households to obtain information on composition and type of household and income level. The results from the first sample were used to draw a final sample highly stratified on type and income level. The final questionnaire was very long and detailed and directed at particular classes and the additional gain from the stratification introduced by the preliminary sample was worthwhile [24:30].

Double sampling has important uses other than the facilitation of stratification. In nonrepetitive or single samples a definite decision is always reached when all the stages are completed and not until then. But in double sampling, according to Deming, a small sample would first be taken: if the results are decisive, no further investigation is required. But if the results are not decisive, a further sample would be taken. The results of the first sample would nearly always provide the necessary estimates ... by which the second sample could be very economically planned and made neither too large nor too small to provide definite and sufficient evidence for a rational decision [8:548–49].

After a small first sample is taken, if the results are not decisive, the next sample taken may also be small. The results of the first and second samples can be combined. If these are not decisive, another sample can be taken, etc. Each sample may be so selected, for example, that taking observations of those elements it includes constitutes a day's work. Computations can then be made to determine whether another sample is required. Such a procedure is called *group sequential sampling*. It can be used profitably where the treatment of the data is relatively simple and additional samples can be drawn very quickly or are prepared beforehand.

The method of sequential sampling just discussed suggests the following question: Would it be possible to make only one observation at a time and decide whether or not the results up to that point are decisive? Such a procedure *is* feasible and is in use. It is simply called *sequential sampling*. In sequential sampling the size of the sample is not determined in advance, but the results of each observation are used to determine whether or not an additional observation is necessary in order to come to one of a set of specified conclusions. On the average, fewer observations are required by this procedure than by single or double sampling relative to a fixed error. In some cases only half the sample size required in single sampling will yield equally good results if sequential sampling is used.

The sequential procedure cannot be used in all cases. The general conditions for its application are the following: (a) random sampling can be conducted for any sample size or for subgroups of samples, and (b) the number of observations can be increased indefinitely at any stage of the procedure. Condition (a) fails to apply in those cases where we doubt that a very small sample can even approximately represent the population. That is, wherever stratification or multistage sampling is desirable, in general, sequential sampling is not an efficient procedure to use. For example, if we were to examine a number of persons for their preferences with respect to some article, we would want to make sure that we had examined several professions, several levels of income, etc., before we came to any conclusion; hence, we would not apply sequential sampling, at least not until a minimum sample had been obtained. Condition (b) fails if it is not possible to draw additional items into a sample after the research has begun. This is true of most social surveys, since it is usually very difficult or expensive to increase the number of subjects during the course of the survey.

Despite these restrictions, there are many cases in which this method is applicable in the social sciences. For example, in one project it was necessary to determine whether the percentage of inmates in a state mental institution who had a certain characteristic was significantly different from 1.5 per cent. For each patient there was a large envelope on file which contained, among other things, his medical history. This history was generally quite long and required considerable time for a complete reading. In such a case, where the sample was drawn from the file and could be increased with no great difficulty, sequential methods were extremely efficient.

In general, sequential procedures are applicable only where the observations can be made one at a time or in groups without considerable loss of time between observations. This means that in most cases the subjects or data concerning them should be concentrated in a relatively small area and hence be easily accessible. The individual subjects must be uniquely identifiable so that there is no ambiguity about which one is selected in each drawing. In effect, this method requires the ability to manipulate efficiently the sample elements, whether these be records, individuals, or groups. It is apparent that satisfactory sequential sampling conditions are most likely to be encountered in social research in which records or very small concentrated populations are involved.

The analysis of data obtained by sequential sampling is different from that applied to single sampling procedures. A discussion of analyses applicable to sequential procedures can be found in (1:iii), (9:278–88), (10:xvii), (44), and (53).

9. Judgment Sampling

The probability sampling procedures which have thus far been discussed involve either a complete count or a random sample at each stage of the procedure. Because all these methods have been based on random sampling, we can say that they *tend* toward representativeness. We can determine for each procedure presented the probability that an estimate of a population characteristic based on that procedure deviates by any specified amount from the true value of the characteristic under investigation. This is not true for all methods of sampling.

In some cases there are well-defined subgroups of a population which seem to be representative of the population to be studied. In other cases practical considerations seem to preclude the use of probability sampling, and the researcher looks for a representative sample by other means. That is, he looks for a subgroup which is *typical* of the population as a whole. This subgroup is used as a "barometer" of the population. Observations are then restricted to this subgroup, and conclusions from the data obtained are generalized to the total population. This is a type of common-sense procedure. For example, for a number of years the United States believed with respect to presidential elections that "as Maine goes, so goes the nation." This belief turned out to be ill founded, but it expressed a conviction at the time that Maine's voting behavior was typical of the nation as a whole. An election forecaster who restricted his observations to Maine would have taken a *judgment* (or purposive) sample.

Judgment sampling is very precarious, because much stronger assumptions must be made about the population and the selection procedure than are required in probability sampling. For example, to select a typical city in a study of consumer purchases for the nation, the researcher may look for a city whose income distribution is similar to that of the nation as a whole, whose industries are typical of the nation as a whole, etc. In effect, he selects a community which is typical with respect to a set of properties, A, B, . . . , N, from which he assumes that the community is typical with respect to the characteristic X which he is investigating. Now it does not follow that, because a city is typical with respect to A, B, . . . , N, it is typical with respect to X, unless A, B, . . . , N completely determine X. No social researcher ever pretends that the properties he uses as guides in his selection completely determine the value he is investigating. At most he argues that they are highly correlated; that is, values of X tend to change in the same way that values of A, B, . . . , N do. Furthermore, even if the correlation assumption is true, the city selected may be *a*typical with respect to the way X is related to A, B, . . . , N. Hence the further assumption is required that in the city selected the relationship between A, B, . . . , N and X is typical. Assumptions such as these are likely to be very doubtful, and their validation is likely to require research beyond the scope of most research agencies.

Judgment sampling has another shortcoming: sampling errors and biases cannot be computed for such samples. For this reason judgment sampling should be restricted to the following situations: (1) the possible errors are not serious and (2) probability sampling is practically impossible. Data from judgment samples at best *suggest* or *indicate* conclusions, but in general they cannot be used as the basis of statistical testing procedures.

An application of judgment—or, as it is sometimes called, "purposive"—sampling in studies of the American soldier is described by Stouffer as follows:

The selection of [military] units involved purposive rather than strictly random sampling. If a cross section of enlisted men in the United States or a theatre was required, the standard procedure was to select the units such that each branch of service was represented in as nearly as possible the correct proportions. Within a given branch of service, effort was made to get units in various stages of training or with various types of Army experience in their correct proportions, in so far as this could be inferred from available data. For example, among infantrymen in the United States, some would be in Replacement Training Centers, some in newly activated divisions, some in divisions scheduled for early shipment overseas. The proportion of men in each type of unit could be roughly calculated, and the sample was designed to maintain these proportions [50:715].

For a more complete discussion of judgment sampling see (8:9–11 and 23) and (37:219, 236–38).

9.1. Quota Sampling

One of the most commonly used methods of sampling in marketing surveys and election polls is the method of *quota* sampling. This method combines aspects of probability sampling and judgment sampling. It usually consists of three steps: (1) a classification of the population in terms of properties known or assumed to be pertinent to the characteristic(s) being studied; (2) a determination of the proportion of the population falling into each class on the basis of the known, assumed, or estimated composition of the population; and (3) a fixing of quotas for each observer or interviewer who has the responsibility of selecting subjects or respondents so that the total sample observed or interviewed contains the proportion of each class as determined in (2).

The observers or interviewers are given their quotas; that is, they are instructed to observe or interview a specified number of individuals in each class. The individuals to be observed or interviewed are not identified by the research designer. The observer or interviewer must select the subjects, that is, individuals who fall into the specified class. Hence the observer or interviewer has the final say in the selection of the subjects. The final selection is a judgment selection, even though the initial stage is similar to that of proportionate stratified sampling. Judgment, however, replaces random selection at the last stage.

Quota sampling may produce serious errors. First, the quotas may not be set up proportionate to the true distribution of properties in the population.

Data for fixing quotas must be estimated from previous census results and certain current sources. When drastic changes are taking place in the economy, as during the depression of the last decade . . . estimated quotas may be seriously in error. Thus wrong controls are imposed on the sample, with the possibility of serious errors resulting [24:27].

Second, a good deal depends on the observer or interviewer, more than in probability sampling. In general, the observer or interviewer can be assumed to fill his quotas in a manner which suits his own convenience, whether intentionally or not.

As a result, even though the sample contains the proper quotas of each class of the population, it may contain too many people of the same nationality, educational level, or avocational interests of the enumerator [interviewer or observer], and too few third floor apartments, single family dwellings, or multiple worker families [24:27].

That is, those selected from each class are likely to be unrepresentative of their class. Furthermore, the observer rather than the researcher must classify the subjects, and, since he seldom is as well informed as the researcher concerning the over-all research design, he is likely to introduce a bias into the classification procedure. The observer may therefore introduce two biases—a bias of classification and a bias of nonrandom selection within each classification.

The results of quota sampling may not be seriously in error, but whether or not they are is extremely difficult to establish. The difficulty is that, at best, we can only know of a quota sample that it is representative with respect to some (but practically never all) of the pertinent population characteristics. Hence, we can have no assurance that the sample is representative with respect to the properties being measured. Since random sampling is not involved at any stage, the errors of the method cannot be determined by statistical procedures.

These [quota sampling] specifications cannot provide sample estimates for which the risk of error can be measured because they do not provide for the selection of persons in a way that permits knowing the probability of selection [15:185].

This [difficulty] may be concretized by a hypothetical survey in which it is desired to ascertain the reading habits of the population. Let us assume that in such a survey, age, sex, color, and income level of the population have been controlled. The respondents selected as the sample may have the proper proportions of each age, sex, color, and income group but if they have an improper representation of educational level, which may well be the case, the reading habits of the sample may not at all represent the reading habits of the universe. If we control on educational levels also, there may still be other points of difference.

In light of the limitations and the risks of serious bias in this type of sample design, it is certainly to be avoided whenever better designs are available at a reasonable price [24:28–29].

10. Populationing versus Sampling

In the formulation of a problem we specify a population, not a sample. In the practical design of research directed toward solving that problem, a sample may be selected from the specified population in order to draw inferences about the population from it. We cannot draw a sample efficiently unless we have a well-defined population. In a good deal of research, social researchers study a small population in its entirety and, having drawn conclusions about this population, generalize to more inclusive populations. They begin with what they consider to be a sample and look for a population that this sample can be said to represent. Such *populationing* (as opposed to sampling) and the generalizations based on it are among the most common methodological errors committed in the social sciences. There are no controlled methods available for starting with representatives and determining the represented. To do so we would require complete information on all pertinent properties of potentially selectable populations as well as of the "sample." If we knew this, we would have no need to start with the sample in the first place.

E. S. Marks eloquently warns against populationing and illegitimate generalization:

The matter of definition of a population is fundamental and has, in many statistical studies, been given inadequate attention. All too frequently, research workers draw their samples and their conclusions from different populations. We start with a study of the "relation between birth order and feelings of insecurity"; secure fifty to one hundred subjects through a sympathetic friend who happens to be superintendent of schools in a conveniently located city and conclude that "feelings of insecurity are not correlated with birth order." I have no particular quarrel with such a conclusion—it may well be true for many populations—but it has nothing to do with the data collected. From a group of cases picked up without consideration of what population is represented, we can conclude nothing about any population other than the cases actually observed.

. . . Our difficulties in drawing sound conclusions from samples stem from our own over-ambitiousness. We are not content with reporting our conclusions as applying to our own school or university or local community—we insist on discussing our results as if they apply to every human population.

If our sample is restricted to a school, group of schools, a community, a city or a state, our statistical conclusions must be similarly restricted. . . . Speculations on applicability to other populations are entirely proper and may be extremely valuable, but they should be labelled as speculations and not as statistical inferences [36:87].

The importance of this warning cannot be overemphasized, since illegitimate generalization is such a common error. For example, in a recent social-psychological study of ulcer patients (42), Ruesch and his associates selected (on the basis of availability) forty-two Navy ulcer patients and twenty civilian ulcer patients. The following is a typical set of observations:

	Per Cent Navy Ulcer Patients	Per Cent Civilian Ulcer Patients
Oldest child........	19	15
Youngest child.....	33	20

From these data the following conclusion was drawn: "Ulcer patients have more older siblings because they are later born children in the family" (42:45). Such a conclusion is completely unjustified *on the basis of these data*, since we have no way of knowing whether or not the group observed is a random sample from the total population of ulcer patients.

In another study conducted by Detroit's Harper Hospital in 1950, twenty-one available ulcer patients were similarly studied. Of these, 38 per cent were oldest children and 19 per cent were youngest. Despite the apparent contradiction between these and Ruesch's data, no conclusions can be drawn even about the contradiction relative to the population of ulcer patients. As a matter of fact, all that can be said is that the two studies dealt with populations (not samples) which differed in the respect noted.

Errors such as the one committed by Ruesch and his associates would not occur if the research problem were formulated in the manner discussed in chapter ii and if an ideal research procedure were designed in the manner called for in chapter iii. Furthermore, even a casual conversation with a sampling expert would prevent such errors.

11. Summary

In this chapter we have considered the various ways of selecting a portion of the total population—a portion which may be observed so as to provide information concerning the total population. For practical as well as purely scientific purposes it is necessary to use selection procedures whose errors are measurable. A procedure should be capable of characterization relative to bias and variability. The fundamental procedure satisfying these conditions is simple random sampling, a method in which each individual has an equal chance of being selected. Simple random sampling is performed with the aid of random numbers, while systematic sampling is a variation which proceeds from a random start to select elements at a preset interval.

By breaking the population into subgroups, we may select a sample in stages. If a random sample is selected at each stage, we have a multistage random sample. If a complete count of sampling units is taken at one stage other than the last, we have a stratified sample. If a complete count is made at the last stage, we have a cluster sample. The probability of selecting any subgroup may be made proportionate to some function of the size of the subgroup, and the number of units selected from any subgroup may also be made proportionate to some such function. Proportionate sampling tends to reduce sampling errors. Stratification and clustering can be combined to yield efficient samples, particularly where stratification and/or clustering is based on geographic properties (i.e., in area sampling). Area sampling reduces the complexity of preparing sampling lists and permits the clustering of subjects so that they come in bunches.

In double sampling a first sample can be used to provide information which can in turn be used to design an efficient second sample. Such sampling can also be used to reduce the number of observations required, on the average, for

TABLE 14

SAMPLING CHART

Type of Sampling	Brief Description	Advantages	Disadvantages
A. Simple random	Assign to each population member a unique number; select sample items by use of random numbers	1. Requires minimum knowledge of population in advance 2. Free of possible classification errors 3. Easy to analyze data and compute errors	1. Does not make use of knowledge of population which researcher may have 2. Larger errors for same sample size than in stratified sampling
B. Systematic	Use natural ordering or order population; select random starting point between 1 and the nearest integer to the sampling ratio (N/n); select items at interval of nearest integer to sampling ratio	1. If population is ordered with respect to pertinent property, gives stratification effect, and hence reduces variability compared to A 2. Simplicity of drawing sample; easy to check	1. If sampling interval is related to a periodic ordering of the population, increased variability may be introduced 2. Estimates of error likely to be high where there is stratification effect
C. Multistage random	Use a form of random sampling in each of the sampling stages where there are at least two stages	1. Sampling lists, identification, and numbering required only for members of sampling units selected in sample 2. If sampling units are geographically defined, cuts down field costs (i.e., travel)	1. Errors likely to be larger than in A or B for same sample size 2. Errors increase as number of sampling units selected decreases
1. With probability proportionate to size	Select sampling units with probability proportionate to their size	1. Reduces variability	1. Lack of knowledge of size of each sampling unit before selection increases variability
D. Stratified 1. Proportionate	Select from every sampling unit at other than last stage a random sample proportionate to size of sampling unit	1. Assures representativeness with respect to property which forms basis of classifying units; therefore yields less variability than A or C 2. Decreases chance of failing to include members of population because of classification process 3. Characteristics of each stratum can be estimated, and hence comparisons can be made	1. Requires accurate information on proportion of population in each stratum, otherwise increases error 2. If stratified lists are not available, may be costly to prepare them; possibility of faulty classification and hence increase in variability
2. Optimum allocation	Same as 1 except sample is proportionate to variability within strata as well as their size	1. Less variability for same sample size than 1	1. Requires knowledge of variability of pertinent characteristic within strata
3. Disproportionate	Same as 1 except that size of sample is not proportionate to size of sampling unit but is dictated by analytical considerations or convenience	1. More efficient than 1 for comparison of strata or where different errors are optimum for different strata	1. Less efficient than 1 for determining population characteristics; i.e., more variability for same sample size

TABLE 14—*Continued*

Type of Sampling	Brief Description	Advantages	Disadvantages
E. Cluster	Select sampling units by some form of random sampling; ultimate units are groups; select these at random and take a complete count of each	1. If clusters are geographically defined, yields lowest field costs 2. Requires listing only individuals in selected clusters 3. Characteristics of clusters as well as those of population can be estimated 4. Can be used for subsequent samples, since clusters, not individuals, are selected, and substitution of individuals may be permissible	1. Larger errors for comparable size than other probability samples 2. Requires ability to assign each member of population uniquely to a cluster; inability to do so may result in duplication or omission of individuals
F. Stratified cluster	Select clusters at random from every sampling unit	1. Reduces variability of plain cluster sampling	1. Disadvantages of stratified sampling added to those of cluster sampling 2. Since cluster properties may change, advantage of stratification may be reduced and make sample unusable for later research
G. Repetitive: multiple or sequential	Two or more samples of any of the above types are taken, using results from earlier samples to design later ones, or determine if they are necessary	1. Provides estimates of population characteristics which facilitate efficient planning of succeeding sample, therefore reduces error of final estimate 2. In the long run reduces number of observations required	1. Complicates administration of field work 2. More computation and analysis required than in nonrepetitive sampling 3. Sequential sampling can only be used where a very small sample can approximate representativeness and where the number of observations can be increased conveniently at any stage of the research
H. Judgment	Select a subgroup of the population which, on the basis of available information, can be judged to be representative of the total population; take a complete count or subsample of this group	1. Reduces cost of preparing sample and field work, since ultimate units can be selected so that they are close together	1. Variability and bias of estimates cannot be measured or controlled 2. Requires strong assumptions or considerable knowledge of population and subgroup selected
1. Quota	Classify population by pertinent properties; determine desired proportion of sample from each class; fix quotas for each observer	1. Same as above 2. Introduces some stratification effect	1. Introduces bias of observers' classification of subjects and nonrandom selection within classes

coming to a conclusion. When double sampling is generalized, it yields sequential sampling, a method of drawing one item or set of items at a time and using the data obtained to decide whether to continue sampling or not.

All sampling methods based exclusively on random selection and complete counts are probability samples. They yield measurable errors. This is not true of judgment samples which rely on the researcher's judgment rather than on controlled methods of selection.

The ultimate basis for selecting a sampling procedure should be the minimization of the cost of getting the sample and the expected cost of errors which may result from using the method. Expert assistance should be employed in making such evaluations; in general, such evaluations require technical knowledge which the social researcher does not have.

Table 14 summarizes in a very brief way the description, advantages, and disadvantages of the various sampling procedures discussed.

DISCUSSION TOPICS

1. Suppose the members of a five-person population are aged 20, 21, 22, 22, and 25 years old, respectively. How many simple random samples of size three could be selected with replacement? What is the expected value of the sample averages? How would you estimate the sum of the ages of the group from a sample of three? What is the expected value of the estimated sum?

2. What methods would you use for obtaining a sample of the following and why?

   a) Children less than one year old who were born in a specified city.
   b) The words in this book.
   c) The books in a library.
   d) The hotels in a city.
   e) The houses in a city.
   f) Twice-married males in a city.
   g) Restaurant waitresses in a county.
   h) Classes meeting at a specific hour in a university.
   i) The automobiles passing through a specified intersection from noon to midnight.

3. Suppose one desired to sample a population of students to determine whether or not their parents are foreign-born. Should one select only students whose last names begin with "S"? Would this yield a biased estimate?

4. How can a sample be designed to determine the frequency with which words in the English language are used in the United States?

5. If one wanted a sample of Army troops in the United States, what kind of clusters could be used? What would be the advantages and disadvantages of each?

6. Define the following terms: (a) simple random sample; (b) bias; (c) probability sample; (d) multistage random sample; (e) stratified sample; (f) judgment sample; (g) quota sample; (h) populationing.

7. What are some critical social research problems in which sequential sampling could be used?

EXERCISES

1. Design three different type samples for the problem which you formulated at the end of chapter ii and for which you prepared an idealized model at the end of chapter iii.

2. Select a systematic sample of thirteen words from those which appear in the statement of this problem. Determine the average number of letters per word in the sample. Is this an unbiased estimate of the average number of letters per word in the population? Show that this is or is not unbiased.

3. A population is divided into the following strata: (1, 4) and (9, 11, 15, 20). Select a proportionate stratified sample of three elements and determine what percentage of the possible samples yield estimates that deviate by no more than 1 unit from the population average. Select a simple random sample of three elements from the same population and compare the variability of the results obtained with those obtained by proportionate stratified sampling.

4. Select a sample (with probability proportionate to size) of two out of four primary units which contain 329, 473, 615, and 178 persons, respectively. Use the random numbers given on page 95.

5. Suppose we have two bowls: bowl (1) has one white and four red balls in it and bowl (2) has three white balls in it. Suppose we use the following method of obtaining a sample of two balls: select one ball from bowl (1). If it is white, select a ball from bowl (2), but, if it is red, select another ball from bowl (1). Would this method give us an unbiased estimate of the proportion of red and white balls in the population?

SUGGESTED READINGS

For those who have just been introduced to the subject of sampling, the following are recommended for getting further into the subject: Hansen (12) and (13); Hansen and Hauser (15); Hansen and Hurwitz (20) and (21); and Stephan (47) and (48). A new introduction to sampling theory and its application will be provided by Hansen, Hurwitz, and Madow (23).

Those who have had advanced training in statistics and/or mathematics should familiarize themselves with Cochran (5), Deming (8), or Yates (55). To catch up on recent developments and trends see Cochran (4), Hansen and Hurwitz (17) and (19), Mahalanobis (35), and Yates (54).

For detailed discussions of some sampling designs see Cornell (6), Hansen and Hurwitz (18), Hansen, Hurwitz, and Gurney (22), Mahalanobis (33) and (35), and Sampling Staff (43).

REFERENCES AND BIBLIOGRAPHY

1. CHURCHMAN, C. W. *Statistical Manual: Methods of Making Experimental Inferences*. 2d rev. ed. Philadelphia: Pittman-Dunn Laboratory, Frankford Arsenal, 1951.
2. COCHRAN, W. G. "The Use of Analysis of Variance in Enumeration by Sampling," *Journal of the American Statistical Association*, XXXIV (1939), 492–510.
3. ———. "Sampling Theory When the Sampling Units are of Unequal Sizes," *ibid.*, XXXVII (1942), 199–212.

4. ——. "Recent Developments in Sampling Theory in the United States." Washington, D.C.: International Statistical Institute, 1947. (Mimeographed.)

5. ——. "Sample Survey Techniques." Raleigh: North Carolina State College, 1948. (Mimeographed.)

6. CORNELL, F. G. "A Stratified Random Sample of a Small Finite Population," *Journal of the American Statistical Association*, XLII (1947), 523–32.

7. DEMING, W. E. "On Training in Sampling," *Journal of the American Statistical Association*, XL (1945), 307–16.

8. ——. *Some Theory of Sampling*. New York: John Wiley & Sons, 1950.

9. DIXON, W. J., and MASSEY, F. J., JR. *Introduction to Statistical Analysis*. New York: McGraw-Hill Book Co., 1951.

10. EISENHART, CHURCHILL; HASTAY, M. W.; and WALLIS, W. A. *Techniques of Statistical Analysis*. New York: McGraw-Hill Book Co., 1947.

11. FISHER, R. A., and YATES, FRANK. *Statistical Tables for Biological, Agricultural, and Medical Research*. London: Oliver & Boyd, Ltd., 1943.

12. HANSEN, M. H. "Sampling Human Populations." Washington, D.C.: International Statistical Institute, 1947. (Mimeographed.)

13. ——. "The Use of Sampling in Opinion Surveys." Washington, D.C.: United States Bureau of the Census, 1947. (Mimeographed.)

14. HANSEN, M. H., and DEMING, W. E. "On Some Census Aids to Sampling," *Journal of the American Statistical Association*, XXXVIII (1943), 343–57.

15. HANSEN, M. H., and HAUSER, P. M. "Area Sampling—Some Principles of Sampling Design," *Public Opinion Quarterly*, IX (1945), 183–93.

16. HANSEN, M. H., and HURWITZ, W. N. "Relative Efficiencies of Various Sampling Units in Population Inquiries," *Journal of the American Statistical Association*, XXXVII (1942), 89–94.

17. ——. "On the Theory of Sampling from Finite Populations," *Annals of Mathematical Statistics*, XIV (1943), 333–62.

18. ——. "A New Sample of the Population," *Estadistica*, II (1944), 483–97.

19. ——. "On the Determination of Optimum Probabilities in Sampling," *Annals of Mathematical Statistics*, XX (1949), 426–32.

20. ——. "Dependable Samples for Marketing Surveys," *Journal of Marketing*, XIV (1949), 362–72.

21. ——. "Modern Methods in the Sampling of Human Populations," *American Journal of Public Health*, XLI (1951), 662–68.

22. HANSEN, M. H.; HURWITZ, W. N.; and GURNEY, MARGARET. "Problems and Methods of Sample Survey of Business," *Journal of the American Statistical Association*, XLI (1946), 173–89.

23. HANSEN, M. H.; HURWITZ, W. N.; and MADOW, W. G. *Sample Survey Methods and Theory*. New York: John Wiley & Sons, Inc., 1953.

24. HAUSER, P. M., and HANSEN, M. H. "On Sampling in Marketing Surveys," *Journal of Marketing*, IX (1944), 26–31.

25. HENDRICKS, W. A. "The Relative Efficiencies of Groups of Farms as Sampling Units," *Journal of the American Statistical Association*, XXXIX (1944), 366–76.

26. HILGARD, E. R., and PAYNE, S. L. "Those Not at Home—Riddle for Pollsters," *Public Opinion Quarterly*, VIII (1944), 254–61.

27. HORTON, H. B. *Random Decimal Digits.* Washington, D.C.: Interstate Commerce Commission, 1949.
28. JESSEN, R. J. *Statistical Investigation of a Sample Survey for Obtaining Farm Facts.* Iowa State College Experimental Station Research Bull. 304. Ames, 1942.
29. KENDALL, M. G., and SMITH, B. B. "Randomness and Random Sampling of Numbers," *Journal of the Royal Statistical Society,* CI (1938), 147–66.
30. ———. *Tables of Random Sampling Numbers.* "Tracts for Computers," No. 24. Cambridge: Cambridge University Press, 1940.
31. MADOW, L. H. "Systematic Sampling and Its Relation to Other Sampling Design," *Journal of the American Statistical Association,* XLI (1946), 204–17.
32. MADOW, W. G. and L. H. "On the Theory of Systematic Sampling," *Annals of Mathematical Statistics,* XV (1944), 1–24.
33. MAHALANOBIS, P. C. "A Sample Survey of the Average Acreage under Jute in Bengal," *Sankyā,* IV (1940), 511–30.
34. ———. "On Large Scale Sampling Surveys," *Philosophical Transactions of the Royal Society,* Ser. B, *Biological Sciences,* CCXXXI (1941), 329–451.
35. ———. "Recent Experiments in Statistical Sampling in the Indian Statistical Institute," *Journal of the Royal Statistical Society,* CIX, Part IV (1946), 325–78.
36. MARKS, E. S. "Some Sampling Problems in Educational Research," *Journal of Educational Psychology,* XLII (1951), 85–96.
37. MOSER, C. A. "The Use of Sampling in Great Britain," *Journal of the American Statistical Association,* XLIV (1949), 231–59.
38. NEYMAN, JERZY. "On the Two Aspects of the Representative Method," *Journal of the Royal Statistical Society,* XCVII (1934), 558–606.
39. ———. "Contributions to the Theory of Sampling Human Populations," *Journal of the American Statistical Association,* XXXIII (1938), 101–16.
40. NORDIN, J. A. "Determining Sample Size," *Journal of the American Statistical Association,* XXXIX (1944), 497–506.
41. PARTEN, M. B. *Surveys, Polls, and Samples.* New York: Harper & Bros., 1950.
42. RUESCH, JURGEN, *et al. Duodenal Ulcer.* Berkeley: University of California Press, 1948.
43. SAMPLING STAFF. *A Chapter in Population Sampling.* Washington, D.C.: United States Bureau of the Census, 1947.
44. STATISTICAL RESEARCH GROUP. *Sequential Analysis of Statistical Data: Application.* New York: Columbia University Press, 1946.
45. STEPHAN, F. F. "Representative Sampling in Large-Scale Surveys," *Journal of the American Statistical Association,* XXXIV (1939), 343–52.
46. ———. "Stratification in Representative Sampling," *Journal of Marketing,* VI (1941), 38–46.
47. ———. "History of the Uses of Modern Sampling," *Journal of the American Statistical Association,* XLIII (1948), 12–39.
48. ———. "Sampling," *American Journal of Sociology,* LV (1950), 371–75.
49. STOCK, J. S., and FRANKEL, L. R. "The Allocation of Sampling among Strata," *Annals of Mathematical Statistics,* X (1939), 288–93.
50. STOUFFER, S. A., *et al. Measurement and Prediction.* Princeton: Princeton University Press, 1950.

51. TEPPING, B. J.; HURWITZ, W. N.; and DEMING, W. E. "On the Efficiency of Deep Stratification in Block Sampling," *Journal of the American Statistical Association*, XXXVIII (1943), 93–100.

52. TIPPETT, L. H. C. *Tables of Random Sampling Numbers*. "Tracts for Computers," No. 15. Cambridge: Cambridge University Press, 1927.

53. WALD, ABRAHAM. *Sequential Analysis*. New York: John Wiley & Sons, 1947.

54. YATES, FRANK. "A Review of Recent Statistical Developments in Sampling and Sampling Surveys," *Journal of the Royal Statistical Society*, CIX (1946), 12–32.

55. ———. *Sampling Methods for Censuses and Surveys*. London: Chas. Griffin Co., Ltd., 1949.

CHAPTER V

The Logic of Statistical Procedures

1. Introduction

If a sample of a population of individuals or events is used in research, some method is required to draw conclusions about (i.e., infer) characteristics of the population from characteristics of the sample. The great advantage of probability samples is that they permit such inferences to be made with measurable error. The methods of drawing such inferences are *statistical* in character. Thus sampling and statistical inference are inseparable: they are two phases of the same process.

The model of statistical procedures has its complicated mathematical side, just as do many other aspects of modern science which have "grown up" with our development in mathematical thinking. The research scientist has found that the tools of the mathematician are extremely useful in making precise the methods and theories of science, so that it is only natural that the modern-day statisticians should have made full use of these tools. But the *logic* that lies behind these mathematical procedures can be understood without any advanced mathematical training. All that is required is an understanding of the basic ideas. Though these ideas have been given rigid mathematical meanings by the specialists in statistical theory, it is not necessary for our purposes to take a rigid mathematical approach to them. We shall, as far as possible, consider the concepts of modern statistics in a nontechnical manner.

2. The Function of Statistics

In the introduction to the problems of sampling we noted that there are two kinds of sampling: (1) sampling from the population of observations that could be made on a single individual and (2) sampling from a population of individuals or events. In that discussion it was pointed out that social research generally deals with populations of the latter type, and hence we concentrated on applications of sampling to populations of individuals and events. The same emphasis

131

will also characterize the discussion in this chapter, but again it should be realized that the same methods are applicable to both types of problems.

It is not necessary to consider sampling from a population of items and sampling from a population of observations of one item as an "either-or" choice. It is possible to take a sample of observations on a sample of items. But, as we noted earlier, if we repeatedly subject a "human item" to the same stimulus, the first response may affect the second, the second may affect the third, etc. For example, if we give a person the same I.Q. test several times, we will expect his score to change, because he changes during the test in a way that affects his subsequent responses; that is, he is learning. Unless we have some systematic way of correcting for this change in the subject, taking more than one observation will not increase our accuracy. In general, then, repeated observations of the response of the same subject to the same stimulus will only increase our accuracy if either (1) we know the effect of repeated stimulation and can *adjust* the observations or (2) each response is unaffected by previous responses, that is, if successive responses are *independent*. We shall see later how a test of independence can be conducted.

Since no one observation is ever completely accurate, we ideally would like to take more than one observation, assuming that a better estimate (of the true value of the characteristic observed) can be made where we have more than one observation. But an infinite number of observations are possible, and we cannot take them all. Hence, one function of statistics is to enable us to make the best possible estimates of the true property (or properties) of an individual from a probability sample of independent observations. If we had all the possible independent observations, we would have no need for statistics; it is only because we have fewer observations than we would ideally like that we have need for statistical methods.

If we *assume* our observations on each member of a population of items to be perfectly accurate, and if we observe every member of the population, again we will have no need for statistical methods. But, if we observe only a sample of the population, then, even if each observation is perfectly accurate, statistics is required to make the best possible estimate of population characteristics.

Statistical estimates of individual or group characteristics are always subject to error. The advantages of making such estimates, however, are (1) that they can be made with the *least possible error* and (2) that this error is *measurable*. By providing us with measures of error, statistical methods give us an explicit criterion in terms of which scientific progress can be measured. It is quite commonplace, for example, to define scientific progress in terms of the reduction of error. But we must be careful not to think of error as a purely statistical concept; statistics may help us measure error, but by itself it cannot define error. To define error, we must have recourse to the nonstatistical specification of "mistakes" such as concerned us earlier. Later in this chapter we shall bring the concepts of "mistake" and "error" together and show how they are used to answer the questions: What errors can be tolerated? How do we analyze the sample data and draw inferences from them?

The function of statistics, then, is to enable us to make the best possible inferences from characteristics of a sample to characteristics of a population. A necessary prerequisite for the use of statistics is that the sample used as a basis for such inferences be a probability sample.

3. Discrepancy of Data

We indicated in the discussion of sampling that it is possible to improve an estimate of a property of an individual by increasing the number of independent or adjusted observations made on the individual. We hope these observations will be "in agreement," but we do *not* expect them all to be identical. As a matter of fact, if all the independent or adjusted observations* on a single individual are exactly the same, we would be just as suspicious of them as we would be if there were no agreement among them. This is true even in the physical sciences. If, for example, we were to weigh an object several times and each time get exactly the same reading, we would be likely to conclude either that the weighing instrument does not make fine enough readings, that it is jammed, or that we are reading the instrument incorrectly. For some purposes we may be satisfied with crude readings, and hence we may not be bothered by complete agreement of readings; but, where we want to become as accurate as possible, we keep trying to develop finer and finer observational instruments. The point here is that, when we make repeated observations on a single subject, we do not expect to get identical readings; and, if we do get them, we attribute the agreement to the crudity of either the instruments or the observer. In effect, where our objective is to increase our accuracy, we insist on discrepancy of observations, but we seek constantly to reduce the amount of discrepancy (e.g., by pushing out to more and more decimal places).

Where we make one or more observations on each of a number of different subjects, we also expect discrepant observations. For example, we do not expect each member of a group to have the same I.Q., to have the same annual income, to be equally heavy, or to have been born in the same year. Thus we have discrepancy between observations on one or many subjects. How can we answer questions about individual or group properties where such discrepancy exists?

---

* Unless otherwise indicated, the term "observations" will henceforth refer to independent or adjusted observations.

This is where statistics comes to our aid; as a matter of fact, it is necessary and applicable only where such discrepancy exists.

4. Pattern of the Data

Suppose we are interested in studying the average weight of male students at a university. We would hardly expect to find that all the students have the same weight. But we would expect to find some pattern in the weights. For example, we might find that there are very few who weigh less than 100 pounds and few who weigh more than 200 pounds. We might also find that most of the students weigh about 150 pounds. If we selected a simple random sample of 270 students, we might get results such as are shown in Table 15.

TABLE 15

WEIGHTS OF 270 MALE STUDENTS

Weight (in Pounds)	Frequency	Relative Frequency*
100–109 . . .†	1	0.004
110– 19 . . .	1	.004
120– 29 . . .	6	.022
130– 39 . . .	38	.141
140– 49 . . .	80	.296
150– 59 . . .	83	.307
160– 69 . . .	39	.145
170– 79 . . .	17	.063
180– 89 . . .	2	.007
190– 99 . . .	2	.007
200–209 . . .	0	.000
210– 19 . . .	1	0.004
Total	270	1.000

* Relative frequency equals the class frequency divided by the total frequency. Thus, in the first class the relative frequency is equal to 1/270, or 0.004.

† This interval includes weights equal to or greater than 99.5 pounds but less than 109.5 pounds; that is, "up to but not including 109.5 pounds."

This table gives the *frequency distribution* of the data. The data are so grouped in the table as to bring out the pattern in the most effective way. The table shows that only 1 of the 270 students weighs less than 110 pounds, while only 1 weighs more than 209.5 pounds. Most of the students' weights fall in between these extremes, and actually over one-half of them weigh between 140 and 160 pounds.

This suggests that there is a very definite pattern in the data obtained, and it also suggests how these data can be used for purposes of predicting the weights of those whom we did not weigh. We expect that, even if we weighed many more students, we would find few who weighed less than 100 pounds. This prediction is based not only on the fact that only 1 student in 270 weighed came anywhere near weighing this little but also on the fact that the distribution of weights shows that there is a definite tendency to weigh more.

5. Distribution of Data

The set of data obtained on the weights of male students shows a definite pattern in the way that the data are distributed. The distribution of the data turns out to be very fruitful in predicting many things. For example, in the illustration of college students given above, it may be very important to obtain the normal or average weight for purposes of judging whether a certain student is "overweight" or "underweight." Again, a physicist who is taking a series of measurements on the same object will usually be interested in the value around which most of his data cluster, for he assumes that, by using this central value, he is less likely to make a large error than a small one. He argues that this central value lies close to the true value which he is seeking.

Whatever may be the motive behind the collection of the data, it will be clear that the pattern of the data is extremely important. It will also be clear that, if we weighed more students selected at random, we would not expect to get the same type of pattern; we might find that there are more students whose weights fall around the central values than we had found in the case of the original 270, or we might find that some weigh less than anyone whom we had originally weighed. It does seem reasonable, however, to expect that, as we increase the number of randomly selected observations, the pattern of the data will become more and more stable, and experience and theory justify this expectation.

Let us follow an example in which more and more data are collected to see how the pattern develops. Just how far one would want to go in this sort of thing is a practical matter, but we will suppose that the researcher is willing to take a great many observations of students' weights in order to be surer and surer of the pattern of the data.

The original data on weights have already been given in Table 15. In order to follow the development of the pattern of the data, it is convenient to plot a graph such as that shown in Figure 6. This type of graph is called a *histogram* and is a very useful way of recording this kind of data, for it shows quite clearly the nature of the pattern.

Along the base of the histogram is the scale which represents the various weights. This scale has been divided into convenient intervals, which match the intervals in Table 15. Along the vertical axis of the histogram is plotted, in blocklike style, the number of students whose weights fall in a given interval. The higher a column is over an interval on the base scale, the greater is the number of students whose weights fall in that interval. A glance at the histogram shows how the data tend to "rise" toward the middle and to fall off rather sharply at either end.

If the number of observations is increased, a direct comparison of the shapes of the new and old histograms is made difficult because of the different heights of

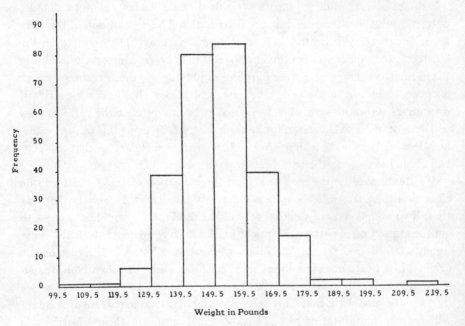

Weight in Pounds

FIG. 6.—Weights of 270 male students

columns. Comparisons are made easier if, instead of plotting the *number* (frequency) of students with weights in each interval, we plot the *relative frequency*. The relative frequency of students whose weights fall into a specified interval is simply the proportion of the students observed whose weights fall in that interval. In the example there are 80 of the 270 students whose weights are within the interval 140–49 . . . pounds; the relative frequency of students with weights in the interval 140–49 . . . pounds is 80/270, or 0.296. This may also be expressed as 29.6 per cent.

The histogram shown in Figure 6 can be replotted in terms of relative frequency. The result is shown in Figure 7. Note that the two histograms show exactly the same pattern; the only difference is that the vertical axis now represents *relative* frequency instead of the absolute frequency (i.e., the actual number observed).

Suppose now that an additional 730 randomly selected students were weighed, so that the total number weighed becomes 1,000. Table 16 shows the results for the entire 1,000. As before, we may plot a histogram to represent the data in the form of relative frequencies. The histogram is shown in Figure 8.

Note that in the new histogram the "spread" of the data is greater than it was in the original 270 observations: some students weigh less than any of those previously weighed. The relative frequencies of weights, however, remain about the same as before. In the original observations not one person weighed less than 100 pounds, so that the relative frequency was, of course, 0.000. In the larger sample only one student weighed less than 100 but more than 90 pounds,

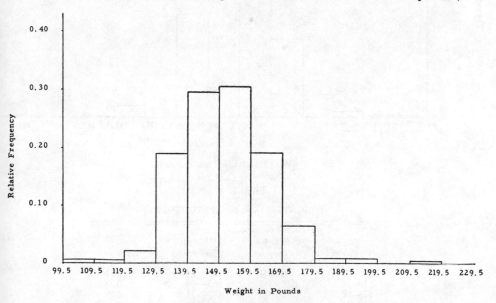

Fig. 7.—Weights of 270 male students

TABLE 16

Weights of 1,000 Male Students

Weight (in Pounds)	Relative Frequency	Weight (in Pounds)	Relative Frequency
90– 99 . . .*	0.001	160– 69 . . .	0.172
100–109 . . .	.001	170– 79 . . .	.072
110– 19 . . .	.008	180– 89 . . .	.012
120– 29 . . .	.042	190– 99 . . .	.002
130– 39 . . .	.135	200–209 . . .	.000
140– 49 . . .	.276	210– 19 . . .	0.001
150– 59 . . .	0.278		

*"90–99 . . ." = "from 89.5 pounds up to but not including 99.5 pounds."

so that the relative frequency is 1/1,000, or 0.001. Similar comparisons can be made for any of the other intervals, and it will be found that the relative frequencies do not differ widely.

In effect, then, the two patterns of the data—the one shown in Figure 7 and the other in Figure 8—do not differ to any great extent. But it is apparent that the histogram in Figure 8 is "smoother" than the histogram of Figure 7. This

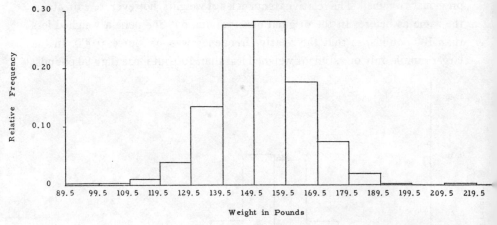

Fɪɢ. 8.—Weights of 1,000 male students

TABLE 17

Wᴇɪɢʜᴛs ᴏꜰ 270 Mᴀʟᴇ Sᴛᴜᴅᴇɴᴛs

Weight (in Pounds)	Relative Frequency	Weight (in Pounds)	Relative Frequency
105– 9 . . .	0.004	160– 64 . . .	0.074
110–14 . . .	.004	165– 69 . . .	.070
115–19 . . .	.000	170– 74 . . .	.045
120–24 . . .	.011	175– 79 . . .	.019
125–29 . . .	.011	180– 84 . . .	.007
130–34 . . .	.030	185– 89 . . .	.000
135–39 . . .	.111	190– 94 . . .	.004
140–44 . . .	.118	195– 99 . . .	.004
145–49 . . .	.178	200–204 . . .	.000
150–54 . . .	.147	205– 9 . . .	.000
155–59 . . .	0.159	210– 14 . . .	0.004

difference in smoothness is all the more apparent if we attempt to refine these histograms further. We can do this by subdividing the intervals. For example, instead of determining the relative frequencies for intervals of 10 pounds, suppose we determine them for intervals of 5 pounds. In this case we would get the results shown in Tables 17 and 18 and plotted in Figures 9 and 10.

Note that, when we subdivide the intervals in this manner, the 270 observa-

TABLE 18

WEIGHTS OF 1,000 MALE STUDENTS

Weight (in Pounds)	Relative Frequency	Weight (in Pounds)	Relative Frequency
95– 99 . . .	0.001	155– 59 . . .	0.133
100–104 . . .	.000	160– 64 . . .	.103
105– 9 . . .	.001	165– 69 . . .	.069
110– 14 . . .	.003	170– 74 . . .	.050
115– 19 . . .	.005	175– 79 . . .	.022
120– 24 . . .	.017	180– 84 . . .	.011
125– 29 . . .	.025	185– 89 . . .	.001
130– 34 . . .	.057	190– 94 . . .	.002
135– 39 . . .	.078	195– 99 . . .	.000
140– 44 . . .	.125	200–204 . . .	.000
145– 49 . . .	.151	205– 9 . . .	.000
150– 54 . . .	0.145	210– 14 . . .	0.001

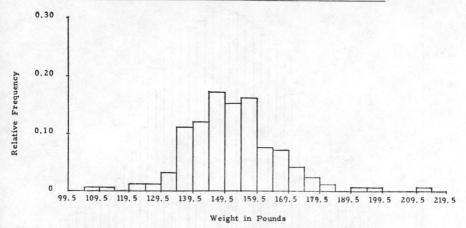

Fig. 9.—Weights of 270 male students

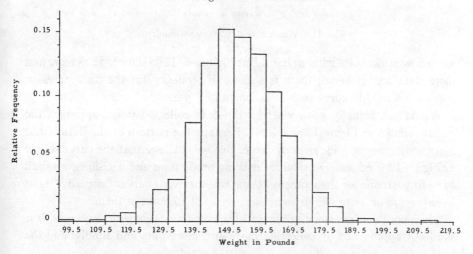

Fig. 10.—Weights of 1,000 male students

tions fall into a more irregular pattern than do the 1,000 observations. Suppose we continued to subdivide the intervals and to increase the number of observations. Then, for example, if 10,000 students were weighed, and $2\frac{1}{2}$-pound intervals were chosen, a histogram such as that shown in Figure 11 would be obtained.

It becomes clear from the succession of figures that the histograms can be made to approach smooth curves by decreasing the interval and increasing the number of observations. The "limiting" smooth curve, of course, could be drawn only if the intervals were decreased in size beyond any limit and the total

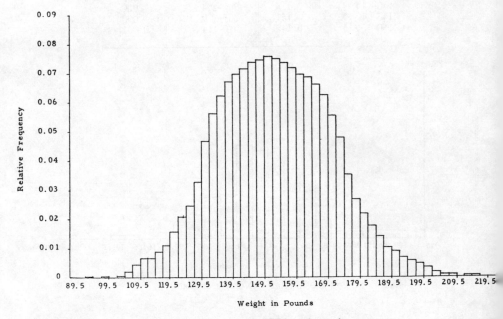

Fɪɢ. 11.—Weights of 10,000 male students

sample were increased without limit. But Figures 6–11 do show that, as more and more data are gathered, there is a definite tendency for the histograms to approach a smooth curve such as is shown in Figure 12.

We do not actually know whether the data collected would approach the picture shown in Figure 12 as a limit. Perhaps the pattern of the data is not approaching any specific smooth curve. But we shall see that the curve shown in Figure 12 is extremely useful for making predictions and decisions; we shall have to postpone for the moment asking whether such curves "actually" exist in nature, in order to see just what use we want to make of them.

The smooth curve shown in Figure 12 is called a *relative frequency curve;* it is the limit approached by collecting more and more data and subdividing the intervals indefinitely. The mathematical equation which describes the relative frequency curve is called a *distribution function.**

Not all relative frequency curves need to look like the one shown in Figure 12. For example, the census data on the distribution of females by income shown in Table 19 and plotted in the histogram in Figure 13 have a quite

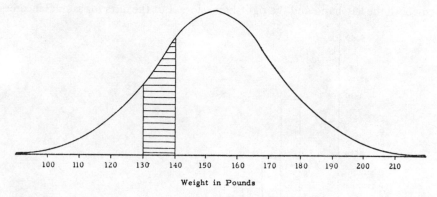

Weight in Pounds

Fig. 12.—Smooth curve for weights of male students

TABLE 19

Distribution of Females with Income, Fourteen Years of Age and Over, by Total
Money Income Level, 1947

(Sample Size = 12,000)

Total Money Income Level	Relative Frequency
Loss	0.002
$ 1–$ 499 ...	.298
$ 500–$ 999 ...	.195
$1,000–$1,499 ...	.160
$1,500–$1,999 ...	.156
$2,000–$2,499 ...	.104
$2,500–$2,999 ...	.038
$3,000–$3,499 ...	.021
$3,500–$3,999 ...	.009
$4,000–$4,499 ...	.006
$4,500–$4,999 ...	.003
$5,000–$5,999 ...	.003
$6,000–$9,999 ...	.003
$10,000 and over	0.003

different pattern. A possible smooth curve of these data is shown in Figure 14. You will notice that there is a decided tendency for this curve to "lag" to the

* More precisely, this equation is called a *probability density function*. The term *distribution function* is technically applied to the equation which describes the cumulative frequency curve. But, since either function can be derived from the other, this distinction is not important for our purposes.

right. This is to be expected from such data as these; there are a large number of females having low incomes, and hence the relative frequency curve of incomes rises rather sharply at first. But there is a wider "spread" on the right-hand side of the distribution. The data collected on the weights of male students were symmetrically distributed, since the curve drops equally sharply from the peak on both the left-hand and the right-hand sides. But the data for annual incomes

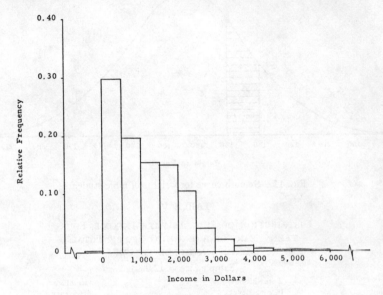

Fɪɢ. 13.—Histogram for Table 19

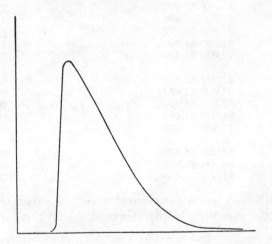

Fɪɢ. 14.—Type of curve approached by Fig. 13

are "skewed to the right," which means that the curve drops far less rapidly on the right than it does on the left. Thus, if we have a curve with one peak and if the frequency decreases more slowly on one side than the other, it is skewed on the side which decreases at the slower rate.

Other types of distribution patterns are shown in Figure 15 with the names that are usually employed to describe them. In the subsequent discussion we shall restrict ourselves mainly to symmetrical functions, although it should be realized that we need not be so restricted in practice.

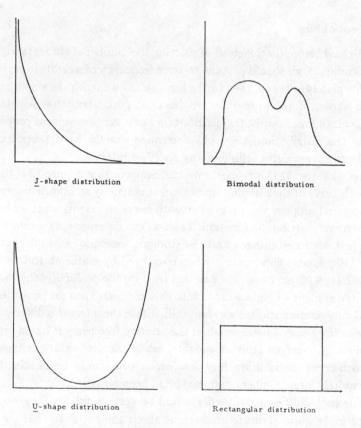

J-shape distribution

Bimodal distribution

U-shape distribution

Rectangular distribution

Fig. 15.—Types of distribution patterns

Perhaps the most commonly used symmetrical distribution is that one called the *normal*. This distribution has a number of properties that make it easy to use for predictive purposes, as will be shown below. The normal distribution always has a pattern similar to that shown in Figure 12. It has only one peak, it is symmetrical, and, the farther we go out on either side away from the peak, the closer the curve comes to the base line.*

In order to talk about the normal and other distributions, it will be convenient to introduce some related terms. This will save us the trouble of repeating a lot of words every time we want to express a certain idea about a distribution pattern. In order to introduce these terms, we will suppose that we know the distribution function, as illustrated by the smooth curves in Figures 12, 14, and 15.

6. Probability

We said before that, instead of plotting the number of students with weights in an interval, we should plot the relative frequency of weights in each interval. If this plan is followed, then in the limit, when we reach the smooth curve, we have a plot of the proportion of the total population that will fall in any interval. In other words, the distribution has a very convenient property: if we knew the distribution, we could determine exactly what proportion of the students have weights falling in any specified interval.

Let us see what this property means. Suppose that Figure 12 is the limiting smooth curve of the distribution of data obtained by an infinitely large random sample and suppose also that the smooth curve represents what we have called a "normal" distribution function. Then we can determine, as we shall presently see, just what percentage of all the students weigh, for example, between 130 and 140 pounds. This fraction when computed by mathematical techniques is 0.0902 (or 9.02 per cent). We call this fraction the *probability* that a randomly selected student's weight will fall into this interval. Thus the probability that a randomly selected student's weight falls within the interval is different from the *relative frequency* of these weights; the relative frequency is based on a limited number of observed student weights, while the probability is based on the smooth-curve distribution function which could only be obtained after an indefinitely large number of students had been observed.

The probabilities undoubtedly would be very useful, for they would enable us to make quite accurate predictions about the population. If we knew the true distribution function of the weights of male students, for example, we could

---

* The properties are not sufficient to define the normal curve; it is defined rigorously in the following equation:

$$Y = \frac{1}{\sqrt{2\pi}\,\sigma}\; e^{-(X-\mu^2)/2\sigma^2},$$

where $\pi = 3.1416$ and $e = 2.7183$; μ and σ will be defined below. X is the abscissa, the measurement or score marked on the horizontal axis; Y is the ordinate, the height of the curve corresponding to an assigned value of X.

say how probable it is that any randomly selected student will have a weight falling in any specified interval.

If we knew the normal distribution function, how could we determine these probabilities? The determination of the probabilities is equivalent, as one can see from the figures, to the determination of a certain area under the relative frequency curve. The shaded portion in Figure 12 represents the area under the relative frequency curve from 130 to 140 pounds; this area is only a part of the total area under the curve. Actually, it is 0.0902 of the total area; that is, the portion of the total area which lies between 130 and 140 pounds is the same as the probability.

Hence, we now have a graphic way of representing probabilities. We can represent the probability that an event will take place by an area under the relative frequency curve. We need some technique, however, for determining the size of these areas. This can be done by the mathematical techniques of integral calculus when the curve is a smooth one such as is shown in Figures 12, 14, and 15. But, in the case of the normal distribution, the areas have been worked out and tabulated in a very convenient way. In order to use these tables, and hence to apply normally distributed data to determining probability of events, we must first consider some important properties of distribution functions.

7. Measures of Central Tendency

One way of describing the pattern of the data represented by the curve in Figure 12 is to say that the curve reaches its one and only "peak" at 152.5 pounds. The value on the base line directly below the peak of the curve is called the true *mode* of the distribution. The location of the mode is important in the description of data of these kinds, for by means of it we can tell where most of the observations lie.

The true mode, then, is called a *measure of central tendency*, for it describes the point around which the data tend to cluster. In the case of the normal distribution, there is only one true mode, and the distribution is therefore called *unimodal*. Distributions with more than one mode (*polymodal*) are sometimes met in practice.

The mode is not the only, or even the most important, measure of central tendency. Many others have been developed. For example, there is the *median;* this is the value on the base line (abscissa) whose ordinate divides in half the area under the curve representing the distribution function. That is, there is an equal probability that an observation will fall on either side of the median. In unimodal symmetrical distributions the mode and median are the same.

For our purposes, the most important measure of central tendency is the *arithmetic mean*, or simply the *mean*. The mean of a distribution of data is very much like the center of gravity of an object, and we actually use the same techniques for estimating both. The center of gravity of a body is a point at which the mass of the body is "effectively" concentrated. If we suspend a steel bar at the location of its center of gravity, it will balance perfectly. We can use this physical analogue to help grasp the conception of the mean. Suppose we have the smooth curve representing the pattern of a set of data, as shown in Figures 12, 14, and 15. Now suppose we were to take a scissors and cut out the figure bounded by the smooth curve and the base line. Suppose the figure were made rigid, for example, by tracing it on a piece of cardboard and cutting out the cardboard similarly. Then we could locate a knife blade perpendicular to the base line at the point where the cardboard figure balances. Then, if the cardboard is made of uniform material, the point on the base line at which the figure balances is the "true" or "population mean" of the distribution of the data. We shall symbolize the *true* or *population mean* by the Greek letter μ.

If we were to try the above procedure on the curve shown in Figure 12, we would find that the figure balances at the point where the mode occurs. This is always true for unimodal symmetrical distributions and hence for the normal distribution function: the mean, the mode, and the median are located at the same point along the base line.

But note that, if a steel bar is irregular in shape, it will not necessarily balance at the point where it is bulkiest, or, to use a term already introduced, at the "mode" of its mass. A dumbbell, for example, has two "mass modes" at either end, but it balances at a point in the center of the handle.

In the same manner, a set of data need not balance at the point where the peak is located. This is clearly shown in Figure 14. The peak is located at $255; but, if we cut out the curve shown in Figure 14 and make the piece of paper rigid, the curve will balance not at the mode but at a point to the right of the mode. In the same manner, bimodal distributions will usually balance in between the two peaks.

8. Estimating the Mean

The true or population mean of a distribution of observations can be found only if we know the distribution function itself; but the distribution function can be known only when we have taken all possible observations. In practice, then, we need some definite technique for *estimating* the true mean on the basis of a finite number of observations; that is, on the basis of a sample. This estimate need not be the exactly correct one; indeed, we will rarely expect it to be. But, in common language, the estimate should come "somewhere near" the true value.

Now there are a number of ways of estimating the true mean of a distribution, most of which can be used in practice. We could, for example, take the value halfway between the highest and the lowest reading obtained. This halfway point would in the long run come fairly close to the true value of the mean, when the frequency distribution (plotted on the basis of a sample) is symmetrical. Or, again, for such symmetrical distributions, we could take the true mean to lie at the mode of the sample, for, as we have already remarked, the mode and the mean are the same for symmetrical distribution curves.

The estimate of the true mean, which is most frequently used with several types of random sampling, because it has some important practical advantages, is obtained by adding up the values of all the observations obtained from the sample and dividing by the total number of observations made; that is, the arithmetic average of the observed values.* It is convenient to symbolize this operation. Let x_1, x_2, x_3, etc., stand for the first, the second, the third, etc., observation. We let x_i stand for *any* observation of the set. The subscript i then stands for any one of the subscript numbers, 1, 2, 3, etc. We introduce the symbol Σ to stand for the operation of adding and let $\sum\limits^{n} x_i$ mean the sum of the n observed values, from the first to the nth (the last). That is,

$$\sum^{n} x_i = x_1 + x_2 + x_3 + \ldots + x_n \, .$$

We let $\bar{x}$ stand for the above-mentioned estimate of the true mean, μ; then

$$\bar{x} = \frac{1}{n} \sum^{n} x_i \, .$$

This formula asserts that $\bar{x}$ is the sum of the observed values divided by the total number of observations. Note that $\bar{x}$ is only an *estimate* of the true mean, μ; it is a *sample mean*, whereas μ is the *population mean*.

It should be noted that this estimate of the population mean, if based on an unrestricted random sample, is unbiased. That is, the expected value of the estimates ($\bar{x}$) can be shown to be equal to the population mean (μ), whether the population is finite or infinite, and whether the sample is drawn with or without replacement.

The method just described is suitable for computing $\bar{x}$ from a set of ungrouped (i.e., unclassified) observations. Note 1 at the end of this chapter

---

* The arithmetic average is the "center of gravity" of the observed values and hence can serve as an estimate of the population's "center of gravity."

describes a method for computing $\bar{x}$ from a set of grouped or classified data such as we had in the case of the students' weights.

9. Measures of Dispersion

The measures of central tendency are not the only ways of describing the pattern of a set of data. This is clearly shown in Figure 16*a*. Here are two relative frequency curves, both of them symmetrical and both having exactly the same population means (μ). But the observations for curve B do not cluster around the mean as closely as do those of curve A. The more a set of observations cluster around the mean, the less *dispersed* and the more *precise* they are said to be; the less they cluster around the mean, the more dispersed and the

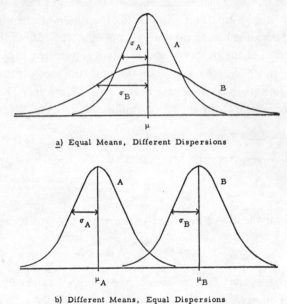

a) Equal Means, Different Dispersions

b) Different Means, Equal Dispersions

Fig. 16.—Comparison of normal distributions

less precise they are said to be. We may have two populations both of which have the same mean but different dispersions. For example, the average I.Q. in a small town may be equal to the national average, but we would expect the small-town I.Q.'s to be less varied than the nation's I.Q.'s. On the other hand, we can have two populations with different means but the same dispersion around their respective means, as is shown in Figure 16*b*.

Hence, to describe a pattern of possible observations, we must know not only where the mean lies but also something about the dispersion of the observations.

There are many ways of measuring dispersion. One such measure might be the "range" of possible values; that is, the distance between the lowest and highest possible values. But in some cases there will be no highest or lowest possible value (i.e., these may be infinitely large or small). One measure that suggests itself is based on the fact that the more dispersed are a set of data, the more the observations seem to deviate from their mean. It might seem, therefore, that a good measure of dispersion would consist of taking the average of the deviations of the observations from the mean. But the sum of the deviation of a set of observations from their mean is always zero. For example, the arith-

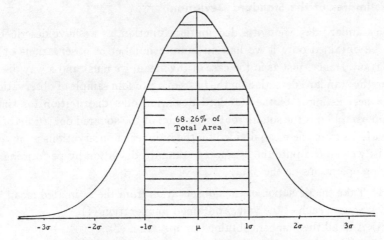

68.26% of
Total Area

-3σ -2σ -1σ μ 1σ 2σ 3σ

FIG. 17.—Graphic representation of the standard deviation

metical mean of 2, 4, 6, 8, 10, and 12, is 7. The deviations from the mean are -5, -3, -1, 1, 3, and 5. The total of these deviations is equal to zero. This difficulty can be avoided either by making the sign of each deviation positive or by squaring the deviations. (The squares of the deviations would all be positive.) The procedure of squaring the deviations and taking the average of these squares yields a measure of dispersion called the *variance*. The square root of the variance is another measure of dispersion; it is called the *standard deviation*. The variance and the standard deviation are by no means the only measures of dispersion in use, but they are probably the most widely employed.

The standard deviation can be represented graphically on a normal distribution function as the distance from the mean to the *inflection points*, the points on both sides of the curve at which the direction of the curvature changes. If we drew two ordinates through these points, the area between them would be 68.26 per cent of the total area under the curve (see Fig. 17).

The more closely the observations cluster around the mean, the smaller is the standard deviation. If the standard deviation were zero, then all the observations would lie at exactly the same point, and there would be no dispersion. The curve of the students' weights shown in Figure 12 has been drawn so that the standard deviation is 20.5 pounds. Suppose the population or "true" mean (μ) of the weight data is 152.5 pounds. Then, by the meaning of the standard deviation, 68.26 per cent of randomly selected students' weights in the long run would lie within 20.5 pounds of the mean, 152.5 pounds; that is, 68.26 per cent would lie between 132.0 and 173.0 pounds.

10. Estimates of the Standard Deviation

The standard deviation of a distribution function, as we have described it, could be obtained only if we had an infinite number of observations of the population. Hence, just as in the case of the mean, we must find a way of estimating the standard deviation on the basis of a random sample of observations.

The best estimate of the standard deviation of a distribution for simple random sampling is the square root of the sum of the squared deviations of the observations from the mean divided by the number of observations minus one. That is, we can compute the estimated standard deviation by performing the following operations on the data:

(1) Take the deviation of each observation from the estimated mean, $\bar{x}$.

(2) Square each of the values obtained in operation (1).

(3) Add all the numbers obtained in operation (2).

(4) Divide the total obtained in operation (3) by $(n-1)$,* that is, one less than the total number of observations.

(5) Take the square root of the result obtained in operation (4).

The *population* or *true* standard deviation is represented by the Greek letter σ, and the estimate of the standard deviation obtained by the operations enumerated above, by the letter s. The estimated standard deviation, s, can be represented by the following formula:

$$s = \sqrt{\frac{\sum_{}^{n} (x_i - \bar{x})^2}{n-1}}.$$

The reader should verify this formula according to the instructions which are given above.

The computation of the standard deviation following the instructions given above is sometimes very complicated. The value of the estimated mean, $\bar{x}$, may

* $(n-1)$ represents the "degrees of freedom" of s. This concept and its use are explained in Sec. 5 of the next chapter.

involve several decimal places so that the numbers obtained in the first operation involve several digits, and hence the squares of the numbers according to operation (2) are difficult to compute. For this reason the following set of operations yield exactly the same value for s and can be used wherever the above set of operations appear complicated:

(1) Examine the figures and guess in round numbers what the mean is (it does not matter if your guess is a bad one).
(2) Subtract your guessed value from each of the observations retaining plus and minus signs.
(3) Square all the numbers obtained in operation (2).
(4) Add all the squares of operation (3) and divide by $(n - 1)$.
(5) Add all the numbers obtained in operation (2), paying attention to plus and minus signs, and square the result.
(6) Divide the square obtained in operation (5) by $n(n - 1)$.
(7) Subtract the number obtained in (6) from the number obtained in (4).
(8) Take the square root of the result in (7). (The result obtained in operation [7] is s^2 and is called the estimated or sample *variance*. Thus the population variance is σ^2, the square of the population standard deviation, σ.)

There are more operations in this procedure than in the previous one, but they are much simpler to follow, since the numbers used are easier to manipulate. The reader may verify that the formula for s according to the eight operations given above is as follows:

Let x_0 represent the guessed mean, then

$$s = \sqrt{\frac{\sum_{i}^{n} (x_i - x_0)^2}{n - 1} - \frac{\left[\sum_{i}^{n} (x_i - x_0)\right]^2}{n (n - 1)}} \,. \quad *$$

These operations are illustrated below on a set of weights of college students.

* It can be proved that

$$\sqrt{\frac{\sum_{i}^{n} (x_i - x_0)^2}{n - 1} - \frac{\left[\sum_{i}^{n} (x_i - x_0)\right]^2}{n (n - 1)}} = \sqrt{\frac{\sum_{i}^{n} (x_i - \bar{x})^2}{n - 1}} \,.$$

Furthermore, if $x_0 = 0$, then

$$\sqrt{\frac{\sum_{i}^{n} (x_i - x_0)^2}{n - 1} - \frac{\left[\sum_{i}^{n} (x_i - x_0)\right]^2}{n (n - 1)}} = \sqrt{\frac{\sum_{i}^{n} x_i^2}{n - 1} - \frac{\left(\sum_{i}^{n} x_i\right)^2}{n (n - 1)}} \,.$$

This latter form is the easiest to use if a computing machine is available.

CALCULATION OF THE VARIANCE AND STANDARD DEVIATION
FOR A SET OF WEIGHTS OF COLLEGE STUDENTS

ORIGINAL DATA (x_i)

142, 156, 184, 169, 153, 172, 135, 162

(1). Guessed mean, $x_0 = 160$

(2). Subtract 160 from each observation

$$(x_i - x_0)$$

$$
\begin{array}{r}
-18 \\
- 4 \\
+24 \\
+ 9 \\
- 7 \\
+12 \\
-25 \\
+ 2 \\
\hline
\end{array}
$$

$$\sum_{}^{n} (x_i - x_0) = -7$$

(3). Square numbers obtained in (2)

$$(x_i - x_0)^2$$

$$
\begin{array}{r}
324 \\
16 \\
576 \\
81 \\
49 \\
144 \\
625 \\
4 \\
\hline
\end{array}
$$

$$\sum_{}^{n} (x_i - x_0)^2 = 1{,}819$$

(4). $1{,}819/7 = 259.9$.

(5) and (6). $(-7)^2/(8)(7) = 49/56 = 0.9$.

(7). $259.9 - 0.9 = 259.0 = s^2$.

(8). $\sqrt{259.0} = 16.1$.

The same operations can be represented in the following formula:

$$s = \sqrt{\frac{\sum_{}^{n} (x_i - x_0)^2}{n-1} - \frac{\left[\sum_{}^{n} (x_i - x_0)\right]^2}{n(n-1)}} = \sqrt{\frac{1{,}819}{(8-1)} - \frac{(-7)^2}{8(8-1)}} = 16.1.$$

The method for computing s for grouped data is described in Note 1 at the end of the chapter.

s^2 is an unbiased estimate of σ^2, if s^2 is computed from a simple random sample drawn from an infinitely large population or from a finite population *with replacement*. If, however, the sample is drawn *without replacement*, s^2 is not an unbiased estimate of σ^2. An unbiased estimate of σ^2 in sampling without replacement is

$$\frac{N-1}{N} s^2 ,$$

where N is the size of the population and s^2 is computed in the same manner described above. Note that, as N increases, the term $(N-1)/N$ approaches 1 as a limit. Hence, for very large populations this term has little effect on the value of s^2.

11. Distribution of Estimated Means

In terms of the distribution functions of observations, we can phrase what is involved in the statistical phase of scientific investigation. In this phase we are always interested in the true properties of the distribution function which are not known because we use a sample of the total population. The problem of statistical inference, then, is to make assertions about the properties of the unknown distribution on the basis of information provided by the sample and the assumptions we are willing to bring to bear on the problem.

The basic logic of the statistical approach to this problem is revealed in the way the statistical problem is formulated. Using common sense, we might ask, "Is the true mean (μ) of a population equal to (say) 100?" But in statistics we ask, "*If* the true mean of the population is equal to 100, then how likely are we to get a given set of observations?" If it is very likely that we would get the specified observations, we may accept the hypothesis, $\mu = 100$; otherwise we would reject it. Thus, the task of statistical analysis consists of determining the probability of obtaining any given set of observations assuming a specific hypothesis to be true.

Suppose that on the basis of a psychological theory we conclude that the average score of normal adults on a certain psychological test should be 100. We want to determine whether this conclusion is valid or not, so we frame it as a hypothesis: $\mu = 100$. Our aim is to test the hypothesis, and to this end we set up the research situation, select a random sample of 100 adults, give them the test, and determine their scores. We want to know now if these 100 observations check the hypothesis. If the hypothesis were true, we ask, how likely would we be to get the set of observations we did? In this manner we seek to determine whether the results confirm or refute the hypothesis.

Suppose the sample mean, $\bar{x}$, is 101.2, a deviation of 1.2 from what we would expect if the hypothesis were exactly confirmed. But this deviation by itself means nothing, for we do not know the likelihood of such a deviation between the sample mean and the population mean if the latter is equal to 100. The determination of this likelihood, or probability, depends, as we shall see, on the dispersion of the observations.

We can now reformulate the statistical problem as follows. Suppose a patient scientist were to give the intelligence tests to a large number of samples, each sample consisting of 100 adults. That is, the researcher would collect his test scores into groups of 100 each and would collect a large number of these samples of 100. For each group he would calculate the estimated (or sample) mean, just as we have done for the first group. Now, what we want to know is: What is the distribution pattern of the estimated means? We do not expect these estimated means to agree exactly, just as we do not expect the individual observations to agree exactly. Hence, just as in the case of the observations, we can prepare a frequency distribution and a histogram of the estimated means. The larger the number of samples we take, the closer we will tend to come to the true distribution pattern of the estimated means.

It is not necessary, however, to go to all this trouble. If we know or can make good estimates of the values of μ and σ of the distribution function of a variable in a population, we can use mathematical techniques to determine the distribution pattern of the estimated means. In particular, one of the convenient features involved in dealing with variables which are normally distributed in a population is that estimated means computed from random samples taken from such a population are also normally distributed.* But the normal patterns are not exactly the same. The distribution pattern of the estimated means has the same true mean as does the distribution pattern of the variable; that is, $\mu_{\bar{x}} = \mu$. The difference between the two distributions lies in the fact that the estimated means are not as dispersed as is the variable. That is, $\sigma_{\bar{x}}^2$, the variance of the distribution of the estimated means, is less than σ^2, the variance of the distribution of the variable (for sample sizes greater than one); that is, $\sigma_{\bar{x}}^2 < \sigma^2$, for $n > 1$. The same, of course, is true for the standard deviation.

This similarity and this difference between the distribution of the estimated means and the variable itself can be grasped more easily by reference to an illustration. Suppose we draw three samples of two observations each:

Sample 1	Sample 2	Sample 3
2	4	6
8	10	12

Then the first sample mean, $\bar{x}_1$, is equal to $(2 + 8)/2$, or 5, and similarly $\bar{x}_2$ is equal to 7, and $\bar{x}_3$ is equal to 9.

---

* It can be shown that the distribution of estimated means taken from a population in which the variable of interest is not normally distributed tends toward normality as the size of the sample (from which the estimates are made) increases.

Now let us take the mean of these sample means. (The mean of the sample means is symbolized by $\bar{\bar{x}}$.)

$$\bar{x}_1 = 5$$
$$\bar{x}_2 = 7$$
$$\bar{x}_3 = 9$$
$$\bar{\bar{x}} = 21/3 = 7$$

The sample variance, $s_{\bar{x}}^2$, of these sample means can easily be determined. It is equal to 8/2, or 4.

Let us now group the six original observations together and compute their mean ($\bar{x}$) and variance (s^2).

x_i	$(x_i - \bar{x})$	$(x_i - \bar{x})^2$
2	−5	25
8	+1	1
4	−3	9
10	+3	9
6	−1	1
12	+5	25
42	0	70

Then $\bar{x} = 42/6$, or 7; and $s^2 = 70/5$, or 14. Note that the estimated variance of the sample means ($s_{\bar{x}}^2$) is less than the estimated variance of the original observations of the variable (s^2) but that $\bar{x}$ and $\bar{\bar{x}}$ are equal.

This fact can also be illustrated by a common-sense example. Suppose we recorded the age of each student at some university. We would not be surprised to have these ages range from about 16 to 65 years. But now suppose we found one hour at which every student was in class, and we determined the average age of each class at that hour. We would hardly expect the averages to cover so wide a range of ages as the ages themselves; that is, we do not expect as much dispersion among the class averages as among the individuals.

We can represent this aspect of the distribution of the estimated means pictorially. In Figure 18 are shown the distribution curves of an original set of observations and estimated means computed from samples of 10, 100, and 10,000 observations, respectively.

You will notice that the distribution curve of the original observations has a wider dispersion than the other curves. The distribution pattern of the estimated means of groups of 10 observations, 100, and 10,000 are also shown. These curves demonstrate what is meant by the assertion that the estimated mean is more "precise" than the observations. If we go as high as 10,000 observations, the estimated means will generally fall very close to the true value, even though the original observations are widely dispersed. The relation between the dispersion of the original observations and the dispersion of the estimated means can be expressed in precise mathematical terms. Let $\bar{x}$ represent an estimate of the mean computed from a simple random sample drawn from either an infinitely large population or from a finite population with replacement. Further, let σ^2 represent the true variance of the distribution of the variable in the population, and $\sigma_{\bar{x}}^2$ represent the true variance of the distribution of estimated means. Then it can be shown that

$$\sigma_{\bar{x}}^2 = \frac{\sigma^2}{n} , \quad *$$

where n is equal to the size of the sample from which $\bar{x}$ is computed. Thus, if we make an estimate of the mean on the basis of 10 observations, the estimated

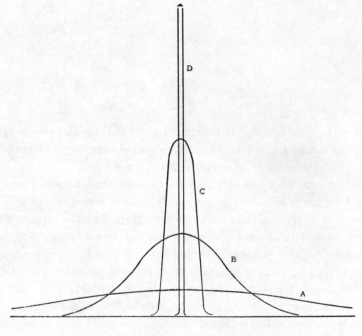

A. Normally Distributed Data
B. Estimated Means of Samples of 10.
C. Estimated Means of Samples of 100.
D. Estimated Means of Samples of 10,000.

Fig. 18.—Distribution patterns

mean has a variance of $\sigma^2/10$ and a standard deviation of $\sigma/\sqrt{10}$. We can increase the precision of the estimate of the mean by increasing the sample size to, say, 100 observations. In this case the variance of the estimate is $\sigma^2/100$ and the standard deviation is $\sigma/10$.

If $\bar{x}$ represents an estimate of the mean computed from an unrestricted

* s^2/n is an unbiased estimate of this value.

random sample drawn from a finite population without replacement, then it can be shown that

$$\sigma_{\bar{x}}^2 = \frac{N-n}{N-1}\frac{\sigma^2}{n},$$

where N is equal to the size of the population. Thus, if we make an estimate of the mean on the basis of 10 observations from a population containing 50 elements, the estimated mean has a variance equal to

$$\frac{50-10}{50-1}\frac{\sigma^2}{10}.\quad\dagger$$

The standard deviation or variance of the estimated mean, $\sigma_{\bar{x}}$ or $\sigma_{\bar{x}}^2$, represents the variability of the sampling method with respect to such estimates. That is, it is a measure of the variability (of the sampling method) to which we referred in chapter iv. $\sigma_{\bar{x}}$ and $\sigma_{\bar{x}}^2$, then, are measures of sampling errors. The method given above for estimating this error is applicable to simple random samples and, hence, is specifically a measure of simple random sampling error relative to estimates of the mean. Other methods are available for computing corresponding errors for other sampling methods and other estimates (see [4]).

12. Tests of Hypotheses concerning the Mean

Let us return, now, to the illustration of the researcher who is trying to check the hypothesis that the average intelligence score of a specific population of adults is equal to 100. We want to know whether the sample mean, $\bar{x}$, of 101.2 is likely to occur if the true mean, μ, is exactly 100. As we have said, this depends not only on the value of the estimated mean, $\bar{x}$, but also on its precision (the sampling error) as well; that is, on $\sigma_{\bar{x}}^2$. Suppose the true variance of the variable in the population (σ^2) turns out to be 25.00. Then we argue that the true variance of the means ($\sigma_{\bar{x}}^2$) of groups of 100 observations is 25.00/100, or 0.25. We now have to decide whether the estimated mean "checks" the hypothetical value of exactly 100.

The basis for the answer to this question can be found in the distribution of the estimated means. This can be done by determining how likely one is to get an estimated mean test score of 101.2 when the population mean is 100 and the true variance of the sample means is 0.25. If it is very unlikely that one would obtain an estimated mean so far from the hypothetical value, then we would be inclined to infer that the observations do not check the theory. On the other hand, if the deviation of the sample mean from the hypothetical mean is very

$\dagger\ \dfrac{N-n}{N}\dfrac{s^2}{n}$ is an unbiased estimate of this value.

likely to occur, then we would be inclined to say that the observations are in
agreement with the hypothesis.

We noted earlier that sample means computed from data taken from a normal population are themselves normally distributed. Let us assume, then, that
the population of estimated mean test scores is normally distributed about a
mean of 100 with a variance of 0.25. The standard deviation would be equal to
$\sqrt{0.25}$, or 0.5. From this information we can construct Figure 19.

For convenience the abscissa has been divided into $\sigma_{\bar{x}}$ units. We can deter-

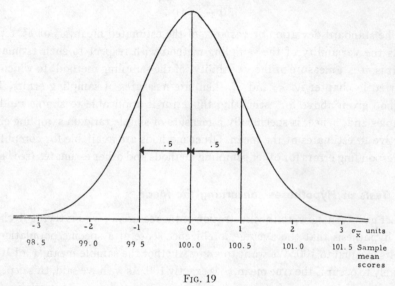

FIG. 19

mine how many $\sigma_{\bar{x}}$ units the sample mean, $\bar{x} = 101.2$, is away from the hypothetical mean, $\mu = 100$, by dividing the difference between them by $\sigma_{\bar{x}}$. This
value is represented by the symbol z.

$$z = \frac{|\bar{x} - \mu|}{\sigma_{\bar{x}}} = \frac{|101.2 - 100|}{0.5} = \frac{1.2}{0.5} = 2.40 \,.$$

The expression $|\bar{x} - \mu|$ means "the absolute difference between $\bar{x}$ and μ"; that
is, the difference independent of sign. If $\mu = 101.2$ and $\bar{x} = 100$, then $|100 -
101.2|$ would still be equal to 1.2.

Now $\bar{x}$ can be located on the curve shown in Figure 20. Since $\bar{x}$ is greater than
μ, it will lie to the right of μ on the curve.

The shaded area to the right of $\bar{x}$ in Figure 20 represents the probability of
obtaining a sample mean which is greater than 101.2. To put it another way, it
represents the probability of obtaining a sample mean that is farther away in a
positive direction from the hypothetical mean than 2.40 $\sigma_{\bar{x}}$ units. If we go

2.40 $\sigma_{\bar{x}}$ units to the left of μ and put in another shaded area (see Fig. 20), then the sum of these equal shaded areas represents the probability of obtaining a sample mean which deviates from the hypothetical mean (in either a positive or a negative direction) by more than 2.40 $\sigma_{\bar{x}}$ units.

How can we determine what proportion of the total area under the normal curve in Figure 20 is shaded? By using the equation of the normal curve, we could determine this proportion for the shaded area on the right by adding up

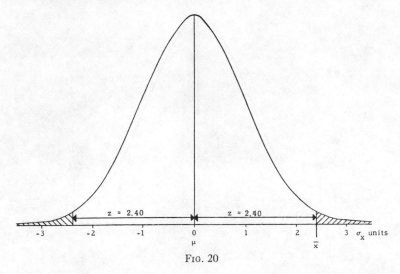

FIG. 20

the area under the curve to the right of 2.40. The same can be done for the shaded area on the left by adding up the area to the left of -2.40. These computations, however, are not necessary, since the results are provided in tables which are readily available. Appendix Table I gives the proportions for various z values. We read down the first column until we come to the z value 2.40. Then, on a line with 2.40 in the second column, the proportion of the area *above* $\bar{x}$ (since $\bar{x}$ is greater than μ) is given (i.e., 0.0082). The entry in the third column gives us the proportion of the area below $\bar{x}$ (i.e., 0.9918). Note that these values total to 1.000.

The total of the two shaded areas in Figure 20 is 2 $\times$ 0.0082, or 0.0164. Now we can say that, if the true mean were equal to 100, we would in the long run get a sample mean from 100 random observations which deviates from 100 by more than 2.40 $\sigma_{\bar{x}}$ units, 1.64 per cent of the time. Hence, if the population mean were 100 and its variance were 25, one would expect a sample mean from 100 observations which deviates by 1.2, 1.64 per cent of the time. The fact that we obtained a sample mean of 101.2 can be interpreted to mean either that the population mean is 100 and that deviations larger than that observed occur with a probability of 0.0164 or that the population mean is not equal to 100. We can never be absolutely certain which is the case, but there is a systematic way of making a "best" decision. In effect, we must decide how probable the occurrence of greater-than-the-obtained deviation must be for us to accept the hypothesis, $\mu = 100$. The probability selected for this purpose is called the *significance level*, which is represented by a. We shall see, in Section 14 of this chapter, how this decision can be made.

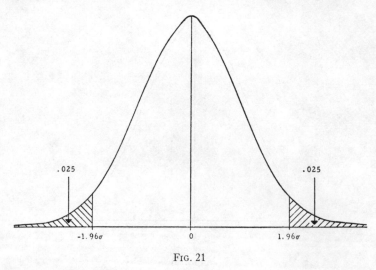

FIG. 21

Let us suppose for the moment that we have selected an 0.05 significance level. Now we ask, "Are deviations between $\bar{x}$ and μ which are greater than the deviation obtained likely to occur at least 5 per cent of the time?" If they are likely to occur at least 5 per cent of the time, then we will accept the hypothesis; if not, we will reject it. In the illustration above, deviations greater than 1.2 were found to be likely to occur only 1.64 per cent of the time; hence, we would reject the hypothesis that $\mu = 100$.

This procedure can be put in another way. The significance level represents the sum of two equal areas at the tails of the normal distribution. Each of these two areas is equal to 0.05/2, or 0.025 (see Fig. 21). From Appendix Table II we can determine the corresponding value of $z_{0.05}$. It is 1.960. In the example above, the z was 2.40. If z is greater than $z_{0.05}$, then we reject the hypothesis (as we would here); otherwise we would accept it.

If we were to use a 0.10 significance level, the corresponding $z_{0.10}$ value would be 1.282. In this case we would also reject the hypothesis, $\mu = 100$. If, on the other hand, we were to use a 0.01 significance level, the corresponding $z_{0.01}$ value would be 2.576, and we would accept the hypothesis.

The procedure just described has nothing final about it. The hypothesis *could* be true after all; we are simply noting that, *if* it were true, then the result obtained is a very unlikely event. The result is *not* impossible, for we can obtain any deviation from an expected or predicted value if the distribution patterns are normal. But there is a limit to our credibility. If a man guesses the card you have drawn from a pack, you may think that he has done so just by chance. But if he does the same thing several times in succession, you give up the notion that he is guessing by chance. You admit that he *might* have made all the guesses just by chance, but this is so unlikely that you do not hold to this explanation any longer.

There are, as we shall see, many ways of testing hypotheses, but the logic underlying all of them is similar to that in the illustration just completed. But now we want to examine the statistical model that is entailed in the process of inference we have just outlined. We are accepting and rejecting hypotheses on the basis of a specific procedure, but we shall certainly want to see the reasoning behind the process before we accept it as a sound basis for inference.

The formal argument goes as follows: Suppose the hypothesis to be tested is true and that the observations have a normal distribution. Suppose we take a random sample of observations, and the resulting value of z is greater than the z_a corresponding to the significance level. Then we say that, *if* the hypothesis is true, we have obtained an extremely improbable result. Hence, the hypothesis is not to be accepted.

This pattern of argument is similar to (but not identical with) what the logicians call the "destructive hypothetical syllogism" (*modus tollens*). In the case of the destructive hypothetical syllogism, we argue as follows: *if* a certain hypothesis is true, a certain consequence must also be true (e.g., *if* all chairs have four legs, then no chair has five legs). Now suppose the consequence is false (i.e., suppose there are five-legged chairs). Then formal logic tells us that we can argue that the hypothesis is false (i.e., it would be false that all chairs have four legs). In the statistical case we argue: if the hypothesis is true, then a certain conclusion must be true (i.e., certain values of z should result). But, if the conclusion is very *improbable*, statistical theory tells us to reject the hypothesis. Note that the statistical theory does not tell us that the hypothesis is false; it merely tells us to reject the hypothesis on the grounds that accepting it leads to the conclusion that the observations are very erratic. The hypothesis may, after all, be perfectly true, and the results obtained may be rare events that inevitably occur if we repeat the process long enough. Actually, if the value of z is just slightly above 1.96, we will reject the hypothesis by the above scheme about 5 per cent of the time *when it is true*. That is, if we repeated the procedure in the illustration by taking many samples of 100 test scores, 5 per cent of the time we would reject the hypothesis ($\mu = 100$) when it is true. Note that there is nothing said here about the "probability" of the hypothesis. The hypothesis is either true or false. The only way a probability consideration enters is in terms of the observations.

If we used the 0.10 significance level, then we would reject the hypothesis when it is true about 10 per cent of the time. It might seem, therefore, that we should always use the 0.05 significance level in preference to the 0.10, since the possibility of making a mistake is less. But this is not necessarily true; for not only do we want to *accept a hypothesis when it is true* but we also want to *reject it when it is false.* We also want to know, for example, when the hypothesis, the average score is 100, is false. And, as we shall see, we are more likely to accept a hypothesis when it is false if we use the 0.05 rather than the 0.10 significance level.

Thus, in an idealized research procedure, we would like to be able to do two things: we would like to reject a hypothesis whenever it is false and to accept it whenever it is true. We cannot hope to be perfect in either respect; hence, we are always susceptible to two types of error:

Type I error: the error of rejecting the hypothesis when it is true.

Type II error: the error of accepting the hypothesis when it is false.

The significance level specifies the Type I error for the procedures given above. The significance level gives the probabilities of making a Type I error if the procedure is used as a basis of accepting or rejecting the hypothesis.

The Type II error, however, is another matter, because its meaning depends on the fact that the hypothesis in question is false. But hypotheses can be false in many ways. If a man tells you he owes you $3.00 when he actually owes you $3.05, his assertion is false, but not by (what we would ordinarily consider to be) a serious amount. But if he says he owes you $3.00 when he actually owes you $30.00, then he is making a more serious mistake. And so it is in scientific research. If we predict the average test score for a population to be 100, and it is actually 101, then the hypothesis is false, but not "very" false. The actual difference may not be serious at all. But if the true average is 110, and we take it to be equal to 100, the consequences might be quite serious.

The procedure we have been describing is rather poor for detecting small degrees of falsity of the hypothesis but good in detecting large degrees. In general, if we use this and similar procedures, we are very likely to accept the hypothesis when it is "slightly" false but not when it is false in any great degree.

13. Operating Characteristic Curves

We can represent the situation with respect to the Type II error in a very precise way by means of an "Operating Characteristic Curve" (see [7]). Figure 22 shows such an "OC" curve for the two-sided z test* which we have described above. The horizontal axis represents various "true" possibilities which we are willing to consider as alternatives to the hypothesis. To make use of this curve, the hypothesis, H_0, is stated in the form that the true mean is equal to a (i.e., H_0: $\mu = a$). In the case considered above, the hypothesis was that $\mu = 100$. The alternative values which μ could have (λ) are represented along the abscissa. The units of λ are given in terms of the true standard deviation of the population (i.e., σ units). Deviations from a, which is 0 on the abscissa, can be both positive and negative. Hence the curves are really bell-shaped. But, since they are symmetrical, positive and negative deviations can be shown on one side. We can therefore ignore the sign of the deviation of the true value of μ from a. Thus, one unit away from the zero point on the scale represents the event in which the true mean of the population (μ) is one standard deviation (σ) away from the value which the hypothesis asserts (a). For example, if the true standard deviation of the readings of the set of data above is 5, then one unit along the base line represents the possible natural situation in which the true average test score actually is 95 or 105. Two units would represent the possibility that the true average is 110 or 90, etc.

The curve drawn in Figure 22 represents the probability that we will accept the hypothesis for each possible value the true mean may have. When the hypothesis is actually true (and hence, $\mu = a$), if we use the 0.05 significance level, the curve passes through the 0.95 probability point. This means that, when the hypothesis is true, the probability is 0.95 that it will be accepted, and hence the probability is $1 - 0.95$, or 0.05, that it will be rejected when it is true. As we move to the right, and consider possible Type II errors, the probability of acceptance begins to drop. We observe that the behavior of this curve depends upon how large the sample is. If, for example, we have only three observations, then the probability of acceptance is about 0.58 when we move out one σ unit, whereas if the sample size is ten, the probability of acceptance is about 0.11.

We can now see the advantage of an increased sample size: the larger the sample, the less probable it is that we will accept a hypothesis which is extremely far off from the true state of affairs. Figure 22 shows how the OC curve drops much more sharply for larger samples. For the very small samples of two or

---

* This test is called "two-sided" because the areas above and below z on both sides of the distribution curve are taken into account.

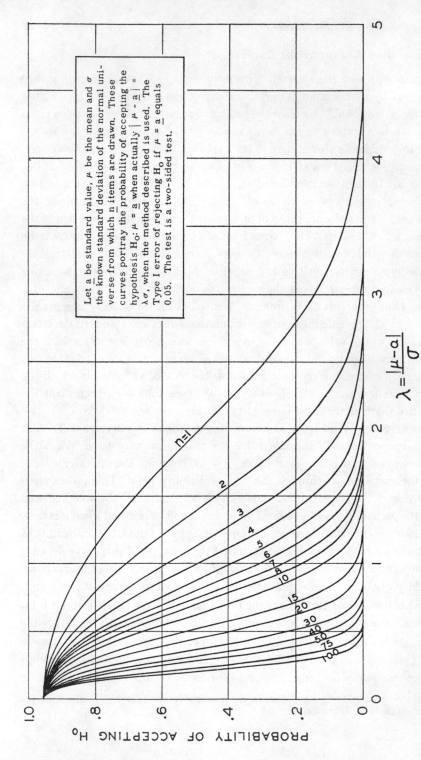

The box within the figure reads:

Let a be standard value, μ be the mean and σ the known standard deviation of the normal universe from which n items are drawn. These curves portray the probability of accepting the hypothesis H_0: $\mu = a$ when actually $\left|\ \mu - a\ \right| = \lambda\sigma$, when the method described is used. The Type I error of rejecting H_0 if $\mu = a$ equals 0.05. The test is a two-sided test.

PROBABILITY OF ACCEPTING H_0

$\lambda = \dfrac{|\mu - a|}{\sigma}$

FIG. 22.—Operating Characteristic Curves of the two-sided normal (z) test (applicable to Tests 1 and 12 in chap. vi). (Reproduced from C. D. Farris, F. E. Grubbs, and C. L. Weaver, "Operating Characteristics for the Common Statistical Tests of Significance," *Annals of Mathematical Statistics*, XVII [1946], 178–92, by kind permission of the authors and the editor.)

three items the probability of accepting the erroneous hypothesis is still quite high even when we go out as far as two σ units.

Returning to our illustration involving intelligence-test scores: if the true standard deviation of the population of test scores is 5, and we make only 5 observations, then the curve in Figure 22 tells us the following:

(1) If the true average is 105, we will accept the hypothesis that it is exactly 100 about 39 per cent of the time. In frequency terms, this means that, if we set a number of testers to work, and tell each one to test 5 people selected at random from the population, and if the true mean is 105, then if the researchers used the above procedures for accepting or rejecting the hypotheses, about 39 per cent of them would accept the hypothesis that the true mean is 100.

(2) If the true mean is 102.5, the probability of accepting the hypothesis is about 0.80. (This is half of one σ unit away from a.)

(3) If the true mean is 110, the probability of acceptance is almost zero. (This is two σ units away from a.)

The OC curve is very useful in the design of research. By means of it we can begin to judge how confident we can be in a given hypothesis we have accepted; if the sample size is small, we would normally say that our confidence is low and that the OC actually enables us to express this kind of confidence quantitatively. Of course, we would all like to have as high a confidence as possible. But the cost of a high degree of confidence is an increase in the sample size; hence, research designers should weigh the increased cost of taking a larger sample against the need for more confidence, that is, the need for an OC curve which drops very sharply when the true state of nature deviates widely from the hypothesis. Let us see how this weighing can be accomplished.

14. The Use of OC Curves

OC curves are not yet available for all statistical testing procedures; but, where they are, we can efficiently and self-consciously reach decisions with respect to the following four statistical questions:

(1) What are the critical Type II errors? That is, for how large a deviation of the hypothesis being tested from the true value should we be practically certain to reject the hypothesis?

(2) What statistical testing procedure should be used?

(3) At what level should the Type I error be set; that is, how often should we be willing to reject the hypothesis being tested when it is true?

(4) How many observations should be made?

These questions are all interrelated and cannot be considered independently. Their answering requires referring constantly to the formulation of the problem; in particular, to the weighting of the seriousness of the possible mistakes. We shall soon consider how to provide a statistical reformulation of the hypotheses formulated at an earlier stage. But we will temporarily postpone this discussion, since the method of answering the four questions listed is quite general and applies to many statistical formulations of hypotheses. We shall consider here, for illustrative purposes, hypotheses of the form: a property of a population (Q) is equivalent to some specified amount (a). The methods discussed, however, will be applicable to all other types of hypotheses as well.

In the formulation of the problem in the formal model we may have been satisfied with formulating two alternative hypotheses in the form: $H_0: Q = a$, $H_1: Q \neq a$. But now we know that $Q \neq a$ can mean many things, since, if $Q \neq a$, Q can take on many values. Consequently, we must expand our original formulation of the alternatives.

The first task is to determine the *critical value* of the Type II error. The critical value of the Type II error is that deviation from the hypothetical value (a), for which we want to be practically certain that the hypothesis, $Q = a$, is not accepted. For example, if we are testing the hypothesis that the mean I.Q. of a population is 100, we must decide for what true value of μ we practically never want to accept the hypothesis, $\mu = 100$. This is only one way the critical value can be defined; that is, in terms of practical certainty of rejection. Actually, any probability of rejection could be used; for example, that deviation from a for which we want to accept ($Q = a$) no more than 50 per cent of the time. But we are usually more concerned with the mistake we are practically never willing to make, and hence we will use this definition.

The problem now is how we decide for what value of Q we want *practically no chance* of accepting the hypothesis in question. To answer this, we must refer back to the mistakes which can be made and to what happens to the seriousness of the mistake associated with accepting H_0, as the true value of Q deviates more and more from a. Let us consider, first, the case where there is only one research objective, O; two hypotheses, H_0 and H_1; and their corresponding courses of action, C_0 and C_1. Let us assume further that H_0 is in the form $Q = a$; and H_1 is $Q \neq a$. Now let us consider what happens to the seriousness of selecting C_0 for O, as the true value of Q deviates more and more from a. Specifically, what we want to know is: What is the minimum deviation of Q from a for which the seriousness of using C_0 for the objective O is maximum. It will be recalled that the seriousness of a mistake relative to one objective, O, is a function of the inefficiency of the course of action and the importance of the objective. The importance of the objective, however, does not change as the true value of Q

changes; only the efficiency of the course of action changes. Therefore, the seriousness of the mistake is maximum where the inefficiency of the course of action is maximum (i.e., where the efficiency of C_0 is equal to zero). Consequently, to find that deviation from a for which the seriousness of the mistake is maximum, we must determine that value of Q for which the efficiency of C_0 is practically zero.

There is, of course, generally more than one objective, so we should find the value of Q for which the efficiency of the course of action is practically zero for *all* the objectives. This value of Q can be taken to be the critical value. The determination of the efficiency of the course of action for the objective for the various values of Q can be made in the same manner as was discussed earlier (p. 29).

Suppose, for example, we are interested in determining if the average I.Q. (μ) of a class is equal to a specified value (a), in order to determine if the class should be given a special advanced training program (C_0). This program is designed, let us say, to provide for the maximum education possible to the class, that is, within the limits of its capacity. If we accept $H_0: \mu = a$, we will give the class the special program. We might decide that, if the true average is below 90, it would be so harmful to the students to subject them to the special program that it would completely defeat our purposes. Then, this deviation of 10 can be taken to be the critical value.

Once the critical value has been selected, we turn to the OC curve or table to determine which test should be used to evaluate the hypothesis. For each alternative available test, we should, where possible, determine how many observations are required (for any fixed significance level) to make the Type II error equal to practically zero at the critical value.

In order to use the OC curve in this manner, the critical value should be expressed in σ units, where σ is the true standard deviation of the variable to be investigated. If σ is not known and no previous observations have been taken which can provide an estimate of it, we can make the following type of rough approximation: We can estimate the largest deviation we might reasonably expect to occur between two observations of population items and divide this estimated deviation by 6, and the result will be a rough approximation of σ. In the two-sided z test σ is known or assumed, and hence this approximation would not have to be made. If, however, we were determining the average I.Q. of a certain population for which σ is not known, the approximation might be required. It might be roughly estimated in this case, for example, that the lowest and highest scores would be approximately 85 and 115. Thus there is a difference of 30, which, divided by 6, yields an estimated σ of 5.

A preferable method for estimating σ is to take a small probability sample of the population from which s can be computed. That is, double sampling can be used where the first sample (or *pretest*) is used to provide estimates on the basis of which an efficient second sample and testing procedure can be selected. Pretests will be considered in some detail in chapter x.

However, when a value of σ is obtained, we can divide it into the critical value to obtain what might be called the *critical deviation*. In the illustration, the critical value is 10, and we say that σ is equal to 5; then the critical deviation is equal to 10/5, or 2. Now we can take the family of OC curves for a given test and mark this critical deviation on the abscissa. Each curve in the family is designated by the number of observations (n) which yields that curve. We select the smallest n whose curve is practically zero at the critical deviation. In the I.Q. illustration the critical deviation is equal to 2. Using the OC curves for the two-sided z test (Fig. 22) we will find that the n which satisfies these conditions is 5. This means that, if we select a random sample of 5 out of the population and test the hypothesis that the average I.Q. is equal to 100, we will be practically certain not to accept this hypothesis if the true average is 90 or lower (or 110 or higher).

This process should be repeated for each alternative testing procedure and its family of OC curves. In general, we should select the test which requires the least number of observations. There is an exception, however; certain test procedures, though they require less observation, require more computation. In such cases the total costs of observation *and* computation have to be compared, where cost involves the expenditure of time and effort as well as expenditure of money. In some instances where the cost of observation is relatively low but the cost of computation relatively high, it may be desirable to employ a test requiring more observations and fewer computations.

Those tests which require fewer observations to assure some assigned Type II error for any value of Q are said to be "more powerful" tests. There are some tests for which it can be shown that no other test could require fewer observations for some assigned Type II error for any value of Q; these tests are said to be "uniformly most powerful." The z test is a uniformly most powerful test. There is no other test for the same hypotheses ($\mu = a$, where σ is known or assumed) which has an OC curve that dips down closer to the base lines than does the OC curve of the z test, for *any* value of Q. The term "uniformly most powerful" is misleading, however, for such tests may not actually be most economical relative to the research objectives. In the last few years there has been considerable work done in developing the so-called "inefficient tests," which are less powerful than uniformly most powerful tests but which are more economical in some circumstances. These "inefficient tests" may be more economical even though they require more observations, because they require less "treatment" of the data; that is, less collation, tabulation, and computation. Some of these tests will be given in the next two chapters (see [5:xv], [12], and [22]).

The following is a general procedure for selecting (1) the test to be used; (2) the acceptable Type I error; and (3) the number of observations to be made.

Once the critical value has been established, we should determine the best that can be done with each of the alternative testing procedures. We have considered how to make such a determination relative to a specific Type I error. But in any given testing procedure, as the Type I error is decreased, the number of observations required to provide practically no Type II error at the critical value increases. What we want, then, is an "optimum balance" between the Type I error and the number of observations for each test. But what is an "optimum balance"?

We can begin to answer this question by considering an example. Suppose that for a given test 96 observations are required at the 0.05 significance level (Type I error) and that 165 observations are required at the 0.01 significance level to get practically no Type II error at a critical value. Suppose we were to conduct the test at each significance level; then what would be the total expected cost for each procedure? By "total expected cost" is meant the average cost per test that would be incurred if the test were to be repeated an indefinitely large number of times. This total expected cost can be computed as follows:

(1) Determine the cost ($c_{0.05}$) of taking 96 observations and the cost ($c_{0.01}$) of taking 165 observations.

(2) Determine the cost (C) of rejecting the hypothesis when it is true. Then the expected cost associated with this error at the 0.05 significance level is equal to $0.05C$ (i.e., the probability of making the error times the cost of the error). This means, for example, that, if we were to conduct this test 100 times, we would *expect* to make this error 5 times. The expected cost by trial then would be 5/100, or 0.05 times the cost of the error. Similarly, the expected cost associated with the Type I error at the 0.01 significance level is equal to $0.01C$.

(3) Determine the cost (K) associated with treating the data obtained at each significance level. Since more observations are required at the 0.01 level than at the 0.05 level, $K_{0.01}$ will, in general, be greater than $K_{0.05}$.

(4) The total expected cost (TC) of each procedure would then be

$$TC_{0.05} = c_{0.05} + 0.05C + K_{0.05}$$
$$TC_{0.01} = c_{0.01} + 0.01C + K_{0.01}$$

(5) Select the significance level for which the total cost is minimum.
We can generalize this procedure for the two-hypothesis test as follows:
(1) Prepare the following chart:

		0.001	0.01	0.05	etc.
1. Type I error (significance level)	a				
2. Cost of rejecting H_0 when it is true	C				
3. Product of entries in 1 and 2	aC				
4. No. of observations required	n				
5. Cost of observations	c				
6. Cost of treating the data	K				
7. Total cost: sum of entries in 3, 5, and 6	TC				

(2) Select that Type I error for which the entry in line 7 is minimum.

Let us illustrate this procedure by considering a simplified example. Suppose we are conducting a survey and that our observations consist of an interview question. Suppose, further, that we have selected the critical value and the test to be used. We consult OC curves for the test selected and find the following number of observations required for three different significance levels:*

$$0.05 - 96$$
$$0.01 - 165$$
$$0.001 - 270$$

Suppose now that the cost of an interview is $0.50 and is independent of the number of interviewers. Suppose also that the cost of rejecting the hypothesis H_0 when it is true is $1,000.00. Assume that the cost of treating the data is $10.00 for 96 observations, $15.00 for 165, and $20.00 for 270. Then we can prepare the tabulation shown on page 171. Then, in this case, since $107.50 is the minimum entry on line 7, the optimum Type I error for this test is 0.01 with 165 observations. In this case, of course, the difference between the 0.01 and 0.05 significance levels is insignificant.

The procedure just described enables us to estimate the best that we can expect to do with any specific testing procedure. That is, relative to a specific critical value, it enables us to determine the optimum (least costly) significance level and number of observations for any testing procedure for which OC curves

* Actually we should use all the significance levels for which OC curves are available. Only three are used here in order to simplify the illustration.

are available. By a simple generalization we can also use this method to select a testing procedure: select that combination of (a) testing procedure, (b) significance level, and (c) number of observations for which the total cost is minimum.

Where more than two hypotheses are involved in the research, the rejection of one hypothesis may mean the acceptance of any one of several others. Hence, the cost of rejecting one hypothesis when it is true varies depending on which false hypothesis is accepted. To take a common multihypothesis situation,

1. Type I error (significance level)	0.001	0.01	0.05
2. Cost of rejecting H_0 when it is true	$1,000.00	$1,000.00	$1,000.00
3. Product of entries in 1 and 2	$ 1.00	$ 10.00	$ 50.00
4. No. of observations required	270	165	96
5. Cost of observations	$ 135.00	$ 82.50	$ 48.00
6. Cost of treating the data	$ 20.00	$ 15.00	$ 10.00
7. Total cost: sum of entries in 3, 5, and 6	$ 156.00	$ 107.50	$ 108.00

suppose we have three hypotheses, H_1, H_2, and H_3. Then, if we reject H_1, we may accept either H_2 or H_3. But the cost of accepting H_2 when H_1 is true may not be equal to the cost of accepting H_3 when H_1 is true.

When there are more than two hypotheses, the procedure outlined above becomes cumbersome, and quite frequently the researcher is concerned with many more than two hypotheses. We have already referred to such problems as ones of estimation. Methods which can be used for obtaining estimates will be discussed in chapter viii. The logic underlying the statistical design of an estimation procedure, however, can be considered before taking up specific methods for computing estimates.

In a problem of estimation there are three practical research design decisions which should be made. These involve (1) the sampling method to be used; (2) the estimation procedure to be used; and (3) the sample size to be used.

The best available method for making these decisions involves a rather complex use of mathematics, an illustration of which is given in Appendix IV. But the underlying logic has already been presented in chapter iv, Section 2.4. It would be a lengthy and costly procedure, indeed, to evaluate all possible sampling and estimation procedures that could be used in the research. But all this work is not necessary. With experience in sampling and estimation comes knowledge of the inefficiency of certain procedures in certain types of situations. A sampling expert, for example, can generally select only the likely candidates for selection and thereby considerably simplify the design procedure.

In specific cases the procedure may still be complex, since the various mathematical functions put into the equations may make the equations difficult or impossible to solve at present. Furthermore, it may be difficult to represent the costs as a function of possible errors, particularly if several objectives are involved and the monetary scale is not suitable for determining costs relative to some of these objectives. These practical difficulties will be reduced by future methodological and statistical developments. The desirability of using the type of logical approach described, however, is unaffected by the difficulties mentioned.

15. Summary

In this chapter we have attempted to expose the logic underlying the use of statistical methods for drawing inferences from a sample's characteristics to a population's characteristics. We saw how the data obtained from a sample can be organized into the tabular form of a frequency distribution and the graphic form of a histogram. As the sample size is increased and the classification-interval decreased, the histogram approaches a smooth frequency curve as a limit. This curve represents a distribution function. Distributions can take on many forms, one of the most important of which is that bell-shaped symmetrical distribution called the *normal*. The proportion of the area under the normal curve which lies between two ordinates at points A and B represents the *probability* of obtaining an observation between A and B. These values are computed from the equation of the normal curve and are given in the normal table (Appendix Table I).

The normal distribution can be defined by two parameters, the mean (μ) and the standard deviation (σ), which are measures of central tendency and dispersion of data, respectively. The best estimates ($\bar{x}$ and s) of these parameters which can be made from a random sample were defined as

$$\bar{x} = \frac{\sum\limits_{}^{n} x_i}{n},$$

and

$$s = \sqrt{\frac{\sum\limits_{}^{n} (x_i - \bar{x})^2}{n-1}}.$$

Next we considered the method of testing the hypothesis, $\mu = a$. We saw that the estimates ($\bar{x}$) of μ are themselves normally distributed with true mean equal to μ and standard deviation ($\sigma_{\bar{x}}$) equal to the standard deviation of the observations (σ) divided by the square root of the number of observations in the sample ($\sqrt{n}$); that is,

$$\sigma_{\bar{x}} = \frac{\sigma}{\sqrt{n}}.$$

We converted the deviation between an estimated mean ($\bar{x}$) and a hypothetical value of the mean (a) into standard units (z); that is,

$$z = \frac{|\bar{x} - a|}{\sigma_{\bar{x}}}.$$

The values of z are also normally distributed, and hence the probability of obtaining a deviation of $\bar{x}$ from a greater than any given amount (z) can be determined from the normal tables. This probability is used as the basis of accepting or rejecting the hypothesis.

Acceptance or rejection of a hypothesis depends on the errors we can tolerate. Two types of error are involved: (I) the probability of rejecting a hypothesis when it is true (which is expressed as a significance level) and (II) the probability of accepting a hypothesis when it is false. The Type II error varies from test to test and can be expressed as a function of possible true values of the variable in question; that is, as an Operating Characteristic Curve.

By use of our earlier computations of the seriousness of mistakes we can determine a "critical value" which represents that Type II error which we want to be practically certain not to make. This value can be converted into a "critical deviation" by dividing it by a known or estimated σ of the population. By using the critical deviation and the OC curves, it is possible to make an optimum selection of (1) the test to be used, (2) the Type I error (significance level) to be employed, and (3) the number of observations to be made.

The procedures described for making these optimum selections are cumbersome where more than two hypotheses are involved. In this case estimation procedures can be used. But here, too, an optimum selection can be made.

Throughout this discussion we have assumed that the hypotheses have been given a statistical reformulation. In the next chapter we shall consider the various types of statistical formulations that can be given to hypotheses. This reversal of order is deliberate, for an understanding of the nature of statistical tests is required to understand the meaning of statistical hypotheses and the methods for testing them.

NOTE 1.—*Method for computing* $\bar{x}$ *and* s *for grouped data, where class intervals are equal:*

The method will be illustrated on a sample of 100 test scores grouped into class intervals.

(1) Test Scores	(2) Fre- quency f_i	(3) Class Mid- point x_i	(4) Unit De- viation u_i	(5) $f_i u_i$	(6) $f_i u_i^2$
0– 9	2	4.5	−4	− 8	32
10–19	4	14.5	−3	−12	36
20–29	6	24.5	−2	−12	24
30–39	17	34.5	−1	−17	17
40–49	26	44.5	0	0	0
50–59	20	54.5	1	20	20
60–69	11	64.5	2	22	44
70–79	6	74.5	3	18	54
80–89	5	84.5	4	20	80
90–99	3	94.5	5	15	75
Total	100			46	382

The class intervals of the test scores are given in column 1, and the number of test scores falling into each class is given in column 2.

PROCEDURE:

(1) Determine the midpoint of each class (x_i) and enter the result in column 3. To find the midpoint, subtract the lower class limit from the upper class limit and divide by 2 and add the result to the lower limit of the class. For example, in the first class $(9 − 0)/2 = 4.5$.

(2) Select one of the class midpoints about halfway down column 3 and enter a "0" beside it in column 4. This is the guessed mean (x_0). The final result of this procedure is independent of which midpoint is selected. In this case the midpoint 44.5 was selected.

(3) Since all the classes cover equal intervals, we can measure the difference of any class midpoint from the midpoint that serves as the guessed mean, in terms of the number of class intervals it is above $(+)$ or below $(−)$ this guessed mean. Therefore, count up from the zero entry in a negative direction, down in a positive direction, and enter consecutive integers and the appropriate signs in column 4.

(4) For each class multiply the entry in column 2 by the entry in column 4; that is, $f_i u_i$. Enter results in column 5.

(5) Multiply the entry in column 4 by the entry in column 5; that is, $f_i u_i u_i$ or $f_i u_i^2$. Enter results in column 6.

(6) Total column 2 $(\Sigma f_i = 100)$, column 5 $(\Sigma f_i u_i = 46)$, and column 6 $(\Sigma f_i u_i^2 = 382)$.

(7) Compute $\bar{x}$ using the following formula:

$$\bar{x} = k \frac{\Sigma f_i u_i}{\Sigma f_i} + x_0,$$

where k is the difference between class midpoints (in this case, 10) and x_0 is the class midpoint which was selected as the provisional mean.

Using the above data, we obtain

$$\bar{x} = (10)\frac{46}{100} + 44.5 = 4.6 + 44.5 = 49.1.$$

(8) Compute s using the following formula:

$$s = k\sqrt{\frac{\sum f_i u_i^2}{n-1} - \frac{(\sum f_i u_i)^2}{n(n-1)}}.$$

Using the above data, we obtain

$$s = 10\sqrt{\frac{382}{99} - \frac{(46)^2}{(100)(99)}} = 17.2.$$

DISCUSSION TOPICS

1. What is the function of statistical procedures? What are their advantages?

2. What is meant by the following terms: (a) frequency distribution; (b) histogram, (c) distribution function; (d) normal distribution; (e) mode; (f) median; (g) mean; (h) standard deviation; (i) variance; (j) probability; (k) Type I error; (l) Type II error; (m) critical value; (n) critical deviation; (o) OC curve; (p) z; (q) uniformly most powerful test; (r) inefficient test.

3. What is the difference between $\bar{x}$ and μ, and s and σ?

4. What is the logic underlying statistical testing procedures?

5. What costs should be taken into account in selecting a statistical testing procedure?

EXERCISES

1. Compute $\bar{x}$ and s for the following sets of data:

a) Annual income of ten randomly selected members of a population

$4,700	$6,400
5,300	7,100
3,200	5,100
3,900	3,900
4,800	4,200

b) Ages of fifteen students selected at random

21	21
19	20
20	25
21	23
28	21
18	20
18	19

c)

Test Scores	Frequency
20–29	1
30–39	3
40–49	2
50–59	5
60–69	9
70–79	12
80–89	10
90–99	4

2. Suppose you want to test the hypothesis that $\mu = 71$. The standard deviation of the population is known to be 4. How many observations should be made using the two-sided z test if the critical value is (*a*) 67; (*b*) 77; (*c*) 79; (*d*) 62; (*e*) 83?

3. Determine the z values for the following data:

    a) $\mu = 40$, $\bar{x} = 34$, $\sigma = 12$, $n = 16$

    b) $\mu = 11.2$, $\bar{x} = 13.1$, $\sigma = 2.8$, $n = 10$

    c) $\mu = \$3,500$, $\bar{x} = \$3,100$, $\sigma = \$1,200$, $n = 150$

4. From Appendix Table I determine the probability of getting a deviation of $\bar{x}$ from μ greater than that obtained in each part of Problem 3.

SUGGESTED READINGS

On the logic of statistical methods see Churchman (1:Introd.) and (2), Neyman and Pearson (13), Shewhart (14), and Wald (16), (17), (18), (19), and (20). With the exception of (1), these presentations are advanced.

For a good and (not advanced) over-all picture of statistical methods see Dixon and Massey (5). Mood (11) is a more advanced presentation.

On the mathematical foundations of statistics see Cramér (3), Feller (6), Hoel (8), and Kendall (9). These are also advanced presentations.

There are many very elementary introductions to statistical methods. Several are Mode (10), Walker (21), and Wilks (23).

The social researcher should become familiar with some journals which deal with statistical methods. The most useful to the social researcher is the *Journal of the American Statistical Association*. Others are *Biometrika, Biometrics Bulletin*, and the *Journal of the Royal Statistical Society* and its *Supplement*. The *Annals of Mathematical Statistics* is a more technical journal than any of these but is worth the attention of those with advanced mathematical and statistical training.

REFERENCES AND BIBLIOGRAPHY

1. Churchman, C. W. *Statistical Manual: Methods of Making Experimental Inferences.* 2d rev. ed. Philadelphia: Pittman-Dunn Laboratory, Frankford Arsenal, 1951.

2. ———. *Theory of Experimental Inference.* New York: Macmillan Co., 1948.

3. Cramér, Harald. *Mathematical Methods of Statistics.* Princeton: Princeton University Press, 1945.

4. Deming, W. E. *Some Theory of Sampling.* New York: John Wiley & Sons, 1950.

5. Dixon, W. J., and Massey, F. J., Jr. *Introduction to Statistical Analysis.* New York: McGraw-Hill Book Co., 1951.

6. Feller, William. *An Introduction to Probability Theory and Its Applications.* New York: John Wiley & Sons, 1950.

7. Ferris, C. D.; Grubbs, F. E.; and Weaver, C. L. "Operating Characteristics for the Common Tests of Significance," *Annals of Mathematical Statistics*, XVII (1946), 178–97.

8. Hoel, P. G. *Introduction to Mathematical Statistics.* New York: John Wiley & Sons, 1947.

9. KENDALL, M. G. *Advanced Theory of Statistics*. 2 vols. London: Chas. Griffin & Co., Ltd., 1947.

10. MODE, E. B. *The Elements of Statistics*. New York: Prentice-Hall, Inc., 1941.

11. MOOD, A. M. *Introduction to the Theory of Statistics*. New York: McGraw-Hill Book Co., 1950.

12. MOSTELLER, FREDERICK. "On Some Useful 'Inefficient' Statistics," *Annals of Mathematical Statistics*, XVII (1946), 377–408.

13. NEYMAN, JERZY, and PEARSON, E. S. "On the Problem of the Most Efficient Tests of Statistical Hypotheses," *Philosophical Transactions of the Royal Society*, Ser. A, CCXXXI (1933), 289–337.

14. SHEWHART, W. A. *Statistical Methods from the Viewpoint of Quality Control*. Washington, D.C.: United States Department of Agriculture, 1939.

15. SNEDECOR, G. W. *Statistical Methods*. 4th ed. Ames: Iowa State College Press, 1946.

16. WALD, ABRAHAM. "Contributions to the Theory of Statistical Estimation and Testing Hypotheses," *Annals of Mathematical Statistics*, X (1939), 299–326.

17. ————. *On the Principles of Statistical Inference*. "Notre Dame Mathematical Lectures," No. 1. Notre Dame, Ind.: Notre Dame University, 1942.

18. ————. "Statistical Decision Functions Which Minimize the Maximum Risk," *Annals of Mathematics*, XLVI (1945), 265–80.

19. ————. "Foundations of a General Theory of Sequential Decision Functions," *Econometrica*, XV (1947), 279–313.

20. ————. "Statistical Decision Functions," *Annals of Mathematical Statistics*, XX (1949), 165–205.

21. WALKER, H. M. *Elementary Statistical Methods*. New York: Henry Holt & Co., 1943.

22. WILCOXON, FRANK. *Some Rapid Approximate Statistical Procedures*. Rev. ed. Stamford, Conn.: Stamford Research Laboratories, American Cyanamid Co., 1949.

23. WILKS, S. S. *Elementary Statistical Analysis*. Princeton: Princeton University Press, 1948.

CHAPTER VI

1. Introduction

The hypotheses constructed in the formulation of the problem state the conditions under which we will accept each of the alternative courses of action. The hypotheses make assertions about the efficiency of these alternative courses of action. In the idealized model we subsequently formulated the conditions under which each hypothesis would ideally be accepted as valid. Since practical considerations usually prevent us from making observations on the entire population, the validation of the hypotheses depends on sampling the population and drawing statistical inferences from the sample to the population. This requires that the hypotheses be reformulated in a way which makes them susceptible to statistical evaluation, that is, to statistical testing.

The number of statistical tests has expanded considerably in the last twenty years and has become so large that not even a professional statistician can keep all of them at his fingertips. As these tests have become more numerous, so have the kinds of hypotheses which can be tested by statistical procedures.

In this chapter we will consider various types of statistical hypotheses and methods for testing them. A number of useful tests will be described and illustrated. The presentation of these tests is not intended to be a substitute for familiarity with a good statistics text. (A number of good texts are listed in the "Suggested Readings" at the end of the chapter.) The tests described are intended to serve as an invitation to a more complete study of statistical methods in sources which deal with them in more detail. On the other hand, the descriptions and illustrations of the tests are designed to provide the newcomer to statistics with some appreciation and understanding of statistical methods. The tests and illustrations may also serve as helpful reminders for those already familiar with these methods.

In the last chapter we discussed one type of question that can be answered by some tests of hypotheses: If a population has a certain property Q, is it likely that we would obtain a given set of observations from a random sample taken from that population? The set of observations are themselves describable by one or more measurable properties, which are called *statistics*. Properties of the population's (as opposed to the sample's) distribution which define that distribution are called *parameters*. Thus, in the normal distribution, μ and σ are parameters. We have considered several statistics also, the most important of which were the sample mean $\bar{x}$, the sample standard deviation s, and the sample variance s^2. These are estimates of the population parameters μ, σ, and σ^2, respectively. We have also considered another important statistic, z, which is a function of $\mu, \bar{x}, \sigma$, and n (the size of the sample) and which is very important in statistical testing. It would serve us well to re-examine its role and to consider several other "functional" statistics which are important in testing hypotheses: t, χ^2 (chi square), and F.

2. z

In the illustration worked out in the last chapter we asked, "If a population mean μ is equal to a quantity a, how likely are we to obtain a random sample of observations whose mean $\bar{x}$ deviates from a by an amount greater than $|\bar{x} - a|$? To find this likelihood (or probability), we first had to determine how the sample means were distributed. Further, we converted $\bar{x}$ into a deviation from the population mean expressed as units of the standard deviation of $\bar{x}$, $\sigma_{\bar{x}}$. ($\sigma_{\bar{x}}$ is called the *standard error* of the estimated mean.) We assigned the symbol z to this deviation. Since z itself is normally distributed, we can find the probability of obtaining a z value equal to or exceeding any amount by using the normal tables. Thus, by use of the statistic z we can determine (where σ is known) the probability of getting a random sample of observations whose mean $\bar{x}$ deviates from the population mean by more than any given amount. Hence, the test of the hypothesis $\mu = a$ (where σ is known) is called a z test.

The exact definition of z can be given symbolically as follows:

$$z = \frac{|x_i - \mu|}{\sigma},$$

where x_i is any observation taken from a normal population. If we consider the distribution of sample means ($\bar{x}$) rather than discrete observations, then

$$z_{\bar{x}} = \frac{|\bar{x} - \mu|}{\sigma_{\bar{x}}} = \frac{|\bar{x} - \mu|}{\sigma / \sqrt{n}},$$

since $\sigma_{\bar{x}} = \sigma / \sqrt{n}$.

3. t

The symbol t plays a role very similar to that of z; it is also a measure of the deviation of a sample mean from the population mean. But, instead of measuring this deviation in σ units, it measures it in s units, units of the estimated or sample standard deviation. Thus, the t value of a single observation x_i is given by

$$t = \frac{|x_i - \mu|}{s}.$$

The t value of $\bar{x}$ is given by

$$t_{\bar{x}} = \frac{|\bar{x} - \mu|}{s_{\bar{x}}} = \frac{|\bar{x} - \mu|}{s/\sqrt{n}},$$

since $s_{\bar{x}} = s/\sqrt{n}$.

In cases where the population standard deviation is not known or cannot be assumed, the deviation of a sample mean from the population mean can be expressed in units of the sample's standard deviation, that is, in terms of t. Unlike z, t is not normally distributed. Though the distribution of t was discovered in the latter part of the nineteenth century, it was not until 1908, when it was rediscovered, that it was made available for statistical use. It was rediscovered by the British statistician, W. S. Gosset, who wished to conceal his identity from his employer and signed his presentation with the pseudonym "Student." Hence, this statistic is usually referred to as *"Student's"* t.

Strictly speaking, the true standard deviation (σ) of a normal population would only be known if an accurate observation could be made of every member of the population. But the estimate (s) of the standard deviation tends to become increasingly accurate as the sample from which it is computed increases in size. (The standard error of s is equal to $\bar{\sigma}/\sqrt{2n}$, where $\bar{\sigma}$ is the mean of σ's computed on the basis of n observations, and, hence, tends to decrease as n increases.) Therefore, when n is large, s can be used in place of σ without any serious error, and the z test can be applied. Before "Student" rediscovered the t distribution, however, there was no way of conducting tests on small samples.

The idea behind the t distribution is a very simple one, though its derivation is quite complex. Consider a normal population whose standard deviation is not known. Suppose we could take an infinite number of samples of, say, five observations from this population and compute $\bar{x}$, s, and hence t for each sample. What would be the distribution of these t's? "Student" answered this question by mathematical analysis. The distribution is shown in Figure 23.

The shaded portion of the figure is 1 per cent, or .01, of the total area under the curve. It is the area below $t = -4.604$ and above $t = 4.604$. The t values below and above which the areas total to .05 of the entire area under the curve is 2.7764. These values can be read from the t table (Appendix Table III). We look down the DF column to that value equal to the number of observations minus one, $n - 1$, or 4,* and across to the column headed by .05. It is apparent

* For an explanation of the use of $n - 1$ rather than n see Sec. 5 below.

from the table that similar distributions have been worked out for other sample sizes and that the values for various significance levels have been tabulated.

As the size of the sample increases, the distribution of t approaches a normal distribution. Hence, it can be seen that the t values given opposite ∞ at the bottom of the table are the same as appear in the normal table. Where the sample size is greater than 123, the normal distribution can be used; that is, s can be substituted for σ.

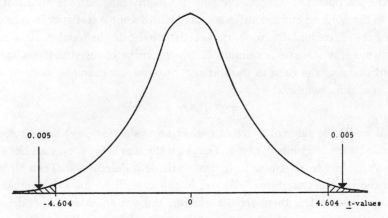

0.005   0.005

-4.604   0   4.604   t-values

Fig. 23.—Distribution of t for samples of 5

4. χ^2 and F

The symbols χ^2 and F are more complex statistics than the two just considered. A complete understanding of them requires more knowledge of mathematics and statistics than this book presupposes. It will be useful, however, to characterize them briefly so that the reader has an idea, even though a vague one, concerning their nature.

Chi square (χ^2) is a measure of the compatibility between an observed frequency of an event or property and a theoretical frequency expected on the basis of an assumed distribution. Suppose, for example, a theory predicts that the variance (σ^2) of a distribution should be equal to a quantity a. We draw a random sample from the pertinent population and compute s^2. The ratio of s^2 to the predicted value of σ^2, multiplied by a suitable factor (in this case, the sample size minus one) is equal to χ^2. (For details see [2:xiii].)

Suppose now we draw two samples from the same normal population and compute the variance of the first, s_1^2, and of the second, s_2^2. Then

$$F = \frac{s_1^2}{s_2^2},$$

that is, F is equal to the ratio between the two sample variances.

The sampling distributions of both χ^2 and F, like those of z and t, have been put into tabular form and are shown in Appendix Tables V and VI, respectively. (For details on the F distribution see [2:viii].)

5. Degrees of Freedom

In the description of statistical testing procedures constant reference will be made to the "degrees of freedom" associated with a sample statistic. In general, the degrees of freedom of a computed statistic indicate the number of factors (from which the statistic is computed) which can be changed independently without changing the value of the statistic. Suppose, for example, we compute the sum of three numbers:

$$x + y + z = S.$$

Now, if we fix the value of S, we can select any value for (say) x and y, but, once x and y are determined, so is z. That is, if the sum is fixed, once all but one of the variables are determined, the last variable is determined. Then all but one of the variables are "free." Hence, in this case, there are two degrees of freedom. In general, if there are n variables, and one equation which defines the statistic computed, there are $n - 1$ degrees of freedom. If we compute $\bar{x}$ from ten observations, for example, there are nine degrees of freedom associated with $\bar{x}$. If we compute s^2 from twenty-one observations, it has twenty degrees of freedom.

Now suppose we have two equations with two variables in each:

(1) $x + y = S$

(2) $x - y = T$

Then both x and y are determined once S and T are determined. For example, if $S = 15$ and $T = 5$, then $x = 10$ and $y = 5$. If we add another variable, z:

(1) $x + y + z = S$

(2) $x + y - z = T$

only one of the variables has any freedom. For example, if $S = 15$, $T = 5$, let x be assigned the value of 5. We now have

(1) $5 + y + z = 15$

(2) $5 + y - z = 5$

or

(1) $y + z = 10$

(2) $y - z = 0$

and y and z are then determined and must both be equal to 5. If there are n variables and two equations which define the statistic computed, there are $n - 2$ degrees of freedom. In general, if there are n variables and k equations which define the statistic computed, there are $n - k$ degrees of freedom.

Degrees of freedom will be symbolized by "DF."

6. Hypotheses concerning the Value of a Single Property of a Single Population

Many questions that researchers ask can be translated into questions about one of the following three properties of a population: (1) the mean value of a specified property; (2) the dispersion of a specified property; and (3) the percentage or proportion of the population which has a specified property.

For example, the following are typical questions which can be translated into these forms, respectively:

(1) Is the average I.Q. of graduating seniors at Harvard greater than 120?
(2) Is the variance in income among General Motors employees less than $10,000,000?
(3) Do 60 per cent of the voting population of the United States favor universal military training?

Each of these three questions can be translated into the following type of hypothesis:

(1) $H_0: Q = a$,

where Q is the property of the population being investigated, and a is the "hypothetical" value derived from theory or previous observations. In the usual two-hypothesis type of research, the alternative hypothesis is

$$H_1: Q \neq a.$$

H_0 is called the "null hypothesis," since it is this hypothesis that the testing procedure is designed to nullify or support.

Alternative pairs of hypotheses are

(2) $H_0: Q \leq a$ (Q is less than or equal to a; i.e., Q is no greater than a)
$H_1: Q > a$ (Q is greater than a)
(3) $H_0: Q \geq a$ (Q is greater than or equal to a; i.e., Q is at least as large as a)
$H_1: Q < a$ (Q is less than a)

Tests 1–11 will deal with these three types of pairs of hypotheses.

NOTE: To simplify the presentation of the tests, the following abbreviated statements of what is known or assumed will be made:

Randomness means that the observations are known or assumed to be obtained from a random sample. Any type of probability sample can be used in these tests, but in some the pertinent statistics must be computed differently than in the case of simple random samples.

Normality means that the collection of all possible pertinent observations (i.e., the *universe*) is known or assumed to be normally distributed.

σ or σ^2 means that the value of σ or σ^2 (the standard deviation or variance of the universe) is known or assumed.

TEST 1* $H_0: \mu = a$

$H_1: \mu \neq a$

KNOWN OR ASSUMED: Randomness, normality, and σ.

PROCEDURE:

(1) Compute $\bar{x}$, the sample mean.
(2) Compute

$$z = \frac{|\bar{x} - a|}{\sigma} \sqrt{n},$$

where n is the number of observations.
(3) Select from Appendix Table II the appropriate value of z_a.
(4) If $z \leq z_a$, accept H_0; otherwise accept H_1.

EXAMPLE: We predict that the mean scores obtained on a new test by members of a specified population will equal 100. This prediction is based on experience with a similar test given to the same population. We see no reason why the dispersion of scores on the two tests should differ, hence we assume that σ is equal to 20, the value obtained on the older test. We draw a random sample of 25 people from the population and give them the new test. The mean of the 25 scores obtained is 106. We want to determine whether we should accept the hypothesis, $\mu = 100$, at (say) the .05 significance level.

$$H_0: \mu = 100$$

$$H_1: \mu \neq 100$$

Solution:

(1) $\bar{x} = 106$.
(2) $z = \dfrac{106 - 100}{20} \sqrt{25} = 1.50$.
(3) $z_{.05} = 1.96$.

* The OC curves for this test (at the .05 significance level) are shown in Fig. 22 (p. 164).

(4) $z < z_{.05}$ (i.e., $1.50 < 1.96$); therefore, accept H_0.

TEST 2
$$H_0: \mu \le a$$
$$H_1: \mu > a$$

KNOWN OR ASSUMED: Randomness, normality, and σ.

PROCEDURE:

(1) Compute $\bar{x}$.

(2) Compute
$$z = \frac{(\bar{x} - a)}{\sigma} \sqrt{n} \, .$$

Note: Do not use the absolute value of $(\bar{x} - a)$.

(3) Multiply the significance level by 2, i.e., $2a$.*

(4) Select from Appendix Table II the value of z_{2a} corresponding to the quantity obtained in step (3).

(5) If $z \le z_{2a}$, accept H_0; otherwise accept H_1.

EXAMPLE: On the basis of past observations we predict that the average number of years of school completed by housewives in a certain city is not any more than 10. We know that the standard deviation of number of years of school completed over the entire community is 4 years. We assume this standard deviation to hold for the population of housewives. We draw a random sample of 100 housewives and determine how many years of school each completed. The sample mean is 10.5 years. Is our prediction supported at the .05 significance level?

$$H_0: \mu \le 10$$
$$H_1: \mu > 10$$

Solution:

(1) $\bar{x} = 10.5$.

(2) $z = \dfrac{(10.5 - 10.0)}{4} \sqrt{100} = 1.25$.

(3) $2a = 2(.05) = .10$.

(4) $z_{.10} = 1.645$.

(5) $z < z_{.10}$ (i e., $1.25 < 1.645$); therefore, accept H_0.

* In this test we will reject H_0 only if $\bar{x}$ is greater than we would expect a specified percentage of the time if $\mu \le a$. Hence, $\bar{x}$ cannot be too small in this case, and the area of rejection is all on the positive side of the distribution of $\bar{x}$'s. But, if we use Appendix Table II and look up the value of z_a, we obtain the distance out on either side (in $\sigma_{\bar{x}}$ units) to the areas of size $a/2$. Hence, in this case we use $2a$ and only the positive z-value.

TEST 3 $H_0: \mu \geq a$

$H_1: \mu < a$

KNOWN OR ASSUMED: Randomness, normality, and σ.

PROCEDURE:

(1) Compute $\bar{x}$.

(2) Compute

$$z = \frac{(\bar{x} - a)}{\sigma} \sqrt{n} .$$

(3) Compute $2a$.

(4) Select from Appendix Table II the value of z_{2a}.

(5) If $z \geq -z_{2a}$, accept H_0; otherwise accept H_1.

EXAMPLE: Suppose that in another city (see "Example" in Test 2) it is predicted that the average number of years of school completed by housewives is no less than 10. Suppose a random sample of 64 housewives is drawn. The mean number of school years completed for the sample is 8.0, and σ is still assumed to be equal to 4. Is this prediction supported at the .10 significance level?

$$H_0: \mu \geq 10$$

$$H_1: \mu < 10$$

Solution:

(1) $\bar{x} = 8.0$.

(2) $z = \dfrac{(8.0 - 10)}{4} \sqrt{64} = -4.0$.

(3) $2a = 2(.10) = .20$.

(4) $z_{.20} = 1.282$.

(5) $z < -z_{.20}$ (i.e., $-4.0 < -1.282$); therefore, reject H_0 and accept H_1.

TEST 4* $H_0: \mu = a$

$H_1: \mu \neq a$

KNOWN OR ASSUMED: Randomness and normality.

* In this and all succeeding tests which use an estimated standard deviation of the population (s), if an unrestricted random sample is drawn without replacement from a finite population, then use $s\sqrt{(N - n)/N}$ in place of s. This replacement is illustrated in Test 5. Correspondingly, in place of s^2 use $s^2 (N - n)/N$.

PROCEDURE 1:†

(1) Compute $\bar{x}$ and s, the sample mean and standard deviation.
(2) Compute

$$t = \frac{|\bar{x} - a|}{s} \sqrt{n}.$$

(3) Compute the degrees of freedom, DF, where DF $= n - 1$.
(4) Go down the DF ("Degrees of Freedom") column of Appendix Table III until you come to the value closest to that computed for DF in step (3). Read across horizontally to the column whose heading corresponds to the significance level used and select the value of t_a under that column.
(5) If $t \leq t_a$, accept H_0; otherwise accept H_1.

EXAMPLE: Workers in a factory on the average do not change their weight in the month of January. Sixteen randomly selected workers are put on a special diet for this month. The average amount gained was 1.50 pounds, and the sample standard deviation of weight changes was 2.00 pounds. Is there any reason to believe at the .01 significance level that the diet produced an increase in the workers' weights?

$$H_0: \mu = 0$$
$$H_1: \mu \neq 0$$

Solution:

(1) $\bar{x} = 1.50$ and $s = 2.00$.
(2) $t = \dfrac{|1.50 - 0|}{2.00} \sqrt{16} = 3.00$.
(3) DF $= 16 - 1 = 15$.
(4) $t_{.01} = 2.9467$.
(5) $t > t_{.01}$ (i.e., $3.00 > 2.9467$); therefore, reject H_0 and accept H_1; that is, there is reason to believe that diet produced an increase in the workers' weights.

PROCEDURE 2: The following is (in the statistical sense) a less efficient test than the first. Where $n < 5$, it is about as good as the first procedure. It does not require the computation of s and hence saves time.

(1) Compute $\bar{x}$.
(2) Compute R, the difference between the largest and smallest observations in the sample.

† The OC curves for this procedure (at the .05 significance level) are shown in Appendix Figure I.

(3) Compute

$$t' = \frac{|\bar{x} - a|}{R}.$$

(4) Select from the left half of Appendix Table IV the t'_a value opposite the sample size used and under the appropriate significance level.

(5) If $t' \leq t'_a$, accept H_0; otherwise accept H_1.

EXAMPLE: Consider the same example as given for Procedure 1. The greatest gain in weight was 4.00 pounds, the least was a loss of 1.00 pound.

$$H_0: \mu = 0$$
$$H_1: \mu \neq 0$$

Solution:

(1) $\bar{x} = 1.50$.

(2) $R = |4.00 - (-1.00)| = 5.00$.

(3) $t' = \frac{|1.50 - 0|}{5.00} = .30$.

(4) $t'_{.01} = .212$.

(5) $t' > t'_{.01}$ (i.e., $.30 > .212$); therefore, reject H_0 and accept H_1.

TEST 5 $H_0: \mu = a$
                                      $H_1: \mu \neq a$

KNOWN OR ASSUMED: Randomness, normality, and sample drawn without replacement from a small finite universe.

PROCEDURE:

(1) Compute $\bar{x}$ and s.

(2) Compute

$$s_{\bar{x}} = \frac{s}{\sqrt{n}} \sqrt{\frac{N - n}{N}},$$

where N is the size of the population, and n is the size of the sample.

(3) Compute

$$t = \frac{|\bar{x} - a|}{s_{\bar{x}}}.$$

(4) Proceed as in steps (3)–(5) of Procedure 1 in Test 4.

EXAMPLE: In an office containing 110 employees, the average number of days of sick leave taken in 1950 was 6. A random sample of 9 employees took an average of 8 days' sick leave with a standard deviation of 5 days. Is there reason to believe at the .05 significance level that the average number of days of sick leave over the whole office has changed?

$$H_0: \mu = 6$$
$$H_1: \mu \neq 6$$

Solution:

(1) $\bar{x} = 8$ and $s = 5$.

(2) $s_{\bar{x}} = \dfrac{5}{\sqrt{9}}\sqrt{\dfrac{110-9}{110}} = 1.60$.

(3) $t = \dfrac{|8-6|}{1.60} = 1.25$.

(4) DF $= 9 - 1 = 8$.

(5) $t_{.05} = 2.3060$.

(6) $t < t_{.05}$ (i e., $1.25 < 2.3060$); therefore, accept H_0; that is, there is no reason to believe the average annual sick leave has increased.

TEST 6　　　　　　　　$H_0: \mu \leq a$

　　　　　　　　　　　$H_1: \mu > a$

KNOWN OR ASSUMED: Randomness and normality.

PROCEDURE:

(1) Compute $\bar{x}$ and s.

(2) Compute

$$t = \frac{(x - a)}{s} \sqrt{n} .$$

Do not take absolute difference between $\bar{x}$ and a.

(3) Compute DF $= n - 1$.

(4) Compute $2a$.

(5) Select from Appendix Table III the t_{2a} value opposite the appropriate DF and under the column headed by $2a$.

(6) If $t \leq t_{2a}$, accept H_0, otherwise accept H_1.

EXAMPLE: On the basis of an examination of census statistics, it is argued that the average number of inhabitants per house in neighborhood A is no greater than 4.5. A random sample of 100 houses is drawn from neighborhood A; the sample mean is found to be 5.3, and the standard deviation to be 2.0. Is the argument substantiated at the .05 significance level?

$$H_0: \mu \leq 4.5$$
$$H_1: \mu > 4.5$$

Solution:

(1) $\bar{x} = 5.3$ and $s = 2.0$.

(2) $t = \dfrac{(5.3 - 4.5)}{2.0} \sqrt{100} = 4.0$.

(3) DF $= 100 - 1 = 99$.

(4) $2a = 2(.05) = .10$.

(5) $t_{.10} = 1.66$.

(6) $t > t_{.10}$ (i.e., $4.0 > 1.66$); therefore, reject H_0 and accept H_1.

TEST 7 $H_0: \mu \geq a$

$H_1: \mu < a$

KNOWN OR ASSUMED: Randomness and normality.

PROCEDURE:

(1)–(5) Same as in Test 6.

(6) If $t \geq -t_{2a}$, accept H_0; otherwise accept H_1.

EXAMPLE: It is argued that the average number of absences of boys from elementary school per month is at least as great as 2.2. A random sample of 25 boys has an average absence of 2.5 days per month with a standard deviation of 1.2. Is the argument justified at the .25 significance level?

$$H_0: \mu \geq 2.2$$
$$H_1: \mu < 2.2$$

Solution:

(1) $\bar{x} = 2.5$ and $s = 1.2$.

(2) $t = \dfrac{(2.5 - 2.2)}{1.2} \sqrt{25} = 1.25$.

(3) DF $= 25 - 1 = 24$.

(4) $2a = 2(.25) = .50$.

(5) $t_{.50} = .68485$.

(6) $t > -t_{.50}$ (i.e., $1.25 > -.68485$); therefore, accept H_0; that is, the boys are absent at least as much as 2.2 days per month on the average.

TEST 8 $H_0: \sigma^2 = a$

$H_1: \sigma^2 > a$

$H_2: \sigma^2 < a$

KNOWN OR ASSUMED: Randomness and normality.

PROCEDURE:

(1) Compute s^2.

(2) Compute $DF = n - 1$.

(3) Compute $.5a$ and $(1.00 - .5a)$.

(4) Compute

$$\chi^2 = \frac{DF\, s^2}{a}.$$

(5) Use Appendix Table V. Read down the DF column until you come to the value computed in step (2). Read across to the column headed by the value equal to $.5a$, and select the $\chi^2_{.5a}$ value. If $\chi^2 > \chi^2_{.5a}$, accept H_1. If not, read across to the column headed by the value equal to $(1.00 - .5a)$ and select this $\chi^2_{(1.00-.5a)}$. If $\chi^2 < \chi^2_{(1.00-.5a)}$, accept H_2; otherwise accept H_0.

EXAMPLE: It is known on the basis of observations made last year that it takes the workers in a factory an average of 4.5 minutes to perform a certain operation, with a variance of .75 minute. A random sample of 25 workers is selected, and it is found that an average of 4.2 minutes is required for the operation, with a variance of .60 minute. Is there reason to believe, at the .10 significance level, that the variance has changed?

$$H_0: \sigma^2 = .75$$
$$H_1: \sigma^2 > .75$$
$$H_2: \sigma^2 < .75$$

Solution:

(1) $s^2 = .60$.

(2) $DF = 25 - 1 = 24$.

(3) $.5a = .5(.10) = .05$, and $(1.00 - .5a) = (1.00 - .05) = .95$.

(4) $\chi^2 = \dfrac{(24)(.60)}{.75} = 19.20$.

(5) $\chi^2_{.05} = 36.415$.

$\chi^2_{.95} = 13.848$.

$\chi^2_{.95} < \chi^2 < \chi^2_{.05}$ (i.e., $13.848 < 19.20 < 36.415$); therefore, accept H_0; that is, there is no reason to believe the variance has changed.

TEST 9* $\qquad\qquad\qquad H_0: \sigma^2 \leq a$
$\qquad\qquad\qquad\qquad\qquad\quad H_1: \sigma^2 > a$

KNOWN OR ASSUMED: Randomness and normality.

PROCEDURE:

(1) Compute s^2.

(2) Compute $DF = n - 1$.

* The OC curves for this test (at the .05 significance level) are shown in Appendix Figure II.

(3) Compute

$$\chi^2 = \frac{\mathrm{DF}\, s^2}{a}.$$

(4) Select from Appendix Table V the χ_a^2 value opposite the appropriate DF and under the appropriate a.

(5) If $\chi^2 \leq \chi_a^2$, accept H_0; otherwise accept H_1.

EXAMPLE: In the past it was observed that the variance in the daily attendance at a city's art museum was 7,000. On the basis of a random sample of 15 days a sample variance of 7,500 was determined. Should one assert, at the .05 significance level, that the variance is no more than 7,000?

$$H_0: \sigma^2 \leq 7,000$$
$$H_1: \sigma^2 > 7,000$$

Solution:

(1) $s^2 = 7,500$.

(2) DF $= 15 - 1 = 14$.

(3) $\chi^2 = \dfrac{(14)(7,500)}{7,000} = 15.0$.

(4) $\chi^2_{.05} = 23.685$.

(5) $\chi^2 < \chi^2_{.05}$ (i.e., $15.0 < 23.685$); therefore, accept H_0; that is, the variance of daily attendance has not increased.

TEST 10* $H_0: \sigma^2 \geq a$

                                   $H_1: \sigma^2 < a$

KNOWN OR ASSUMED: Randomness and normality.

PROCEDURE:

(1)–(3) Same as Test 9.

(4) Select from Appendix Table V the χ^2_{1-a} opposite the appropriate DF and under the value equal to $(1 - a)$.

(5) If $\chi^2 \geq \chi^2_{1-a}$, accept H_0; otherwise accept H_1.

EXAMPLE: The average monthly civilian labor force in a major city from 1940 to 1950 fluctuated about a mean with a variance of 25,000,000. A random sample of 11 months taken since 1950 yields a variance of the monthly averages of 20,000,000. Is there reason to believe, at the .01 significance level, that this variance has decreased?

$$H_0: \sigma^2 \geq 25,000,000$$
$$H_1: \sigma^2 < 25,000,000$$

* The OC curves for this test (at the .05 significance level) are shown in Appendix Figure III.

Solution:

(1) $s^2 = 20,000,000$.

(2) $DF = 11 - 1 = 10$.

(3) $\chi^2 = \dfrac{(10)(20,000,000)}{25,000,000} = 8.0$.

(4) $\chi^2_{.99} = 2.558$.

(5) $\chi^2 > \chi^2_{.99}$ (i.e., $8.0 > 2.558$); therefore, accept H_0; that is, the variance has not decreased.

TEST 11 $\qquad\qquad\qquad H_0: p = a$

$\qquad\qquad\qquad\qquad\qquad H_1: p \neq a$

KNOWN OR ASSUMED: The events observed are independent (i.e., have no effect on each other) and have the same probability of occurring. The sample should in general be of such a size that $np > 5$; in general, p should be less than .90.

PROCEDURE:

(1) Compute $\bar{p}$, the observed relative frequency of the occurrences of the event; that is, the ratio of the total number of times the event occurred to the total number of observed cases.

(2) Compute

$$\sigma = \sqrt{\frac{a(1-a)}{n}}.$$

(3) Compute

$$z = \frac{|\bar{p} - a|}{\sigma}.$$

(4) Select from Appendix Table II the appropriate value of z_a.

(5) If $z \leq z_a$, accept H_0; otherwise accept H_1.

EXAMPLE: We predict on the basis of past experience that the proportion of professionals who survive age fifty is .400. We draw a random sample of histories of 1,000 professionals and determine that .417 of them lived at least fifty years. Does this contradict the prediction at the .05 significance level?

$$H_0: p = .400$$
$$H_1: p \neq .400$$

Solution:

(1) $\bar{p} = .417$.

(2) $\sigma = \sqrt{\dfrac{.400(1-.400)}{1,000}} = .015$.

(3) $z = \dfrac{|.417 - .400|}{.015} = 1.13$.

(4) $z_{.05} = 1.96$.

(5) $z < z_{.05}$ (i.e., $1.13 < 1.96$); therefore, accept H_0; that is, the prediction is not contradicted.

7. Hypotheses concerning Differences between the Same Property of Different Populations

Many questions a researcher asks can take the form: Is one population similar to another or several others with respect to some specified property? For example:

(1) Is the average intelligence of the senior class at Harvard the same as the average intelligence of the senior class at Yale? That is, does μ_H equal μ_Y?

(2) Is there equal variation in income among employees of Chrysler and Ford? That is, does σ_C^2 equal σ_F^2?

(3) Is the proportion of Detroiters in favor of universal military training equal to the proportion of New Yorkers in favor of such training? That is, are p_D and p_{NY} equal?

There is no restriction on the number of populations which can thus be compared, though the methods used for more than two populations sometimes differ from those used where only two populations are compared. In addition to asking about the equality of two populations, we can also ask, for example, whether the mean of one population is larger or smaller than the mean of another. Similar questions can also be asked about the variance and proportions.

TEST 12* $H_0: \mu_1 = \mu_2$

$H_1: \mu_1 \neq \mu_2$

KNOWN OR ASSUMED: Both samples are random and are drawn from normal universes and σ^2.

PROCEDURE:

(1) Compute the mean of each sample, $\bar{x}_1$ and $\bar{x}_2$.

(2) Compute

$$z = \frac{|\bar{x}_1 - \bar{x}_2|}{\sqrt{\dfrac{\sigma_1^2}{n_1} + \dfrac{\sigma_2^2}{n_2}}} ,$$

* The OC curves for this test (at the .05 significance level) are shown in Fig. 22, where $\mu = \mu_1 - \mu_2$, $\sigma^2 = \sigma_1^2 + \sigma_2^2$.

where σ_1^2 and σ_2^2 are the known variances of the two populations, and n_1 and n_2 are the sizes of the samples from the two populations.

(3) Select from Appendix Table II the appropriate value of z_α.

(4) If $z \leq z_\alpha$, accept H_0; otherwise accept H_1.

EXAMPLE: We want to determine whether the students at two different schools have the same average I.Q. On the basis of past tests it is assumed that the variance in one school is 100 and in the other it is 144. A random sample of 10 students is drawn from the first school and given the test. Their average score is 104. A random sample of 24 students is drawn from the second school and given the test. Their average score is 98. Should we assert that the two schools have the same average I.Q. at the .05 significance level?

$$H_0: \mu_1 = \mu_2$$
$$H_1: \mu_1 \neq \mu_2$$

Solution:

(1) $\bar{x}_1 = 104$ and $\bar{x}_2 = 98$.

(2) $z = \dfrac{|104 - 98|}{\sqrt{\dfrac{100}{10} + \dfrac{144}{24}}} = 1.50$.

(3) $z_{.05} = 1.96$.

(4) $z < z_{.05}$ (i.e., $1.50 < 1.96$); therefore, accept H_0; that is, the two schools have the same average I.Q.

TEST 13
$$H_0: \mu_1 \leq \mu_2$$
$$H_1: \mu_1 > \mu_2$$

KNOWN OR ASSUMED: Randomness, normality, and σ^2 relative to each sample (i.e., σ_1^2 and σ_2^2).

PROCEDURE:

(1) Compute $\bar{x}_1$ and $\bar{x}_2$.

(2) Compute

$$z = \frac{(\bar{x}_1 - \bar{x}_2)}{\sqrt{\dfrac{\sigma_1^2}{n_1} + \dfrac{\sigma_2^2}{n_2}}}.$$

Do *not* take the absolute difference between $\bar{x}_1$ and $\bar{x}_2$.

(3) Compute 2α.

(4) Select from Appendix Table II the value of $z_{2\alpha}$.

(5) If $z \leq z_{2\alpha}$, accept H_0; otherwise accept H_1.

EXAMPLE: A random sample of 100 graduates of the class of 1940 is taken from two different universities. The average annual income of the first sample is $7,000; of the second, $7,775. Both population variances are assumed to be equal to 1,000,000. Is there reason to believe, at the .20 significance level, that the average of the class from the first university is no more than that from the second?

$$H_0: \mu_1 \leq \mu_2$$
$$H_1: \mu_1 > \mu_2$$

Solution:

(1) $\bar{x}_1 = 7,000$ and $\bar{x}_2 = 7,775$.

(2) $z = \dfrac{7,000 - 7,775}{\sqrt{\dfrac{1,000,000}{100} + \dfrac{1,000,000}{100}}} = -5.48$.

(3) $2a = 2(.20) = .40$.

(4) $z_{.40} = .842$.

(5) $z < z_{.40}$ (i.e., $-5.48 < .842$); therefore, accept H_0; that is, the average from the first university is no more than that from the second.

TEST 14 $H_0: \mu_1 \geq \mu_2$
                                 $H_1: \mu_1 < \mu_2$

KNOWN OR ASSUMED: Randomness, normality, and σ^2 relative to each sample.

PROCEDURE:

(1)–(4) Same as Test 13.

(5) If $z \geq -z_{2a}$, accept H_0; otherwise accept H_1.

EXAMPLE: Same situation as given in "Example" of Test 13. Is there reason to believe, at the .05 significance level, that the average of the class from the first university is less than that from the second?

$$H_0: \mu_1 \geq \mu_2$$
$$H_1: \mu_1 < \mu_2$$

Solution:

(1) $\bar{x}_1 = 7,000$ and $\bar{x}_2 = 7,775$.

(2) $z = \dfrac{7,000 - 7,775}{\sqrt{\dfrac{1,000,000}{100} + \dfrac{1,000,000}{100}}} = -5.48$.

(3) $2a = 2(.05) = .10$.

(4) $z_{.10} = 1.645$.

(5) $z < -z_{.10}$ (i.e., $-5.48 < -1.645$); therefore, reject H_0 and accept H_1; that is, the average from the first university is less than that from the second.

TEST 15 $H_0: \mu_1 = \mu_2 = \ldots = \mu_k$

$\qquad$ $H_1: \mu_i \neq \mu_j$ (i.e., at least two of the means are not equal)

KNOWN OR ASSUMED: Random samples of equal size from normal universes whose variances are known or assumed and equal.

PROCEDURE:

(1) Compute $\bar{x}$ for each sample.

(2) Compute

$$\sum_{}^{k} (\bar{x} - \bar{\bar{x}})^2 = \Sigma \bar{x}^2 - \frac{(\Sigma \bar{x})^2}{k},$$

where k = the number of samples.

(3) Compute

$$\chi^2 = \frac{n \sum_{}^{k} (\bar{x} - \bar{\bar{x}})^2}{\sigma^2},$$

where n = the number of items in each sample.

(4) Compute DF = $k - 1$.

(5) Select from Appendix Table V the χ_a^2 value opposite the appropriate DF and under the appropriate a.

(6) If $\chi^2 \leq \chi_a^2$, accept H_0; otherwise accept H_1.

EXAMPLE: Five observers in a laboratory are tested for their consistency in determining the percentage of a certain chemical in a specified compound. The variance of the readings is known to be independent of the observers and to be equal to .0001. Two determinations are made by each observer, the computed averages of which are .460, .465, .469, .461, and .463. Are the observers consistent at the .05 significance level?

$$H_0: \mu_1 = \mu_2 = \mu_3 = \mu_4 = \mu_5$$
$$H_1: \mu_i \neq \mu_j$$

Solution:

(1) $\bar{x}_1 = .460$, $\bar{x}_2 = .465$, $\bar{x}_3 = .469$, $\bar{x}_4 = .461$, and $\bar{x}_5 = .463$. For computational ease reduce each $\bar{x}$ by .460. This will not affect the results.

Therefore, let $\bar{x}_1 = .000$, $\bar{x}_2 = .005$, $\bar{x}_3 = .009$, $\bar{x}_4 = .001$, and $\bar{x}_5 = .003$.

(2) $\displaystyle\sum_{}^{k} (\bar{x} - \bar{\bar{x}})^2 = (.000)^2 + (.005)^2 + (.009)^2 + (.001)^2 + (.003)^2$

$$- \frac{(.000 + .005 + .009 + .001 + .003)^2}{5} = .000051.$$

(3) $\chi^2 = \dfrac{2\,(.000051)}{.0001} = 1.02$.

(4) $DF = 5 - 1 = 4$.

(5) $\chi^2_{.05} = 9.488$.

(6) $\chi^2 < \chi^2_{.05}$ (i.e., $1.02 < 9.488$); therefore, accept H_0; that is, the observers are consistent.

TEST 16 $\qquad\qquad H_0: \mu_1 = \mu_2$

$\qquad\qquad\qquad\qquad\quad H_1: \mu_1 \neq \mu_2$

KNOWN OR ASSUMED: Randomness and normality. The variances are unknown but equal (i.e., $\sigma_1^2 = \sigma_2^2$).

PROCEDURE 1:*

(1) Compute $\bar{x}_1$, $\bar{x}_2$, s_1^2, and s_2^2.

(2) Compute

$$s = \sqrt{\frac{(n_1 - 1)\, s_1^2 + (n_2 - 1)\, s_2^2}{n_1 + n_2 - 2}},$$

where n_1 and n_2 are the two sample sizes.

(3) Compute

$$t = \frac{|\,\bar{x}_1 - \bar{x}_2\,|}{s\sqrt{\dfrac{1}{n_1} + \dfrac{1}{n_2}}}.$$

(4) Compute $DF = n_1 + n_2 - 2$.

(5) Select from Appendix Table III the t_a value opposite the appropriate DF and under the appropriate a.

(6) If $t \leq t_a$, accept H_0; otherwise accept H_1.

EXAMPLE: The average duration of 15 randomly selected work stoppages in city A in 1951 was 25.7 days, with a sample variance of 20. The average duration of 10 randomly selected work stoppages in city B in 1951 was 19.5 days,

* The OC curves for this test (at the .05 significance level) are shown in Appendix Figure I, where $\mu = \mu_1 - \mu_2$, $\sigma^2 = \sigma_1^2 + \sigma_2^2$.

with a sample variance of 25. Is there reason to believe, at the .05 significance level, that the average work stoppages in the two cities are equal?

$$H_0: \mu_A = \mu_B$$
$$H_1: \mu_A \neq \mu_B$$

Solution:

(1) $\bar{x}_1 = 25.7$, $\bar{x}_2 = 19.5$, $s_1^2 = 20$, and $s_2^2 = 25$.

(2) $s = \sqrt{\dfrac{(15-1)\,20 + (10-1)\,25}{15 + 10 - 2}} = 4.69$.

(3) $t = \dfrac{|\,25.7 - 19.5\,|}{4.69\sqrt{\dfrac{1}{10} + \dfrac{1}{15}}} = 3.24$.

(4) DF $= 15 + 10 - 2 = 23$.

(5) $t_{.05} = 2.0687$.

(6) $t > t_{.05}$ (i.e., $3.24 > 2.0687$); therefore, reject H_0 and accept H_1; that is, the average durations of work stoppages in the two cities are not equal.

PROCEDURE 2: Where $n_1 = n_2$ the following simplified but less efficient test can be used. The remarks made in Test 4, Procedure 2, pertain here.

(1) Compute $\bar{x}_1$ and $\bar{x}_2$.

(2) Compute R_1 and R_2, the ranges in each sample.

(3) Compute

$$t' = \frac{|\,\bar{x}_1 - \bar{x}_2\,|}{.5\,(R_1 + R_2)}\,.$$

(4) Select from the right half of Appendix Table IV the t'_a value equal to $n = n_1 = n_2$, and under the appropriate a.

(5) If $t' \leq t'_a$, accept H_0; otherwise accept H_1.

EXAMPLE: A study similar to that made in the example for the first procedure is made in two other cities, C and D. A random sample of 10 work stoppages is taken in each city. The sample mean in city C is 26.1 and in city D, 21.3. The least and greatest stoppages in the first sample are 10 and 40 days, respectively. In the second they are 3 and 37 days, respectively. Is there reason to believe, at the .05 significance level, that the mean work stoppages are equal?

$$H_0: \mu_C = \mu_D$$
$$H_1: \mu_C \neq \mu_D$$

Solution:

(1) $\bar{x}_1 = 26.1$ and $\bar{x}_2 = 21.3$.

(2) $R_1 = 40 - 10 = 30$. $R_2 = 37 - 3 = 34$.

(3) $t' = \dfrac{|26.1 - 21.3|}{.5\,(30+34)} = .15$.

(4) $t'_{.05} = .3 \mathrm{C4}$.

(5) $t' < t'_{.05}$ (i.e., $.15 < .304$); therefore, accept H_0; that is, the average work stoppages are equal.

TEST 17 $H_0: \mu_1 \leq \mu_2$

$H_1: \mu_1 > \mu_2$

KNOWN OR ASSUMED: Randomness and normality. The variances are unknown but equal (i.e., $\sigma_1^2 = \sigma_2^2$).

PROCEDURE:

(1)–(2) Same as Test 14.

(3) Compute

$$t = \frac{(\bar{x}_1 - \bar{x}_2)}{s\sqrt{\dfrac{1}{n_1} + \dfrac{1}{n_2}}}.$$

Do *not* take the absolute difference between $\bar{x}_1$ and $\bar{x}_2$.

(4) Compute DF $= n_1 + n_2 - 2$.

(5) Compute $2a$.

(6) Select from Appendix Table III the t_{2a} value opposite the appropriate DF and under the column headed by $2a$.

(7) If $t \leq t_{2a}$, accept H_0; otherwise accept H_1.

EXAMPLE: We want to determine which of two typists can type the greatest number of words per minute. They are each timed at a random selection of 10 intervals during the day. The average number of words typed by typist A is 42 per minute, with a variance of 20. Typist B has an average of 37 words per minute, with a variance of 40. Is typist A faster than typist B at the .025 significance level?

$$H_0: \mu_A \leq \mu_B$$

$$H_1: \mu_A > \mu_B$$

Solution:

(1) $\bar{x}_A = 42$, $\bar{x}_B = 37$, $s_A^2 = 20$, and $s_B^2 = 40$.

(2) $s = \sqrt{\dfrac{(9)(20) + (9)(40)}{18}} = 5.48$.

(3) $t = \dfrac{(42 - 37)}{5.48\sqrt{\dfrac{2}{10}}} = 2.04$.

(4) DF $= 10 + 10 - 2 = 18$.

(5) $2\alpha = 2(.025) = .05$.

(6) $t_{.05} = 2.1009$.

(7) $t < t_{.05}$ (i.e., $2.04 < 2.1009$); therefore, accept H_0; that is, typist A is not faster than typist B.

TEST 18 $\qquad\qquad\qquad\qquad$ H_0: $\mu_1 \geq \mu_2$

$\qquad\qquad\qquad\qquad\qquad\qquad\quad$ H_1: $\mu_1 < \mu_2$

KNOWN OR ASSUMED: Randomness and normality. The variances are unknown but equal (i.e., $\sigma_1^2 = \sigma_2^2$).

PROCEDURE:

(1)–(6) Same as Test 17.

(7) If $t \geq -t_{2\alpha}$, accept H_0; otherwise accept H_1.

EXAMPLE: It is desired to determine whether city B has a larger number of petty crimes reported per day than does city A. A random sample of 50 days is examined in city A, and the sample mean and variance are 140 and 1,000, respectively. A random sample of 25 days is examined in city B, and the sample mean and variance are 125 and 2,500, respectively. Is the average number of petty crimes committed per day in city B greater, at the .05 significance level, than the corresponding number in city A?

$$H_0\text{: } \mu_A \geq \mu_B$$
$$H_1\text{: } \mu_A < \mu_B$$

Solution:

(1) $\bar{x}_A = 140$, $\bar{x}_B = 125$, $s_A^2 = 1,000$, and $s_B^2 = 2,500$.

(2) $s = \sqrt{\dfrac{(49)(1,000) + (24)(2,500)}{50 + 25 - 2}} = 38.6$.

(3) $t = \dfrac{(140 - 125)}{38.6\sqrt{\dfrac{1}{50} + \dfrac{1}{25}}} = 1.59$.

(4) DF $= 50 + 25 - 2 = 73$.

(5) $2a = 2(.05) = .10$.

(6) $t_{.10} = 1.67$ (approximately).

(7) $t > -t_{.10}$ (i.e., $1.59 > -1.67$); therefore, accept H_0; that is, the average number of petty crimes reported in city B is no greater than that in city A.

TEST 19 $H_0: \mu_1 = \mu_2 = \ldots = \mu_k$

$H_1: \mu_i \neq \mu_j$ (at least two of the means are not equal)

KNOWN OR ASSUMED: Randomness and normality. The variance of each universe is unknown, but $\sigma_1^2 = \sigma_2^2 = \ldots = \sigma_k^2$.

PROCEDURE:

(1) Compute $\bar{x}$ and s^2 for each sample.

(2) Compute

$$\sum^k (\bar{x} - \bar{\bar{x}})^2 = \Sigma \bar{x}^2 - \frac{(\Sigma \bar{x})^2}{k},$$

where $k =$ the number of samples.

(3) Compute

$$\bar{s}^2 = \frac{\Sigma s^2}{k}.$$

(4) Compute

$$F = \frac{n\Sigma (\bar{x} - \bar{\bar{x}})^2}{(k - 1) \bar{s}^2}.$$

(5) Compute $DF_1 = k - 1$ and $DF_2 = k(n - 1)$.

(6) Select from that part of Appendix Table VI which is headed by the appropriate a the F_a value opposite the appropriate DF_2 and under the appropriate DF_1.

(7) If $F \leq F_a$, accept H_0; otherwise accept H_1.

EXAMPLE: Random samples of 6 students each are taken from 4 different schools and tested for a certain aptitude. The computed averages and variances are as follows:

$$\bar{x}_1 = 105 \qquad\qquad s_1^2 = 8.3$$
$$\bar{x}_2 = 100 \qquad\qquad s_2^2 = 11.2$$
$$\bar{x}_3 = 107 \qquad\qquad s_3^2 = 12.0$$
$$\bar{x}_4 = 102 \qquad\qquad s_4^2 = 8.5$$

Is there reason to believe, at the .01 significance level, that the means of the schools are not the same?

$$H_0: \mu_1 = \mu_2 = \mu_3 = \mu_4$$
$$H_1: \mu_i \neq \mu_j$$

Solution:

(1) For computational ease reduce the sample means by 100:

$$\bar{x}_1 = 5, \ \bar{x}_2 = 0, \ \bar{x}_3 = 7, \text{ and } \bar{x}_4 = 2.$$

(2) $\displaystyle\sum^k (\bar{x} - \bar{\bar{x}})^2 = (5^2) + (0^2) + (7^2) + (2^2) - \frac{(5+0+7+2)^2}{4} = 29.$

(3) $\displaystyle \bar{s}^2 = \frac{40.0}{4} = 10.0.$

(4) $\displaystyle F = \frac{(6)(29)}{(3)(10)} = 5.80.$

(5) $DF_1 = 4 - 1 = 3. \ DF_2 = 4(6 - 1) = 20.$

(6) $F_{.01} = 4.9382.$

(7) $F > F_{.01}$ (i.e., $5.80 > 4.9382$); therefore, reject H_0 and accept H_1; that is, the means are not equal.

TEST 20 $\qquad\qquad H_0: \sigma_1^2 = \sigma_2^2$
$$H_1: \sigma_1^2 \neq \sigma_2^2$$

KNOWN OR ASSUMED: Randomness and normality.

PROCEDURE:

(1) Compute s_1^2 and s_2^2.
(2) Compute

$$F = \frac{s_1^2}{s_2^2}$$

if $s_1^2 > s_2^2$; otherwise reverse their positions and subscripts; that is, let the subscript 1 represent the sample with the greater s^2.
(3) Compute $DF_1 = n_1 - 1$ and $DF_2 = n_2 - 1$.
(4) Compute $.5\alpha$.
(5) Select from that part of Appendix Table VI which is headed by the value equal to $.5\alpha$ the $F_{.5\alpha}$ value opposite the appropriate DF_2 and under the appropriate DF_1.
(6) If $F \leq F_{.5\alpha}$, accept H_0; otherwise accept H_1.

EXAMPLE: Two track men have raced the same distance repeatedly. A random sample of 8 races of runner A has a variance of 26 (seconds squared). A random sample of 8 races of runner B has a variance of 15. Is there reason to assert, at the .10 significance level, that A's speed varies differently than B's?

$$H_0: \sigma_A^2 = \sigma_B^2$$
$$H_1: \sigma_A^2 \neq \sigma_B^2$$

Solution:

(1) $s_A^2 = 26$ and $s_B^2 = 15$.

(2) $F = 26/15 = 1.73$.

(3) $DF_1 = 8 - 1 = 7$ and $DF_2 = 8 - 1 = 7$.

(4) $.5\alpha = .5(.10) = .05$.

(5) $F_{.05} = 3.7870$.

(6) $F < F_{.05}$ (i.e., $1.73 < 3.7870$); therefore, accept H_0; that is, there is no reason to believe that A's and B's speeds vary differently.

TEST 21* $H_0: \sigma_1^2 \leq \sigma_2^2$

                                               $H_1: \sigma_1^2 > \sigma_2^2$

KNOWN OR ASSUMED: Randomness and normality.

PROCEDURE:

(1) Compute s_1^2 and s_2^2.

(2) Compute

$$F = \frac{s_1^2}{s_2^2}.$$

s_1^2 need not be the greater of the two.

(3) Compute $DF_1 = n_1 - 1$ and $DF_2 = n_2 - 1$.

(4) Select from that part of Appendix Table VI which is headed by the appropriate value of α the F_α value opposite the appropriate DF_2 and under the appropriate DF_1.

(5) If $F \leq F_\alpha$, accept H_0; otherwise accept H_1.

EXAMPLE: Two random samples are drawn from two army divisions, 21 from division A, 51 from division B. The sample variance of ages in A is 24.6 and in B is 30.0. Can one infer, at the .01 significance level, that the spread of ages in A is no more than in B?

$$H_0: \sigma_A^2 \leq \sigma_B^2$$
$$H_1: \sigma_A^2 > \sigma_B^2$$

* The OC curves for this test (at the .05 significance level) are shown in Appendix Figures IV–VI.

Solution:

(1) $s_A^2 = 24.6$ and $s_B^2 = 30.0$.

(2) $F = 24.6/30.0 = .82$.

(3) $DF_1 = 21 - 1 = 20$ and $DF_2 = 51 - 1 = 50$.

(4) $F_{.01} = 2.26$ (approximately).

(5) $F < F_{.01}$ (i.e., $.82 < 2.26$); therefore, accept H_0; that is, the ages in division A are no more dispersed than in division B.

TEST 22 $H_0: \sigma_1^2 = \sigma_2^2 = \ldots = \sigma_k^2$

            $H_1: \sigma_i^2 \neq \sigma_j^2$ (at least two of the variances are not equal)

KNOWN OR ASSUMED: Randomness and normality.

PROCEDURE:

(1) Compute for each sample separately

$$\sum_{i}^{n} (x_i - \bar{x})^2 = \sum_{i}^{n} x_i^2 - \frac{\left(\sum_{i}^{n} x_i \right)^2}{n}.$$

(2) Add the results of (1); that is, compute

$$\sum_{i}^{k} \left[\sum_{i}^{n} (x_i - \bar{x})^2 \right].$$

(3) Compute $DF_i = n_i - 1$ for each sample.

(4) Compute $\sum_{i}^{k} DF_i$.

(5) Compute

$$\sum_{i}^{k} DF_i \ln \frac{\sum_{i}^{k} \left[\sum_{i}^{n} (x_i - \bar{x})^2 \right]}{\sum_{i}^{k} DF_i},$$

that is, (4) $\ln [(2)/(4)]$, where (2) represents the results obtained in step (2), etc., and "ln" is the natural logarithm.

(6) Compute for each sample separately

$$s_i^2 = \frac{\sum_{i}^{n} (x_i - \bar{x})^2}{DF_i};$$

that is, (1)/(3).

(7) Compute $\ln (s_i^2)$ for each sample separately.

(8) Compute $DF_i \ln (s_i^2)$ for each sample; that is, (3) (7).

(9) Add the results of (8); that is, compute

$$\sum_{i}^{k} DF_i \ln(s_i^2).$$

(10) Compute $M = (5) - (9)$.

(11) Consult Appendix Table VII:

    a) If M is less than the smallest entry opposite the appropriate k, accept H_0.

    b) If M is greater than the largest entry opposite the appropriate k, accept H_1.

    c) If M lies between the smallest and the largest entry, compute

$$C_1 = \sum^{k} \frac{1}{DF_i} - \frac{1}{\sum^{k} DF_i},$$

and consult the appropriate C_1 column. If M is less than or equal to the value shown, accept H_0; otherwise accept H_1.

Note.—If some DF_i are small (less than or equal to 2) and others are large (equal to or greater than 12), and great accuracy is required, consult (10). For discussion and illustrations of other methods of testing these hypotheses see (6:80–81).

Example: It is desired to determine whether the variation in time required to perform a certain task is different in five different factories. Data are collected from random samples drawn from each factory with the following results and computations:

(1) Sample	(2) n_i	(3) DF_i	(4) $\sum^{n} (x_i - \bar{x})^2$	(5) s_i^2	(6) $\ln(s_i^2)$	(7) $DF_i \ln(s_i^2)$	(8) $1/DF_i$
1......	14	13	845	65	4.17	54.21	.077
2......	22	21	1,491	71	4.26	89.46	.048
3......	20	19	1,045	55	4.01	76.19	.053
4......	10	9	378	42	3.74	33.66	.111
5......	14	13	884	68	4.22	54.86	.077
Total	80	75	4,643	.....	....	308.38	.366

At the .05 significance level test the following hypotheses:

$$H_0: \sigma_1^2 = \sigma_2^2 = \sigma_3^2 = \sigma_4^2 = \sigma_5^2$$

$$H_1: \sigma_i^2 \neq \sigma_j^2$$

Solution:

(1) Column 4.

(2) $\displaystyle\sum^{5}\left[\sum^{n}(x_i - \bar{x})^2\right] = 4,643$.

(3) Column 3.

(4) $\displaystyle\sum^{5} DF_i = 75$.

(5) $\displaystyle\sum^{5} DF_i \ln\frac{\displaystyle\sum^{5}\sum^{n}(x_i - \bar{x})^2}{\displaystyle\sum^{5} DF_i} = (75)\ln\frac{4,643}{75} = 75(4.1257)$

$= 309.43$.

(6) Column 5.

(7) Column 6.

(8) Column 7.

(9) $\displaystyle\sum^{5} DF_i \ln(s_i^2) = 308.38$.

(10) $M = 309.43 - 308.38 = 1.05$.

(11) The smallest value opposite $k = 5$ in Appendix Table VII is 9.49. Since $1.05 < 9.49$, accept H_0; that is, the variances are equal.

TEST 23
$$H_0: p_1 = p_2$$
$$H_1: p_1 \neq p_2$$

KNOWN OR ASSUMED: Equal random samples from both populations. The probability of occurrence in each sample of the event examined remains constant throughout the sampling. Thus, if the population is small, sampling with replacement is necessary.

PROCEDURE:

(1) Prepare the following table (called a "double dichotomy"):

	Number of Occurrences	Number of Non-occurrences	Total
Sample from first population........	a	b	$a+b$
Sample from second population......	c	d	$c+d$
Total.....................	$a+c$	$b+d$	$a+b+c+d=2n$

where a represents the number of occurrences in the first sample, b the number of nonoccurrences, etc.

(2) Compute

$$z = \sqrt{\frac{2n(ad - bc + n)^2}{(a + c)(b + d)(a + b)(c + d)}}.$$

(3) Select from Appendix Table II the appropriate z_a value.

(4) If $z \leq z_a$, accept H_0; otherwise accept H_1.

EXAMPLE: It is desired to determine (at the .01 significance level) whether one government agency employs a larger percentage of World War II veterans than another. In agency A, 30 out of a random sample of 100 are veterans; in agency B, 40 out of a similar sample are veterans.

$$H_0: p_A = p_B$$
$$H_1: p_A \neq p_B$$

Solution:

(1)

	Number of Oc- currences	Number of Non- occur- rences	Total
Sample from A	30	70	100
Sample from B	40	60	100
Total.........	70	130	200

(2) $z = \sqrt{\dfrac{200(30 \times 60 - 70 \times 40 + 100)^2}{(70)(130)(100)(100)}} = 1.33.$

(3) $z_{.01} = 2.58.$

(4) $z < z_{.01}$ (i.e., $1.33 < 2.58$); therefore, accept H_0; that is, the percentages are the same.

TEST 24 $\qquad\qquad H_0: p_1 \leq p_2$

$\qquad\qquad\qquad\quad H_1: p_1 > p_2$

KNOWN OR ASSUMED: Same as Test 23.

PROCEDURE:

(1)–(2) Same as Test 23.

(3) Compute $2a$.

(4) Select from Appendix Table II the appropriate z_{2a} value.

(5) If $z \leq z_{2a}$, accept H_0; otherwise accept H_1.

EXAMPLE: It is desired to determine whether hospital patients with ulcers (A) tend more than those without ulcers (B) to come from families which contain at least one alcoholic. A random sample of 50 ulcer patients contains 40 who have an alcoholic in their families, whereas the sample of 50 drawn from other patients contains 20 who have an alcoholic in their families. At the .05 significance level is there a significantly larger percentage of alcoholics in families with ulcers than in the families of other types of patients?

$$H_0: p_A \leq p_B$$
$$H_1: p_A > p_B$$

Solution:

(1)

	Number of Oc-currences	Number of Non-occur-rences	Total
Sample from A.....	40	10	50
Sample from B.....	20	30	50
Total.........	60	40	100

(2) $z = \sqrt{\dfrac{100\,(40 \times 30 - 10 \times 20 + 50)^2}{(60)\,(40)\,(50)\,(50)}} = 4.29$.

(3) $2a = 2(.05) = .10$.

(4) $z_{.10} = 1.645$.

(5) $z > z_{.10}$ (i.e., $4.29 > 1.645$); therefore, reject H_0 and accept H_1; that is, the ulcer patients have a greater tendency to come from families with at least one alcoholic than do other patients.

The hypotheses $(H_0: p_1 \geq p_2)$ and $(H_1: p_1 < p_2)$ can be tested in the same manner as just described with a difference only in the fifth step:

(5) If $z \geq -z_{2a}$, accept H_0; otherwise accept H_1.

8. Hypotheses concerning Relational Properties

Many experiments are concerned with problems of the following types:

(1) How can changes in one variable Y be expressed as a function of changes of another variable X?

  (2) Do changes in one variable tend to be accompanied by changes in another variable?

To answer such questions, the methods of regression and correlation analysis have been developed.

8.1. Regression Analysis

  Suppose we were interested in making a study of the distribution of scores obtained on a certain ability test by employees of a certain agency relative to the number of years of school that they have completed. Suppose also that no employee has completed less than six years or more than eighteen years of school. We could begin by grouping the employees by the number of years of school completed and give the test to each group. We could then determine the distribution of scores for each group and compute the mean and variance of the distribution for each group. We could plot each of the thirteen means obtained on a graph in which the horizontal axis (X) represents the number of years of school completed and the vertical axis (Y) represents the scores. The points which represent the means of each group could be connected by a curve. This would be the *regression curve* of Y on X, or of scores on number of years of school completed. In this case the scores are the *dependent* variable and the years are the *independent* variable.

  In some cases the regression curve may be a straight or approximately straight line. If it is, it is called a *linear regression*.

  Consider the following example of a linear regression. Suppose the variances of the distribution of scores in each year-group (σ_{yx}^2) are equal and the means of the scores (y) for each year (x), μ_{yx}, have the following values:

Number of years of school completed (x)	6	7	8	9	10	11	12	13	14	15	16	17	18
Mean test score (μ_{yx})	70	75	80	85	90	95	100	105	110	115	120	125	130

  It is convenient to express the number of years of school completed (x) as deviations from the mean of this set of values (μ_x); that is, as ($x - \mu_x$). In this case μ_x is equal to 12 years. The data can now be retabulated as follows:

($x - \mu_x$)	−6	−5	−4	−3	−2	−1	0	1	2	3	4	5	6
μ_{yx}	70	75	80	85	90	95	100	105	110	115	120	125	130

  Note that the mean of the μ_{yx} values (μ_y) is 100 and occurs in combination with the mean of the X values (12 years). This can be shown to always be the case in linear regressions. The values are plotted in Figure 24.

Any regression line can be expressed by an equation in the following form:

$$\mu_{yx} = \mu_y + B(x - \mu_x),$$

where B is the slope of the line; that is, the number of units by which μ_{yx} changes when x changes by one unit. B is called the *regression coefficient*. In this case B is equal to 5. If B is equal to zero, then the regression line is horizontal. In such a case changes in Y values do not tend to be associated with

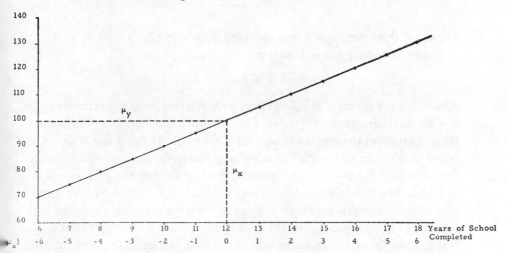

FIG. 24.—Linear regression of test scores on number of years of school completed

changes in X values; that is, the variable Y is independent of X. The presence of a slope indicates that there is such an association. It is misleading, however, to say that Y is dependent on X where a slope exists. Such a statement implies that changes in X cause changes in Y, and this is not necessarily so. All that can be properly asserted (where a slope exists [$B_{yx} \neq 0$]) is that changes in Y are associated with changes in X.

To see how the regression equation works, suppose we want to determine the value of μ_{y8}; that is, the mean score of those who have completed only eight years of school. Then, since $\mu_y = 100$, $B = 5$, and $\mu_x = 12$, we obtain

$$\mu_{yx} = 100 + 5(8 - 12) = 100 - 20 = 80.$$

One use of such an equation becomes apparent. If we want to predict the score that a randomly selected member of any specified X group will obtain, we would do best to use the mean score of the group (μ_{yx}) as the estimate. This follows from the fact that the values of y for a specified x cluster around their mean.

Now suppose that we do not know the equation for the regression line in the illustration and that we want to estimate it on the basis of a sample selected from the population. To estimate the regression line, we must first obtain estimates of μ_y and B_{yx}. For μ_x we can use the mean of the x's ($\bar{x}$) selected in the sample. The unbiased estimates of μ_y and B_{yx} which have minimum variance are $\bar{y}$ and b_{yx}, respectively, where

$$b_{yx} = \frac{\sum x_i y_i - \dfrac{\sum x_i y_i}{n}}{\sum x_i^2 - \dfrac{(\sum x_i)^2}{n}}.$$

The use of this estimate will be considered in Section 8.2.

The estimated regression equation is

$$\bar{y}_x = \bar{y} + b_{yx}(x_i - \bar{x}),$$

where $\bar{y}_x$ is the estimate of μ_{yx}. This value is referred to as the estimate of Y and is sometimes represented by y_E. The line which this equation describes has the property that the sum of the squares of the vertical deviations $[\Sigma(y_x - \bar{y}_x)]$ is less than the corresponding sum for any other straight line which can be drawn through the points. Consequently, this line is called the *least squares* fit.

It should be kept in mind that we may not know that there is a linear regression when we use this equation. If there is, then the equation yields the best estimate of it. The question might arise as to whether Y is independent of X. If it is, then B_{yx} will be equal to zero. To answer this question, then, we can test the hypothesis $H_0: B_{yx} = 0$. The procedure is described in Test 25.

Suppose we want to study the distribution of test scores not only relative to the number of years of school completed but also relative to income groups. Then we would want to determine the regression of scores on two independent variables. This would involve a *multiple regression*. Techniques for estimating such regressions will not be considered here, but they are discussed in (5:xiv).

The regression of Y on X may or may not be linear; it may be curvilinear. Techniques are also available for such cases. It is possible to test the hypothesis that a regression is linear. Such a test is described in (2:160–62).

In the illustration used above the population was grouped relative to the number of years of school completed (X), and the distribution of test scores (Y) was determined for each group. It is possible to group the population relative to their scores and determine the distribution of years for each score group. This would give us a regression of X on Y. It is also possible to study the relationship between the regression of Y on X and the regression of X on Y. Such a study is called *correlation analysis*. The significance and techniques of such a study are discussed in Section 8.3 of this chapter.

Now let us turn to a specific illustration of the use of linear regression and consider the procedure for estimating the regression equation and testing hypotheses for the significance of the slope. Suppose we draw a sample of ten members of the employee population whose test scores and numbers of years of school completed are as follows:

Subjects	School Years Completed (X)	Scores (Y)
1........	13	104
2........	10	96
3........	18	124
4........	12	120
5........	8	95
6........	7	122
7........	11	110
8........	10	90
9........	6	85
10........	12	104

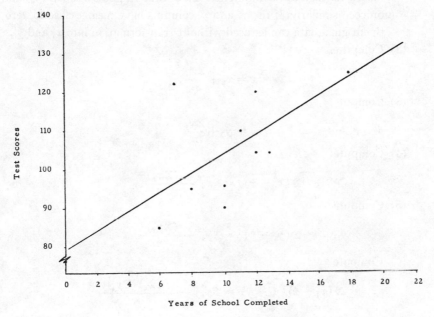

FIG. 25.—Scatter diagram and estimated regression line of y on x

These values can be plotted graphically. They are shown in Figure 25. Such a plot is called a *scatter diagram*. The procedure for estimating the regression line for these data follows.

8.2. Procedure for Determining Linear Regression Equation

Given: a set of paired observations, x_i and y_i, such that there is one and only one y_i associated with each x_i.

(1) Prepare the following chart:

	x_i	y_i	x_i'	y_i'	$x_i'^2$	$y_i'^2$	$x_i'y_i'$
1.........							
2.........							
.							
.							
.							
n.........							
Total							

To obtain x_i', guess a mean (x_0) of the x_i column. Subtract x_0 from each x_i and enter the result in the x_i' column (i.e., $x_i' = x_i - x_0$), and record the sign of the difference. To obtain y_i', guess a mean (y_0) and proceed similarly. If the x_i and y_i columns have means close to zero, the original data can be used without transformation into x_i' and y_i'.

(2) Compute

$$\bar{x} = x_0 + \frac{\Sigma x_i'}{n}.$$

(3) Compute

$$\bar{y} = y_0 + \frac{\Sigma y_i'}{n}.$$

(4) Compute

$$\Sigma (x_i - \bar{x})^2 = \Sigma x_i'^2 - \frac{(\Sigma x_i')^2}{n}.$$

(5) Compute

$$\Sigma (y_i - \bar{y})^2 = \Sigma y_i'^2 - \frac{(\Sigma y_i')^2}{n}.$$

(6) Compute

$$\Sigma (x_i - \bar{x})(y_i - \bar{y}) = \Sigma x_i'y_i' - \frac{(\Sigma x_i')(\Sigma y_i')}{n}.$$

(7) Then the regression line of Y on X is described by the equation:

$$\bar{y}_x = \bar{y} + \frac{\Sigma (x_i - \bar{x})(y_i - \bar{y})}{\Sigma (x_i - \bar{x})^2} (x_i - \bar{x}),$$

where $\bar{y}_x$ is the predicted value of Y for a given value of X. The estimated regression coefficient (b_{yx}) is obtained from

$$b_{yx} = \frac{\Sigma (x_i - \bar{x})(y_i - \bar{y})}{\Sigma (x_i - \bar{x})^2},$$

hence, $\bar{y}_x = \bar{y} + b_{yx}(x_i - \bar{x})$.

The true or population regression coefficient is represented by B. The estimated standard error of the predicted value $(\bar{y}_x)$ is obtained from

$$s_{yx} = \sqrt{\frac{\Sigma (y_i - \bar{y})^2 - \dfrac{\Sigma (x_i - \bar{x})(y_i - \bar{y})^2}{\Sigma (x - \bar{x})^2}}{n - 2}}.$$

The estimated standard error of b_{yx} is obtained from

$$s_{b_{yx}} = \frac{s_{yx}}{\sqrt{\Sigma (x_i - \bar{x})^2}}.$$

EXAMPLE: Regression equation of test scores on years of school completed based on 10 paired observations.

(1)

OBSERVA-TION	YEARS OF SCHOOL COMPLETED x_i	TEST SCORES					
		y_i	x_i'	y_i'	$x_i'^2$	$y_i'^2$	$x_i' y_i'$
1........	13	104	1	4	1	16	4
2........	10	96	-2	-4	4	16	8
3........	18	124	6	24	36	576	144
4........	12	120	0	20	0	400	0
5........	8	95	-4	-5	16	25	20
6........	7	122	-5	22	25	484	-110
7........	11	110	-1	10	1	100	-10
8........	10	90	-2	-10	4	100	20
9........	6	85	-6	-15	36	225	90
10........	12	104	0	4	0	16	0
Total.			-13	50	123	1,958	166

$x_0 = 12$ and $y_0 = 100$.

(2) $\bar{x} = 12 + (-13)/10 = 10.7$.

(3) $\bar{y} = 100 + 50/10 = 105$.

(4) $\Sigma(x_i - \bar{x})^2 = 123 - 169/10 = 106.1$.

(5) $\Sigma(y_i - \bar{y})^2 = 1,958 - 2,500/10 = 1,708$.

(6) $\Sigma(x_i - \bar{x})(y_i - \bar{y}) = 166 - (-13)50/10 = 231$.

(7) $\bar{y}_x = 105 + 231/106.1(x_i - 10.7) = 105 + 2.18(x_i - 10.7)$.

$b_{yx} = 2.18$.

$$s_{yx} = \sqrt{\frac{1,708 - (231)^2/106.1}{8}} = 12.3.$$

$$s_{b_{yx}} = \frac{12.3}{\sqrt{106.1}} = 1.19.$$

TEST 25

$$H_0: B_{yx} = 0$$
$$H_1: B_{yx} \neq 0$$

KNOWN OR ASSUMED: The regression of Y on X is linear, Y is normally distributed with equal variance for any given value of X, and the observed values of Y are selected at random for each fixed value of X.

    (1) Compute b_{yx}. If b_{yx} is negative ignore the sign in subsequent computations.

    (2) Compute s_{yx}.

    (3) Compute $s_{b_{yx}}$.

    (4) Compute

$$t = \frac{b_{yx}}{s_{b_{yx}}}.$$

    (5) Compute DF $= n - 2$.

    (6) Select from Appendix Table III the appropriate t_a value.

    (7) If $t \leq t_a$, accept H_0; otherwise accept H_1.

EXAMPLE: Use data in Section 8.2. Test at .05 significance level.

$$H_0: b_{yx} = 0$$
$$H_1: b_{yx} \neq 0$$

Solution:

    (1) $b_{yx} = 2.18$.

    (2)–(3) $s_{b_{yx}} = 1.42$.

    (4) $t = 2.18/1.42 = 1.54$.

    (5) DF $= 10 - 2 = 8$.

    (6) $t_{.05} = 2.306$.

    (7) $t < t_{.05}$ (i.e., $1.54 < 2.306$); therefore, accept H_0; that is, the regression coefficient is not significant.

8.3. Correlation Analysis

In correlation analysis the regression of Y on X *and* the regression of X on Y are (in effect) both determined and the relationship between them is measured by a quantity called the *correlation coefficient*. The true or population correlation coefficient is symbolized by the Greek letter rho (ρ), and estimates of this value are represented by r.

First, let us take a nonmathematical approach to the meaning of correlation. Suppose we obtain for each individual in a population both a score on a reading ability test (x_i) and a score on a vocabulary test (y_i). We would expect to find that a person who does well on one test is more apt than not to do well on the other. We would also expect that individuals who do poorly on one test do likewise on the other. That is, we expect high and low scores on one test to be accompanied by high and low scores respectively on the other. If we prepared a graph on which we plotted for each individual a point defined by his two test scores, we would expect to get a distribution of points something like that shown in Figure 26. These two variables would be said to be *positively* correlated.

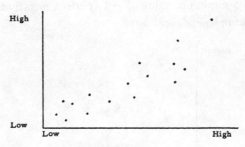

FIG. 26.—Positively correlated variables

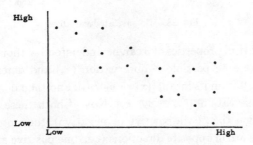

FIG. 27.—Negatively correlated variables

Not all variables are positively correlated. A high value of one variable, for example, may tend to be accompanied by a low value of the other. If we were to determine for a group of individuals their incomes and the amount of physical energy required in their work, we would expect to find that as income increases, the amount of physical exertion required tends to decrease. Graphically, we would expect to obtain a set of points such as is shown in Figure 27. This set of paired observations would be said to be *negatively* correlated.

Finally, the two variables may change *independently;* that is, a high value of one is just as likely to be accompanied by a low as a high value of the other. For example, we would expect that the number of children born in New York City each year is independent of the amount of rainfall in Peru. That is, we would expect to find no tendency for values of these variables to change in either the same or opposite directions. Graphically we would expect to obtain a set of points such as is shown in Figure 28. These variables would be said to be *uncorrelated*.

It was mentioned that the correlation coefficient expresses the relationship between the regression of X on Y (B_{XY}) and the regression of Y on X (B_{YX}). Specifically,

$$\rho = \sqrt{B_{XY}B_{YX}}.$$

This value can be shown to have a maximum value of 1 (perfect positive correlation) and a minimum value of -1 (perfect negative correlation). Zero represents perfect independence.

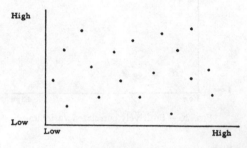

FIG. 28.—Uncorrelated variables

The mathematical properties of ρ can be understood without much difficulty. Suppose we take each possible X observation (x_i) and determine how many σ_x units it is away from its mean, $[(x_i - \mu_x)/\sigma_x]$; and then do the same for each associated Y observation, $[(y_i - \mu_x)/\sigma_x]$. Now if both these deviations are in the same direction (i.e., both positive or negative), their product is positive. If the deviations are in opposite directions (i.e., one positive and one negative), their product is negative. Now suppose we determined these products for each possible pair of observations and obtained their total:

$$\sum^{N} \frac{(x_i - \mu_x)}{\sigma_x} \frac{(y_i - \mu_y)}{\sigma_y}.$$

If this sum is positive, it indicates a tendency of the variables to change in the same direction. If it is negative, it indicates a tendency to change in opposite directions. The more consistent this tendency, the larger the sum.

It is convenient to consider the average product of these deviations rather than the sum because the average enables comparisons to be made between different sized sets of paired observations. Hence the correlation coefficient can be defined as follows:

$$\rho = \frac{1}{N} \sum^{N} \frac{(x_i - \mu_x)}{\sigma_x} \frac{(y_i - \mu_y)}{\sigma_y}.$$

The estimate of ρ is then defined as follows:

$$r = \frac{1}{n} \sum^{n} \frac{(x_i - \bar{x})}{s_x} \frac{(y_i - \bar{y})}{s_y}.$$

This formula may be transformed to enable simpler computations to be made. The more complex looking but simpler to use form of this equation is given in Section 8.5, step (2).

8.4. Misuses of Correlation Analysis

In the social sciences the use of correlation has become a standard procedure, although in many cases there is little consideration given to the advantages of using one type of estimate of correlation rather than another. Since this subject is so complex, consultation with a mathematical statistician is frequently desirable.

There are two common misuses of correlation analysis against which the social scientist should be warned. The first consists of taking the estimated correlation coefficient, r, to have some meaning by itself. A sample correlation coefficient has no meaning by itself. We must determine how likely such an estimate is to be obtained if the true coefficient has some specified value; that is, we must determine whether or not the estimate is significant. For example, we might ask: If the true correlation coefficient is equal to zero, how likely are we to get a specified estimate? In practice many researchers automatically take r to be significant if it is equal to or greater than some specified amount (e.g., .85). Such conclusions are not always sound; in some instances even where r is less than .85 it is significant, and where r is more than .85 it may be insignificant. That is, even if the true correlation coefficient is equal to zero, in some cases we are quite likely to get values of r greater than .85. We shall consider some of the common tests for significance below.

The second common error is one to which we have already referred (in chap. iii). It consists in asserting that, because X and Y are correlated, one is either the cause or the effect, the producer or the product, of the other. Such an inference cannot be based on correlation analysis alone. The conditions and operations required to establish such a relationship have been discussed previously.

It should be noted that we are not restricted to two variables in correlation analysis. Methods are available for handling large numbers of variables simultaneously.

Finally, it should be noted that there are some very useful but relatively unknown measures of association between variables. Three particularly useful measures for the social sciences are (1) the coefficient of concordance, which measures the agreement of rankings with some pre-established standard; (2) the coefficient of consistence, which indicates how consistent a judge or observer is in his preferences where he makes paired comparisons; and (3) the coefficient of agreement, which measures the agreement of a number of judges in making paired comparisons. These measures and tests for their significance are discussed in (8:I, xvi). For further discussion of correlation see (5), (7), (9), and (10).

8.5. Procedure for Computing Linear Correlation Coefficient

(1) Prepare the same table as required in the first step in computing the linear regression coefficient. (See Sec. 8.2.)

(2) Compute

$$r = \sqrt{\frac{[n\Sigma x_i' y_i' - (\Sigma x_i')(\Sigma y_i')]^2}{[n\Sigma x_i'^2 - (\Sigma x_i')^2][n\Sigma y_i'^2 - (\Sigma y_i')^2]}}.$$

EXAMPLE: Use the same data as is given in Section 8.2.

(1) See page 215.

(2) $r = \sqrt{\dfrac{[(10)(166) - (-13)(50)]^2}{[(10)(123) - (-13)^2][(10)(1,958) - (50)^2]}} = .54$.

TEST 26 $H_0: \rho = 0$

                                       $H_1: \rho \neq 0$

KNOWN OR ASSUMED: The pairs of observations are drawn at random and are normally distributed.

PROCEDURE:

(1) Compute r.

(2) Compute DF $= n - 2$.

(3) Select from Appendix Table VIII the r_a value opposite the appropriate DF and under the appropriate a.

(4) If $r \leq r_a$, accept H_0; otherwise accept H_1.

EXAMPLE: Use data in Section 8.2. Test at .05 significance level.

$$H_0: \rho = 0$$
$$H_1: \rho \neq 0$$

Solution:

(1) $r = .54$. (See Sec. 8.4.)

(2) $DF = 10 - 2 = 8$.

(3) $r_{.05} = .6319$.

(4) $r < r_{.05}$ (i.e., $.54 < .6319$); therefore, accept H_0; that is, the correlation coefficient is not significant.

TEST 27 $H_0: \rho = 0$

                                         $H_1: \rho \neq 0$

KNOWN OR ASSUMED: The observations consist of two sets of rankings of the same set of items.

PROCEDURE:

(1) Prepare the following table:

Item	A_1	A_2	. . .	A_n
Ranking 1......	X_1	X_2	. . .	X_n
Ranking 2......	Y_1	Y_2	. . .	Y_n

where $A_1, A_2, \ldots, A_n$ identify the items ranked; X_1 is the ranking given to the first item in ranking 1, Y_1 is the ranking given to the same item in the second ranking, etc.

(2) Determine the X ranking for the item ranked first in the Y-ranking. Suppose the X ranking were 4. Then count the number of items (A's) to the right of A_4 (i.e., $n - 4$) and subtract from this the number of items to the left of A_4 (i.e., 3). Call this value d_1. Cross out A_4. Repeat this process for item ranked second in the Y ranking, third, etc., up to the next-to-the-last Y ranking. That is, compute $d_2, d_3, \ldots, d_{n-1}$.

(3) Compute

$$S = \sum_{i=1}^{n-1} d_i .$$

(4) Compute

$$r = \frac{2S}{n(n-1)} ,$$

where $n =$ the number of items ranked.

(5)

    a) If $n \leq 10$, select from Appendix Table IX the probability opposite the S value obtained in (3) and under the appropriate n. If this probability is greater than or equal to $.5a$, accept H_0; otherwise accept H_1.

   b) If $n > 10$:

      (i) Compute

$$t = r\sqrt{\frac{n-2}{1-r^2}}.$$

      (ii) Compute $DF = n - 2$.

     (iii) Select from Appendix Table III the t_a value opposite the appropriate DF and under the appropriate a.

     (iv) If $t \leq t_a$, accept H_0; otherwise accept H_1.

EXAMPLE: Two corporation executives independently rank 10 of their subordinates with respect to executive ability. The results are as follows:

	A_1	A_2	A_3	A_4	A_5	A_6	A_7	A_8	A_9	A_{10}
Executive A's ranking......	1	3	4	6	2	7	8	9	10	5
Executive B's ranking......	5	1	4	6	7	8	9	3	2	10

What is the rank correlation? Is it significant at the .05 significance level?

$$H_0: \rho = 0$$
$$H_1: \rho \neq 0$$

Solution:

   (1) See tabulation above.

   (2) $d_1 = +5$ $d_6 = 0$

        $d_2 = -8$ $d_7 = +3$

        $d_3 = -7$ $d_8 = 0$

        $d_4 = +2$ $d_9 = -1$

        $d_5 = +5$

   (3) $S = -1$.

   (4) $r = 2(-1)/(10)(9) = .0222$.

   (5) From Appendix Table IX the probability is equal to .500.

      Since $.500 > .5(.05)$, accept H_0; that is, the rankings are not significantly correlated.

TEST 28 $H_0: \rho = a$

                             $H_1: \rho \neq a$

KNOWN OR ASSUMED: The pairs of observations are drawn at random and are normally distributed.

PROCEDURE:

(1) Compute r.
(2) Select from Appendix Table X the z' value corresponding to r. If r is negative, place a minus sign in front of the value indicated.
(3) Select from Appendix Table X the z' value corresponding to a. If a is negative, place a minus sign in front of the value indicated. Let $\bar{z}'$ represent this value.
(4) Compute

$$\sigma_z' = \frac{1}{\sqrt{n-3}}.$$

(5) Compute

$$z = \frac{|z' - \bar{z}'|}{\sigma_z'}.$$

(6) Select from Appendix Table II the appropriate z_a value.
(7) If $z \leq z_a$, accept H_0; otherwise accept H_1.

EXAMPLE: A sample of 10 observations yields $r = .59$. For $a = .01$, test the following hypotheses:

$$H_0: \rho = .800$$
$$H_1: \rho \neq .800$$

Solution:

(1) $r = .59$.
(2) $z' = .678$.
(3) $\bar{z}' = 1.099$.

(4) $\sigma_z' = \dfrac{1}{\sqrt{10-3}} = .378$.

(5) $z = \dfrac{1.099 - .678}{.378} = 1.11$.

(6) $z_{.01} = 2.576$.
(7) $z < z_{.01}$ (i.e., $1.11 < 2.576$); therefore, accept H_0.

TEST 29
$$H_0: \rho_1 = \rho_2$$
$$H_1: \rho_1 \neq \rho_2$$

KNOWN OR ASSUMED: The pairs of observations in each sample are drawn at random and are normally distributed.

PROCEDURE:

(1) Compute r_1 and r_2.

(2) Select from Appendix Table X the value of z' corresponding to r_1 (z'_1), and the value of z' corresponding to r_2 (z'_2). If either r is negative, the corresponding z' value should be given a negative value.

(3) Compute

$$z = \frac{|z'_1 - z'_2|}{\sqrt{\dfrac{1}{n_1 - 3} + \dfrac{1}{n_2 - 3}}}.$$

(4) Select from Appendix Table II the appropriate z_a value.

(5) If $z \leq z_a$, accept H_0; otherwise accept H_1.

EXAMPLE: A random sample of doctors is chosen from two cities, A and B, and a correlation coefficient is obtained for each with respect to their income and the number of years they have been in practice. The results are: $r_A = .65$, $r_B = .56$. The sample sizes are $n_A = 53$, $n_B = 28$. Test at the .05 significance level the hypotheses:

$$H_0: \rho_A = \rho_B$$
$$H_1: \rho_A \neq \rho_B$$

Solution:

(1) $r_A = .65$ and $r_B = .56$.

(2) $z'_A = .775$ and $z'_B = .633$.

(3) $z = \dfrac{|.775 - .633|}{1/50 + 1/25} = .46$.

(4) $z_{.05} = 1.96$.

(5) $z < z_{.05}$ (i.e., $.46 < 1.96$); therefore, accept H_0; the correlation coefficients are equal.

TEST 30 $H_0: \rho_1 = \rho_2$

$H_1: \rho_1 \neq \rho_2$

KNOWN OR ASSUMED: Random samples from the same population, the pairs normally distributed, and three observations on each individual. Let $\rho_1 = $ the correlation between observations on X_i and Z_i, and let $\rho_2 = $ the correlation between observations Y_i and Z_i; that is, Z is a standard for comparison.

PROCEDURE:

(1) Compute r_{xz}, r_{yz}, and r_{xy}.

(2) Compute

$$F = \frac{(r_{xz} - r_{yz})^2 (n-3)(1+r_{xy})}{2(1 - r_{xy}^2 - r_{xz}^2 - r_{yz}^2 + 2 r_{xy} r_{xz} r_{yz})}.$$

(3) Let $DF_1 = 1$. Compute $DF_2 = n - 3$.

(4) Select from the appropriate part of Appendix Table VI the F_a value opposite the appropriate DF_2 and under $DF_1 = 1$.

(5) If $F \leq F_a$, accept H_0; otherwise accept H_1.

EXAMPLE: A random sample of 53 students were given three tests, a reading test (X), a vocabulary test (Y), and an intelligence test (Z). The correlation coefficients between the scores on these tests were as follows:

$$r_{xy} = .72, r_{xz} = .80, \text{ and } r_{yz} = .64.$$

At the .05 significance level determine which of the following hypotheses should be accepted:

$$H_0: \rho_{xz} = \rho_{yz}$$

$$H_1: \rho_{xz} \neq \rho_{yz}$$

Solution:

(1) $r_{xy} = .72, r_{xz} = .80,$ and $r_{yz} = .64$.

(2) $F = \dfrac{(.80 - .64)^2 (50)(1 + .72)}{2[1 - (.72)^2 - (.80)^2 - (.64)^2 + 2(.72)(.80)(.64)]} = 6.5$.

(3) $DF_1 = 1$ and $DF_2 = 53 - 3 = 50$.

(4) $F_{.05} = 4.03$.

(5) $F > F_{.05}$ (i.e., $6.5 > 4.03$); therefore, reject H_0 and accept H_1.

DISCUSSION TOPICS

1. What is the difference between the distribution of z and t? What is the difference in their use?

2. Suppose the true mean of a population is known. A sample is drawn and its mean is computed. How can one test the assertion that the sample was selected at random from the population?

3. How do regression analyses and correlation analyses differ? When would you use each?

4. What does *statistically significant* mean?

EXERCISES

1. We predict that the average number of rooms per house in a certain neighborhood is equal to 6. A random sample of 25 houses is selected, and the average number

of rooms for the sampled houses is 4.75. On the basis of previous studies we assume that $\sigma = 1.50$. Is the prediction supported at the .01 significance level?

2. Ten students, selected at random from a freshman class, have a point average of 1.32. Last year's freshman class had an average of 1.56. The variance is assumed to be unchanged since last year and to be equal to 0.72. Can one infer, at the .05 significance level, that this year's class is inferior to last year's class?

3. The average number of children attending kindergarten in 16 randomly selected schools in a county is equal to 45. The sample variance is 220. The state as a whole has an average kindergarten attendance of 32. Is the county significantly different from the state as a whole? Let $\alpha = .05$. Suppose the smallest class in the sample contained 20 children, and the largest 53. Answer the question without using the sample variance.

4. Suppose a sample of 21 individuals has an $\bar{x} = 21.2$ and $s^2 = 14$. Is there reason to believe that the population from which the sample is drawn has a mean at least as great as 20.0? Let $\alpha = .005$.

5. A random sample of 8 is selected from a class of 40. The sample mean and variance are, respectively, 95 and 38. Can one infer, at the .10 significance level, that the class mean is equal to 100?

6. If observations on a random sample of 25 persons have a variance equal to 1,264, should one infer that the population has a variance less than, equal to, or greater than 1,300? Let $\alpha = .10$.

7. Suppose observations on a random sample of 17 persons have a variance of 17.5. Should one conclude that the population variance is at least 20? Let $\alpha = .01$.

8. If a random sample of households in a city indicates that 52 per cent of the 1,200 children (in the sample) between five and six years old attend school, can one infer that the city is typical if the national percentage is 43? Let $\alpha = .20$.

9. Suppose two random samples of 33 (n_1) and 40 (n_2) individuals have the following sample means and true variances: $\bar{x}_1 = 9.2$, $\sigma_1^2 = 3.4$, $\bar{x}_2 = 11.1$, and $\sigma_2^2 = 4.3$. Should one infer, at the .10 significance level, that the populations from which the samples are drawn have the same means?

10. The following are data obtained from samples taken from two populations:

A	B
32	24
22	48
40	36
25	.52
51	

Can one infer, at the .05 significance level, that the mean of population A is as great as that of B?

11. Samples of 35 are taken from 4 different universities. The observations from each university are known to have the same variance: 6,200. The sample means are 92, 87, 71, and 104. Can one infer that the population means are equal? Let $\alpha = .01$.

12. A random sample of 50 undergraduates and 25 graduates are tested for mathematical proficiency. The former obtain a mean score of 45.6, with a sample variance of 6.1. The latter obtain a mean score of 52.5, with a sample variance of 8.7. Are the undergraduates and graduates equally proficient? Let $\alpha = .005$.

13. Same type of situation as in Problem 12. Here $n_1 = 15$, $\bar{x}_1 = 47.3$ with $R_1 = 15.0$, and $n_2 = 15$, $\bar{x}_2 = 54.2$ with $R_2 = 22.0$. Test $H_0: \mu_1 = \mu_2$ at the .05 significance level.

14. Suppose random samples of 11 each are drawn from four populations with the following results: $\bar{x}_1 = 12.1$, $s_1^2 = 6.2$, $\bar{x}_2 = 10.8$, $s_2^2 = 8.1$, $\bar{x}_3 = 11.3$, $s_3^2 = 5.3$, $\bar{x}_4 = 13.5$, and $s_4^2 = 7.1$. Is there reason to believe that these samples are drawn from populations with equal means? Let $a = .01$. (The true variances are assumed to be equal.)

15. Two salesmen are selling the same product in different areas. The following are the number of sales in randomly selected weeks for each:

A	B
45	61
51	72
44	73
48	54

Can one infer that their sales have equal variance from week to week? Let $a = .05$.

16. The sample variance in income of 41 randomly selected architects is 16,000,000. The sample variance in income in a sample of 61 engineers is 22,000,000. At the .25 significance level can we conclude that the income of engineers is more widely dispersed than that of architects?

17. A random sample of 100 persons in neighborhood A contains 75 per cent who are in favor of rent control. In neighborhood B, where a sample of 50 is taken, 70 per cent are in favor of such control. At the .05 significance level can we infer that A and B have the same percentage in favor of rent control?

18. A certain characteristic is possessed by 58 per cent of a population. A sample of 100 is drawn, of which only 41 per cent have this characteristic. At the .01 significance level can this sample be considered to be selected at random from the population?

19. Compute the regression coefficient of income on age for the following data and determine if it is significant at the .05 level.

Age	Income (Weekly)
27	98
34	37
56	28
32	38
47	104
65	120
39	56
58	75

20. Determine the correlation coefficient of the following data and determine if it is significant at the .01 level.

X	Y
17	54
26	85
19	41
18	40
21	67
22	71
15	50
17	55
14	32
2	5

21. Suppose a sample of 40 is selected in which age and income have a correlation coefficient equal to .57 and in which age and family size have a correlation coefficient

equal to .69. At the .05 significance level is there reason to believe that the population correlations with respect to these properties are equal?

22. The correlation between scores on attitude tests given to a random sample of 20 persons is .31. It is believed that the population correlation is .40. Is this belief substantiated at the .01 significance level?

23. Five finalists in a talent show are rated by two different judges as follows:

	FINALIST				
	1	2	3	4	5
Ranking A	2	5	3	1	4
Ranking B	3	5	1	2	4

Are these rankings significantly correlated at the .10 level?

SUGGESTED READINGS

Good reference books for the social scientist on statistical tests are Churchman (1), Dixon and Massey (2), Edwards (3), and Johnson (5).

The latter three cover aspects of correlation not discussed here. A very elementary treatment of regression and correlation can be found in Mode (8). For advanced and detailed treatments see Ezekiel (4) and Kendall (6).

REFERENCES AND BIBLIOGRAPHY

1. CHURCHMAN, C. W. *Statistical Manual: Methods of Making Experimental Inferences.* 2d rev. ed. Philadelphia: Pittman-Dunn Laboratory, Frankford Arsenal, 1951.
2. DIXON, W. J., and MASSEY, F. J., JR. *Introduction to Statistical Analysis.* New York: McGraw-Hill Book Co., 1951.
3. EDWARDS, A. L. *Experimental Designs in Psychological Research.* New York: Rinehart & Co., 1950.
4. EZEKIEL, M. J. B. *Methods of Correlation Analysis.* 2d ed. New York: John Wiley & Sons, 1949.
5. JOHNSON, P. O. *Statistical Methods in Research.* New York: Prentice-Hall, Inc., 1949.
6. KENDALL, M. G. *Rank Correlation Methods.* London: Chas. Griffin & Co., Ltd., 1948.
7. ———. *Advanced Theory of Statistics.* London: Chas. Griffin & Co., Ltd., 1947.
8. MODE, E. B. *The Elements of Statistics.* 2d ed. New York: Prentice-Hall, Inc., 1951.
9. SPURR, W. A. "A Short-Cut Method of Correlation," *Journal of the American Statistical Association,* XLVI (1951), 89–94.
10. THOMPSON, C. A., and MERRINGTON, M. "Tables for Testing the Homogeneity of a Set of Variances," *Biometrika,* XXXIII (1943–46), 296–304.

CHAPTER VII

Tests of Hypotheses (2): The Analysis of Variance and Covariance

1. Introduction

In recent years a number of very useful statistical tools have been made available to the social researcher. Of these, perhaps the most important have been the analysis of variance and the analysis of covariance. These methods are more complex than most of those discussed in the last chapter. Only the relatively simple and common uses of the methods will be discussed. Further study of the methods by the social scientist is likely to be very rewarding.

2. The Analysis of Variance

A large number of research projects are concerned with determining whether one variable (V_1) "significantly affects" another variable (V_2); that is, whether changes in V_1 produce changes in V_2. It will be recalled (from chap. iii) that the traditional model for making such determinations consists of keeping all variables other than V_1 and V_2 at a fixed value, varying V_1, and observing changes in the value of V_2. There are several disadvantages to this traditional model even if we assume that all the pertinent variables other than V_1 and V_2 can be held constant. The use of this model may yield *unrealistic* results. That is, it may tell us that changes in V_1 are followed by changes in V_2 relative to a situation in which all the other pertinent variables have a specified fixed value. But outside the laboratory such a situation may never exist; that is, either the values of the other pertinent variables change or, if not, they remain constant at values other than the ones used in the laboratory. Suppose, for example, that we want to determine if one textbook produces better results than another. We could set up two "matched classes" in the same university, have the same teacher instruct both, etc. The results would enable us to evaluate the text only for *this* teacher, *this* university, *this* age group, etc.

One suggestion in this last illustration is to repeat the experiment for different teachers, different universities, etc. The procedure then becomes very lengthy and requires a good deal of effort, time, and money. In addition, it may still not yield usable results. Suppose, for example, that we want to determine whether a variable, V_3, is a function of variables V_1 and V_2. Two separate traditional experiments might be conducted: one to determine how V_3 varies for changes in V_2 while V_1 is held constant at some one value, and another to determine how V_3 varies for changes in V_1 while V_2 is held constant at some one value. From data obtained in this way it could not be inferred how V_3 changes for combined changes in V_1 and V_2 unless it were known that any possible effects V_1 and V_2 have on V_3 are independent. That is, V_1 and V_2 may *interact;* for example, they may tend to cancel out each other's effect. To determine whether or not this is the case, we would have to determine how V_3 changes for variations in V_1 relative to a number of different values of V_2. Hence the complexity of the experiment increases considerably.

It becomes obvious, then, that there would be a considerable advantage to a method which would simultaneously determine (*a*) if each of a set of variables (V_1, V_2, . . . , V_n) produces significant effects on another variable (V_x) and (*b*) if each of the variables independently affects V_x or interacts with other variables in the set. That is, to paraphrase R. A. Fisher, it is more desirable to ask nature many questions in one interview than to ask one question in each of a series of interviews.

This desire is as old as science, but only within the last few decades has an efficient method for satisfying it been available. The method is called the *analysis of variance*, or ANOVA, and it is in large part due to Fisher (7) and (8).

The analysis of variance has particular importance to the social sciences, since it is seldom possible in these sciences even approximately to hold all but one variable at a constant value. That is, even if it were desirable to do so, the social scientist can seldom manipulate his subjects and their environment so as to satisfy these conditions. For example, if he wants to use the same classroom for two different classes, the two classes cannot be given simultaneously, and hence the time variable has a different value for each class. This change may be accompanied by a change in the observed results. But, if the researcher can determine the extent of the effect on the results, he can adjust for it and need not be concerned with holding the time variable constant.

Suppose we have two pertinent independent variables, V_1 and V_2, and we are concerned with two values of each. Then there are four types of situations of concern to the researcher. These can be shown in a simple matrix on p. 231. The researcher may be able to find such situations already set up and hence not need to manipulate the variables. If he cannot find them, it may still be easier to produce the four situations of this type than to produce one or two of another type. For example, it would be impossible to have two classes meet at the same hour in the same room but quite simple to have them meet in the same room at different hours or in different rooms at the same hour. If, in such situations, we can determine the change in the observed results which accompany the changes in the independent variables, we can control the research situation, even though we cannot manipulate the variables.

		V_1	
		A	B
V_2	a	Aa	Ba
	b	Ab	Bb

The logic underlying the analysis of variance is not too complex, although the mathematics in which it is expressed is sometimes cumbersome. Consider the four-cell matrix given above. Suppose one observation is made in each cell; then there are three variances which could be estimated:

$\sigma_{V_1}^2$: the variance between the means of the columns, of which there are two.
$\sigma_{V_2}^2$: the variance between the means of the rows, of which there are two.
$\sigma_{V_3}^2$: the variance of the population of observations, of which there are four.

Hence, $\sigma_{V_1}^2$ represents the variance in the values of V_3 which is associated with changes in the variable V_1, and $\sigma_{V_2}^2$ represents the corresponding variance relative to V_2. If the sum of these two variances is not equal to the total variance, $\sigma_{V_3}^2$, then the difference can be attributed to the uncontrolled (or chance) variables. The portion of the total variance not accounted for by V_1 and V_2 is called the *residual* variance, σ_r^2. Then

$$\sigma_r^2 = \sigma_{V_3}^2 - (\sigma_{V_1}^2 + \sigma_{V_2}^2),$$

or

$$\sigma_{V_3}^2 = \sigma_{V_1}^2 + \sigma_{V_2}^2 + \sigma_r^2.$$

Suppose that $\sigma_{V_1}^2 = \sigma_r^2$. This would mean that controlled changes in V_1 are accompanied by no more variation than occurs by chance due to the uncontrolled variables. Hence, we would conclude that changes in V_1 are not accompanied by significant changes in V_3. If, on the other hand, $\sigma_{V_1}^2 \neq \sigma_r^2$, then the changes in V_3 accompanying changes in V_1 cannot be attributed to chance.

Now, what the analysis of variance does is the following: (1) It provides separate estimates of the variance in the observed results associated with changes in each controlled variable and an estimate of the variance associated with the chance variations in all the uncontrolled variables. (2) It provides a test to determine whether or not the controlled and chance variations are significantly different. (3) It provides a test to determine whether the variance associated with combinations of the controlled variables is different from what one would expect if these variables were independent.

This third aspect of the method is directed toward determining whether or not any of the controlled variables interact. Two controlled variables interact if the effect which one has on the dependent variable is itself dependent on the value of the other controlled variable. To take a prosaic example of inter-action, the amount of comfort or discomfort a person feels is dependent on temperature and humidity. But the effect of temperature and humidity on comfort are not independent. A small increase in temperature when the hu-midity is high may produce more discomfort than a greater rise in temperature when the humidity is lower. Conversely, the effect of changes in humidity on comfort depends on temperature.

If the analysis of variance indicates that the variance associated with changes in a controlled variable (V_1) is significantly different from the variance asso-ciated with the uncontrolled variables, it does not necessarily follow that V_1 produces changes in the dependent variable (V_x). V_1 may not be the producer of changes in V_x; in fact, it may be that V_x produces changes in V_1 or that V_1 and V_x are merely correlated. For example, if we observe that changes in school grades are accompanied by changes in amount of time devoted to study, we cannot determine from this alone which variable is the producer and which the product. Consider an example used earlier: let V_1 represent the amount of soot-fall in a neighborhood and let V_x represent the percentage of inhabitants of a neighborhood who have tuberculosis. The analysis of variance would show that the variance associated with V_1 is significantly larger than chance variation. Yet soot-fall does not produce tuberculosis. It will be recalled from the earlier discussion that tuberculosis is produced by dietary deficiency, among other things. Dietary deficiency is produced by low income. People with low income live in low-rent districts, and low rent is produced by soot-fall. This relationship can be shown diagrammatically as follows:

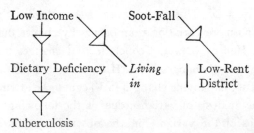

To establish that soot-fall produces tuberculosis, it would be necessary to show not only that variations in soot-fall are accompanied by variations in tuberculosis but also that changes in soot-fall *precede* changes in tuberculosis There is nothing in the analysis of variance to tell us this; such precedence must be established by other means.

There is one further misuse of the analysis of variance against which the reader should be warned. Different values of the variables tested must be used. There is little danger in not using different values of the variable if the variable is clearly quantitative; but, if it is qualitative and the underlying scale is not made explicit, an error may be made. Suppose we want to determine the effect of teachers on student performance. It would be necessary to test *different* teachers; to assure that the teachers selected are different, the scale along which the difference is established should be made explicit. It is common practice simply to draw a sample of teachers and assume that they are different. Sampling cannot assure this difference; hence, the teachers selected may be alike with respect to the critical variable. If the analysis of variance then showed that there was no "teacher effect," it would not be valid to apply this conclusion to the population of teachers from which the sample is drawn.

It should also be noted that conclusions based on the analysis of variance are applicable only to the range of values of the controlled variables which are used. If, for example, I.Q. is used as a controlled variable, and values between 80 and 110 are used, conclusions drawn from an analysis are applicable only to this range of values.

There are many different ways of conducting the analysis of variance; that is, there are many different designs for the use of the method. It is very much worth the social scientist's while to become familiar with as many of these designs as possible. Here we shall consider two of the more commonly used designs: the *factorial* and the *Latin square*.

2.1. Factorial Designs

A factorial design consists of a research plan in which the values of two or more controlled variables are grouped into two or more categories. A matrix is formed (as was done above) so that there is a cell for each possible combination of the different categories. Observations are made for each of the cells. Any number of variables may be involved, and any number of categories for each may be used, although the complexity of the analysis increases as does the number of variables and categories.

Only the two-variable factorial design will be considered here. The generalization to more than two variables is an easy one. We will first take up the case where only one observation is made in each cell and then the case where several observations are made in each cell.

2.1.1. Hypotheses and Assumptions in Factorial Designs

If we have a set of controlled variables, V_1, V_2, . . . , V_n, and a dependent variable V_x, then by use of the analysis of variance we can test the following hypotheses:

H_0: As V_1 changes (within a specified range, R_1), V_x does not change.
H_1: As V_1 changes (within R_1), V_x does change.
H_0': As V_2 changes (within R_2), V_x does not change.
H_1': As V_2 changes (within R_2), V_x does change.
Etc.

If it is known or assumed that changes in a variable, V_i, precede changes in V_x, then the above hypotheses may be formulated in the following form:

H_0: Changes in V_i (within R_i) do not produce changes in V_x.
H_1: Changes in V_i (within R_i) produce changes in V_x.

If repeated observations are made in each cell, we can test the following sets of hypotheses, in addition to the ones listed above:

H_0: V_1 and V_2 do not interact.
H_1: V_1 and V_2 interact.
H_0': V_2 and V_3 do not interact.
H_1': V_2 and V_3 interact.
.
.
.
H_0: V_1, V_2, and V_3 do not interact.
H_1: V_1, V_2, and V_3 interact.
Etc.

The assumptions underlying the analysis of variance are quite complex. We shall consider them only briefly here. For details see (3), (4), and (7). The assumptions for the two-variable factorial design are as follows:

(1) Any observation can be considered to be the sum of four components: (*a*) a constant value μ which is not affected by V_1 or V_2; (*b*) a value due to the possible influence of V_1; (*c*) a value due to the possible influence of V_2; and (*d*) a value due to the chance (or residual) variables.

(2*a*) The observations are all randomly drawn from normal populations. (2*b*) They all have the same variances. (If assumption [2*b*] is not justified, serious errors may result. Hence, if there is reason to doubt its validity, Test 20 can be used to check it.)

(3) The "residual effects" (errors due to the uncontrolled variables) are normally distributed, are independent, and have the same variance for all observations. Further, the mean of the residual effects is as-

sumed to be zero; that is, in the long run the negative and positive residual effects tend to cancel out.

Note on symbolism.—In the subsequent presentation of analysis of variance and covariance test procedures, it will be convenient to use X and Y to represent individual observations, $\overline{X}$ and $\overline{Y}$ to represent sample means, x to represent $(X - \overline{X})$, and y to represent $(Y - \overline{Y})$. The following subscripts will also be used:

I = Categories of V_1; that is, columns.

i = Categories of V_2; that is, rows.

j = Categories of V_3.

in = Interaction.

re = Residual.

st = Subtotal.

w = Within group.

The lack of a subscript represents a value pertinent to all the observations made on the variable.

2.1.2. Factorial Design, Two Variables, Single Observations

TEST 31 H_0: As V_1 changes (within R_1), V_3 does not change.
                H_1: As V_1 changes (within R_1), V_3 does change.
                H_0': As V_2 changes (within R_2), V_3 does not change.
                H_1': As V_2 changes (within R_2), V_3 does change.

KNOWN OR ASSUMED: See 2.1.1.

PROCEDURE:

(1) Prepare the following matrix:

			V_1			
		A	B	$\ldots$	K	Total
	a	X_{Aa}	X_{Ba}	$\ldots$	X_{Ka}	T_a
	b	$X_{\cdot b}$	X_{Bb}	$\ldots$	X_{Kb}	T_b
V_2	$\cdot$	$\cdot$	$\cdot$		$\cdot$	$\cdot$
	$\cdot$	$\cdot$	$\cdot$		$\cdot$	$\cdot$
	$\cdot$	$\cdot$	$\cdot$		$\cdot$	$\cdot$
	k	X_{Ak}	X_{Bk}	$\ldots$	X_{Kk}	T_k
Total		T_A	T_B	$\ldots$	T_K	T = Grand Total

(2) Compute the sum of the squares of deviations of column means $(\overline{X}_I)$ from the grand mean of all the observations $(\overline{X})$:

$$\Sigma \bar{x}_I^2 = \sum^{K} (\overline{X}_I - \overline{X})^2 = \frac{1}{k}(T_A^2 + T_B^2 + \ldots + T_K^2) - \frac{T^2}{Kk}.$$

(3) Compute the sum of the squares of deviations of row means $(\overline{X}_i)$ from the grand mean:

$$\Sigma \bar{x}_i^2 = \sum^{k} (\overline{X}_i - \overline{X})^2 = \frac{1}{K}(T_a^2 + T_b^2 + \ldots + T_k^2) - \frac{T^2}{Kk}.$$

(4) Compute the (total) sum of squares of the individual observations (X_{Ii}) from the grand mean:

$$\Sigma x^2 = \sum^{K} \sum^{k} (X_{Ii} - \overline{X})^2 = (X_{Aa}^2 + X_{Ab}^2 + \ldots + X_{Ak}^2 + X_{Ba}^2$$
$$+ \ldots + X_{Kk}^2) - \frac{T^2}{Kk}.$$

(5) Compute the residual sum of squares of deviations:

$$\Sigma x_{re}^2 = \Sigma x^2 - \Sigma \bar{x}_I^2 - \Sigma \bar{x}_i^2 = (4) - (3) - (2).$$

(6) Prepare the following table:

	Sum of Squares of Deviations	DF	Mean Square Deviation	F
Column Means...	(2)	$DF_I = K - 1$	$\bar{d}_I^2 = (2)/DF_I$	$F_I = \bar{d}_I^2/\bar{d}_{re}^2$
Row Means......	(3)	$DF_i = k - 1$	$\bar{d}_i^2 = (3)/DF_i$	$F_i = \bar{d}_i^2/\bar{d}_{re}^2$
Residual.......	(5)	$DF_{re} = DF - DF_I - DF_i$	$\bar{d}_{re}^2 = (5)/DF_{re}$	
Total......	(4)	$DF = Kk - 1$		

(7) Select from the appropriate part of Appendix Table VI the F_a value opposite DF_{re} and under DF_I.

(8) If $F_I \leq F_a$, accept H_0; otherwise accept H_1.

(9) Select from the appropriate part of Appendix Table VI the F_a value opposite DF_{re} and under DF_i.

(10) If $F_i \leq F_a$, accept H_0'; otherwise accept H_1'.

EXAMPLE: Four individuals $(A, B, C,$ and $D)$ with I.Q.'s of 80, 90, 100, and 110, respectively, are given the same problem on three successive days. Are the variations in I.Q. and number of previous tries accompanied by changes in the time required to solve the problem? The data are given below in step (1). Let $a = .05$.

H_0: Changes in I.Q. (between 80 and 110) are not accompanied by changes in time required to solve problem.

H_1: Changes in I.Q. (between 80 and 110) are accompanied by changes in time required to solve problem.

H_0': Changes in the number of previous tries (between 0 and 2) are not accompanied by changes in time required to solve problem.

H_1': Changes in the number of previous tries (between 0 and 2) are accompanied by changes in time required to solve problem.

Solution:

(1)

Number of Previous Tries	I.Q.				Total
	110	100	90	80	
0..........	2.6	2.8	2.3	3.1	10.8
1..........	2.1	2.2	2.5	2.0	8.8
2..........	1.8	2.2	1.9	2.2	8.1
Total...	6.5	7.2	6.7	7.3	27.7

(2) $\Sigma \bar{x}_I^2 = \frac{1}{3}(6.5^2 + 7.2^2 + 6.7^2 + 7.3^2) - \dfrac{27.7^2}{(4)(3)} = 0.15$.

(3) $\Sigma \bar{x}_i^2 = \frac{1}{4}(10.8^2 + 8.8^2 + 8.1^2) - \dfrac{27.7^2}{(4)(3)} = 0.98$.

(4) $\Sigma x^2 = (2.6^2 + 2.1^2 + 1.8^2 + \ldots + 2.2^2) - \dfrac{27.7^2}{(4)(3)} = 1.59$.

(5) $\Sigma x_{re}^2 = 1.59 - 0.15 - 0.98 = 0.46$.

(6)

	Sum of Squares of Deviations	DF	Mean Square Deviation	F
Column Means.	0.15	4−1=3	.15/3 = .05	$F_I = .05/.08 = .63$
Row Means....	0.98	3−1=2	.98/2 = .49	$F_i = .49/.08 = 6.13$
Residual......	0.46	11−3−2=6	.46/6 = .08	
Total.....	1.59	12−1=11		

(7) $F_{.05} = 4.7571$ ($DF_1 = 3, DF_2 = 6$).

(8) $F_1 < F_{.05}$ (i.e., $.63 < 4.7571$); therefore, accept H_0.

(9) $F_{.05} = 5.1433$ ($DF_1 = 2, DF_2 = 6$).

(10) $F_i > F_{.05}$ (i.e., $6.13 > 5.1433$); therefore, reject H_0' and accept H_1'.

2.1.3. Factorial Design, Two Variables, Equal Number of Repeated Observations in Each Cell

Since there are repeated observations in each cell, it is possible to compute an estimate of the variance within the cells; that is, of the within-group variance, σ_w^2. Furthermore, since possible effects of the controlled variables are canceled out in the computation of this estimate, it must be produced by the uncontrolled variables. Now suppose it is assumed that there is no within-group variance; then the observations within each cell can be treated as a single observation (i.e., their sum can be treated as a single observation). An estimate of the variance of these sums (the subtotal variance, σ_{st}^2) can be computed in the same manner as the total variance was estimated in the last test. The column variance (σ_l^2) and row variance (σ_i^2) can also be estimated as in the last test. Now the difference $\sigma_{st}^2 - \sigma_l^2 - \sigma_i^2$ cannot be taken to be the variance due to the uncontrolled variables, since this was canceled out by treating only the cell sums. Therefore, it can be due only to the interaction between the controlled variables. The interaction variance, σ_{in}^2, can then be defined as follows:

$$\sigma_{in}^2 = \sigma_{st}^2 - \sigma_l^2 - \sigma_i^2 .$$

Returning to the original observations, the variance for all the observations (i.e., the total variance σ^2) can be estimated. The difference between the total and subtotal variances must be due to the uncontrolled variables; that is, it is the within-group variance σ_w^2. Hence,

$$\sigma_w^2 = \sigma^2 - \sigma_{st}^2 .$$

Once estimates for these variances are obtained, their significance can be determined by the use of the F statistic as in the last test.

TEST 32 H_0: As V_1 changes (within R_1), V_3 does not change.

H_1: As V_1 changes (within R_1), V_3 does change.

H_0': As V_2 changes (within R_2), V_3 does not change.

H_1': As V_2 changes (within R_2), V_3 does change.

H_0'': There is no interaction between V_1 and V_2.

H_1'': There is interaction between V_1 and V_2.

KNOWN OR ASSUMED: See 2.1.1.

PROCEDURE:

(1) Prepare the following matrix:

	A	B	$\ldots$	K
a	X_{Aa1} X_{Aa2} . . . X_{Aan}	X_{Ba1} X_{Ba2} . . . X_{Ban}	$\ldots$ $\ldots$ $\ldots$	X_{Ka1} X_{Ka2} . . . X_{Kan}
b	X_{Ab1} X_{Ab2} . . . X_{Abn}	X_{Bb1} X_{Bb2} . . . X_{Bbn}	$\ldots$ $\ldots$ $\ldots$	X_{Kb1} X_{Kb2} . . . X_{Kbn}
.	.	.	.	.
.	.	.		.
.	.	.		.
k	X_{Ak1} X_{Ak2} . . . X_{Akn}	X_{Bk1} X_{Bk2} . . . X_{Bkn}	$\ldots$ $\ldots$ $\ldots$	X_{Kk1} X_{Kk2} . . . X_{Kkn}

(2) Total the observations in each cell and prepare the following matrix:

	A	B	$\ldots$	K	Total
a	T_{Aa}	T_{Ba}	$\ldots$	T_{Ka}	T_a
b	T_{Ab}	T_{Bb}	$\ldots$	T_{Kb}	T_b
.	.	.		.	.
.	.	.		.	.
.	.	.		.	.
k	T_{Ak}	T_{Bk}	$\ldots$	T_{Kk}	T_k
Total	T_A	T_B	$\ldots$	T_K	T

(3) Compute the sum of squares of deviations of column means from $\overline{X}$:

$$\Sigma \bar{x}_I^2 = \frac{1}{kn}(T_A^2 + T_B^2 + \ldots + T_K^2) - \frac{T^2}{Kkn}.$$

(4) Compute the sum of squares of deviations of row means from $\overline{X}$:

$$\Sigma \bar{x}_i^2 = \frac{1}{Kn}(T_a^2 + T_b^2 + \ldots + T_k^2) - \frac{T^2}{Kkn}.$$

(5) Compute the sum of squares of deviations of all the observations from $\overline{X}$:

$$\Sigma x^2 = (X^2_{Aa1} + X^2_{Aa2} + \ldots + X^2_{Kkn}) - \frac{T^2}{Kkn}.$$

(6) Compute the sum of squares of deviations of subtotals from $\overline{X}$:

$$\Sigma x^2_{st} = \frac{1}{n}(T^2_{Aa} + T^2_{Ab} + \ldots + T^2_{Kk}) - \frac{T^2}{Kkn}.$$

(7) Compute the interaction sum of squares:

$$\Sigma x^2_{in} = \Sigma x^2_{st} - \Sigma \bar{x}^2_I - \Sigma \bar{x}^2_i = (6) - (3) - (4).$$

(8) Compute the with in-group sum of squares:

$$\Sigma x^2_w = \Sigma x^2 - \Sigma x^2_{st} = (5) - (6).$$

(9) Prepare the following table:

	Sum of Squares	DF	Mean Square	F
Column Means.....	(3)	$DF_I = K-1$	$\bar{d}^2_I = (3)/DF_I$	$F_I = \bar{d}^2_I/\bar{d}^2_w$ *
Row Means........	(4)	$DF_i = k-1$	$\bar{d}^2_i = (4)/DF_i$	$F_i = \bar{d}^2_i/\bar{d}^2_w$ *
Interaction.......	(7)	$DF_{in} = (DF_I)(DF_i)$	$\bar{d}^2_{in} = (7)/DF_{in}$	$F_{in} = \bar{d}^2_{in}/\bar{d}^2_w$
Subtotal.........	(6)	$DF_{st} = Kk-1$		
Within Groups...	(8)	$DF_w = DF - DF_{st}$	$\bar{d}^2_w = (8)/DF_w$	
Total.........	(5)	$DF = Kkn-1$		

* In practice, the value of F_I and F_i are frequently computed by taking $\bar{d}^2_I/\bar{d}^2_{in}$ and $\bar{d}^2_i/\bar{d}^2_{in}$ rather than as is done in the table. For a discussion of the advantages of so doing see (10: Secs. 14.6, 14.9, and 14.10).

(10) Select from the appropriate part of Appendix Table VI the F_a value opposite DF_w and under DF_I.

(11) If $F_I \leq F_a$, accept H_0; otherwise accept H_1.

(12) Select from the appropriate part of Appendix Table VI the F_a value opposite DF_w and under DF_i.

(13) If $F_i \leq F_a$; accept H'_0; otherwise accept H'_1.

(14) Select from the appropriate part of Appendix Table VI the F_a value opposite DF_w and under DF_{in}.

(15) If $F_{in} \leq F_a$, accept H''_0; otherwise accept H''_1.

If the interaction is significant, this may be due to any one or more of the following factors:

    (a) The two controlled variables are together producing an effect neither would produce separately.

    (b) There is an important uncontrolled variable which should be taken into account, a variable which is changing in some systematic way from cell to cell.

    (c) The samples in the cells are not drawn at random.

    (d) There is no interaction, and the apparent significance is a result of Type I error.

Possibilities (b) and (c) should be thoroughly investigated by a re-examination of the research model and the sampling procedure. A duplication of the research with the same result would reduce the possibility of (d) being the case.

EXAMPLE:* Suppose we have the set of data shown in step (1) below. Test the hypotheses given above at the .05 significance level.

Solution:

    (1)

		A	B	C
a		2	0	3
		5	1	4
		3	0	2
b		7	6	8
		6	5	6
		6	3	5

    (2)

	A	B	C	Total
a	10	1	9	20
b	19	14	19	52
Total	29	15	28	72

$$(3)\ \ \Sigma \bar{x}_I^2 = \frac{1}{(2)(3)}(29^2 + 15^2 + 28^2) - \frac{72^2}{(3)(2)(3)} = 20.33\,.$$

$$(4)\ \ \Sigma \bar{x}_i^2 = \frac{1}{(3)(3)}(20^2 + 52^2) - \frac{72^2}{(3)(2)(3)} = 56.89\,.$$

$$(5)\ \ \Sigma x^2 = 2^2 + 5^2 + \ldots + 5^2 - \frac{72^2}{(3)(2)(3)} = 96.00\,.$$

$$(6)\ \ \Sigma x_{st}^2 = \tfrac{1}{3}(10^2 + 19^2 + \ldots + 19^2) - \frac{72^2}{(3)(2)(3)} = 78.67\,.$$

* This example is adopted from one given by Dixon and Massey (4:134–37).

(7) $\Sigma x_{in}^2 = 78.67 - 20.33 - 56.89 = 1.45$.

(8) $\Sigma x_w^2 = 96.00 - 78.67 = 17.33$.

(9)

	Sum of Squares	DF	Mean Square	F
Column Means....	20.33	2	10.17	$F_I = 10.17/1.44 = 7.06$
Row Means.......	56.89	1	56.89	$F_i = 56.89/1.44 = 39.51$
Interaction.......	1.45	2	.72	$F_{in} = .72/1.44 = .50$
Subtotal........	78.67	5		
Within Groups	17.33	12	1.44	
Total........	96.00	17		

(10) $F_{.05} = 3.8853$ (DF$_1$ = 2, DF$_2$ = 12).

(11) $F_I > F_{.05}$ (i.e., 7.06 > 3.8853); therefore, reject H_0 and accept H_1; that is, changes in V_1 are accompanied by changes in V_3.

(12) $F_{.05} = 4.7472$ (DF$_1$ = 1, DF$_2$ = 12).

(13) $F_i > F_{.05}$ (i.e., 39.51 > 4.7472); therefore, reject H_0' and accept H_1'; that is, changes in V_2 are accompanied by changes in V_3.

(14) $F_{.05} = 3.8853$ (DF$_1$ = 2, DF$_2$ = 12).

(15) $F_{in} < F_{.05}$ (i.e., .50 < 3.8853); therefore, accept H_0''; that is, there is no significant interaction between V_1 and V_2.

Note.—If there is only one variable of classification, the test procedure is similar to that just described except for a few minor changes. Only Column Means, Within Groups, and Total Sum of Squares of Deviations are computed. Column Means Sum of Squares is equal to

$$\sum_{}^{K} \frac{T_I}{n_I} - \frac{T^2}{\sum\limits^{K} n_I},$$

where n_I is the number of observations in the Ith column. Total Sum of Squares is computed as above. Within Groups Sum of Squares is equal to the difference between Column Means and Total Sum of Squares. DF$_w$ is equal to DF $-$ DF$_I$, where DF$_I = K - 1$, and DF $= \sum\limits^{K} n_I - 1$.

2.2. Latin Square and Greco-Latin Square Designs

Suppose we have three variables (V_1, V_2, and V_3) and three values of each which we want to incorporate into a factorial design. To do so we would have to construct a three-dimensional matrix with $3 \times 3 \times 3$, or 27 cells. If we had three variables and four values of each we would require a $4 \times 4 \times 4$, or 64 cells.

It is frequently impractical to use so many cells because of the large number of observations required and the many different situations which must be found or constructed. To overcome this difficulty, a modification in the factorial design was developed—one which requires a smaller number of cells but which yields a larger error than does the usual factorial design. This method is called the *Latin Square* design.

Let A, B, and C represent the three categories of V_1; a, b, and c represent the three categories of V_2; and 1, 2, and 3 represent the three categories of V_3. Then we can set up a nine-cell matrix as follows:

	A	B	C
a	1	2	3
b	2	3	1
c	3	1	2

The meaning of this matrix becomes clear by illustration. Suppose we want to measure the performance of groups of three different sizes (A, B, and C) doing the same task under three different sets of conditions (a, b, and c). The order in which the groups do the tasks may affect their performance. Hence, the order may be made the third controlled variable. Group A will first do the task under condition a, then b, and then c. Group B will first do the task under condition c, then a, and then b. Group C will first do the task under condition b, then c, and then a. An analysis can now be made which determines the effect of the order and which permits the difference between groups and conditions to be determined independently of order. The procedure for doing so is similar to that used in a factorial design and is given below.

Notice that in the above matrix each number appears in each column and each row only once. The arrangement shown is not the only one which has this property; there are a number of others, any of which would do equally as well. For example:

	A	B	C
a	3	1	2
b	2	3	1
c	1	2	3

Note also that the number of categories of each variable is the same.

Suppose that in the above example we also want each group to use a different one of three instruments (α, β, and γ) on each trial. A fourth variable has been introduced. The fourth variable can be incorporated into the above design by a simple generalization. The generalized method is called a *Greco-Latin Square* design. The revised matrix would look as follows:

	A	B	C
a	1α	2β	3γ
b	2γ	$3a$	1β
c	3β	1γ	$2a$

Note that none of the Greek letters appears more than once in any row or column or more than once in combination with the same number. There are many other usable arrangements which would also satisfy these conditions.

The procedure of analysis in both methods is very similar, hence the procedure for the Greco-Latin Square will not be given. For details see (4:x).

TEST 33 (LATIN SQUARE)

H_0: As V_1 changes (within R_1), V_4 does not change.
H_1: As V_1 changes (within R_1), V_4 does change.
H_0': As V_2 changes (within R_2), V_4 does not change.
H_1': As V_2 changes (within R_2), V_4 does change.
H_0'': As V_3 changes (within R_3), V_4 does not change.
H_1'': As V_3 changes (within R_3), V_4 does change.

KNOWN OR ASSUMED: Same as in 2.1 except for generalization to three variables.

PROCEDURE:

(1) Prepare the following matrix:

		V_1			
		A	B	. . .	K	Total
V_2	a	X_{Aa1}	X_{Ba2}	. . .	X_{Kam} *	T_a
	b	X_{Ab2}	X_{Bb3}	. . .	X_{Kb1}	T_b
	.	.	.		.	.
	.	.	.		.	.
	.	.	.		.	.
	k	X_{Akm}	X_{Bk1}	. . .	$X_{Kk(m-1)}$	T_k
	Total	T_A	T_B	. . .	T_K	T

* m = the number of categories of V_3. Note that $K = k = m$.

(2) Compute

$$T_1 = X_{Aa1} + X_{Bk1} + \ldots + X_{Kb1}.$$
$$T_2 = X_{Ab2} + X_{Ba2} + \ldots + X_{Kc2}.$$
$$\vdots$$
$$T_m = X_{Akm} + \ldots + X_{Kcm}.$$

(3) Compute

$$\Sigma \bar{x}_I^2 = \frac{1}{k}(T_A^2 + T_B^2 + \ldots + T_K^2) - \frac{T^2}{Kk}.$$

(4) Compute

$$\Sigma \bar{x}_i^2 = \frac{1}{K}(T_a^2 + T_b^2 + \ldots + T_k^2) - \frac{T^2}{Kk}.$$

(5) Compute

$$\Sigma \bar{x}_j^2 = \frac{1}{m}(T_1^2 + T_2^2 + \ldots + T_m^2) - \frac{T^2}{Kk},$$

where j represents any category of V_3.

(6) Compute

$$\Sigma x^2 = X_{Aa1}^2 + X_{Ab2}^2 + \ldots + X_{Kk(m-1)}^2 - \frac{T^2}{Kk}.$$

(7) Compute

$$\Sigma x_{re}^2 = \Sigma x^2 - \Sigma \bar{x}_I^2 - \Sigma \bar{x}_i^2 - \Sigma \bar{x}_j^2.$$

(8) Prepare the following table:

	Sum of Squares	DF	Mean Square	F
Column Means.....	(3)	$DF_I = K-1$	$\bar{d}_I^2 = (3)/DF_I$	$F_I = \bar{d}_I^2/\bar{d}_{re}^2$
Row Means........	(4)	$DF_i = k-1$	$\bar{d}_i^2 = (4)/DF_i$	$F_i = \bar{d}_i^2/\bar{d}_{re}^2$
V_3 Means.........	(5)	$DF_j = m-1$	$\bar{d}_j^2 = (5)/DF_j$	$F_j = \bar{d}_j^2/\bar{d}_{re}^2$
Residual.........	(7)	$DF_{re} = DF - DF_I - DF_i - DF_j$	$\bar{d}_{re}^2 = (7)/DF_{re}$	
Total.........	(6)	$DF = Kk-1$		

(9) Select from the appropriate part of Appendix Table VI the F_a value opposite DF_{re} and under DF_I.

(10) If $F_I \leq F_a$, accept H_0; otherwise accept H_1.

(11) If $F_i \leq F_a$, accept H_0'; otherwise accept H_1'.

(12) If $F_j \leq F_a$, accept H_0''; otherwise accept H_1''.

EXAMPLE: Suppose a random selection of three groups of 5, 10, and 15 Boy Scouts is made from the Boy Scouts in a certain city. They are given the same task to perform at three different times—morning, afternoon, and night. In this case, changes in the three variables (size of group, number of previous trials, and time of day) precede the performance of the job. Then, given the design and data shown below, test the following hypotheses at the .05 significance level:

H_0: Changes in the size of the group (between 5 and 15) do not produce changes in performance time.

H_1: Changes in the size of the group (between 5 and 15) do produce changes in performance time.

H_0': Changes in the time of day do not produce changes in performance.

H_1': Changes in the time of day do produce changes in performance.

H_0'': Changes in the number of previous trials (between 0 and 2) do not produce changes in performance time.

H_1'': Changes in the number of previous trials (between 0 and 2) do produce changes in performance time.

Solution:

(1)

TIME OF TEST	SIZE OF GROUP			TOTAL
	15	10	5	
9:00 A.M.	2(0)*	6(1)	1(2)	9
3:00 P.M.	1(1)	7(2)	6(0)	14
9:00 P.M.	7(2)	1(0)	9(1)	17
Total	10	14	16	40

* Numbers in parentheses indicate number of preceding trials.

(2) $T_0 = 2 + 1 + 6 = 9.$

$T_1 = 1 + 6 + 9 = 16.$

$T_2 = 7 + 7 + 1 = 15.$

(3) $\Sigma \bar{x}_I^2 = \frac{1}{3} (10^2 + 14^2 + 16^2) - \frac{40^2}{3^2} = 6.22.$

(4) $\Sigma \bar{x}_i^2 = \frac{1}{3} (9^2 + 14^2 + 17^2) - \frac{40^2}{3^2} = 10.89.$

(5) $\Sigma \bar{x}_j^2 = \frac{1}{3} (9^2 + 16^2 + 15^2) - \frac{40^2}{3^2} = 9.55.$

(6) $\Sigma x^2 = 2^2 + 1^2 + \ldots + 9^2 - \frac{40^2}{3^2} = 80.22.$

(7) $\Sigma x_{re}^2 = 80.22 - 6.22 - 10.89 - 9.55 = 53.56.$

(8)

	Sum of Squares	DF	Mean Square	F
Column Means...	6.22	2	3.11	$F_I = 3.11/26.78 = .1161$
Row Means......	10.89	2	5.45	$F_i = 5.45/26.78 = .2035$
V_3 Means........	9.55	2	4.78	$F_j = 4.78/26.78 = .1785*$
Residual........	53.56	2	26.78	
Total.......	80.22	8		

* Actually, if a computed F value is less than 1, no test need be run, unless one tests to determine if the residual is significant compared to the other means; i.e., is there too much conformity between columns, rows, or V_3 categories? If there is, then there may be a constraining influence on the controlled variables.

(9) $F_{.05} = 19.00$ (DF$_1$ = 2, DF$_2$ = 2).

(10) $F_I < F_{.05}$ (i.e., .1161 < 19.00); therefore, accept H_0.

(11) $F_i < F_{.05}$ (i.e., .2035 < 19.00); therefore, accept H_0'.

(12) $F_j < F_{.05}$ (i.e., .1785 < 19.00); therefore, accept H_0''.

3. The Analysis of Covariance

The analysis of covariance is an extremely useful extension of the analysis of variance. It is also largely due to R. A. Fisher. This method is applicable to situations in which a variable affects the observed results but in which the subjects tested cannot be assigned equal values of that variable prior to making the observations. For example, suppose that "initial ability" conditions the observed performance of a set of subjects but that the subjects cannot be selected beforehand so that they have equal "initial ability." If, during the research, one can determine each subject's initial performance, then the observed results can be adjusted for this source of variation. Or suppose a source of variation arises during the course of the research, one which was not anticipated but is recognized once it occurs. During the course of the research, for example, it might become apparent that the performances of the subjects are affected by their education. If we can determine the amount of education they have had, then by use of the analysis of covariance the results can be adjusted for this source of variation.

Suppose that we want to determine whether values of a variable (Y) change for various values of a controlled variable (V_1). Suppose further that there is another variable (X) which is suspected of having an effect on Y, but values of X cannot be assigned before the research has begun. The values of X, however, can be determined for each Y observation. The problem, then, is to cancel out the effect of X on Y so that the relationship between V_1 and Y can be determined independently of any effect that X may have on Y.

Let V_1 be broken into three categories, A, B, and C. Then, assuming four paired observations for each V_1 value, the data obtained can be arranged as follows:

	V_1							
	A		B		C			
	X	Y	X	Y	X	Y		
	2	8	4	10	0	6		
	1	7	3	11	2	5		
	0	7	1	6	4	8		
	1	10	4	13	2	5	T_X	T_Y
Totals	4	32	12	40	8	24	24	96
Means	1	8	3	10	2	6	2	8
							$\bar{X}$	$\bar{Y}$

These data can be graphed in such a way as to let the abscissa represent X values, and the ordinate represent Y values, and the point of origin represent $\bar{X}$ and $\bar{Y}$ (Fig. 29). A similar plot can be made separately for each class, A, B, and C (Fig. 30). The three plots obtained in Figure 30 can be superimposed to obtain the plot shown in Figure 31. By so doing, the means of each X column have been equated, and so have the means of each Y column. Now the regression line of Y on X can be computed for Figure 29 and Figure 31. The regression coefficient of the former (b_t) is applicable to the observations taken as a whole.

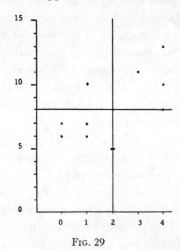

FIG. 29

The regression coefficient of the latter (b_w) is the within-group regression, since the plot in Figure 31 has canceled out between group variance.

If the dispersion about the regression line in Figure 31 is significantly less than in Figure 29, then equating the means of the subgroups has had a significant effect on the data. From this it can be inferred that the means of the V_1 categories (μ_A, μ_B, and μ_C) are significantly different in the original data. Hence it can be concluded that changes in the value of V_1 are accompanied by changes in Y.

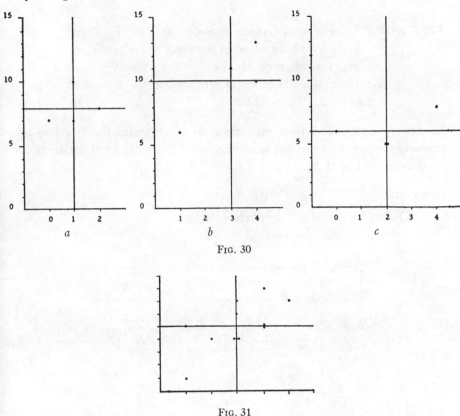

FIG. 30

FIG. 31

The computational procedure of the analysis of covariance is directed toward obtaining (a) an estimate of the variances about the regression line with coefficient b_t and (b) an estimate of the variance about the regression line with coefficient b_w. The difference, $b_t - b_w$, is attributable to the dispersion of the means whose effect is canceled out in computing b_w. Then the following F ratio is determined:

$$\frac{b_t - b_w}{b_w}.$$

If this is significant, one can infer that the contribution to the variance by the column means is significant relative to the chance (within-group) variance.

The analysis of covariance can be used where there are several controlled variables, though it will be illustrated here only for the one-variable-of-classification case. It can also be applied where there is more than one observation per cell. Furthermore, it can also be used where there are several variables like X in the above example. For details on the method see (4:xiii), (5:333 ff.), and (9:216 ff.).

TEST 34 H_0: There is no difference in mean value for Y values which have been adjusted (by the Y value predicted from the regression equation: $\bar{Y} + b_w[X - \bar{X}]$).

H_1: There is a difference in mean value for Y values which have been adjusted.

KNOWN OR ASSUMED: Within each group of observations the Y values are normally distributed about the same regression line with equal variances for the different values of X.

PROCEDURE:

(1) Prepare the following matrix:

V_1								
A		*B*		. . .	*K*			
X_{A1}	$Y_{\cdot 1}$	X_{B1}	Y_{B1}	. . .	X_{K1}	Y_{K1}		
X_{A2}	Y_{A2}	X_{B2}	Y_{B2}	. . .	X_{K2}	Y_{K2}		
.	.	.	.		.	.		
.	.	.	.		.	.		
.	.	.	.		.	.		
$X_{\cdot n}$	Y_{An}	X_{Bn}	$Y_{Bn}\cdot$	. . .	X_{Kn}	Y_{Kn}		
Total T_{x_A}	T_{Y_A}	T_{x_B}	T_{Y_B}	: . .	T_{x_K}	T_{Y_K}	T_X	T_Y

Y_i are observations of the variable of primary interest.

(2) Compute the total sum of products, $\displaystyle\sum_i \sum_j (X_{ij} - \bar{X})(Y_{ij} - \bar{Y})$:

$$\Sigma xy = (X_{A1})(Y_{A1}) + (X_{A2})(Y_{A2}) + \ldots + (X_{Kn})(Y_{Kn}) - \frac{(T_X)(T_Y)}{Kn},$$

where $x = (X - \bar{X})$ and $y = (Y - \bar{Y})$.

(3) Compute the among-means sum of products, $n\Sigma(\overline{X}_i - \overline{X})(\overline{Y}_i - \overline{Y})$:

$$\Sigma\bar{x}_i\bar{y}_i = \frac{1}{n}[(T_{X_A})(T_{Y_A}) + (T_{X_B})(T_{Y_B}) + \ldots + (T_{X_K})(T_{Y_K})] - \frac{(T_X)(T_Y)}{Kn}.$$

(4) Compute the within-group sum of products, $\displaystyle\sum_i \sum_j (X_{ij} - \overline{X}_i)$

$\times (Y_{ij} - \overline{Y}_i)$:
$$\Sigma(xy)_w = \Sigma xy - \Sigma\bar{x}_i\bar{y}_i.$$

(5) Compute the total sum of squares (as in the analysis of variance):

(a) $\Sigma x^2 = (X_{A1})^2 + (X_{A2})^2 + \ldots + (X_{Kn})^2 - \dfrac{T_X^2}{Kn}.$

(b) $\Sigma y^2 = (Y_{A1})^2 + (Y_{A2})^2 + \ldots + (Y_{Kn})^2 - \dfrac{T_Y^2}{Kn}.$

(6) Compute the sum of squares of (column) means (as in the analysis of variance):

(a) $\Sigma\bar{x}_i^2 = \dfrac{1}{n}(T_{X_A}^2 + T_{X_B}^2 + \ldots + T_{X_K}^2) - \dfrac{T_X^2}{Kn}.$

(b) $\Sigma\bar{y}_i^2 = \dfrac{1}{n}(T_{Y_A}^2 + T_{Y_B}^2 + \ldots + T_{Y_K}^2) - \dfrac{T_Y^2}{Kn}.$

(7) Compute the sum of squares within groups:

(a) $\Sigma x_w^2 = \Sigma x^2 - \Sigma\bar{x}_i^2 = (5a) - (6a).$

(b) $\Sigma y_w^2 = \Sigma y^2 - \Sigma\bar{y}_i^2 = (5b) - (6b).$

(8) Compute the total sum of squares about regression line, $\Sigma(Y - Y_X)^2$:

$$\Sigma y'^2 = \Sigma y^2 - \frac{(\Sigma xy)^2}{\Sigma x^2} = (5b) - \frac{(2)^2}{(5a)}.$$

(9) Compute the sum of squares about regression line for within groups:

$$\Sigma y_w'^2 = \Sigma y_w^2 - \frac{[\Sigma(xy)_w]^2}{\Sigma x_w^2} = (7b) - \frac{(4)^2}{(7a)}.$$

(10) Compute the sum of squares of means about regression line:
$$\Sigma\bar{y}_i'^2 = \Sigma y'^2 - \Sigma y_w'^2 = (8) - (9).$$

(11) Prepare the following table:

	DF	Σx^2	Σxy	Σy^2	DF'	$\Sigma y'^2$	Mean Square
Among Means	$K-1$	(6a)	(3)	(6b)	$\mathrm{DF}'_w = K(n-1)-1$	(10)	$\bar{a}_i^2 = (10)/\mathrm{DF}'_i$
Within Groups	$K(n-1)$	(7a)	(4)	(7b)	$\mathrm{DF}_w = K(K-1)-1$	(9)	$\bar{a}_w^2 = (9)/\mathrm{DF}'_w$
Total......	$Kn-1$	(5a)	(2)	(5b)	$\mathrm{DF}' = Kn-2$	(8)	

(12) Compute

$$F_i = \frac{\bar{d}_i^2}{\bar{d}_w^2}.$$

(13) Select from the appropriate part of Appendix Table VI the F_a value opposite DF_w' and under DF_i'.

(14) If $F_i \leq F_a$ accept H_0; otherwise accept H_1.

EXAMPLE: Using the data given in step (1) below, test at the .025 significance level the following hypotheses:

H_0: There is no significant difference in mean value for Y values which have been adjusted.

H_1: There is a significant difference in mean value for Y values which have been adjusted.

Solution:

(1)

	V_1						
	A		B		C		
	X	Y	X	Y	X	Y	
	2	8	4	10	0	6	
	1	7	3	11	2	5	
	0	7	1	6	4	8	
	1	10	4	13	2	5	T_X T_Y
Total	4	32	12	40	8	24	24 96

(2) $\Sigma xy = (2)(8) + (1)(7) + \ldots + (2)(5) - \dfrac{(24)(96)}{(3)(4)} = 24$.

(3) $\Sigma \bar{x}_i \bar{y}_i = \frac{1}{4} [(4)(32) + (12)(40) + (8)(24)] - \dfrac{(24)(96)}{(3)(4)} = 8$.

(4) $\Sigma(xy)_w = 24 - 8 = 16$.

(5) (a) $\Sigma x^2 = 2^2 + 1^2 + \ldots + 2^2 - \dfrac{24^2}{(3)(4)} = 24$.

(b) $\Sigma y^2 = 8^2 + 7^2 + \ldots + 5^2 - \dfrac{96^2}{(3)(4)} = 70$.

(6) (a) $\Sigma \bar{x}_i^2 = \frac{1}{4} (4^2 + 12^2 + 8^2) - \dfrac{24^2}{(3)(4)} = 8$.

(b) $\Sigma \bar{y}_i^2 = \frac{1}{4} (32^2 + 40^2 + 24^2) - \dfrac{96^2}{(3)(4)} = 32$.

(7) (a) $\Sigma x_w^2 = 24 - 8 = 16$.

    (b) $\Sigma y_w^2 = 70 - 32 = 38$.

(8) $\Sigma y'^2 = 70 - \dfrac{24^2}{24} = 46.00$.

(9) $\Sigma y_w'^2 = 38 - \dfrac{8^2}{9} = 30.89$.

(10) $\Sigma \bar{y}_i'^2 = 46.00 - 30.89 = 15.11$.

(11)

	DF	Σx^2	Σxy	Σy^2	DF′	$\Sigma y'^2$	Mean Square
Among Means....	2	8	8	32	2	15.11	7.56
Within Groups...	9	16	16	38	8	30.89	3.86
Total........	11	24	24	70	10	46.00	

(12) $F_i = 7.56/3.86 = 1.96$.

(13) $F_{.025} = 6.0595$ (where $DF_1 = 2$, $DF_2 = 8$).

(14) $F_i < F_{.025}$ (i.e., $1.96 < 6.0595$); therefore, accept H_0.

This test can also be conducted for unadjusted Y values. In this case,

$$\bar{d}_i^2 = 32/2 = 16, \text{ and } \bar{d}_w^2 = 38/9 = 4.22.$$

Then $F_i = 16/4.22 = 3.79$. This result would also be insignificant, since $F_{.025} = 5.7147$, where $DF_1 = 2$ and $DF_2 = 9$.

DISCUSSION TOPICS

1. In what types of social research might the analysis of variance be particularly useful? Give examples. The analysis of covariance? Give examples.

2. Once the analysis of variance has shown that the effect of a variable on the observations is significant, how could one go about determining the extent to which that effect varies for changing values of the variable?

3. How can one "cancel out" the effect of a variable by using the analysis of variance? By using the analysis of covariance?

4. Design an experiment using the analysis of variance to determine which of three textbooks on the same subject is the best.

5. Why is there an equal number of categories of each variable in the Latin Square design? How many possible arrangements are there if each variable is broken into three categories?

6. Define "interaction" and "within-group variance."

7. In your own words explain the logic underlying (a) the analysis of variance and (b) the analysis of covariance.

EXERCISES

1. Three equivalent experimental groups (A, B, and C) which have been trained for different lengths of time are given the same job to perform under two measurably different sets of conditions (a and b). The number of minutes required to do the job is determined for each case:

	A	B	C
a	45	37	51
b	29	36	42

Do the training periods and conditions affect the performance time? Let $a = .05$

2. Given the following set of data, determine (a) if changes in either of the two variables are accompanied by changes in the variable observed and (b) if the two variables interact. Let $a = .01$.

	A	B	C
a	7 3	31 40	20 27
b	10 16	37 33	29 31
c	8 21	48 52	50 45
d	24 20	60 59	31 27

3. Suppose four individuals (A, B, C, and D) with different levels of educational attainment take each of four different examinations (a, b, c, and d). The results and the order in which taken are indicated below. Is there a significant difference between the individuals? Is a change in tests accompanied by a change in scores? Does the order in which they are taken make a difference? Let $a = .10$.

	A	B	C	D
a	25(1)	7(2)	22(3)	10(4)
b	20(2)	3(3)	15(4)	19(1)
c	18(3)	0(4)	32(1)	23(2)
d	13(4)	9(1)	26(2)	23(3)

4. Three groups are formed. Each consists of five randomly selected individuals from a certain population. The members of each group are given the test. The number of mistakes made by each individual is recorded in the X column below. The

groups are then placed in environments A, B, and C, which differ with respect to noise level. They are given the same test again. The number of mistakes is recorded in the Y column below. Does the noise level produce a significant effect on the number of mistakes made? Let $a = .05$.

A		B		C	
X	Y	X	Y	X	Y
13	8	6	9	10	10
10	8	8	7	14	13
8	5	2	6	11	12
9	3	4	3	8	7
5	4	4	6	15	13

SUGGESTED READINGS

For introductory treatments of the analysis of variance and covariance see Dixon and Massey (4), Johnson (9), and, in particular, Edwards (5), which has a rather extensive discussion.

More advanced treatments are found in Cochran and Cox (3), Mann (10), and Mood (11).

REFERENCES AND BIBLIOGRAPHY

1. CHURCHMAN, C. W. *Statistical Manual: Methods of Making Experimental Inferences.* Philadelphia: Pittman-Dunn Laboratory, Frankford Arsenal, 1951.
2. COCHRAN, W. G. "Some Consequences When the Assumptions for the Analysis of Variance Are Not Satisfied," *Biometrics*, III (1947), 22–38.
3. COCHRAN, W. G., and COX, G. M. *Experimental Designs.* New York: John Wiley & Sons, 1950.
4. DIXON, W. J., and MASSEY, F. J., JR. *Introduction to Statistical Analysis.* New York: McGraw-Hill Book Co., 1951.
5. EDWARDS, A. L. *Experimental Designs in Psychological Research.* New York: Rinehart & Co., 1950.
6. EISENHART, CHURCHILL. "The Assumptions Underlying the Analysis of Variance," *Biometrics*, III (1947), 1–21.
7. FISHER, R. A. *Statistical Methods for Research Workers.* London: Oliver & Boyd, Ltd., 1948.
8. ———. *The Design of Experiments.* London: Oliver & Boyd, Ltd., 1949.
9. JOHNSON, P. O. *Statistical Methods in Research.* New York: Prentice-Hall, Inc., 1949.
10. MANN, H. B. *Analysis and Design of Experiments.* New York: Dover Publications, Inc., 1949.
11. MOOD, A. M. *Introduction to the Theory of Statistics.* New York: McGraw-Hill Book Co., 1950.

CHAPTER VIII

Tests of Hypotheses (3) and Estimation Procedures

1. Introduction

In this chapter several loosely related types of tests are considered. First, some methods for testing hypotheses concerning qualitative data are considered. Then tests of hypotheses concerning distributions and testing methods which make no assumptions concerning underlying distributions are considered. Finally, procedures for estimating values of several population characteristics are presented.

This chapter will conclude the discussion of hypothesis testing and estimation procedures.

2. Qualitative Analysis

In most of the tests discussed up to this point, the data have consisted of measurements along some scale. In the tests involving proportions or percentages (i.e., those involving p) the observations are not measurements but consist of counts of items having a specified property. For this reason, tests involving p are said to deal with *enumeration statistics*. The observed frequency of an event (f_i) is also an enumeration statistic. It can, of course, be converted into an estimate of p by dividing it by the total number of observations (Σf_i). That is,

$$\bar{p}_i = \frac{f_i}{\Sigma f_i} \quad \text{or} \quad f_i = \bar{p}_i \Sigma f_i.$$

Enumeration statistics are very commonly used where the pertinent variables are treated qualitatively, as attributes. Opinion polls, for example, may count the number of people "for" or "against" a candidate or issue.

The *binomial* and *Poisson* distributions are particularly useful in treating qualitative data. Each of these will be considered together with some additional tests of hypotheses involving enumeration statistics.

2.1. The Binomial Distribution

Consider the case in which we seek to test a hypothesis concerning the expression of verbal preference. Each of a set of individuals may be asked whether he likes or dislikes a certain object. He answers either "Yes" or "No," and hence each observation is qualitative. Suppose a random sample of twenty persons is selected and an estimate is made of the probability of preference on the basis of this sample. The estimate, of course, is likely to be inaccurate, since it is based on a sample. To obtain an idea of how inaccurate such an estimate might be, a histogram can be constructed similar to the ones considered in chapter v. The histogram could be obtained by repeating the process of selecting twenty persons at random and plotting the number of times a given proportion of "Yes" responses is obtained (see Fig. 32).

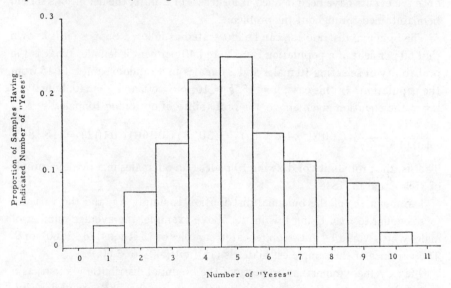

Fig. 32.—Histogram of preference data (100 samples of 20)

The frequency curve (or distribution function) which this histogram approaches as the number of samples is increased is called the *binomial distribution*. This distribution is not a smooth curve, since a discontinuous scale is involved; that is, there may be one or two "Yeses," but not $1\frac{1}{2}$ or $2\frac{1}{2}$, etc.

The equation which defines the binomial distribution is

$$P_k = \frac{n!}{k!\,(n-k)!}\, p^k q^{n-k},$$

where P_k = the probability of obtaining exactly k successes.

n = the number of observations in the sample.

$n!$ (read "n factorial") $= n(n-1)(n-2) \ldots 1$. For example,
$6! = (6)(5)(4)(3)(2)(1) = 720$. (NOTE: $0! = 1$.)

k = the number of successes.

$k! = k(k-1)(k-2) \ldots 1$.

p = the probability of obtaining a success on a single observation.

$q = (1-p)$, the probability of not obtaining a success on a single observation.

If a set of events can be classified into two categories such that each observation must fall into one and only one category, then inclusion in either category may be defined as a success, and inclusion in the other may be defined as a failure. In the polling example a "Yes" response could be defined as a success and a "No" response as a failure. The definitions may also be reversed, but, once the events have been defined as a success or failure, the definitions should be maintained throughout the problem.

The binomial distribution can be illustrated as follows. Suppose it is known that 60 per cent of a population is male and 40 per cent is female. What is the probability of selecting 10 males and 5 females in a random sample of 15 from the population? In this case, $n = 15$, $k = 10$, $p = .60$, and $q = .40$. Substituting in the equation given above, the probability of obtaining 10 males is

$$\frac{15!}{10!\,(15-5)!}\ (.60^{10})\ (.40^{(15-10)}) = (3003)(.0060)(.0102) = .1838.$$

That is, the probability of drawing 10 males and 5 females in a random sample of 15 is equal to .1838.

The mean (μ) of the binomial distribution is simply np, and the variance (σ^2) is equal to npq. Using this in the above example, the average number of males which would be drawn on repeated samples of 15 is equal to 15(.60), or 9. The variance of the sample estimates is (15)(.60)(.40), or 3.60.

One extremely important property of the binomial distribution is that, as n approaches infinity, the binomial distribution approaches the normal distribution as a limit. The approach to normality is faster the closer p is to .50. Consequently, the normal distribution can be used to "approximate" the binomial in many cases. The tests of hypotheses involving proportions, which were presented in chapter vi, all made use of this normal approximation. This use of the normal approximation is desirable because the normal distribution is much easier to handle than the binomial. Detailed discussion of the binomial distribution can be found on an elementary level in (8) and on a more advanced level in (4: vi).

Within the past few years, a very useful device based on the binomial distribution has been developed: the *binomial probability paper*. This paper makes it possible to obtain approximate results very rapidly for a number of different problems involving enumeration statistics. It also has "the advantage of visual presentation in pointing out facts or clues which might otherwise be overlooked" (9:174). Some of the uses of this paper are: (*a*) to compare an observed proportion with a theoretical proportion; (*b*) to make estimates of and design sampling plans for binomial populations; and (*c*) to approximate the results obtained by the *t* test and *F* test, including the analysis of variance.

The paper can also be used for tests of goodness of fit and in nonparametric testing, subjects which will be considered below. A complete discussion of this paper can be found in (9).

2.2. The Poisson Distribution

If the value of N (the size of the population) is large, and np, or nq, in the binomial distribution is very small (in general, less than 5), convenient and good approximations can be made to P_k by use of the Poisson distribution. This distribution is defined by the following equation:

$$P_k = \frac{m^k}{k!} e^{-m},$$

where P_k = the probability of k successes.

$m = np$, the theoretical mean.

$e = 2.78 \ldots$

Tables giving values of P_k for various values of m are given in (1), (3), and (5).

One particularly useful application of the Poisson distribution involves determining whether a small minority group is scattered randomly over a population. For example, suppose one wants to determine whether 120 Catholics are scattered randomly over 60 city blocks. The probability of finding k Catholics in any one block, if they are randomly distributed, is given by the equation above. In this case $m = 120/60 = 2$, the expected number of Catholics per block. By use of the Poisson tables we can determine the probability of finding any k number of Catholics in a block. In this case, the following values are obtained:

k	P_k	k	P_k
0	.135	5	.036
1	.271	6	.012
2	.271	7	.003
3	.180	8	.001
4	.090		

If, then, 7 Catholics were found in one block, we would reject (at the .01 significance level) the hypothesis that they are distributed randomly.

2.3. Independence of Attributes

There are many cases in which we wish to determine whether two variables change independently. For example, we may suspect that height and weight are not independent; that is, they are correlated. We could measure the heights and weights of the members of a random sample and run a correlation analysis. There are cases, however, where the variables are treated qualitatively, as attributes. For example, we might want to determine whether the profession of father and profession of son are independent. The following test is applicable to just such cases.

TEST 35 H_0: V_1 and V_2 are independent.

                        H_1: V_1 and V_2 are not independent.

KNOWN OR ASSUMED: Randomness.

PROCEDURE 1 (where there are two categories for each attribute):

(1) Prepare the following "contingency" matrix:

		V_1		
		I	II	Total
V_2	1	a	b	$a+b$
	2	c	d	$c+d$
Total		$a+c$	$b+d$	$a+b+c+d=n$

where a is the number of observations falling into cell I-1, b the number in II-1, etc.

(2) Compute

$$\chi^2 = \frac{(|ad - bc| - n/2)^2 n}{(a+b)(a+c)(b+d)(c+d)}.$$

(3) Select from Appendix Table V the χ_a^2 value opposite DF $= 1$, and under the appropriate α.

(4) If $\chi^2 \leq \chi_a^2$, accept H_0; otherwise accept H_1.

EXAMPLE: A random sample of 76 employees of a corporation is selected. It is desired to determine (at the .10 significance level) whether college graduation and marital stability are independent. The data are given in step (1) below.

H_0: College graduation and marital stability are independent.

H_1: College graduation and marital stability are not independent.

Solution:

(1)

	Divorced	Not Divorced	Total
College graduates.	6	27	33
Not college graduates. .	11	32	43
Total.	17	59	76

(2) $\chi^2 = \dfrac{(\,|\,6.32 - (27)(11)\,| - 76/2\,)^2\,(76)}{(17)(59)(33)(43)} = .2397$.

(3) $\chi^2_{.10} = 2.706$.

(4) $\chi^2 < \chi^2_{.10}$ (i.e., $.2397 < 2.706$); therefore, accept H_0; that is, the variables are independent.

PROCEDURE 2 (where one attribute has two categories, the other more than two):

(1) Prepare the following matrix:

		V_1			
		A	B	Total	
	a	f_{Aa}	f_{Ba}	T_a	f_{Aa}^2/T_a
	b	f_{Ab}	f_{Bb}	T_b	f_{Ab}^2/T_b
V_2	.	.	.	.	.
	.	.	.	.	.
	n	f_{An}	f_{Bn}	T_n	f_{An}^2/T_n
Total		T_A	T_B	T	T'

(2) Compute

$$\bar{p} = T_A/T.$$

(3) Compute

$$\chi^2 = (T' - \bar{p}T_A)/\bar{p}(1 - \bar{p}).$$

(4) Compute DF $= n - 1$.

(5) Select from Appendix Table V the χ^2_α value opposite the appropriate DF and under the appropriate α.

(6) If $\chi^2 \leq \chi^2_\alpha$, accept H_0; otherwise accept H_1.

EXAMPLE: It is desired to determine whether or not the grades obtained on a certain test are independent of the sex of those tested. From past records of the use of the test 160 observations are drawn at random. The results are shown in step (1) below. Is there reason to believe these attributes are independent at the .10 significance level?

H_0: Test grades and sex are independent.

H_1: Test grades and sex are not independent.

Solution:

(1)

Test Grades	Fe-male	Male	Total	
A........	4	18	22	$4^2/22 = 0.727$
B........	9	12	21	$9^2/21 = 3.857$
C........	7	15	22	$7^2/22 = 2.227$
D........	3	26	29	$3^2/29 = 0.310$
E........	6	31	37	$6^2/37 = 0.973$
F.........	5	24	29	$5^2/29 = 0.862$
Total..	34	126	160	8.956

(2) $\bar{p} = 34/160 = .213$.

(3) $\chi^2 = [8.956 - (.213)(34)]/(.213)(.787) = 10.227$.

(4) DF $= 6 - 1 = 5$.

(5) $\chi^2_{.10} = 9.236$.

(6) $\chi^2 > \chi^2_{.10}$ (i.e., $10.227 > 9.236$); therefore, reject H_0 and accept H_1; test grades and sex are not independent.

3. Hypotheses concerning Distributions

At one point in the history of statistical methods a great deal of emphasis was placed on discovering the distribution underlying the observations. This was done because it was felt that one could not correctly apply statistical techniques unless one were sure that the distribution was normal, or binomial, or Poisson, or whatever. For this reason many of the older texts devote considerable space to the methods for testing the normality of a distribution and suggest methods for transforming observations so that the resulting transformed data would be normal. More recently, it has been found that, in many cases where the underlying distribution is not normal, the use of tests which presuppose normality produces no serious error (2). Furthermore, an increasing number of tests have been found which require no presuppositions concerning the nature of the distribution. These will be discussed in the next section.

There are still many problems, however, whose solution requires a known and, specifically, a normal distribution. For example, this is the case in estimating the proportion of a population that lies above or below some value, in so-called "tail" estimation. Furthermore, if a distribution is normal, tests which make use of this information are more efficient than tests which do not. For this reason it is sometimes desirable to transform a distribution which is not normal into one that is. A number of techniques are available for accomplishing such transformations. One common method, for example, consists in using the logarithms of the observations. For a discussion of this and other methods of "normalizing" data see (6:vii).

In situations where it is desirable to determine whether a set of observations comes from a normal or some other specified distribution, the χ^2 test (which will be given in Sec. 3.2) is most commonly used. If the distribution tested is not actually normal, this test has certain disadvantages: it is not sensitive to deviations at the tails of the distribution. Consequently, if the tails are important, the test should not be used. A number of other tests are available (6:viii), but almost all either suffer from the same disadvantage or require very large samples. One of the better of the available tests is given in (7).

For many purposes an approximate method for testing normality is good enough. In such cases *normal probability paper* is very useful. It has the advantage of extreme simplicity but the disadvantage of yielding no measures of error. We shall consider this paper first and then the χ^2 test.

3.1. Normal Probability Paper and the Test for Normality

In presenting this method, we shall depart from the usual procedure for presenting tests. The method will be described by illustration.

The use of normal probability paper for testing normality requires that the data be collected into groups. There are no definite rules as to the number of classes or observations required, but in general it is desirable to have at least ten classes and fifty observations.

Suppose that data are collected from a sample of 200 employees of a certain company and that the age of each employee is determined. These data should then be arranged as shown in the tabulation on the following page.

The cumulative frequency is simply the sum of all frequencies of classes up to and including the class for which it is computed. For example, the cumulative frequency of the fourth class (35–40) is equal to $2 + 6 + 12 + 20$, or 40.

The cumulative relative frequency in per cent for a class is equal to the cumulative frequency divided by the total frequency and multiplied by 100. For example, the cumulative relative frequency in per cent for the fifth class (40–45) is equal to $(80)(100)/(200)$, or 40.

The upper limits are plotted along the abscissa of the normal probability paper (see Fig. 33). The cumulative relative frequency in per cent is then plotted, using the figures on the extreme right for ordinate values. A straight line is then drawn, visually, as close to all the points as possible. If the points come close to the straight line so drawn, the distribution approximates the

Age Group	Upper Limit	Fre-quency	Cumula-tive Fre-quency	Cumula-tive Rela-tive Frequency (Per Cent)
20–25..........	25	2	2	1
25–30..........	30	6	8	4
30–35..........	35	12	20	10
35–40..........	40	20	40	20
40–45..........	45	40	80	40
45–50..........	50	50	130	65
50–55..........	55	36	166	83
55–60..........	60	18	184	92
60–65..........	65	12	196	98
65–70..........	70	4	200	100

normal. The points at the tails will generally deviate more than the others and hence can be discounted except where we are primarily interested in the tails of the distribution. In the illustration none of the points is more than about 2 per cent away from the line drawn, and most are within 1 per cent. This would be considered a good fit for most purposes, and the assumption of normality seems justified. There is no way of measuring the confidence one should place in such a judgment, since this is not a rigid statistical test. But, as has been indicated, it is good enough for many purposes in which the tails are not critical.

3.2. χ^2 Test for Goodness of Fit

The χ^2 test can be used for testing goodness of fit of a set of data to any known distribution. It will be illustrated in a test for normality. It should be remembered, however, that this test is not sensitive to deviations from normality at the tails of the distribution.

A word should be devoted to the method by which the theoretical frequencies are determined. Suppose, for example, a normal population is known or assumed to have a mean (μ) equal to 10 and a standard deviation (σ) equal to 2. Now suppose we want to determine the theoretical relative frequency of ob-

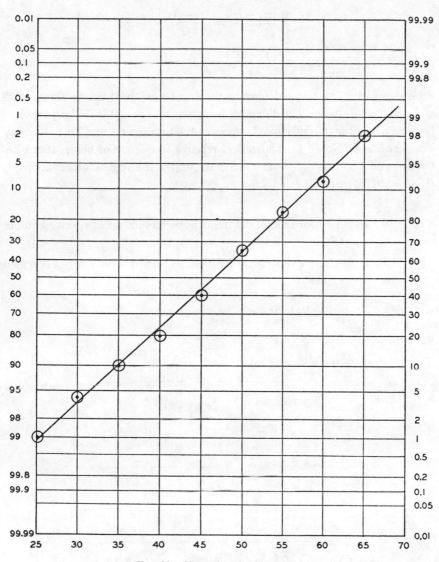

FIG. 33.—Normal probability paper

servations in the interval from 6 to 8. First, 6 and 8 are converted into deviations from the mean expressed as σ units; that is, in terms of z:

$$z_{x_i=6} = \frac{|x_i - \mu|}{\sigma} = \frac{|6 - 10|}{2} = 2.0 .$$

$$z_{x_i=8} = \frac{|8 - 10|}{2} = 1.0 .$$

From Appendix Table I we determine the area below these two z values: .0228 and .1587, respectively. The difference between these values is the proportion of the area under the normal curve between ordinates drawn 1 and 2 σ units away from the mean. Hence the theoretical relative frequency of observations between 1 and 2 σ units (i.e., from 6 to 8 in the unit of the original observations) is .1587 $-$ .0228, or .1359.

TEST 36 H_0: A set of theoretical frequencies have a set of specified values (F_i)

H_1: A set of theoretical frequencies do not have a set of specified values (F_i)

KNOWN OR ASSUMED: Randomness.

PROCEDURE:

(1) Prepare the following table:

DESCRIP-TION	FREQUENCY		$f_i - F_i$	$(f_i - F_i)^2/F_i$
	Observed f_i	Theoretical F_i		
1........	f_1	F_1	$f_1 - F_1$	$(f_1 - F_1)^2/F_1$
2........	f_2	F_2	$f_2 - F_2$	$(f_2 - F_2)^2/F_2$
.	.	.	.	.
.	.	.	.	.
.	.	.	.	.
n........	f_n	F_n	$f_n - F_n$	$(f_n - F_n)^2/F_n$
Total...	$\sum\limits^{n} f_i$	$\sum\limits^{n} F_i$	....	$\sum\limits^{n} (f_i - F_i)^2/F_i = \chi^2$

Note: $\sum\limits^{n} f_i$ should be equal to $\sum\limits^{n} F_i$.

(2) Compute DF $= n - 1$.

(3) Select from Appendix Table V the χ_a^2 value opposite the appropriate DF and under the appropriate a.

(4) If $\chi^2 \leq \chi_a^2$, accept H_0; otherwise accept H_1.

EXAMPLE: We want to determine whether a set of theoretical frequencies are equal to the values shown in the F_i column below. The F_i values were obtained from an assumed normal distribution ($\mu = 47$, $\sigma = 9.5$). At the .05 significance level test the following hypotheses:

H_0: The theoretical frequencies for the classes indicated are equal to the values shown in the F_i column; that is, the distribution is normal, with $\mu = 47$ and $\sigma = 9.5$.

H_1: The theoretical frequencies for the classes indicated are not equal to the values shown in the F_i column.

Solution:

(1)

Age Group	f_i	F_i	$(f_i - F_i)$	$(f_i - F_i)^2 / F_i$
Under 25....	2	2	0	$0/2 = 0.00$
25–30......	6	5	1	$1/5 = 0.20$
30–35......	12	13	-1	$1/13 = 0.08$
35–40......	20	26	-6	$36/26 = 1.38$
40–45......	40	38	2	$4/38 = 0.11$
45–50......	50	40	10	$100/40 = 2.50$
50–55......	36	36	0	$0/36 = 0.00$
55–60......	18	22	-4	$16/22 = 0.73$
60–65......	12	12	0	$0/12 = 0.00$
65 or over...	4	6	-2	$4/6 = 0.67$
Total....	200	200	....	$5.67 = \chi^2$

(2) DF $= 10 - 1 = 9$.

(3) $\chi_{.05}^2 = 16.92$.

(4) $\chi^2 < \chi_{.05}^2$ (i.e., $5.67 < 16.92$); therefore, accept H_0.

4. Nonparametric Tests

Reference was made above to tests which require no presuppositions concerning the nature of the distribution which underlies the data. Such tests are called *nonparametric* because many of them do not involve the use of a distribution's parameters.

Nonparametric tests can be used to determine whether or not there is some real difference between two distributions without making strong assumptions concerning the nature of the distributions. These tests are also particularly useful where the data can be expressed not quantitatively but only as ordered responses. Such is the case where the data consist of rankings and where the underlying distribution is not known. The test for significance of rank correlation given in Test 27 (p. 221) is nonparametric. The χ^2 test for goodness of fit (Test 36) is also nonparametric.

One of the advantages in using nonparameteric tests lies in the fact that they usually require very few computations. This advantage will be very apparent in the two types of nonparametric tests to be considered in this section: *sign tests* and *run tests*.

4.1. The Sign Test

In many social research projects it is desirable to compare two groups or two individuals in a variety of different circumstances. That is, the researcher wants to determine whether or not there is a difference between groups or individuals over a range of situations. In each situation an observation can be made on each group; if two groups are involved, paired observations are obtained. There may be no basis for making any assumptions concerning the underlying distribution of the observations in each or over all the situations. Then a nonparametric test is required. In particular, the sign test can be used in this situation.

The sign test can be used for a variety of different purposes, only some of which will be discussed here (for a more detailed discussion see [3:xvii]). The applications we shall consider are designed to answer such questions as the following (let A and B represent the two groups or individuals involved):

(1) Are A and B different with respect to some specified property over situations 1 to n?

(2) Is A better than B by at least pc per cent?

(3) Is A better than B by at least q units?

These questions are translated into hypotheses concerning the median, m. It will be recalled that the median is that value on the abscissa of a distribution function whose ordinate divides the area under the curve into two equal parts. A sample median, in the case of an odd number of observations in the sample, is that observation which has an equal number of observations in the sample which are both less than and greater than it. In the case of an even number of observations, it is the value halfway between the two middle observations. For example, the median of 3, 9, and 27 is 9; the median of 3, 9, 11, and 27 is 10.

The critical statistic in these tests is the number of times the least frequent sign ($+$ or $-$) occurs in the difference between the paired observations. This statistic is usually represented by r, the same symbol used to represent the sample correlation coefficient. To avoid confusion, the symbol r_s will be used here to represent the sign-test statistic.

The distribution of r_s has been worked out and is given in Appendix Table XI. It will be noted that values are not given for small n. In fact, the values given for n less than or equal to 10 are not reliable in general and should only be used for rough approximations. For more accurate treatment of small samples see (3:252–54).

TEST 37 $H_0: m_x = m_y$

$H_1: m_x \neq m_y$

KNOWN OR ASSUMED: The differences between the pairs of observations are independent.*

PROCEDURE:

(1) Prepare the following table:

x_i	y_i	Sign of $(x_i - y_i)$
x_1	y_1	
x_2	y_2	
.	.	
.	.	
x_n	y_n	

(2) Compute r_s, the number of times the less frequent sign appears.
(3) Select from Appendix Table XI the value of r_{sa} opposite the appropriate n and under the appropriate a.
(4) If $r_s > r_{sa}$, accept H_0; otherwise accept H_1.

EXAMPLE: Two schools (A and B) have competed with each other for a number of years in various types of sports. A random sample of 14 games in which no ties are possible is selected. The scores are listed below. At the .05 significance level are the schools different in their athletic ability?

$$H_0: m_A = m_B$$

$$H_1: m_A \neq m_B$$

---

* Strictly speaking, it is also assumed that no ties occur, that is, no observations in a pair are equal. "In practice, however, even when two ties would not occur if measurements were sufficiently precise, ties do occur because measurements are often made only to the nearest unit or tenth of a unit for example. Such ties should be excluded" (3:248).

Solution:

(1)

A	B	Sign of Difference	A	B	Sign of Difference
7	4	+	28	14	+
2	3	−	18	24	−
3	4	−	6	2	+
49	54	−	64	14	+
21	18	+	19	20	−
32	18	+	26	12	+
12	4	+	31	11	+

(2) $r_s = 5$ (i.e., there are 5 minus signs).

(3) $r_{s.05} = 2$.

(4) $r_s > r_{s.05}$ (i.e., $5 > 2$); therefore, accept H_0; that is, there is no difference between the schools.

TEST 38 $H_0: m_x \geq cm_y$

$H_1: m_x < cm_y$

c is a specified constant

KNOWN OR ASSUMED: The differences between the pairs of observations are independent, and the measurements between pairs are comparable (i.e., along the same scale).

PROCEDURE:

(1) Prepare the following table:

x_i	y_i	cy_i	Sign of Difference $x_i - cy_i$
x_1	y_1	cy_1	
x_2	y_2	cy_2	
.	.	.	
.	.	.	
.	.	.	
x_n	y_n	cy_n	

(2) Compute r_s.

(3) Select from Appendix Table XI the value of r_{sa} opposite the appropriate n and under the appropriate a.

(4) If $r_s > r_{sa}$, accept H_0; otherwise accept H_1.

EXAMPLE: It is argued that one salesman (A) in a store is twice as good as another (B). Both sell the same item. A random sample of 12 records for daily sales is taken. The data are recorded below. Is the argument supported at the .10 significance level?

$$H_0: m_A > 2m_B$$

$$H_1: m_A < 2m_B$$

Solution:

(1)

A_i	B_i	$2B_i$	Sign of $A_i - 2B_i$
47	22	44	+
51	25	50	+
63	27	54	+
49	30	60	−
65	31	62	+
75	37	74	+
43	20	40	+
55	27	54	+
74	35	70	+
50	21	42	+
57	25	50	+
71	34	68	+

(2) $r_s = 1$.

(3) $r_{s.10} = 2$.

(4) $r_s < r_{s.10}$ (i.e., $1 < 2$); therefore, reject H_0 and accept H_1; that is, A is twice as good as B.

TEST 39

$$H_0: m_x = m_y + q$$

$$H_1: m_x \neq m_y + q$$

q is a specified number of units

This test is similar to the preceding one except that the sign of the difference $x_i - (y_i + q)$ is used.

4.2. The Run Test

Reference has been made several times to the difficulty of taking repeated observations on human subjects. The subjects are likely to change under repeated stimulation of the same type, and hence the observations would not be independent or random. Despite this possible difficulty, it is desirable in many projects to make a set of independent observations on the same subject(s) under repetitions of the same stimulus. In such cases it is advisable to test the observations to determine whether they can be taken to be randomly selected from the universe of possible observations.

There are a number of tests for independence and randomness. Most are usable only under special conditions. However, the run test can be used for this purpose in a variety of circumstances, and, like the sign test, it has the virtue of extreme simplicity. The median of the sample is determined, and then the differences between the observations (taken in the order in which they were obtained) and the median are denoted by $+$ or $-$, depending on whether they are above or below the median, respectively. Then each consecutive set of the same sign is designated as a *run*. The number of runs (u) is determined. The probability of obtaining various numbers of runs for different sample sizes has been computed. Appendix Table XII provides the critical values required for conducting run tests at the .05 significance level.

Two run tests will be given below: one to determine if the population median is equal to a specified value, the other to determine if a set of observations can be taken to be a random sample from a single population. For further details and applications see (3:xvii, Sec. 3).

TEST 40 H_0: $m = a$

                                     H_1: $m \neq a$

KNOWN OR ASSUMED: Randomness and the order in which the observations are made.

PROCEDURE:

(1) Prepare the following table:

x_i	x_1	x_2	$\ldots$	x_n
Sign of $x_i - a$				

If any x_i is equal to a, remove it from the list.

(2) Compute u, the number of runs of consecutive $+$ and $-$ signs.

(3) Compute n_1, the number of the less frequently occurring sign, and n_2, the number of the more frequently occurring sign.

(4) Select from Appendix Table XII the $u_{.025}$ and $u_{.975}$ values under the appropriate n_1 and opposite the appropriate n_2.

(5) If $u_{.025} < u \leq u_{.975}$, accept H_0; otherwise accept H_1.

EXAMPLE: A random sample of test scores of 15 subjects is selected. The scores are given below. Is there reason to believe, at the .05 significance level, that the population median score is equal to 75?

$$H_0: m = 75$$
$$H_1: m \neq 75$$

Solution:

(1)

x_i	90	71	64	83	87	76	70	51	62	85	87	95	73	69	81
Sign of $x_i - 75$	+	−	−	+	+	+	−	−	−	+	+	+	−	−	+

(2) $u = 7$.

(3) $n_1 = 7$ and $n_2 = 8$.

(4) $u_{.025} = 4$ and $u_{.975} = 12$.

(5) $u_{.025} < u < u_{.975}$ (i.e., $4 < 7 < 12$); therefore, accept H_0.

TEST 41 H_0: A specified set of observations is drawn at random from a single population.

H_1: A specified set of observations is not drawn at random from a single population.

KNOWN OR ASSUMED: The order in which the observations are made.

PROCEDURE:

(1) Compute the median of the sample, m'.

(2) Prepare the following table:

x_i	x_1	x_2	. . .	x_n
Sign of $x_i - m'$				

where x_1 is the first observation made, x_2 is the second, etc. (This is not the same order used to compute the median.)

(3) Compute u, the number of runs of consecutive + and − signs.

(4) Compute n_1 and n_2 where $n_1 = n_2 = n/2$ if n is even; and $n_1 = n_2 = (n - 1)/2$ if n is odd.

(5) Select from Appendix Table XII the $u_{.025}$ and $u_{.975}$ values under the appropriate n_1 and opposite the appropriate n_2.

(6) If $u_{.025} < u \leq u_{.975}$, accept H_0; otherwise accept H_1.

EXAMPLE: Suppose a subject is repeatedly given the same maze problem to solve at regular intervals. Observations are made on the length of time required to solve the problem. The results for the first 20 trials are given below. Can these observations be taken to be drawn at random from a single population? Let $a = .05$.

H_0: The set of observations is drawn at random from a single population.

H_1: The set of observations is not drawn at random from a single population.

Solution:

(1) The observations ordered by magnitude are:
   54, 53, 51, 47, 46, 45, 42, 41, 36, 34,
   33, 32, 31, 30, 29, 29, 29, 28, 26, 25.
   The sample median, m', is $33 + (1/2)(34 - 33) = 33.5$.

(2)

x_i	54	53	51	47	46	42	45	30	36	41	34	33	29	29	32	31	29	28	26	25
Sign of $x_i - m'$	+	+	+	+	+	+	+	−	+	+	+	−	−	−	−	−	−	−	−	−

(3) $u = 4$.

(4) $n_1 = n_2 = 20/2 = 10$.

(5) $u_{.025} = 6$ and $u_{.975} = 15$.

(6) $u < u_{.025}$ (i.e., $4 < 6$); therefore, reject H_0 and accept H_1; that is, the observations are not drawn at random from a single population.

5. Estimation Procedures

The problem of estimation in statistics is quite similar to the general problem of "description" in the sciences. In common-sense terms, one sometimes describes an aspect of nature by depicting in words certain characteristics of the environment. We say that the description is "accurate" if it truly depicts what is "really" taking place. So, in statistics, one may want to describe one or more properties of a population, and such description is called an "estimate" of the property if it is based on a sample. We would like to have criteria that enable us to determine whether or not an estimate is good or adequate.

We have already considered (in chap. iv) the desirability of estimation procedures which are unbiased and yield minimum variance. However, additional criteria are needed. But there is no one set of *statistical* criteria which assure a best estimate in the practical sense, since "best" depends on the nature of the problem being investigated.

The methods of estimation to be considered in this section are not to be taken as necessarily the "best" in all cases. Most of the methods are based on the principle that the cost of overestimation or the cost of underestimation is proportionate (approximately) to the square of the amount of over- or under-estimation. In the illustration given in Appendix IV a different principle is used: the cost is proportionate to the amount of over- or underestimation and not to its square. The rationale for considering the square is that in many cases it is reasonable to assume that the cost rises more sharply for larger errors than for small. That is, it is four times as serious to err by two units as it is to err by one, nine times as serious to err by three units as to err by one, etc. Further, the principle of minimizing the square of the error (the principle of "least squares") has the advantage of being simpler to handle mathematically than most other methods of estimation, and hence it is often easier to tell just what risks are involved in a least-squares estimate than with other types of estimates. Further, minimizing the squares may minimize other functions of the error as well. Nevertheless, the reader should keep an open mind with respect to the principle of least squares and its application, since in some cases the risks may not be proportionate to the square of the error.

In some cases it may be desirable to obtain a single value or *point* estimate of a variable. In effect, it may be desirable to determine what is the best value to "bet on." One can never be certain that any estimate is perfectly accurate, but one can use methods of estimation which in the long run yield a distribution of estimates whose mean is equal to the true value of the quantity estimated; that is, unbiased methods. The methods of estimation are, of course, closely related to the methods of sampling. For example, the procedure for obtaining an unbiased estimate of the mean from a simple random sample would yield biased estimates if applied, say, to disproportionate stratified samples.

We have already considered a number of point estimates: $\bar{x}$ is a point estimate of the mean; s^2 is an estimate of the variance; s of the standard deviation; $\bar{p}$ of a proportion; b of a regression coefficient; r of the correlation coefficient; etc. All these sample statistics and others which have been discussed are point estimates of population properties, and for many purposes they are the best available.

In general, when the researcher has a problem of estimation, he does not desire a single value but rather an interval; that is, a range of values within which the true value can be taken to lie. One of the advantages of an interval estimate is that it enables the researcher to express quantitatively the amount of confidence that can be placed in the estimate. Hence, interval estimates are said to provide a "confidence interval" in the following sense: a 95 per cent confidence interval, for example, has a probability of .95 of including the true value. A 90 per cent confidence interval has a probability of .90 of including the true value, etc. In other words, if many attempts were made to catch the true value by using the same estimation procedure on many random samples of the same size, then 95 per cent (or whatever percentage is specified) of the estimates would in the long run catch the true value in the calculated range. Note that confidence intervals do not guarantee that the true value is actually in the interval specified. Nor can one predict that future estimates will fall in the same interval. On the basis of the estimate one can only assert that anyone who uses the same method will, with the specified probability, catch the true value.

As in the case of point estimates, the risks in setting up confidence intervals are supposed to be proportionate to the square of the error.*

Some of the more common interval estimates are given below. For further details see (3:viii and ix) and (6:vi).

ESTIMATE 1. *Confidence Interval of the Mean.*

KNOWN OR ASSUMED: Randomness, normality, and σ.

PROCEDURE:

(1) Compute $\bar{x}$.
(2) Compute $a = 1 - (pc/100)$, where pc is equal to the per cent confidence interval desired.
(3) Select from Appendix Table II the appropriate z_a value.
(4) Compute the confidence interval:

$$\left[\bar{x} - \frac{z_a \sigma}{\sqrt{n}}\right] \leq \mu \leq \left[\bar{x} + \frac{z_a \sigma}{\sqrt{n}}\right].$$

EXAMPLE: It is desired to determine the 95 per cent confidence interval of μ for a random sample of 25 test scores. σ is assumed to be equal to 15. $\bar{x}$ is computed and is equal to 104.00.

* R. A. Fisher has suggested that the estimates also provide "maximum information" and that they maximize the likelihood of the observed events (the principle of "maximum likelihood"). In most cases occurring in practice, there is little difference between the least-squares estimates and maximum likelihood estimates and a third type called "minimax estimates" (estimates which minimize the maximum risk that could conceivably occur).

Solution:

(1) $\bar{x} = 104.00$.

(2) $a = 1 - (95/100) = .05$.

(3) $z_{.05} = 1.96$.

(4) $\left[104.00 - \dfrac{(1.96)(15)}{\sqrt{25}} \right] \le \mu \le \left[104.00 + \dfrac{(1.96)(15)}{\sqrt{25}} \right]$,

$98.12 \le \mu \le 109.88$.

ESTIMATE 2. *Confidence Interval of the Mean.*

KNOWN OR ASSUMED: Randomness and normality.

PROCEDURE:

(1) Compute $\bar{x}$ and s.

(2) Compute $a = 1 - (pc/100)$.

(3) Compute DF $= n - 1$.

(4) Select from Appendix Table III the t_a value opposite the appropriate DF and under the appropriate a.

(5) Compute the confidence interval:

$$\left[\bar{x} - \frac{t_a s}{\sqrt{n}} \right] \le \mu \le \left[\bar{x} + \frac{t_a s}{\sqrt{n}} \right].$$

EXAMPLE: What is the 99 per cent confidence interval of the mean age of college students if a random sample of 16 students has an average age of 21 and a standard deviation of 4 years?

Solution:

(1) $\bar{x} = 21$ and $s = 4$.

(2) $a = 1 - (99/100) = .01$

(3) DF $= 16 - 1 = 15$.

(4) $t_{.01} = 2.95$.

(5) $\left[21 - \dfrac{(2.95)(4)}{\sqrt{16}} \right] \le \mu \le \left[21 + \dfrac{(2.95)(4)}{\sqrt{16}} \right]$,

$18.05 \le \mu \le 23.95$.

ESTIMATE 3. *Confidence Interval of the Variance.*

KNOWN OR ASSUMED: Randomness and normality.

PROCEDURE:

(1) Compute s^2.

(2) Compute DF $= n - 1$.

(3) Compute $.5a = (1/2)(1 - pc/100)$ and $1 - .5a$.

(4) Select from Appendix Table V the $\chi^2_{.5a}$ value opposite the appropriate DF and under the column headed by $.5a$; select $\chi^2_{1-.5a}$ opposite the same DF but under $1 - .5a$.

(5) Compute

$$\left[\frac{DF\,s^2}{\chi^2_{.5a}}\right] \leq \sigma^2 \leq \left[\frac{DF\,s^2}{\chi^2_{1-.5a}}\right].$$

EXAMPLE: The sample variance of the income of 30 randomly selected workers is 2,000,000. What is the 90 per cent confidence interval of the population variance?

Solution:

(1) $s^2 = 2,000,000$.

(2) DF $= 30 - 1 = 29$.

(3) $.5a = 1/2(1 - 90/100) = .05$, and $1 - .05 = .95$.

(4) $\chi^2_{.05} = 42.557$, and $\chi^2_{.95} = 17.708$.

(5) $\left[\dfrac{(29)(2,000,000)}{42.557}\right] \leq \sigma^2 \leq \left[\dfrac{(29)(2,000,000)}{17.708}\right]$,

$1,362,878 \leq \sigma^2 \leq 3,275,356$.

ESTIMATE 4. *Confidence Interval of the Difference between Two Means.*

KNOWN OR ASSUMED: Randomness and normality. Means are independent, variances unknown but equal.

PROCEDURE:

(1) Compute $\bar{x}_1$, $\bar{x}_2$, s_1^2, and s_2^2.

(2) Compute DF $= n_1 + n_2 - 2$.

(3) Compute $a = 1 - (pc/100)$.

(4) Select from Appendix Table III the t_a value opposite the appropriate DF and under the appropriate a.

(5) Compute the confidence interval:

$$(\bar{x}_1 - \bar{x}_2) - t_a \sqrt{\frac{n_1 + n_2}{n_1 + n_2 - 2}\left[\frac{(n_1 - 1)\,s_1^2 + (n_2 - 1)\,s_2^2}{n_1 n_2}\right]} \leq (\mu_1 - \mu_2)$$

$$\leq (\bar{x}_1 - \bar{x}_2) + t_a \sqrt{\frac{n_1 + n_2}{n_1 + n_2 - 2}\left[\frac{(n_1 - 1)\,s_1^2 + (n_2 - 1)\,s_2^2}{n_1 n_2}\right]}$$

EXAMPLE: A random sample of 10 meetings of Boy Scout troops A and B is taken. The average attendance at A's meetings is 30, and at B's it is 20. The sample variances are 20 and 10, respectively. What is the 95 per cent confidence interval of the difference between the true attendance-means?

Solution:

(1) $\bar{x}_A = 30$, $\bar{x}_B = 20$, $s_A^2 = 20$, and $s_B^2 = 10$.

(2) DF $= 10 + 10 - 2 = 18$.

(3) $a = 1 - 95/100 = .05$.

(4) $t_{.05} = 2.10$.

$$(5) \quad (30 - 20) - 2.10\sqrt{\frac{10+10}{18}\left[\frac{(10-1)\,20 + (10-1)\,10}{(10)(10)}\right]}$$
$$\leq (\mu_A - \mu_B)$$
$$\leq (30 - 20) + 2.10\sqrt{\frac{10+10}{18}\left[\frac{(10-1)\,20 + (10-1)\,10}{(10)(10)}\right]},$$

$$6.37 \leq (\mu_A - \mu_B) \leq 13.63 \ .$$

This means that at least 6 more people attend A in the long-run average, and at most 13 more attend A. If the lower limit were negative, then (at the level chosen) we would reject a true difference between μ_A and μ_B.

ESTIMATE 5. *Confidence Interval of the Regression Coefficient.*

KNOWN OR ASSUMED: The observations (x_i) are not subject to error, and errors of the observations (y_i) are independent and normally distributed with zero mean.

PROCEDURE:

(1) Compute b and s_b. (See p. 214.)

(2) Compute $a = 1 - (pc/100)$.

(3) Compute DF $= N - 2$.

(4) Select from Appendix Table III the t_a value opposite the appropriate DF and under the appropriate a.

(5) Compute the confidence interval:

$$(b - t_a s_b) \leq B \leq (b + t_a s_b).$$

EXAMPLE: A regression coefficient of the number of psychotics against the size of communities is determined to be 10.4, with a standard error of this estimate equal to 3.9. A sample of 1,000 cases was used. Determine the 95 per cent confidence interval of the true regression coefficient.

Solution:

    (1) $b = 10.4$ and $s_b = 3.9$.

    (2) $a = 1 - 95/100 = .05$.

    (3) DF $= 1,000 - 2 = 998$.

    (4) $t_{.05} = 1.96$.

    (5) $10.4 - (1.96)(3.9) \leq B \leq 10.4 + (1.96)(3.9)$,

        $2.76 \leq B \leq 18.04$.

ESTIMATE 6. *Confidence Interval of the Correlation Coefficient.*

KNOWN OR ASSUMED: The pairs of observations are drawn at random and are normally distributed.

PROCEDURE:

    (1) Compute r.

    (2) Select from Appendix Table X the value of z' corresponding to r.

    (3) Compute $\sigma_{z'} = 1/\sqrt{N - 3}$.

    (4) Compute $a = 1 - (pc/100)$.

    (5) Select from Appendix Table II the appropriate z_a value.

    (6) Compute

$$\bar{z}_1 = z' - z_a \sigma_{z'},$$

    and

$$\bar{z}_2 = z' + z_a \sigma_{z'}.$$

    (7) Select from Appendix Table X the r_1 value corresponding to $\bar{z}_1$, and the r_2 value corresponding to $\bar{z}_2$.

    (8) Then

$$r_1 \leq \rho \leq r_2.$$

EXAMPLE: The correlation coefficient computed from a random sample of ten paired observations is equal to .59. Determine the 99 per cent confidence interval of ρ.

Solution:

    (1) $r = .59$.

    (2) $z' = .678$.

    (3) $\sigma_{z'} = 1/\sqrt{10 - 3}$.

(4) $\alpha = 1 - 99/100 = .01$.

(5) $z_{.01} = 2.576$.

(6) $\tilde{z}_1 = .678 - (2.576)(.377) = -.293$.

$\tilde{z}_2 = .678 + (2.576)(.377) = 1.649$.

(7) $r_1 = -.285$ and $r_2 = .929$.

(8) $-.285 \le \rho \le .929$.

ESTIMATE 7. *Confidence Interval of a Proportion or Percentage.*

KNOWN OR ASSUMED: $n > 30$ and $(.10 < p < .90)$. The events are independent and have an equal probability of occurring.

PROCEDURE:

(1) Compute $\bar{p}$, the observed relative frequency.

(2) Compute $\alpha = 1 - (pc/100)$.

(3) Select from Appendix Table II the appropriate z_a value.

(4) Compute the confidence interval:

$$\left[\bar{p} - z_a \sqrt{\frac{\bar{p}(1-\bar{p})}{n}} \right] \le p \le \left[\bar{p} + z_a \sqrt{\frac{\bar{p}(1-\bar{p})}{n}} \right].$$

Note: If a percentage is used rather than a proportion, substitute the percentage for the proportion in the above procedure and replace 1 by 100 in step (4).

EXAMPLE: In an election poll 60 out of 100 randomly selected individuals are in favor of candidate A. What is the 99 per cent confidence interval of the proportion of the population in favor of A?

Solution:

(1) $\bar{p} = 60/100 = .60$.

(2) $\alpha = 1 - 99/100 = .01$.

(3) $z_{.01} = 2.58$.

(4) $\left[.60 - 2.58 \sqrt{\frac{.60(.40)}{100}} \right] \le p \le \left[.60 + 2.58 \sqrt{\frac{.60(.40)}{100}} \right]$,

$.47 \le p \le .73$.

Social surveys are so frequently concerned with estimates of percentages that it is worth directing more attention toward such estimates.

The standard error (σ) of the estimate of a percentage $(\overline{PC})$ whose true value is a is given by

$$\sigma_{\overline{PC}} = \sqrt{\frac{a(100-a)}{n}}, \tag{1}$$

where n is the sample size. In Test 11 (p. 193) it was seen that the z value of an estimate of a hypothetical value (a) of a percentage is given by

$$z = \frac{\overline{PC} - a}{\sigma_{\overline{PC}}}. \tag{2}$$

Substituting the value of $\sigma_{\overline{PC}}$ given in equations (1) and (2), we obtain

$$z = \frac{\overline{PC} - a}{\sqrt{\dfrac{a\,(100 - a)}{n}}}. \tag{3}$$

Squaring both sides of (3), we get

$$z^2 = \frac{n\,(\overline{PC} - a)^2}{a\,(100 - a)}. \tag{4}$$

Solving for n, we obtain

$$n = \frac{z^2 a\,(100 - a)}{(\overline{PC} - a)^2}. \tag{5}$$

Now $(\overline{PC} - a)$ is equal to the difference between the estimated and the hypothetical value of the percentage. Suppose we know the value of the true percentage (a); then by use of equation (5) we can determine the number of observations required to obtain an estimate within any specified percentage with a given probability.

Suppose, for example, that the true percentage is 50, and we want our estimate to be within 5 per cent (i.e., between 45 and 55 per cent), 95 per cent of the time. Then

$$a = 1 - 95/100 = .05.$$

$$z_{.05} = 1.96.$$

$$\overline{PC} - a = 5.$$

Substituting in (5), we get

$$n = \frac{(1.96)^2\,(50)\,(100 - 50)}{(5)^2} = 384.16 \text{ or } 384\,.$$

Hence, if the true percentage is equal to 50, we would require 384 randomly selected observations to obtain estimates that would come within 5 per cent of this value, 95 per cent of the time. Thus, if we have some notion as to what the true value is, we can determine by use of equation (5) the number of observations required to obtain any specified confidence.

If our original notion of the value of a is shown to be very unlikely on the basis of the estimate, adjustment can be made by using the revised notion of the value of a. That is, we may find that we have either taken too many or too few observations for the desired confidence level. In the former case we will have obtained more confidence than is required; in the latter case, less. If we have obtained less confidence than is desired, a new computation of n can be made on the basis of the revised estimate of a, and the proper number of additional observations can be made.

In Tables 20 and 21 the number of observations required for various possible true values of a percentage is given for the 95 per cent and the 99 per cent confidence levels. In the tables the possible true values of the percentage are paired (e.g., 1–99, 2–98, etc.). This follows from the term $a(100 - a)$ in equation (5). If $a = 1$, then $(100 - a) = 99$, and, conversely, if $a = 99$, then $(100 - a) = 1$.

6. Compounding Errors: A Technical Note

Before leaving the discussion of the statistical aspects of the practical research design, there is one technicality which should be noted; that is, compounding errors.

It was indicated earlier that the great advantage of statistical methods derives from the fact that they provide measures of error involved in the inferences from sample to population. There are cases, however, where part of this advantage is lost in the use of statistical methods—in cases where double testing or estimation procedures are involved. This point can be clarified by illustration.

Suppose one wants to test the hypothesis (H_0: $\mu_1 = \mu_2$) by use of Test 16 (p. 198). In this test it is assumed that the variances of the two populations, though unknown, are equal (i.e., $\sigma_1^2 = \sigma_2^2$). Now the researcher may have some question as to whether or not this assumption is justified and therefore decide to test it. Then, by use of Test 20 (p. 203), he can first test the hypothesis (H_0: $\sigma_1^2 = \sigma_2^2$). In conducting this test for equality of variances, there is always some chance that the hypothesis will be accepted when it is false (Type II error); that is, when actually $\sigma_1^2 \neq \sigma_2^2$. Suppose that as a matter of fact the equality is accepted when it is false. The researcher does not know that this is the case and hence will go ahead and apply Test 16 to H_0: $\mu_1 = \mu_2$, at (say) the .05 significance level. Then, in this case, it can be shown that the hypothesis asserting the equality of the means would be rejected when true with a probability greater than .05. (For a numerical illustration see [6:73–75].)

The point, then, is not to keep from double testing, for it is frequently advantageous, but to realize that, in so doing, one obtains a result which is not necessarily significant at the level (Type I error) at which the second test is conducted.

TABLE 20*

SIZE OF SAMPLE NECESSARY TO OBTAIN ACCURACY WITHIN SPECIFIED LIMITS 99 PER CENT OF THE TIME

LIMITS OF ERROR IN PER CENT + AND −	PERCENTAGES																
	1-99	2-98	3-97	4-96	5-95	6-94	7-93	8-92	9-91	10-90	15-85	20-80	25-75	30-70	35-65	40-60	50-50
.25	15,510	20,807	30,892	40,765	50,425	59,873	69,109	78,133	86,944	95,543	135,352	169,853	199,047	222,933	241,510	254,780	265,396
.50	2,627	5,202	7,723	10,191	12,606	14,968	17,277	19,533	21,736	23,886	33,838	42,463	49,762	55,733	60,378	63,695	66,349
.75	1,168	2,312	3,432	4,529	5,603	6,653	7,679	8,681	9,660	10,616	15,039	18,873	22,116	24,770	26,834	28,309	29,448
1	657	1,300	1,931	2,548	3,152	3,742	4,319	4,883	5,434	5,971	8,459	10,616	12,440	13,933	15,094	15,924	16,587
2		325	483	637	788	936	1,080	1,221	1,358	1,493	2,115	2,654	3,110	3,483	3,774	3,981	4,147
3			215	283	350	416	480	543	604	663	940	1,180	1,382	1,548	1,677	1,769	1,843
4				159	197	234	270	305	340	373	529	664	778	871	943	995	1,037
5					126	150	173	195	217	239	338	425	498	557	604	637	663
6						104	120	136	151	166	235	295	346	387	419	442	461
7							88	100	111	122	173	217	254	284	308	325	339
8								76	85	93	139	166	194	218	236	249	259
9									67	74	104	131	154	172	186	197	205
10										60	85	106	124	139	151	159	166
15											38	47	55	62	67	71	74
20												27	31	35	38	40	41
25													20	22	24	25	27
30														13	17	18	18
35															12	13	14
40																10	10

* From M. Parten, *Surveys, Polls, and Samples* (New York: Harper & Bros., 1950), pp. 314-15.

TABLE 21*

SIZE OF SAMPLE NECESSARY TO OBTAIN ACCURACY WITHIN SPECIFIED LIMITS 95 PER CENT OF THE TIME

LIMITS OF ERROR IN PER CENT + AND −	PERCENTAGES																
	1–99	2–98	3–97	4–96	5–95	6–94	7–93	8–92	9–91	10–90	15–85	20–80	25–75	30–70	35–65	40–60	50–50
.25	6,085	12,047	17,886	23,602	29,195	34,665	40,013	45,237	50,338	55,317	78,366	98,341	115,244	129,073	139,829	147,512	153,658
.50	1,521	3,012	4,471	5,900	7,299	8,666	10,003	11,309	12,585	13,829	19,591	24,585	28,811	32,268	34,957	36,878	38,415
.75	676	1,339	1,987	2,622	3,244	3,852	4,446	5,026	5,593	6,146	8,707	10,927	12,805	14,341	15,537	16,390	17,073
1	380	753	1,118	1,475	1,825	2,167	2,501	2,827	3,146	3,457	4,898	6,146	7,203	8,067	8,739	9,220	9,604
2		188	279	369	456	542	625	707	787	864	1,224	1,537	1,801	2,017	2,185	2,305	2,401
3			124	164	203	241	278	314	350	384	544	683	800	896	971	1,024	1,067
4				92	114	135	156	177	197	216	306	384	450	504	546	576	600
5					73	87	100	113	126	138	196	246	288	323	350	369	384
6						60	69	79	87	96	136	171	200	224	243	256	267
7							51	58	64	71	100	125	147	165	178	188	196
8								44	49	54	77	96	113	126	137	144	150
9									39	43	60	76	89	100	108	114	119
10										35	49	61	72	81	87	92	96
15											22	27	32	36	39	41	43
20												15	18	20	22	23	24
25													12	13	14	15	15
30														9	10	10	10
35															7	8	8
40																6	6

* Ibid.

7. Summary

This chapter brings to a close consideration of the statistical phases of the practical research design. The necessity for statistical design was pointed out in the discussion of the ideal model: the impracticality or impossibility of observing all members of the pertinent population. Out of this arises the need for selecting a sample of the population from which inferences can be drawn to the total population. The various methods for doing so were discussed in chapter iv. The general logic underlying statistical methods for drawing inferences from the sample was discussed in chapter v. In chapters vi, vii, and this one, specific procedures have been considered for various types of hypotheses and estimation problems. A number of different forms of statistical hypotheses have been presented, forms into which the hypotheses originally constructed (chap. ii) can be translated.

The phases of the statistical design of the practical research procedures can then be summarized as follows:

(1) The statistical reformulation of the hypotheses formulated in the problem formulation phase of the research design.
(2) The selection of a method of sampling.
(3) The determination of the size of the sample.
(4) The determination of the acceptable Type I error.
(5) The determination of the acceptable Type II errors.
(6) The selection of a statistical testing or estimation procedure.

These decisions are all interrelated and hence cannot be made independently. They all depend in turn on the determination of the following costs:

(*a*) The cost of preparing the sample.
(*b*) The cost of obtaining observations on the sample units.
(*c*) The cost of treating the data obtained from the sample.
(*d*) The expected cost associated with a Type I error in testing hypotheses or the error of underestimation in estimation procedures.
(*e*) The expected cost associated with Type II errors in testing hypotheses or the error of overestimation in estimation procedures.

That is, the objective of the statistical design is to minimize the total of these costs. It should be apparent that assurance of such minimization can be obtained only by the use of designed procedures.

DISCUSSION TOPICS

1. Why is the binomial distribution important in the social sciences?

2. In what types of situations would the Poisson distribution be useful? Find examples.

3. What are the advantages of nonparametric tests?

4. Define (a) a run; (b) median; (c) goodness of fit; and (d) confidence interval.

5. Can observations made on a sample ever have a perfect normal distribution? Explain.

6. What property of normal probability paper makes it so useful? How can the paper be used to estimate the mean and standard deviation of a set of data?

EXERCISES

1. A random sample of 50 lawyers is taken in a certain city. Of these, 8 are self-employed and vote the Republican ticket; 12 are self-employed and vote the Democratic ticket. Of those who work for others, 17 are Republicans and 13 are Democrats. Are these variables independent at the .10 significance level?

2. Suppose a random sample of members of a club can be broken into groups as follows:

No. of Children	Rent Place They Live In	Own Place They Live In
0.	9	1
1.	8	3
2. . . . . . ,	5	3
3.	2	9
4.	2	8
5.	6	2
6.	2	3
7.	0	1

Are these variables independent at the .20 significance level?

3. Use normal probability paper to determine whether or not the following data can be assumed to come from a normal population.

Age Group	Frequency	Age Group	Frequency
Under 20. . .	.005	50–55.	.123
20–25.	.079	55–60.	.086
25–30.	.135	60–65:.	.042
30–35.	.145	65–70.	.017
35–40.	.134	70–75.	.003
40–45.	.117	75 and over.	.001
45–50.	.113		

4. Toss 5 coins 100 times and note the number of heads which appear each time. Prepare a frequency distribution table and determine whether the distribution you obtained fits the following theoretical frequency distribution at the .05 significance level.

No. of Heads	Theoretical Frequency
0	3.12
1	15.63
2	31.25
3	31.25
4	15.63
5	3.12

5. Two branch offices of the same company sell a number of similar items. A sample of daily sales records for items carried by both places is drawn with the following results:

ITEM	NUMBER OF SALES	
	Store A	Store B
1	63	66
2	58	42
3	12	20
4	76	0
5	63	88
6	98	80
7	56	71
8	26	62
9	5	87
10	89	80

Is there a difference between these stores? (The underlying distribution is not known.) Let $a = .05$.

6. Are student A and student B significantly different if they get the following final grades in a sample of courses they both took? Let $a = .10$.

Course	A	B	Course	A	B
a	72	71	g	80	65
b	87	94	h	95	70
c	73	74	i	90	74
d	83	61	j	92	77
e	98	70	k	91	67
f	95	90			

7. Suppose 11 pairs of members are selected from two different clubs. Their annual income is determined. Is there reason to believe at the .01 significance level that members of club A make a thousand dollars more on the average than do members of club B?

A	B	A	B
$8,857	$5,406	$6,411	$4,143
9,516	9,852	8,699	4,179
8,058	3,730	3,584	9,067
6,047	9,200	8,530	7,152
9,504	4,955	7,160	6,130
4,554	4,967		

8. A random sample of 20 patients in a hospital's wards is drawn in order, and the age of each noted. Should the median age be taken to be 40 years ($\alpha = .05$)? The ages were noted in the following order:

39, 53, 63, 48, 36, 26, 18, 53, 45, 37, 28, 58, 37, 22, 57, 49, 42, 34, 25, 18.

9. The number of telephones in twelve European countries is determined in the order indicated below. Is there sufficient reason to assert this sample has not been randomly selected from a single population? Let $\alpha = .05$.

Country	No. of Telephones	Country	No. of Telephones
Austria..........	281,790	Estonia.........	25,055
Belgium.........	415,522	Finland.........	185,456
Bulgaria........	29,576	France..........	1,589,595
Czechoslovakia...	220,510	Germany........	4,146,489
Denmark.......	442,998	Greece..........	49,872
Eire............	43,086	Hungary........	165,362

10. Determine the 90 per cent confidence interval for the mean if $\bar{x} = 117$, $\sigma = 23$, and $n = 36$.

11. Determine the 95 per cent confidence interval for the mean if $\bar{x} = 27.5$, $s = 4.2$, and $n = 25$.

12. Determine the 98 per cent confidence interval of the variance if $s^2 = 1,042$ and $n = 28$.

13. Determine the 95 per cent confidence interval of a proportion if $\bar{p} = .69$ and $n = 34$.

14. Determine the 90 per cent confidence interval of the difference between two means if $\bar{x}_1 = 23.5$, $\bar{x}_2 = 29.7$, $s_1^2 = 4.9$, $s_2^2 = 5.3$, $n_1 = 71$, and $n_2 = 51$.

15. Determine the 97.5 per cent confidence interval of the regression coefficient if $b = 5.71$, $s_b = 3.20$, and $n = 17$.

16. Determine the 99 per cent confidence interval of the correlation coefficient if $r = .76$ and $n = 19$.

SUGGESTED READINGS

Suggestions have been made throughout this chapter for further reading on each subject. It is worth noting again, however, that good over-all reference works on these and other statistical subjects are Dixon and Massey (3) and Johnson (6).

REFERENCES AND BIBLIOGRAPHY

1. ARKIN, HERBERT, and COLTON, R. R. *Tables for Statisticians.* "College Outline Series." New York: Barnes & Noble, Inc., 1950.
2. BENEPE, O. J. "The Sensitivity of t and F to Departures from Normality." University of Washington Master's thesis. Seattle, 1949.
3. DIXON, W. J., and MASSEY, F. J., JR. *Introduction to Statistical Analysis.* New York: McGraw-Hill Book Co., 1951.
4. FELLER, W. A. *An Introduction to Probability Theory and Its Applications,* Vol. I. New York: John Wiley & Sons, 1950.
5. FISHER, R. A., and YATES, FRANK. *Statistical Tables for Biological, Agricultural, and Medical Research.* London: Oliver & Boyd, 1943.
6. JOHNSON, P. O. *Statistical Methods in Research.* New York: Prentice-Hall, Inc , 1949.
7. MASSEY, F. J., JR. "The Kolmogorov-Smirnov Test for Goodness of Fit," *Journal of the American Statistical Association,* XLVI (1951), 68–78.
8. MODE, E. B. *The Elements of Statistics.* 2d ed. New York: Prentice-Hall, Inc., 1951.
9. MOSTELLER, FREDERICK, and TUKEY, J. W. "The Uses and Usefulness of Binomial Probability Paper," *Journal of the American Statistical Association,* XLIV (1949), 174–212.
10. SWED, F. S., and EISENHART, CHURCHILL. "Tables for Testing Randomness of Grouping in a Sequence of Alternatives," *Annals of Mathematical Statistics,* XIV (1943), 66–87.

CHAPTER IX

The Observational Phase of the Practical
Research Design

1. Introduction

In as much of the practical research design as we have considered up to this point, account has been taken of adjustments regarding the number of subjects (i.e., taking a sample rather than a complete count) and inferences from a sample to a population. Additional practical adjustments in the ideal model may have to be made. These adjustments become apparent as we begin to design the actual conditions under which and operations by which observations are to be made; that is, as we enter the *observational* phase of the practical research design.

To begin with, even though we deal with only a sample, it may not be possible to meet the specifications of the idealized research model with respect to this sample. Some of the sampled elements may not be available for observation, and, of those who are, some may refuse or be unable to co-operate with the observer. The practical research design should take this into account in planning the actual research operations to be performed. Furthermore, it may be either impossible or impractical to observe the designated subjects in the ideally specified environments and under the ideally specified stimuli. Hence, practical substitutes and/or samples of environments and stimuli may also have to be designed.

Each of these possible practical adjustments will be considered in this chapter. The principal design problem in this regard is to prepare ways and means for effectively approximating the ideal and adjusting for the resultant deviations from the ideal. First, consideration will be given to adjustments required because of the subjects. Then observational design problems involving the environments and stimuli will be discussed.

2. Practical Design Decisions Regarding the Subjects

Possible practical problems that might arise in the course of the research and that involve the subjects to be observed can be itemized as follows:

(1) It may not be possible to observe the subject because of his unavailability; he cannot come to or be found in a specified environment or environments. This problem will be referred to as that of *unavailables*.

(2) A subject who is available may refuse to co-operate with the researcher; that is, he may be unwilling to respond to the stimulus provided. For example, he may refuse to answer questions or even have them asked, to take tests, or to be observed under any circumstances. This problem will be referred to as that of *refusals*.

(3) A subject who is available and who is willing to respond may either deliberately or accidentally distort his responses and thereby provide misleading data to the researcher. This problem will be referred to as that of *response error*.

Each of these problems and methods for preventing or overcoming them will be considered in turn.

2.1. Unavailables

In dealing with human subjects, the researcher must either arrange to get the subject into a desired environment or observe him in one in which he is already located. The observer may be able to observe the subject without the subject's knowing it. This may either be arranged by concealment of the observer or by disguise of his (the observer's) role. Concealment is difficult (if not impossible) in most natural situations. In some situations it can be extremely effective, particularly where small groups are involved. Children at school can be observed through one-way mirrors, and so may others in a restricted class of environments. Recording devices, visual (cameras) or auditory, can be "planted" in some cases. In general, such devices are easier to conceal than observers but require more preparation. Disguise of the observer has proved useful in some research; that is, not letting the subject know that the person(s) whom he knows to be present is observing him. Such a procedure is called "participant observation." This method has serious disadvantages arising out of the fact that the observer is required to provide a good deal of interpretation of the data and the conditions under which they were obtained. This means that the research designer who has others do the participant observing exercises little control over the observations, and he has no way of systematically estimating the error of these observations. For details on this method see (16); for examples see (20), (22), and (23).

The more usual research situation is one in which the observer is known by the subject. This means that the researcher must either arrange to have the subject in a prepared environment or to have the observer in an environment occupied by the subject. To bring a subject to an environment to which he would not ordinarily come requires (in a free society) the co-operation of the subject. The subject may refuse or be unable (e.g., because of illness) to do so. Such a refusal creates sampling problems which will be considered below. If the observer must go to an environment in which the subject is expected to be (e.g., his home or place of business), similar difficulties may arise. The subject may not be there; he may be temporarily gone (e.g., on vacation), permanently away (e.g., moved), or unable to respond (e.g., due to illness). These possibilities exist even in the case where the stimulus but not the observer is put into the environment in which the subject is expected to be. For example, in postal or telephone surveys these same dangers (in addition to others) are present.

The following testimony of J. S. Stock provides striking evidence of the extent and seriousness of the problem caused by subjects not being available.

One of the characteristics of area sampling is that you predetermine the person you are going to interview. You know before you start whom you have got to see, and the experience is, in our modern cities especially, that the fellow isn't home. Now area sampling depends on the notion that everybody has a home, and if you sample homes you will have sampled everybody. If you set out a series of people to be interviewed, selected by area sampling, and say that you must see those people, you will find when you are through that the great majority of the people you set out to see you couldn't find, and the social characteristics of the people you have found would be different in many respects from those of the people you did not find.

We performed a number of experiments on this, considering just householders as the unit, and found, for example, by calling back time after time after time that the people we missed were the small family people. Also, the people we missed had a large number of workers in the family, and there was a tendency, therefore, toward a higher income.

We found a striking difference as to the characteristics of migration. For instance, in Washington, D.C., a number of years ago, we set out to interview so many dwelling units to find if that family had lived there a year ago last Christmas, or some such question. On first call we found two per cent said they had not lived there a year ago last Christmas. We were calling them migrants, but there was a large proportion, actually 30 per cent, who were not at home. There was no adult at home who could give us the answer to the question. We called back a second time. Of those we found on the second call we noted four per cent had not lived at that address a year ago last Christmas. On the third call we found that seven per cent had not lived at that address, and finally on the fourth call we found that sixteen per cent were migrants under that definition.

Now this problem of calling back is very expensive. Actually we used to figure that it would cost us a dollar per interview to get the interviewer from the home office out to the person to be interviewed. If the person was not at home, that was two dollars. Before you knew it, there was a tremendous cost involved when you started to make several calls, because we found, using the household as a unit, that in a large city like Philadelphia, in thirty per cent of the households no one was at home.

When we selected individuals, we found it even worse. Sixty per cent of the individuals to be called on were not at home [31:22–23].

2.1.1. Reduction of the Number of Unavailables

The possibility of the unavailability of the designated subjects should be taken into account in the practical design of the research, particularly where probability sampling is used. A large number of "unavailables" can prevent a planned probability sample from actually being a probability sample. This is due to the fact, as Stock mentions above, that the class of "unavailables" is likely to differ from the "availables" with respect to properties which are critical in the research. That is, the omission of unavailables introduces a bias— a tendency away from representativeness. This difficulty cannot be overcome simply by increasing the size of the sample, for the increased sample is still very likely to exclude representation of an important segment of the population if the unavailables are not included. For example, suppose a researcher conducts a survey to determine what percentage of the adult women in a certain neighborhood is employed. If he intends to conduct the interviews in the evening in order to catch most of the women at home, he is likely to miss those working in the evenings and a sizable proportion of unmarried or married and childless employed adult women, because they are more likely (than married employed mothers) to be "out for the evening." Omitting these women would introduce a distortion or bias into the sample. For several illustrations of such results see (25:409–12) and (14).

In general, it is much better to try to prevent the occurrence of unavailables than to try to cure it once it has taken place. A good practical design can reduce the subsequent magnitude of the problem a great deal. There are several rather obvious preventive measures which can be taken, not all of which, however, are practical in every situation.

(1) Appointments with the subjects can be made. This can be done by personal calls, mail, and/or telephone.

(2) Preliminary information can be obtained to determine when the subjects will probably be available. This may be done by a quick preliminary survey.

(3) Notice can be given of the approximate time at which the observer will call, and publicity can be used to enlist the subjects' co-operation.

(4) Selection can be made of times for the observer to call which will minimize the number of not-at-homes.

(5) Selections can be made of interviewers and supervisors who are

intelligent enough and know enough about the population to be able to plan their "calls" efficiently.

Despite such precautions, there is still likely to be a number of unavailables where the sample size is large and where contact with each subject is impractical. Remedial measures may then have to be taken and hence should be planned beforehand.

There is no one "sure" remedial method for handling unavailables. Several methods are available the relative values of which depend on the specific research situation and conditions.

1. In some cases all or part of the information to be obtained from the subject can be obtained from secondhand informants. A relative, friend, or neighbor may be able to supply the needed information. In the use of secondhand informants a great danger lies in the fact that the substitute may be misinformed about the subject and not be aware that he is misinformed. In some cases, however, a substitute may be better than the subject. For example, a parent may be able to provide better information about his or her child than the child itself. Such cases, however, are generally restricted to situations involving only elementary types of information such as age, weight, etc.

2. Calling back on or following up unavailables is the most obvious method and is the best method if cost is not important. That is, an attempt can be made to find out when the individual will be available and call back. If the designated person is no longer at the designated location, his new location may be possible to determine. In the case of postal surveys, follow-ups by postal means or personal call can be used. The costs of call-backs and follow-ups are obviously a function of the number of unavailables and their dispersion. If call-backs and follow-ups are to be made, it is necessary to specify how many call-backs should be made and under what conditions. It is helpful to instruct the observers to make a definite appointment for a call-back where possible (perhaps by phone). A stamped card addressed to the observer or his supervisor can be left at the home or place of business of the unavailable, along with a request that he indicate the time at which he will be available. Follow-ups are generally very expensive, and hence some limit usually has to be placed on the effort to be expended. Planning of call-backs by the interviewer or his supervisor can reduce their cost considerably.

Call-backs and follow-ups may themselves be conducted on a sample basis; that is, attempts can be made to contact only a portion of the unavailables. In such a procedure the cost of observation is reduced, but, since there will also be unavailables in the sample, the bias is not reduced as much as when complete call-backs and follow-ups are made. The basic problem here is to balance two costs against each other: the cost of the call-back or follow-up and the cost of the bias. The researcher should select that sample size which will minimize the sum of these two costs. A method for doing this in mail survey follow-ups is suggested by Hansen and Hurwitz (11). They indicate that, in general, a sample of one out of three unavailables is desirable and that one out of two is better if the interviewing cost of the call-back or follow-up is not high. Birnbaum and Sirkin (4) have made a similar analysis for personal interview surveys.

2.1.2. Adjusting for Unavailables

Obviously, it would be most desirable to be able to avoid having to call back on any of the unavailables. This could only be done if we knew or could make good estimates of the properties of the unavailables. One rather simple and ingenious suggestion for making such estimates was made by H. O. Hartley in (13). A method for making these estimates was independently developed by Politz and Simmons. This method is well worth consideration. Before discussing the procedure involved, it is worth looking at the underlying logic:

Every set of first call interviews of timing A must include respondents who are "not at homes" in another set of interviews of timing B. It must include respondents who are not at home in timing C and it must include respondents who are not at home in timing B and timing C. Statistically, therefore, it must be possible to reconstruct from a present "at home" sample, past samples of "at homes" and "not at homes," if: (a) respondents provide information on their past "at home" performance, and (b) if the individuals in the present "at home" sample are visited at times chosen at random.

Consider, for example, the following three groups, among which all individuals in the population are distributed: 1) those who are at home, on the average, 20% of the time, 2) 50% of the time, and 3) 80% of the time. If the time of visits is determined at random, we would expect to find on the first call about 20% of group (1), 50% of group (2), and 80% of group (3). Now if each person in the sample can only be identified with the group to which he belongs, a correction for the under-representation of each group is clearly indicated. Since only about one-fifth of the persons in the first group are interviewed, this group is assigned a weight of 5. Likewise, the second group receives a weight of 2 because only about half of the persons in this group are found at home, while the third group receives the weight of 1.25. This weighting, of course, does not completely eliminate the bias, for it takes into account only three arbitrarily defined groups. On the other hand, the bias must be reduced because the weighting has at least partially compensated for the under-representation of persons frequently away from home.

The number of such groups, however, need not be restricted to three. With obvious modifications, the above example is applicable to any number of such groups into which the population might be divided, where each group contains persons who are at home any part of the time during which interviewing is in progress [27:11–12].

The Politz-Simmons method consists of the following steps:

(1) Call on each person in the sample only once.

(2) Determine for those who are contacted what number of the interview periods of the preceding week they were at home. For example, if the interviewing takes place in the evenings, and a particular interview is conducted on a Saturday evening, ask:

    (*a*) "Would you mind telling me whether or not you happened to be at home last night at just this time?"

    (*b*) "How about the night before last at this time?"

    (*c*) "How about Wednesday night?"

    (*d*) "How about Tuesday night?"

    (*e*) "Monday night?"

(3) Group all the respondents contacted according to whether they were home 6/6, 5/6, 4/6, 3/6, 2/6, or 1/6 of these evenings.

(4) Compute the estimates for each variable being investigated for each of the six groups separately.

(5) Weight each estimate for each group by the reciprocal of the proportion of the evenings that group was home at the interview time.

(6) Compute the total estimate on the basis of the weighted estimates of the six groups.

For example, suppose we are conducting an investigation to determine the percentage of eligible voters in a city who did not vote in a recent election. A sampling plan is devised, an interview procedure is designed, and interviews are planned for evening hours. One call is made at each household designated in the sample with, say, the following results:

(1) No. of Nights at Home Out of Six	(2) No. of Eligible Voters Con- tacted	(3) No. Who Did Not Vote	(4) Weights	(5) Weighted No. of Eligible Voters Ob- served (Estimated No. of Eligible Voters in Sample)	(6) Weighted No. Who Did Not Vote (Esti- mated No. of Non- voting Eligible Voters in Sample)
1..........	25	15	$6/1 = 6.0$	$6.0 \times 25 = 150$	$6.0 \times 15 = 90$
2..........	50	30	$6/2 = 3.0$	$3.0 \times 50 = 150$	$3.0 \times 30 = 90$
3..........	100	58	$6/3 = 2.0$	$2.0 \times 100 = 200$	$2.0 \times 58 = 116$
4..........	200	100	$6/4 = 1.5$	$1.5 \times 200 = 300$	$1.5 \times 100 = 150$
5..........	400	190	$6/5 = 1.2$	$1.2 \times 400 = 480$	$1.2 \times 190 = 228$
6..........	700	315	$6/6 = 1.0$	$1.0 \times 700 = 700$	$1.0 \times 315 = 315$
Total...	1,475	708	....	1,980	989

Then the adjusted estimated proportion of nonvoting eligible voters is equal to 989/1,980 = .50. (The unadjusted proportion would be equal to 708/1,475 = .48.)

It is clear that the estimate just made does not take account of those who were not at home on any of the six nights. However, Politz and Simmons suggest a method for taking this group into account. First, using the above data, we can compute the regression coefficients of the entries in column 5 on the entries in column 1, and column 6 on column 1. The significance of these coefficients is tested. If they are not significant, then we need not consider those who were out all six nights, since their omission introduces no bias. If the regression is significant, then let the "number of nights at home out of six" be equal to zero and determine from the two regression equations the values to be placed in columns 5 and 6, opposite zero inserted at the top of column 1. Suppose these values were 100 and 70, respectively. Then we would compute 70 + 989, or 1,059, and 1,980 + 100, or 2,080. The new adjusted estimated proportion would then be 1,059/2,080, or .51.*

An obvious question which arises in connection with the Politz-Simmons method is: How reliable are the responses on nights at home? The method, however, can provide an internal check on this reliability. The interviewer can be instructed to keep a record of the percentage he finds and does not find at home. In addition, it is known that the expected percentage of persons at home at a randomly selected time is equal to the average percentage of the time all persons are at home. This latter percentage

may be estimated directly from the information obtained from respondents concerning the number of nights each respondent was at home out of the past six nights. This comparison between two independent estimates of the average per cent of persons at home is usually made in order to check the over-all accuracy of respondents' answers, interviewers' records and any other source of error. The results of this check for the Chicago survey are as follows:

CHICAGO METROPOLITAN AREA

	At Home Per Cent	Not at Home Per Cent
Based on actual interviewers' records of number of persons visited and number found at home............	61.1	38.9
Based on respondents' answers concerning the number of nights they are at home.......................	61.5	38.5

. . . The direct count provides an elegant internal statistical check on the reliability of the response to the not-at-home question, and thereby indirectly, a check on the interviewers' carefulness in dealing with the respondents [27:16].

* This method assumes that the moment at which the observer determines whether or not the subject is at home is selected at random from the population of possible moments at which such determinations can be made. A selection is made, however, of six moments if the questions given above are used. These six moments "are not independently selected at random, but sys-

The Politz-Simmons method for adjusting for not-at-homes is not necessarily the best method to use in any situation. In some situations call-backs may be more efficient. Comparative evaluations of the two methods are required for each different situation; that is, evaluations which take into account (1) bias, (2) the variance of the estimates, and (3) operating costs. The Politz-Simmons method is likely to be advantageous in cases where there is little money available for call-backs, where the survey must be conducted rapidly, and where the population is widely dispersed, thereby making call-backs relatively expensive. In some cases it may be advantageous to combine the two methods. For example, either method may yield serious bias if the property investigated is correlated with the frequency of the subjects' being away from home. In such cases the bias can be reduced somewhat by supplementing the Politz-Simmons method with one or two call-backs. For some studies there may not be enough information available to assure an efficient decision as to how to handle the unavailables. Where this is the case, a pretest can frequently be used to provide the necessary information.

2.2. Refusals

Even when the subject is found in, or brought to the environment in which he is to be observed, he may refuse to respond to the stimulus. Such a refusal may provide information concerning the subject, but, in general, this will not be the information desired. The problem created by refusals is similar in several respects to that created by unavailables, although, in general, there are not so many refusals as there are unavailables. In dealing with the refusal problem, prevention is again worth more than cure. Antirefusal design measures overlap with those taken to minimize the unavailability problem. Some of the obvious preventive measures are:

(1) Good publicity to arouse a co-operative attitude of subjects. Such publicity should emphasize the importance of the results of the research.

(2) Tactful and diplomatic observers who have some understanding and experience with the problem.

---

tematically selected within a randomly selected cluster of six successive nights. An exact statement of probability would involve the intraclass correlation of the probability of an individual being at home on successive nights. However, experience has indicated that this correlation tends to be quite low or even negative because a person is more apt to stay at home on a night following a night on which he goes out. The assumption of a zero correlation is, therefore, realistic" (27:21).

It should also be noted that, if the zero-group characteristic is estimated and used in computing a population estimate, errors are being compounded (see p. 283).

(3) Introductory remarks by the observer which stress the importance of the results and the important role of the subject. In addition, assurance must be given to the subject that the information obtained from or about him will not be used against him in any way.

(4) Inducements to the subjects, particularly when a great deal of time is required of them; that is, some form of compensation or a gift.

(5) Most important, perhaps (and not so obvious), is a procedure of obtaining the data which does not arouse the subjects' antipathy. There are no general principles available which can aid in developing such a procedure. However, a good procedure can be developed by use of pilot study, pretest, and trial run. These methods will be discussed in detail in the next chapter, but it is worth remarking here that such studies frequently result in considerable subsequent savings. Deming asserts (7:36), for example, that pilot studies in which the research instruments are improved and variance and cost studied may well be worth from 5 to 25 per cent of the total cost of the research.

Possible remedial measures are (1) to make further attempts to induce the refusers to co-operate by offering them either greater inducements and/or (2) to give the job to a more experienced observer. In some cases, secondhand informants can be used if the refuser persists. There is no best method for handling refusals, since the reasons for the refusals vary greatly, and as yet there has been little systematic study of the problem.

2.3. Response Error

Even if the subject is available and co-operates with the observer to the extent of responding to the stimulus, it is not necessarily true that the response observed is accurate. Owing to his lack of information, the subject may unknowingly and unintentionally give inaccurate responses, even though he may sincerely want to inform the observer. On the other hand, inaccuracy may be deliberate. This problem is pertinent to nonverbal as well as to verbal responses. Such falsification can be prevented to a certain extent by using procedures which tend to expose inaccuracies to the subject and the observer. But no matter what precautions are taken, some "response error" is likely to remain. Therefore, it is highly desirable to be able to measure it. The practical research procedure can usually be so designed that some measure of this error is possible.

First, consider the case where each sampling unit has a unique value of the property being investigated, for example, age at last birthday. Various types of evidence can be used to determine age. Some types of evidence are more accurate than others. For example, we would expect, in general, that a birth certificate is better evidence of age than is a person's answer to the question: "How old were you on your last birthday?" However, it is generally easier to obtain an answer to the question than to examine a birth certificate. Cost considerations may force us to resort to questioning the subject. Furthermore, we would probably have to question the subject to get the information required to locate his birth certificate; therefore, we might as well ask him his age while we are at it. But, since birth certificates are preferable evidence, responses to age questions can be checked by examination of birth certificates. Such a procedure provides an estimate of the accuracy of responses to the question. If a large number of individuals are involved, this "record-checking" procedure may be very costly. Consequently, such a check on accuracy may be conducted on a sample basis. For example, suppose in a study to estimate the average age of a specified population a random sample of a hundred persons are asked their ages. Then suppose that ten are selected at random out of the one hundred and that their birth records are traced. The difference between the two ages can be determined in each case. Then a test can be conducted to determine if the mean difference between the paired observations is equal to zero. If it is, the verbal responses can be said to be accurate; if not, a correction factor can be determined and applied to the verbal responses. It may be possible to use sequential sampling to advantage in this checking procedure.

In some cases the data obtained by observers on subject responses can be checked by going to other types of records, such as payrolls, school files, immigration forms, etc. In still other cases the subject's response can be checked by questioning others who are familiar with the subject relative to the characteristic under investigation. This method must be used with care, for, in general, "witnesses" are not so reliable as records. In still other cases, measures can be used to check testimony. For example, if a subject is asked to give his height and weight, his responses can be checked by making actual measurements of his height and weight. Or an expression of preference can be checked by observing actual choices under experimental conditions.

There are many properties for which such checking is very difficult, as in some opinion and attitude studies which use verbal tests. In such cases there may be no conveniently obtainable evidence other than the verbal responses of the subject. Here it is possible to design into the stimuli properties which make it possible to determine the consistency or reliability of the responses. In its most direct form this consists of putting the subject under the same stimulus several times to see if his response is the same in each case. If his responses are independent and the same, it does not necessarily follow that his response is accurate, but the researcher can have greater assurance that it is. That is, one can argue that consistency among responses is necessary for accuracy but is not sufficient. A person can, for example, consistently lie as well as tell the truth. Therefore, consistency is a negative check on accuracy in the sense that inconsistency makes the researcher suspicious, and consistency gives him some but not complete assurance. We will discuss measures of reliability in more detail in a later section of this chapter.

3. Practical Design Decisions Regarding Research Environment and Stimuli

We may desire to determine a psychological property of a large number of individuals, say, a trait like ascendance-submission. In the idealized research design the designer should specify an idealized behavioristic test of the trait. This test might be costly and time-consuming and create problems concerning availability of the subjects. The situations in which the subjects can be observed may or may not be close to the idealized situation. First let us consider the case where it is possible to observe and stimulate the subjects in a situation which approximates the ideal.

Consider an analogue from the physical sciences. Suppose a physicist wants to determine the length of a piece of metal in, say, a temperature of $-50°$ F. It may not be practical to construct such an environment. But he can determine the length of the piece of metal in an environment in which the temperature is, say, $70°$ F. It happens that for certain metals he knows the extent to which they are affected by temperature; that is, he knows their "coefficient of expansion." Applying this knowledge to the measurements he can make, he can infer what *would* be observed if he made the measurement under the ideally specified conditions. Suppose he does not know what the coefficient of expansion of this metal is. Then he can find out what it is by taking measurements under various temperatures and by determining the increase or decrease in length per unit change in temperature. This determination can be made under temperatures he can produce.

Similar maneuvers are possible within the social sciences. In some cases the social scientist knows how a dependent and an independent variable are related, and he can make the required adjustment directly. In other cases he does not and will first have to determine that relationship. Consequently, he can convert the idealized research design (which asks only for a value of the dependent variable at a fixed value of the independent variable) by changing the problem to one of determining the functional relationship between two (or more) variables. The statistical tool for determining such a functional relationship is regression analysis.

Suppose, for example, one wants to determine how rapidly a worker will perform a certain job after he has performed it 100 times. It may be impractical to have him do the job 101 times in order to get the answer. On the basis of what is known about the characteristics of learning curves (they are usually S-shaped curves), one can observe the speed of the worker for fewer than 101 times and determine which curve best fits the observed results. This would enable the researcher to extrapolate to the 101st performance and predict the rate at which the 101st job will be done. It may turn out, for example, that after the 10th time the job is done the worker has reached his maximum speed, and all subsequent performances take place at the same rate, assuming that no fatigue or boredom factor sets in.

In cases where approximate environments and stimuli are used, it is necessary for the researcher either to specify explicitly beforehand what practical environments and stimuli are to be constructed or to specify what measurements are to be made in available natural environments so that they can be described in sufficient detail to permit extrapolation or interpolation. Furthermore, the researcher should make explicit the method of extrapolation or interpolation to be used, and the method should be justified by explicit theoretical or factual knowledge or assumptions concerning the relationship between the variables involved. Extrapolation and interpolation presuppose an underlying pattern in this relationship. Unless this pattern and its use are made explicit, there is no way of checking the adequacy of the conclusions drawn.

3.1. Verbal Substitutes

Suppose we want to determine the preferences of a population with regard to a set of instruments all of which have the same function. A market survey may well be of this type. For example, we may want to determine which of a set of alternative brands of laundry soap housewives prefer. Ideally we might decide that we would like to put each sampled housewife in a situation where she wants laundry soap and offer her one but only one of each of the alternative brands. Then we would observe which choice she makes. If the sample of housewives is a large one, this method becomes expensive and impractical. Consequently, it may be necessary to make the following adjustment: to show the housewives the alternatives and *ask* them which they would choose if they had the choice. Finally, if it is difficult to show the alternatives, we might simply name the alternatives and *ask* them which they would select. In either of these two modifications of the ideal design, verbal responses are substituted for what are usually called "overt" responses. In effect, the researcher can provide a verbal substitute for the ideally specified environment and stimulus and accept a verbal substitute for the ideally specified overt response.

The ability of the social scientist to use verbal research instruments is at one and the same time a great advantage and disadvantage. It is an advantage in the sense that it permits the social researcher to conduct inquiries in many situations where practical considerations would otherwise make approximations to the idealized research situation impossible. Two of the more important of these practical considerations are (1) the difficulty of getting individuals and groups into specially constructed environments for extended periods of time and (2), even where this difficulty does not exist, the fact that it is frequently very costly to conduct research under the ideal conditions.

The disadvantage of verbal techniques arises out of the fact that their use introduces many new variables into the research procedure and hence new sources of error. There is a great temptation to ignore these "nuisance" variables and sources of error, since it is frequently difficult to assess their effect on the research. A complete evaluation of verbal techniques requires that society eventually make available to the social scientist the opportunity and funds necessary to conduct extensive tests on nonverbal behavior. In the meantime it is very important to make verbal tests and questionnaires as efficient as possible. This involves our showing, in the design of verbal tests and questionnaires, how adjustments of "verbal responses to verbal stimuli" can be made so as to permit good inferences to the other types of behavior in question.

There is a difference between the verbal *test* and the *questionnaire* which it is helpful to maintain. A test is used to determine a property of an individual or group where it is known or assumed that the subject(s) does not know either (1) whether or not he has that property or (2) to what extent he has it.* A questionnaire is used when it is known or assumed that the subject(s) does know or can estimate these things within certain error limits. For example, if we want to measure an individual's learning ability, personality structure, or intelligence, we use tests, since we do not believe an individual can provide the desired information directly. On the other hand, if we desire to know a person's age, income, and (sometimes) attitudes and opinions, we ask him directly by use of a questionnaire. We shall consider tests and questionnaires separately, although the procedures involved in preparing them are similar.

3.1.1. Test Design

Psychologists, social psychologists, and sociologists have probably spent more time in developing methods of designing tests and questionnaires than in designing any other research instrument. This follows from the fact that these instruments are used so extensively in these sciences. It would take a book

---

* Sometimes "test" is used to refer only to an instrument designed to measure abilities. The use here is more general.

larger than this one merely to describe the various methods which are available, and, in this connection, see, for example, (10); one good summary article on the nature of scales underlying test design is (6). Here we shall consider only one procedure for designing tests—a procedure more lengthy and difficult to apply than most of the available alternatives. This method, however, has several important advantages over most alternative methods: (1) it is completely general (i.e., it can be applied to tests for measuring any psychological or social property); (2) it yields maximum information; and (3) it produces tests whose scores have a well-defined meaning.

Procedures for designing tests such as the prominent ones developed by Thurstone (35), Guttman (32), and Lazarsfeld (32) are easier to use; they yield a test in less time than the method to be presented. Hence they may be preferable if time is critical. But these and most other methods for designing tests provide no way of determining whether the test produced actually measures the characteristic in question. They provide only intuitive assurance that the results obtained are pertinent to the problem under investigation.

3.1.1.1. Use of Definitions in Test Construction

None of the usual methods of test construction systematically employs the definition of the property to be determined in the construction of the test. They use the definition merely as an intuitive guide in the selection of test items. There is little wonder that this is so, for in most cases the definitions are so formulated that they cannot be systematically used in the design procedure. Consider, for example, the following two definitions which were used by Allport and Thurstone, respectively, in the preparation of their well-known tests of a trait and an attitude. Allport, it will be recalled, defines a trait as "a generalized and focalized neuropsychic system (peculiar to the individual), with the capacity to render many stimuli functionally equivalent, and to initiate and guide consistent (equivalent) forms of adaptive and expressed behavior" (2:295). Thurstone defines an attitude as "the sum-total of a man's inclinations and feelings, prejudice or bias, preconceived notions, ideas, fears, threats, and convictions about any specific topic" (35:6–7). Neither of these definitions *directs* the researcher toward a method of answering questions concerning traits or attitudes. That this is so can be shown by attempting to take literally a definition such as Thurstone's. Let us do so briefly.

First it would be necessary to define the pertinent populations of (*a*) inclinations, (*b*) feelings, (*c*) prejudices or biases, (*d*) preconceived notions, (*e*) ideas, (*f*) fears, (*g*) threats, and (*h*) convictions. Then either a complete count of each population or a probability sample would be required. An estimate of the "sum" of these would have to be made, assuming the research obtained comparable measures which could be summed. As a matter of fact, none of this is done or tried, and for obvious reasons. For example, the test items are actually selected because they *seem* pertinent and not because they can be demonstrated to be so on the basis of the definition. Furthermore, the items provide no identifiable measure. In the test for "measuring" attitudes toward the church (36), for example, such items as the following can be found:

"I regard the church as a monument to human ignorance."

"I feel the church is the greatest agency for the uplift of the world."

The subject is instructed to check those statements with which he fully agrees. Such a check or lack of it may *seem* to provide information concerning an attitude as defined above, but no demonstration that this is the case has been provided. The definition does not make it easy to do so.

The first requirement in the test-design procedure presented here is to formulate a *scientific* definition of the property or properties involved. The requirements of a scientific definition were discussed in detail in chapter iii. Briefly, we said a scientific definition was one which made explicit the conditions under which and the operations by which questions concerning the concept defined could be answered scientifically.

Since we are going to illustrate this procedure on the trait ascendance-submission, let us begin by formulating a scientific definition of this trait.

In the ascendant-submissive situation the subject is faced with the following set of conditions: an aggressive act has been committed which decreases the efficiency of the subject's behavior with respect to one of his objectives. In other words, the stimulus is an aggressive act. The response in which we are interested is the subject's attempt to retaliate on the aggressor, that is, to control rather than be controlled by the aggressor. Thus we are interested in whether or not the subject responds to aggression and how he responds.

We can define ascendant-submissive behavior in terms of the following aspects of the subject's behavior:

(1) A response by the subject A to another individual's (B's) act, when B's act has the function of decreasing the efficiency of A's behavior with respect to one of his (A's) ends; that is, when B aggresses on A.

(2) A potential producer of a reduction in the efficiency of B's behavior relative to his (B's) ends.

In terms of these aspects of behavior the following behavior patterns can be defined:

(a) To exhibit both (1) and (2) is an ascendant act.

(*b*) To exhibit (1) and (not-2) is a submissive act.

(*c*) Not to exhibit (1) but to exhibit (2) is an aggressive (but not ascendant act.

(*d*) To exhibit neither (1) nor (2) is neither aggression nor submission.

The "degree of ascendance" of an individual can be defined as the *probability* of his choosing the behavior pattern (*a*), and the "degree of his submission" can be defined as the probability of his choosing the behavior pattern (*b*). The sum of these probabilities we can call his *degree of awareness* or *consciousness* of the aggression.

From the definition of degree of ascendance, we can immediately discern one loss involved in the use of verbal tests rather than staged environments. In the verbal test we ask the subject how often he tends to respond in a certain way when aggression occurs. Such a question will at best elicit information concerning his response to aggression when he is *conscious* of the aggression and his response to it. But many people respond to aggression without being fully conscious either of the aggressive act or of their response. Hence, the verbal questionnaire method will at best gather evidence on the subject's sensitivity to aggression when he is fully conscious of the aggression (in the sense that he can recall the aggression and his response to it). A more general measure of ascendance would depend on evidence other than the subject's verbal testimony or on a method of inferring from conscious responses to nonconscious ones.

The definition of ascendance-submission, which has been offered illustratively, is given in terms of overt behavior. To construct a verbal test of the trait, a translation will have to be made from the overt model to a verbal model.

The definition makes clear that the test items constructed for the ascendance-submission test should permit us to estimate how frequently the subject exhibits a certain type of behavior under specified circumstances. Such a determination cannot be made without error and consequent cost. A verbal testing procedure is therefore only justifiable if the cost of this error plus the cost of giving the test is less than for any other feasible method or combination of methods. In general, the researcher does not know whether or not this is so; he usually assumes that it is. This assumption does not mean that the researcher expects absolutely accurate responses, but it does imply that he expects to obtain the most information for the lowest cost.

It is to be noted that the design method being described does provide an estimate of the precision (reliability) of the subject's responses. The entire test will provide what amounts to repetitions of the same situations, and these repetitions will be the basis for estimating precision.

Although the presupposition of accuracy of verbal response is involved in this test-design procedure, it is important to note reasons why it might fail to hold for the purpose of suggesting subsequent research designed to check the accuracy of the presupposition. For one thing, the particular situation may seem "unreal" to the subject, and consequently he may have difficulty in imagining what he would do in given circumstances. For example, if we ask a man who dislikes intensely to use rail transportation what he would do if someone interfered with him while buying a train ticket, his distaste for the entire situation might distort his notion of what he would actually do. Or if we asked a pauper what he would do if he found someone in a Pullman berth he had reserved, his lack of familiarity with even analogous situations might bias his response. This latter point implies that the situations incorporated into the test must be chosen with an eye to at least the social and economic status of the subjects.

3.1.1.2. Use of Pertinent Attributes and Variables in Test Construction

In defining the property to be measured by means of the test, we have in effect characterized the environment, stimulus, and response to be observed. Now we have to decide whether they are to be held constant or varied and, if they are to be varied, in what respects they are to be changed. Presumably, these decisions would have been made in the design of the ideal model. But let us see how practical modifications might be made in the design of the ascendance-submission test.

The environment is specified in the definition as one in which the observed subject (A) is pursuing some objective (O). Hence this environment can change significantly with respect to how much the subject desires (i.e., intends) the objective he is pursuing. This is obviously a pertinent variable, for it seems clear that, if one person interferes with a second, what the second will do depends on how important he considers the objective he is pursuing. The subject's *degree of intention for* (interest in) *the objective*, then, is one pertinent variable.

The stimulus—the decrease in the subject's efficiency produced by the aggressor's behavior—is also pertinent. It seems clear that what the subject does to the aggressor will depend on the intensity of the aggression. We can measure the intensity of aggression, and hence the intensity of the stimulus, in terms of the decrease in efficiency for which the aggressor is responsible.

Finally, we have the efficiency of the available response of the subject for his end. That is, we want to know not only how frequently an individual chooses ascendant or submissive behavior but how that frequency varies with the effectiveness of the available means for obtaining his objective.

We can characterize each ascendant-submissive situation in terms of (a) the degree of the subject's interest in his objective; (b) the intensity of the aggression stimulus; and (c) the efficiency of the available means for accomplishing his objective.

These are the pertinent properties in the ascendant-submissive situation which we will want to vary. The problem now is how to vary them.

3.1.1.3. Varying the Attributes and Variables in the Test

We have made explicit which variables are pertinent and are to be changed. Now we must decide how they are to be changed. Again these decisions would presumably have been made in earlier stages of the design.

Suppose, for example, we decide that we want to express the property to be observed as a function of the pertinent properties. Then we would want to express the pertinent properties as variables which can take on any value along a specified continuous scale. For example, we may want to express the degree of ascendance-submission as a function of the three variables listed above. If this were our interest, we could design the test so that a multiple "regression analysis" could be conducted. We could determine how many and what values of the three variables would be necessary to get the accuracy and precision required by the research objectives.

On the other hand, we may merely want to determine what the degree of ascendance or submission is, and whether or not each of the pertinent variables affects it separately or in combination with other pertinent variables. We could then use a test design based on an analysis of variance. For our illustration, we are going to consider such a case. This decision merely to test the effect of the variables rather than the actual degree of their effect should, in practice, depend on the purposes of the research.

In the type of test design based on the analysis of variance, the scales along which the three variables change should be split up into intervals. The number of intervals selected will depend on many considerations, all based on the research objectives. One very important consideration is the number of test items that is desirable. For example, if we use the type of analysis of variance presented in Test 32 (p. 238), and, if we decide to use five values of each of the three pertinent variables, we will require a minimum of $5 \times 5 \times 5$, or 125 items.* If we select four of each, we will require $4 \times 4 \times 4$, or 64 items. When this ascendance-submission test was first designed, three values of each variable were used, and each combination was repeated once, making a total of $2(3 \times 3 \times 3)$, or 54 items. This was found to be too long a test for the subjects, and it

---

* The Latin Square and the Incomplete Block Design, both of which require fewer cells, yield a larger error. The cost of the increased error should be weighed against the cost of an increased number of items in selecting the test design.

was subsequently reduced to a breakdown of properties yielding $2(3 \times 2 \times 2)$, or 24 items, which appeared to be a suitable length. The selection of attribute intervals proceeded as follows:

The first property (a), the subject's interest in his objective, can be expressed along a continuous scale running from 0 to 1, where 0 represents complete lack of interest and 1 represents maximum interest. (See [5] for details on this scale.) But the scale can be broken into convenient intervals. Here the intention scale is split into three intervals: high (intense), moderate, and low (disinterested). In effect, this means that high intentions of .67 and over are taken to be essentially the same from the point of view of the research objectives. Of course, the subject is assumed to understand that such terms as "extremely important" and "critical" refer to this interval. In the same manner, intentions ranging from approximately .33 to .67 are considered to be essentially the same (moderate), and the subject is assumed to understand that such words as "moderately interested" refer to this interval. Similar remarks apply to the interval from .00 to .33 (low).

These attribute values can be represented symbolically as follows:

a_1 = low intention
a_2 = moderate intention
a_3 = high intention

The intensity of the stimulus (b) can be measured in terms of the decrease of efficiency in the subject's pursuit of his objective. Since the scale of efficiency also runs between 0 and 1, this measure will also vary between 0 (minimum stimulus) to 1 (maximum stimulus). (See [5] for details on this scale.) Here this scale will be divided into two parts: 0–.5 (low intensity of stimulus) and .5–1.0 (high intensity of stimulus). Assumptions corresponding to those made in the discussion of intention are also made here. These two attributes can be represented as follows:

b_1 = low intensity of stimulus
b_2 = high intensity of stimulus

Finally, there is the variable (c): the efficiency of the responses available to the subject for accomplishing his original objective. That is, the courses of action available to the subject can vary in efficiency relative to the objective he pursues at the time of the aggression. These variations may affect the subject's response to the aggression; for example, if he has little chance of obtaining his objective, he may not "object" so much to an aggressive interruption. This efficiency can also be measured along a probability scale running from 0 to 1.

This scale will be divided into two parts: 0–.5 (low efficiency), and .5–1.0 (high efficiency). These will be represented symbolically as follows:

c_1 = low efficiency

c_2 = high efficiency

Now any ascendant-submissive situation can be described in terms of these three properties and the attributes into which they are divided. Table 22 indi-

TABLE 22

POSSIBLE ASCENDANT-SUBMISSIVE SITUATIONS

Intensity of Stimulus		b_1		b_2	
Intensity of Response		c_1	c_2	c_1	c_2
Degree of Intention	a_1				
	a_2				
	a_3				

cates all the possible situations relative to the breakdown of the properties made above. From this table it can be seen that there are twelve different ascendant-submissive situations if the variables are changed as indicated.

Now it is necessary to decide what characteristics of the subject's response should be observed. It has already been indicated (in the definition of the trait) that our concern is with the probability of selecting an ascendant or submissive act. In a verbal test the subject can be asked to indicate the relative frequency of choice in such qualitative terms as "never," "practically never," "occasionally," "half the time," "frequently," "very frequently," and "always." If the subject is given a set of alternative responses which are supposed to be exhaustive, it is desirable that the sum of the frequencies indicated in his responses is equal to "always," since he must choose one response in each situation. This is very difficult to obtain if qualitative estimates of frequency are used. Hence, in this case it is more efficient to ask the respondent to estimate the percentage of the time he selects each alternative and instruct him that the percentages assigned to the alternatives in any situation should add up to 100.

Actually, the response in any situation is neither purely ascendant nor purely submissive, but it can be characterized by a scale value—its intensity. The extent to which the response affects the aggressor is a measure of its intensity. Thus pure ascendance and pure submission represent the upper and lower limits of this scale of intensity. The value of any response can be characterized by its distance from either limit. Its deviation from the ascendant limit is a measure of submissiveness; its deviation from the submissive limit is a measure of its ascendance.

The subject's response is studied with respect to its effect on the aggressor's behavior, and hence it is desirable to determine the relationship between the probability of responding in a certain way with the *intensity* of the retaliation involved in responding that way. This intensity can be measured by how much the subject decreases the aggressor's efficiency for his end. This scale, which also runs from 0 to 1, is here divided into three intervals:

d_1 = low intensity (0–.33)
d_2 = moderate intensity (.33–.67)
d_3 = high intensity (.67–1.00)

This completes both the specification of the attributes that will be changed and the specification of the values the attributes are to be assigned. It is still necessary to plan the statistical analysis of the responses given by each subject. To determine properties of the population from the sample, we must first be able to characterize each of the subjects in the sample. In this case, we will have to show how to characterize the population on the basis of characterizations of the sampled subjects.

It has already been indicated that in this test the analysis of variance will be used. The particular design to be used requires that there be a test situation corresponding to each of the twelve situations shown in Table 22 and that for each situation a determination is made of the probability of the subject's choosing responses of the alternative intensities.

It is very desirable in the initial test to have estimates of reliability (precision). In this sense, reliability means the dispersion of an individual's answers to the same or equivalent questions. Two situations can be taken to be equivalent if their attribute values are the same; that is, if they fall into the same cell in Table 22. If there are two items for each cell, a measure of reliability can be obtained. Other methods are available for obtaining estimates of reliability (see [15]). Duplication of items is one of the simplest and most informative methods, though it requires more items than other methods. The important thing, however, is that we design the test so that an estimate of reliability can be derived. Measures of reliability will be discussed below (in Sec. 3.1.1.7). But now let us turn to the test items themselves.

3.1.1.4. The Design of the Test Items

The requirements for the individual test items follow from the considerations and decisions we have just gone through. We want to construct twenty-four items, two falling into each one of the cells in Table 22. Each item should contain a description of an ascendant-submissive situation. This involves specifying the nature of the stimulating aggression and the importance of the subject's objective at the time of the aggression. Next should come a set of alternative responses which are all equally efficient for his objective but which vary in the intensity of their effect on the aggressor. And, finally, space should be provided for the subject to indicate how frequently he would select each alternative.

Let us examine one such item and see what has gone into its construction.

Having nothing better to do, you are out to take a relaxing Sunday drive in your automobile. You stop at an intersection to permit a pedestrian to cross the street. A car pulls up behind you, and its driver begins to sound his horn at you in a very annoying way. Would you

(1) Tell him to quiet down or deliberately delay in getting started so as to delay him more than is necessary? ....%
(2) Give him a dirty look but say nothing? ....%
(3) Ignore him and continue as you would normally? ....%

The situational presuppositions of this item are as follows:

    (1) The subject's objective is to relax.
    (2) The degree of intention for this objective is low (a_1); that is, there is "nothing better to do."
    (3) The intensity of the stimulus is high (b_2); that is, "very annoying."
    (4) The efficiency of the alternatives is high (c_2), since the drive will quickly come back to normal no matter what is done.

Therefore, this is an a_1–b_2–c_2 situation.

The response presuppositions on this item are as follows:

    (1) The three responses are equally efficient for the objective, since it is possible to continue the ride undisturbed no matter which choice is made.
    (2) Response (1) is designed greatly to decrease the efficiency of the other driver (d_3); response (2) decreases his efficiency mildly (d_2); and response (3) hardly affects his efficiency at all (d_1).

The order of the alternative responses should be randomized, otherwise the subject might tend to make his entries automatically and hence bias his responses considerably.

Consider another item.

You are reading an enjoyable book in a library, a book that you want very much to finish at the sitting. A boring and persistent acquaintance enters and begins a conversation with you. On the basis of past experience you know that it is practically impossible to discourage him. Would you

(1) Make brief answers and show your annoyance? ....%

(2) Pretend to have an appointment and excuse yourself?   ....%
(3) Enter into the conversation without remarking on the interruption?   ....%

The situational presuppositions of this item are as follows:

(1) The subject's objective is "reading a very enjoyable book."
(2) There is high intention (a_3)—the subject wants to continue reading the book very much.
(3) The intensity of the stimulus is high (b_2)—the interruption reduces the probability of reading the book to virtually zero.
(4) The efficiency of the alternatives is high (c_1), since the situation is such that the reader cannot possibly continue reading the book no matter what he does. That is, we presuppose the subject to be bound by social customs so that it is impossible for him to get up and leave and read the book elsewhere.

The response presuppositions on this item are as follows:

(1) The three responses are equally efficient for the objective, since, by the nature of the situation, none of them is efficient.
(2) Response (1) is of moderate intensity (d_2); response (2) is of high intensity (d_3); and response (3) is of low intensity (d_1).

In comparing any two situations of the sort just given, it will be apparent that they differ with respect to variables which, though not taken into account, may affect the subject's response. For example, in the reading-interruption situation, it would be considered impolite or rude to select the most ascendant response but not necessarily so in the driving situation. Or, again, in one of the two situations a stranger is involved; in the other, an acquaintance. Ideally we want to determine how the subject responds when no such nuisance variables are involved, but practically we cannot eliminate them in any physical sense. By randomizing over all such possible influences, however, we can cancel out their effect. If, for example, the analysis of variance is applied to the responses, it can be used to determine whether or not the controlled variables affect the responses, *providing* the uncontrolled variables vary in a random fashion. If the researcher suspects that an uncontrolled variable is influencing the results in a nonrandom way, he can evaluate each item with respect to that variable and cancel it out by use of the analysis of covariance.

One way of checking for the presence of systematic effects of an uncontrolled variable is to ask respondents (after they have taken the test) why they responded as they did on each item. If a reason consistently appears in these explanations—a reason which is not related to a controlled variable—it is likely to indicate the presence of a nuisance variable. Once such an influence is determined, it can be designed out of the test by using a random selection of values of the variable in the test items. For example, suppose the attribute of the aggressor "friend" or "stranger" is suspected of influencing respondents. Then an equal number of items involving friends and strangers can be used, and the attributes can be assigned to different items at random.

3.1.1.5. General Presuppositions of Test Design

In the test being constructed there are both general presuppositions which are pertinent to the entire project and specific presuppositions (some of which have been given above) which are pertinent to specific items of the test. Some of the presuppositions may appear to be tenuous, but it should be remembered that presuppositions of this type are involved in every research project, psychological, social, or otherwise. In most psychological and social test design, however, the researcher does not explicitly formulate his assumptions and hence does not expose them to critical appraisal.

General Presupposition I: For each of the twelve combinations of attributes there exist three probabilities (P_1, P_2, and P_3) assignable to each of the three alternative responses, respectively, for a given subject. Each P_i is the true measure of the subject's probability of selecting that particular response (i) when all the alternative responses have equal efficiency for his desired end. The sum of these probabilities is equal to one.

It will be recalled that "trait" was defined as typical behavior independent of efficiency. Therefore, it is necessary, if trait behavior is to be isolated, to make the alternative responses in each ascendant-submissive situation equally efficient for the respondent's objective. Then it is assumed here that, for each situation uniquely characterized by the pertinent attributes, there is a true probability of choice of each response characterized by the intensity attribute (d). Furthermore, the alternatives are assumed to be exhaustive; one must always be selected.

General Presupposition II: The expected value of the subject's estimates of the frequency with which he selects each response is equal to the true probability of selecting that response, P_i, presupposed in General Presupposition I above. That is, the subject's method of estimation is assumed to be unbiased.

These two presuppositions are the most general ones. Their validity is necessary to guarantee the pertinence of the entire procedure. They are, however, so general that an examination of their validity is generally too difficult. It is advisable, therefore, eventually to list presuppositions which are special aspects of the two above. These have been listed after the two test items given above.

It is to be understood that some of these presuppositions may fail for a given subject. For example, it is assumed that certain ends have high (or low) intention for almost everyone in a specified class for whom this test is designed. It may happen, however, that for a given individual this general property of the population fails. Thus, by listing the assumptions which were made to justify the inclusion of an item, the researcher is able to decide for specific subjects whether or not his response to the item should be included.

In items such as those illustratively constructed for the ascendance-submission test, it is assumed that the three alternative responses are equally efficient for the subject's objective. Furthermore, each of the responses is assigned an intensity value. The assumption of equal efficiency and the assigned intensity values can also be submitted to the judges for evaluation; it is highly desirable to do so. In this way this assumption can also be checked. A procedure which can be used for this purpose will be described in the next section.

In the ascendance-submission items the pertinent objective in each situation is designated. But obviously there are any number of different sets of other objectives which could accompany the designated objective in any environment. It is presupposed that the subject, when estimating the frequencies of his responses, will randomize over environments in which the behavior patterns will have any efficiency for other objectives. In other words, the natural question that will occur to any subject is that his response depends upon the other possibilities in the situation, and there can be no doubt that it does. But the subject's response is supposed to represent the relative frequency of a certain type of behavior over all possible situations. The instructions for the test should make this point clear to the subjects.

A given test may be suitable only for one population. For example, it may be unreal for farmers or inhabitants of rural areas. Consequently, the test should be designed for the population to be studied. If necessary, the population should be stratified and different tests constructed for each stratum. The explicit and precise definition of the population and strata is necessary for the proper design of the items.

The reality and applicability of test situations can be checked by use of judges who are asked to evaluate the test before it is issued. They can be asked, for example, how frequently they have been in such situations. Those situations which are unfamiliar should be dropped. A subject cannot be relied on to answer only the situations which are real to him. He will reply to others, and his response may consequently be inaccurate.

Once the test items have been selected, it is important that the order they are given in the final test does not introduce a bias in the subjects' responses. The items should not be ordered, for example, from less intense to more intense stimulation. To avoid such ordering, each item can be assigned a number and then be ordered in the test by the use of a table of random numbers. The same random ordering should be applied to the alternative responses. The ascendant response, for example, should not always be listed first among the alternatives. Its position should be varied randomly. Such randomized ordering tends to make the subject consider each item separately and minimizes his guessing or anticipating the next item and his response to it.

Every test, verbal or nonverbal, requires a set of instructions for the subjects. The instructions should be used to strengthen the assumptions involved in the test by anticipating questions the subject might have. In general, a sample item should be included which indicates how he should record his responses. For example, the directions to an ascendance-submission test might be constructed as follows:

DIRECTIONS

In this study you are presented with more or less familiar situations in which you are to choose among three ways of behaving.

Opposite each choice write how much of the time (in percentages) you think you would behave in such a way. Be sure your percentages add up to 100 for each situation.

As far as possible, base your answers on how you *usually behave* in these types of situations.

EXAMPLE: As you start to cross the street, a car stops directly in front of you. As you walk around the car, would you:

(% of
Times)

a) Shout at the driver.................................. ......0....
b) Give him a dirty look............................... ....75....
c) Do nothing.. ....25....

In this case the answers indicate that you would practically never shout at the driver; you would give him a dirty look about 75 per cent of the time; and you would do nothing about it 25 per cent of the time.

In each situation any choice that you would make would be just as efficient as any other; that is, all three choices would have about the same effect in getting you what or where you want.

3.1.1.6. Evaluating Test Items

The researcher who designs the test items can himself evaluate each item with respect to the pertinent attributes. In general, however, he should have some assurance that the subjects will interpret each item in the same way he does. To attain such assurance, a method such as the following may be used:

(1) Select a probability sample from the pertinent population. This sample should not overlap with the sample to which the test is ultimately to be given. This sample shall be referred to as "judges."

(2) Instruct the judges on the purpose and nature of the test, with emphasis on the meaning of attributes and the values of the attributes used.

(3) Provide each of these individuals with a matrix such as that shown in Table 22.

(4) Provide each judge with a numbered list of test items, randomly and differently ordered for each judge. In general, the number of items offered the judges should exceed some multiple of the number of blocks in the table. For example, if 24 items are to be used in the test (2 for each situation), 36 or 48 items in all (that is, 3 or 4 [but not the same number] for each block) should be given to the judges.

(5) Have each judge independently evaluate each item and record the number of the item in what appears to him to be the appropriate block of the table he has been given. It should be made clear to the judges that they need not try to place the same number of items in each block; they may even leave some blocks empty. (A modification of this procedure consists of having a "cannot tell" block for doubtful items; this procedure will, in the main, demand a different analysis of the results.)

(6) After all the items have been evaluated by each judge,

(a) Prepare a table for each item as follows:

JUDGE	(1) RESEARCHER'S EVALUATION				(2) JUDGE'S EVALUATION				(3) DIFFERENCE $[(2)-(1)]$				(4) SQUARE OF DIFFERENCE			
	a	b	$\ldots$	n	a	b	$\ldots$	n	a	b	$\ldots$	n	a	b	$\ldots$	n
1																
2																
.																
.																
n																

For example, suppose we use the four variables given in the ascendance-submission test: a, b, c, d. Suppose the researcher's evaluation of the item is a_1, b_2, c_2, d_1. Suppose the judge's evaluation is a_2, b_2, c_1, d_1. Then the differences between these are

$$\begin{array}{cccc} a & b & c & d \\ +1 & 0 & -1 & 0 \end{array}$$

and the squares are 1, 0, 1, and 0, respectively.

(b) Total the squares in each column under (4) and divide by the number of judges.

(c) If the value obtained in step (b) exceeds .50 for any attribute, it means the item has been judged to be the equivalent of one block away from the researcher's evaluation.*

The item can then be either discarded or given a new evaluation which will reduce this mean square deviation to less than .50 relative to the attribute in question.

Suppose, for example, that the designer gives the item the value a_1 and that each of 10 judges evaluates it as a_2. Each difference would be equal to 1, as would the squares. The mean square deviation would be equal to 10/10, or 1. If half the judges evaluated the item as a_1 and half as a_2, the mean square deviation would be 5/10, or .50. In the first case the item could be changed to an a_2 item, and the mean square deviation would be equal to 0. Suppose half the judges evaluate the item as a_1 and half as a_3. The mean square deviation would still be equal to 1.0, but changing the value of the item to a_1 or a_3 would still yield a mean square deviation of 1.0. The item should then be discarded.

There is nothing compulsory about using .5 as the critical value of the mean square deviation. If more than majority agreement is desired, the value can be decreased.

(d) Repeat step (c) for each attribute and subsequently for each item.

On the basis of this procedure we infer that those who are to be given the test will interpret consistently the situations which survive the judgment; that is, each item will appear the same to most of the sampled subjects. This gives us assurance of the reliability of each item over the population. Furthermore, it provides a measure of reliability of the paired items; it tells us whether or not

* Several aspects of this measure of item adequacy should be noted. First, the measure assumes that the seriousness of an error is equal to n^2, where n is the number of categories by which the judge's evaluation differs from that of the researcher. Other assumptions could be made; for example, making the error equal to n or n^3. The more critical reliability is, the greater the power of n should be. Second, the seriousness of a deviation of n categories is independent of the total number of categories into which the attribute is broken. However, the "distance" between categories along the underlying scale of the property decreases as the number of categories into which the property is broken increases. But it is assumed here that the number of categories used by the researcher reflects the importance of distance along this scale. The difference between two categories (regardless of the range covered by the categories) is therefore considered to be practically (though not metrically) equivalent regardless of the total number of categories involved. Suppose, for example, the underlying scale goes from 0 to 1. If two categories are used, they might be defined as follows: a_1 ranges from 0 to .5 and a_2 ranges from .5 to 1.0. If four categories are used, a_1 may range from 0 to .25, and a_2 from .25 to .50. Hence differences which are not important in the first case are in the second. In other words, a difference of .50 is taken as the critical difference in the first case, and .25 is so taken in the second case. Thus, though these units differ metrically, they are identical practically because they represent in their respective situations equivalent practical units of difference.

we are justified in saying the two items are the same for the population. Finally, it enables us to determine if the unpaired items are different to the population; that is, whether or not the population discriminates between the items.

The procedure just described is similar in some respects to that used by Thurstone (35); it differs from his method in one important respect: the judges are provided with an explicit definition of the attribute values with respect to which they are to make their evaluations. An item is good to the extent to which it receives consistent evaluations by the judges. Hence the variance of the judges' estimates can be converted into a measure of the reliability of the item *with respect to the property involved.*

3.1.1.7. Evaluating the Responses and the Test

A test designed by the method just described yields a good deal of information. Such information can be summarized by various scoring devices. We want to use that method of scoring which best serves the research objectives. Since objectives vary, there is no unique best method of scoring.

One very simple scoring method is the following. Consider each percentage entered beside an ascendant response as positive, and each percentage beside a submissive response as negative. Total these percentages (omitting the entries beside the "neutral" responses). Divide the total by the number of items. The maximum value which can be obtained in this way is 100 per cent, which represents a maximum degree of ascendance (and minimum degree of submission). The minimum value which can be obtained in this way is −100 per cent, which represents the maximum degree of submission (and minimum degree of ascendance). That is, positive values indicate ascendance and negative values indicate submission. Zero represents the lack of a tendency toward either.

Such a scoring method leaves out a good deal of information. We could get slightly more information, for example, by averaging the ascendant, submissive, and neutral percentages separately, and then use all three values. But even in this three-valued score much information would be ignored. By use of the analysis of variance considerably more information could be obtained.

If we apply the analysis of variance to the responses, we can determine which variables, separately or in combination, affect the responses. Such information would be necessary in some research projects. For example, in determining job suitability, it might not be enough to know whether or not a potential supervisor is ascendant. We may also need to know if he tends to become more ascendant the more intense the aggression on him. This knowledge can be provided by an analysis of variance.

The application of an analysis of variance to each test is a lengthy and perhaps costly procedure. Again, the basis of decision as to how to analyze the test scores should be a comparison of the cost of each scoring procedure and the value of the information yielded. An added advantage of the analysis of variance should be kept in mind, however: it enables us to evaluate the test as well as the responses.

First, let us consider an evaluation of the test and the entire sample relative to each other. Suppose, for example, that we have K pairs of items in a test, that is, each item is duplicated. Let a represent one item of the pair and b represent the other. Then, if there are k subjects, a table such as the following could be prepared:

	ITEMS						
SUBJECT	1		2		...	k	
	a	b	a	b	...	a	b
1							
2							
.							
.							
k							

The entry in each cell would consist of the percentage assigned to the ascendant alternative minus the percentage assigned to the submissive alternative.

From these data the estimates of variance (mean square deviation) can be computed for the items (columns), subjects (rows), interaction, and within groups.

If no difference in the responses accompanies differences in the items, then we will infer that the subjects fail to discriminate between the items; that is, there is no real difference between the items for the subjects.

If there is no significant difference in the responses accompanying differences in the subjects, then we will know that the test fails to discriminate between the subjects. It may be, of course, that the subjects are not different with respect to the characteristic tested. However, if the subjects are believed to be different, such a result could mean that the test may not be sensitive to differences as small as exist between the subjects. If the differences between the subjects are believed to be large, then the test would be considered to be inadequate.

If the interaction between subjects and items is not significant, we can infer that the items discriminate in the same way for all the subjects; that is, they are not being interpreted differently by different subjects. If the interaction is significant, it may mean that the items mean different things to different individuals. (For other possible interpretations see p. 240.)

An analysis can also be conducted to determine how reliable are the subjects' responses. There are duplicate items for each cell; the duplication is asserted on the basis of the judges' evaluations. The *a* columns and *b* columns can be grouped and then a test conducted to determine whether there is a significant difference between *a* and *b* columns. If there is no significant difference, we can infer that in general the subjects are consistent (i.e., reliable). If there is a significant difference between the grouped *a* columns and *b* columns, we can infer either that the subjects are not consistent or that the judges were in error and the items are not reliable. These possibilities could be studied further.

The same type of analysis can be made relative to each item; that is, test the difference between the *a* and the *b* column. In this way reliability of the subjects (taken collectively) relative to each separate item can be tested.

The analysis discussed above provides an evaluation of the test relative to the entire sample and an evaluation of the sample relative to the test. A similar procedure can be applied to each individual. By use of the matrix shown on page 321 the responses of each subject can be analyzed separately in order to determine whether each subject discriminates between items and whether each subject is consistent over the duplicates. A more intensive analysis of each subject's responses can be made by recording his responses (the difference between ascendant and submissive percentages) as was done in the matrix on page 311. This matrix provides a three-variable, $3 \times 2 \times 2$ factorial design with replication. By use of the analysis of variance we can determine for each subject (1) whether his degree of ascendance or submission is affected by each of the three variables (intention, intensity of stimulus, and efficiency) taken separately and (2) whether this measure is affected by each of the three possible combinations of two variables and all three variables taken collectively. Such an analysis provides more than the usual descriptive score; it provides explanatory data as well.

Nothing in a verbal test itself provides a measure of the accuracy of the responses, except in the case where the property studied is the ability to attain a certain score on the test itself (e.g., a reading ability or vocabulary test). In most cases verbal test responses are substitutes for other types of behavior, other evidence of which is difficult or costly to obtain. The definition of the property tested, however, should indicate how such observations might be made. If no definition is provided (which is quite common), no way of checking the verbal responses is even imagined. The reliance of the social sciences on verbal tests is so great that it seems wise to make a serious effort to check the accuracy of test results by use of a model situation. A check on even a small sample of the population is likely to be very revealing. There is nothing wrong in relying on the verbal substitutes *providing* this reliance can be justified. Without checking against model testing, we do not even have grounds for saying "verbal tests are the best practical tool available." Furthermore, unless such evaluations of verbal tests are made, we have no basis for adjusting the test responses, that is, correcting for inaccuracy produced by the instrument.

In some cases a check on accuracy can be made. For example, suppose the test is one of attitudes toward compulsory military training. The accuracy of the test can be estimated roughly by giving it to samples from two populations, one known to be in favor of such training, and one known to be opposed. For example, voluntary enlistees in the military service can be taken as a "pro" group, and conscientous objectors as an "anti" group. The test should yield high pro- and anti-scores, respectively, for the two groups.

The use of such an accuracy check involves a number of assumptions. In this illustration it assumes, for example, that a person with a pro-attitude is more likely to enlist in a military service than one with an anti-attitude. This may not be the case. Enlistments may be the product of fear of the draft and the restrictions on the draftee relative to choice of type of military duty rather than the result of a pro-attitude. Another possible type of error is one which arises where the test actually measures an attitude other than the one intended, and it may happen that the attitude measured is characteristic of one of the groups tested and not the other. Unless the attitude tested is clearly defined, and unless the essential producers of the typical pro- and anti-groups are known, this type of check on accuracy may yield deceptive and even false results. But if the researcher is armed with good definitions and knowledge of the producers of his test groups' behavior, this method may be very effective.

It must be remembered that a test which, for example, enables us to predict who will and who will not enlist in military service does not necessarily measure attitudes toward compulsory military training. It may simply measure "inclination to enlist." To get from this inclination to the attitude, a good deal of conceptual, factual, and theoretical information is required. A purely intuitive or common-sense jump may be spectacular, but it is not sound scientific procedure.

In sum, a test score by itself means nothing; it is only a number. It can only derive meaning from the conceptualization which *systematically* enters into the test design and in terms of its accuracy and precision as a measure of the property conceptualized. The test should be so designed as to provide estimates of the precision of the responses and to permit checks on its accuracy. If it is not so designed, either the results are useless or a separate and frequently fruitless research project must be entered into in order to determine possible uses for the scores obtained. Predictability is *not* enough. To know that people who obtain a score of such an amount are likely to do so and so does not by itself add to our *understanding* of the subject or his behavior. Prediction of this sort is a type of numerological witchcraft, not science. Prediction is scientific only if it is based on conceptualization, theory (assumed laws), and data in such a way that the success *or* failure of the prediction adds to our understanding and hence control of natural (including human and social) phenomena. In effect we must know *why* a prediction fails or succeeds, or, more generally, *why* a test score can be used to help solve the research problem. The test design and its scoring and evaluation, discussed herein, have all been directed to producing data which can be *understood* and, hence, systematically improved as science demands.

3.1.2. Questionnaires

Although a good deal has been written on the subject of questionnaire design, most of it has consisted of the obvious. There are as yet few hard methodological principles which can be used. Consequently, this discussion will lack the rigor of that in the last section.

In designing a questionnaire, we assume that the subject can directly give us the value of the property (or properties) being investigated. We must decide, as in test design, just what we want to know (and hence why we want to know it), but the way to go about getting it is different. For example, if we assume an individual knows what his attitude toward a religious group is, then we ask him to express that attitude or to select from a set of alternative expressions that one which most nearly conforms with his attitude. But if we assume that he is not aware of his true attitude, then we must construct an attitude test which will be at least as complex as the trait test discussed in the last section. The economy of time and effort for the designer and respondent is considerable if we can justifiably assume this knowledge and awareness on the part of the respondent.

If a questionnaire is constructed on the basis of an assumed but nonexistent knowledge, needless to say, the results are worthless. We should be careful, then, whenever we use a questionnaire, to examine as best we can the legitimacy of such assumptions. Such examination may be based on previous studies or on a pretest deliberately conducted to check this assumption.

Once we have decided that we can assume the subject has knowledge of the points at issue, the problem is primarily a communicative one. This means that we want to make sure the subject understands the questions as we want him to, that he tries to give a truthful answer, and that we get his answer accurately recorded.

At present we have no organized science of linguistic communication to help us in these problems, though there are contemporary attempts to construct such a science. As yet there are no general criteria to assist in the design of questionnaires. Hence, if we want to evaluate the adequacy of a questionnaire beforehand, in most cases, the best we can bring to bear—other than controlled pretesting—is common sense and past experience. Past experience with questionnaires, however, is by no means meager. There are numerous articles in the journals which provide sound advice for specific types of questions. One of the best of these is authored by Mauldin and Marks (24). A number of the following remarks and illustrations are borrowed from this article.

Response errors to questionnaire items may, in general, be due to two factors: (1) poor communication and (2) poor recall. "Poor communication" may involve either (*a*) the failure of the question or the one who asks it to make its meaning clear or (*b*) the failure of the respondent to make his meaning clear, or, if he makes it clear, the failure of the recorder of the response to grasp the meaning. The failure of the interviewer to make the question clear may be due to his failure to understand it. This, in turn, may be due either to poor training or to lack of ability. Both of these problems will be considered in the next chapter in connection with selection and training of personnel.

It is obvious and trite to say that questions should use language familiar to the subjects, that they should not be too long, and that there should not be too many of them. The problem, of course, lies in the meaning of "familiar," "too long," and "too many." Several attempts have been made to obtain systematic knowledge on these points (34) by employing linguistic scales. But, as yet, the designer must rely primarily on unsystematized familiarity with the population to be questioned, common sense, *and* the pretest. (More about the pretest appears in chap. x.)

If there is any doubt as to whether or not a question or statement contains too much, it is better to break it into two or more questions.

Until recently the Bureau of the Census has asked . . . : "What is the highest grade of school you have completed?" Interpreted literally this question should offer no difficulty for the vast majority of people in answering it correctly. However, many people hear the term "highest grade of school" and immediately think in terms of the highest grade of school they "went to." Some people don't even hear the final word in the question, that is, the word "completed." . . . So we now ask, "What is the highest grade of school you have attended?" Then, the respondent is asked, "Did you finish this grade?" This eliminates part of the response bias for this particular item [24:650].

Respondents tend to give answers they *think* the interviewer wants. They may think incorrectly, in which case the respondent's incorrect anticipation should itself be anticipated. The author, for example, once asked a housewife, "Do you raise poultry?" The response was, "No," but it was accompanied by sounds of chickens in the back yard. Further questioning made clear that the housewife thought the question meant "Do you raise poultry for sale?" She raised poultry only for her own use. The question was subsequently changed to "Do you have any live poultry on this place?" Mauldin and Marks point out that "in evaluating a question it is more important to ask 'How will the respondent interpret this?' than to ask 'What does this question mean?' " (24:650).

In some cases the question is addressed to the interviewer or observer; that is, he is asked to make a judgment concerning a property of that which is observed (e.g., the condition of a house, the status of a person). In such cases, even if "condition of a house" or "status" is defined, the observer may prefer his own notion as to what these terms mean. Where this is the case, it is desirable to break the question down into a set of components which can be answered without involving the concept or the observer's prejudices but from which an accurate and reliable judgment can subsequently be derived. For example, it is better to ask questions to determine the extent to which hot and cold water are available than to ask, "Is the supply of water adequate?"

Errors of recall may be due to lack of knowledge or poor memory. In one study, for example, F. F. Smith (29) asked students to check off those books on a list (which he provided) which they had read. The list contained a number of titles of nonexisting books. But over one-fourth of the students checked one or more of these. For other similar results see (17) and (18).

We cannot expect a respondent to remember too far back. When he says he has read a nonexisting book, he probably is not lying deliberately; the title sounds familiar, and he concludes that he must have read it, or he has doubts and decides to "play safe."

Response errors can be reduced in many cases by several alternative design procedures. To do so may be costly, and the gain in accuracy may not be worth that cost. Consequently,

in considering the reduction of response error, the fundamental question is how accurate the data should be. Frequently an answer to this question will raise the further problem of how much it is worth (in dollars and in effort) to achieve a given level of accuracy. The level of accuracy required is, of course, dependent upon the uses to be made of the data. For example, much greater accuracy on age is required in preparing life tables for actuarial use than would be required in classifying the population into age groups for an analysis of public opinion trends [24:653].

This problem is the analogue of one we have already considered in chapter iii—determining how accurately measurements should be made. Here, as there, we are concerned with two costs: the cost of the inaccuracy a given procedure is expected to yield and the cost of using the procedure. The designer, then, should select a questionnaire and validation procedure which minimizes the sum of these two costs. Research may be necessary to obtain satisfactory estimates of these costs.

Some of the possible validation procedures have already been mentioned, but let us consider the alternatives and their relative advantages and disadvantages.

1. Preventive measures can be taken by attempting to formulate questions that will be interpreted the way the designer wants them to be interpreted. Or questions can be prefaced by explanations which attempt to make their intentions clear. The adequacy of the question and the preface can be determined by the use of pretests. For example, in a pretest of the question, "How far did you go in school?" a number of rural residents gave an answer such as "two miles." The question designer was completely surprised by such responses, for the meaning of the question had seemed clear to *him*. The designer himself is seldom a good judge of the clarity of the question.

The advice and criticism of those who are familiar with the type of question involved, and of those who will use the results of the research, can provide a valuable check on the adequacy of the items. Consultant and advisory committees should be used wherever possible.

2. The questionnaire can be constructed so as to provide internal checks on reliability. The inclusion of false items, referred to above, provides a basis for evaluating responses to true items. Duplication of questions, however, provides a better basis. For example, if we want to determine the age of the respondent, the question, "What was your age at your last birthday?" can be followed (not necessarily immediately) by "What was the month, day, and year of your birth?" We could then determine if the two answers are consistent. Consistency is no proof of validity, but consistent answers are more likely to be accurate than inconsistent ones.

3. Record checks can be used for the validity of some responses. For example, if we determine by use of the questionnaire the place of birth and residence of the parents at the time of birth, we may be able to check birth certificates. Such checks are likely to be costly and time-consuming. This can in part be overcome by checking a sample of such records.

The major drawback of making record checks . . . is that usually a substantial proportion of the cases cannot be "matched." Furthermore, it is very difficult to establish a so-called match if the discrepancy between the survey figure and the "true" figure is large. . . . We do not expect to be able to match more than 80 per cent of the Census data on age with birth certificate data, even if the study is restricted to persons born after 1915 [24:654–55].

The utility of record checks obviously depends on the property checked and the population involved. In one case, a record check on data of naturalization, over 90 per cent of the cases could be matched. In some cases the cost of such checks may not be too high, since the records may be in the possession of the subject (i.e., car titles, mortgages) or in one central agency (e.g., at a bureau in the city hall).

4. An intensive reinterview of a sample of the population may be conducted. Both the interviewers and the questions in such an interview are more carefully selected. Since a smaller sample is involved, fewer interviewers are required, and only the better interviewers can be used. Questions on the original questionnaire can be broken down into several components. The answer to the original question can be checked against the subsequent answer, and, where there is a discrepancy, the interviewer can attempt to determine which answer is correct. Further, he can in many cases determine *why* one response was incorrect. Such explanations provide valuable information in evaluating data and in directing future questionnaire design.

Many questions are "summation" questions; for example, "How many rooms are in this house?" "How many children do you have?" "How many times have you moved in the last five years?" Such questions can be broken down into component parts in an intensive reinterview, or the respondent can be asked to itemize the parts. For example, the respondent can be asked to list the rooms on each floor of his house, including the attic and basement.

Suppose that on reinterviewing it is discovered that a respondent neglected to count one room in his original response. Discussion may reveal that he did not count a recreation room which he built himself in his basement. If such omissions are frequent, we learn that the original question was not adequate. Thus the knowledge gained from such reinterviews can help reduce errors in subsequent research.

4. Summary

In this chapter we have considered a number of practical adjustments in the ideal model which the research designer may be required to make. First we considered problems arising from the unavailability of designated subjects. This problem is most acute where the observer must go to the subjects' usual environment, or else get him on the telephone, or persuade him to respond to a mailed stimulus. The magnitude of the problem can be reduced by making appointments, giving advance notice of calls, selecting efficient times to call, and using efficient personnel. The harm done by unavailables can be partially compensated for by use of substitute respondents, call-backs, and follow-ups. The Politz-Simmons method is a new procedure which can be used in some cases to correct for the bias due to unavailables without making call-backs.

Refusals constitute a problem which can be avoided in part by preventive measures: publicity, good observers, explanations to the subject, inducements, and a method which does not arouse antipathy. Where these fail, substitutes or call-backs can be used.

It may not be possible or practical to observe responses in all the desired environments and under all the desired stimuli. In such cases interpolation and extrapolation can be used on the basis of regression analyses. If none of the conditions can be met in a practical way, verbal substitutes can be used. Of these, there are two types: tests and questionnaires. The latter presupposes knowledge of the property in question on the part of the subject; the former does not.

The design of a test requires a scientific definition of the property being investigated. The pertinent attributes and variables must then be analyzed to determine which of their values should be employed. These values can then be designed into the test to enable determination of the contribution of each variable to be made; for example, by an analysis of variance. Once the test items are designed, they should be evaluated by a set of judges selected from the population to be studied. The results of the judges' evaluations provide a basis for selecting reliable and discriminating items. Once the test has been given, both the items and the responses may be further evaluated for reliability and discrimination. Accuracy may be checked by using populations with "known characteristics" or (preferably) by controlled behavioristic tests.

The questionnaire must make clear to the subject what information the observer desires. The problem is essentially one of communication. Pretests and advisory groups can aid in clarifying questions and preventing ambiguity. Record checks can be used to estimate accuracy of responses, and duplicate questions can provide measures of reliability. Intensive reinterviews of a subsample of the original sample provide information not only on the accuracy of the original data but on how to avoid repetition of such errors in subsequent research.

DISCUSSION TOPICS

1. What are the possible reasons for a person's being unavailable? How would one handle each type of unavailability?
2. What are the possible reasons for refusals? How could one handle each type?
3. Select a test familiar to all members of the group. What evidence is there that the test measures what it is supposed to? Is the evidence adequate? If not, how could one redesign the test?
4. How could one design a test to measure an individual's vocabulary? How could one evaluate the test and the responses?

5. Under what conditions would the following be useful scientific instruments: (*a*) participant observing; (*b*) motion-picture cameras; and (*c*) sound recorders?

EXERCISES

1. Design three ascendance-submission test items. Identify the cell into which each one falls and make explicit the presuppositions of each.

2. Suppose three candidates are running for the same public office. Design a polling questionnaire which can be used to determine the outcome and the extent to which each candidate deprives the others of votes.

3. In an intensive follow-up survey on student income, how could one break down the question: "How much money did you earn last year?" Outline a pretest to determine the adequacy of the breakdown.

4. Suppose that in a study of voting behavior several subjects refuse to answer the question: "Did you vote in the last presidential election?" Write out the remarks one could make to induce the refuser to answer.

5. Prepare an observational model for your course project.

SUGGESTED READINGS

For an introduction to the problem of unavailables see Birnbaum and Sirken (4), Hansen and Hurwitz (11), and Hilgard and Payne (14). For alternative methods of test design see Guilford (10), Stouffer (32), and Thurstone (35). A particularly good discussion of response errors is to be found in Hansen *et al.* (12) and in Marks and Mauldin (24). An excellent discussion of the use of record checks and follow-up surveys is to be found in Eckler and Pritzker (8).

REFERENCES AND BIBLIOGRAPHY

1. ABRAMS, MARK. "Possibilities and Problems of Group Interviewing," *Public Opinion Quarterly*, XIII (1949), 502–6.

2. ALLPORT, G. W. *Personality: A Psychological Interpretation.* New York: Henry Holt & Co., 1937.

3. BEVIS, J. C. "Economic Incentives Used for Mail Questionnaires," *Public Opinion Quarterly*, XII (1948), 492–93.

4. BIRNBAUM, Z. W., and SIRKEN, M. G. "Bias Due to Non-availability in Sampling Surveys," *Journal of the American Statistical Association*, XLV (1950), 98–110.

5. CHURCHMAN, C. W., and ACKOFF, R. L. "An Experimental Definition of Personality," *Philosophy of Science*, XIV (1947), 304–32.

6. COOMBS, C. H. "Mathematical Models in Psychological Scaling," *Journal of the American Statistical Association*, XLVI (1951), 480–89.

7. DEMING, W. E. *Some Theory of Sampling.* New York: John Wiley & Sons, 1950.

8. ECKLER, A. R., and PRITZKER, LEON. *Measuring the Accuracy of Enumeration Surveys.* Washington, D.C.: Bureau of the Census, 1951.

9. EYSENCK, H. J., and CROWN, SIDNEY. "An Experimental Study in Opinion-

Attitude Methodology," *International Journal of Opinion and Attitude Research*, III (1949), 47–86.

10. GUILFORD, J. P. *Psychometric Methods*. New York: McGraw-Hill Book Co., 1936.

11. HANSEN, M. H., and HURWITZ, W. N. "The Problem of Non-response in Sample Surveys," *Journal of the American Statistical Association*, XLI (1946), 517–29.

12. HANSEN, M. H.; HURWITZ, W. N.; MARKS, E. S.; and MAULDIN, W. P. "Response Errors in Surveys," *Journal of the Amercian Statistical Association*, XLVI (1951), 147–90.

13. HARTLEY, H. O., in FRANK YATES, "Review of Recent Statistical Developments in Sampling and Sampling Surveys: Methods of Estimating Sampling Error with Discussion," *Journal of the Royal Statistical Society*, CIX (1946), 12–43.

14. HILGARD, E. H., and PAYNE, S. L. "Those Not at Home: Riddle for Pollers," *Public Opinion Quarterly*, VIII (1944), 254–61.

15. JOHNSON, P. O. *Statistical Methods in Research*. New York: Prentice-Hall, Inc., 1949.

16. LINDEMAN, E. C. *Social Discovery*. New York: Republic Publishing Co., 1924.

17. LUCAS, D. B. "A Rigid Technique for Measuring the Impression Values of Specific Magazine Advertisements," *Journal of Applied Psychology*, XXIV (1940), 778–90.

18. ———. "A Controlled Recognition Technique for Measuring Magazine Advertising Audiences," *Journal of Marketing*, VI (1942), 133–36.

19. LUNDBERG, G. A. *Social Research*. New York: Longmans, Green & Co., 1946.

20. LUNDBERG, G. A.; KOMAROVSKY, MIRRA; and McINERY, M. A. *Leisure: A Suburban Study*. New York: Columbia University Press, 1934.

21. LUNDBERG, G. A., and LARSEN, O. N. "Characteristics of Hard-To-Reach Individuals in Field Surveys," *Public Opinion Quarterly*, XIII (1949), 487–94.

22. LYND, R. S. and H. M. *Middletown*. New York: Harcourt, Brace & Co., 1929.

23. ———. *Middletown in Transition*. New York: Harcourt, Brace & Co., 1938.

24. MAULDIN, W. P., and MARKS, E. S. "Problems of Response in Enumerative Surveys," *American Sociological Review*, XV (1950), 649–57.

25. PARTEN, MILDRED. *Surveys, Polls, and Samples*. New York: Harper & Bros., 1950.

26. PAYNE, S. L. "Case Studies in Question Complexity," *Public Opinion Quarterly*, XIII (1950), 653–58.

27. POLITZ, ALFRED, and SIMMONS, W. R. "An Attempt To Get the Not-at-Homes into the Sample without Call-Backs," *Journal of the American Statistical Association*, XLIV (1949), 9–31.

28. SHEATSLEY, P. B. "An Analysis of Interviewer Characteristics and Their Relationship to Performance," *International Journal of Opinion and Attitude Research*, IV (1950–51), 473–98.

29. SMITH, F. F. "Direct Validations of Questionnaire Data," *Educational Administration and Supervision*, XXI (1935), 561–75.

30. STEMBER, HERBERT, and HYMAN, HERBERT. "How Interviewer Effects Operate through Question Form," *International Journal of Opinion and Attitude Research*, III (1949–50), 493–512.

31. STOCK, J. S. "The Problem of Call Backs," in *Measurement of Consumer Interest*, ed. C. W. CHURCHMAN, R. L. ACKOFF, and MURRAY WAX. Philadelphia: University of Pennsylvania Press, 1947.

32. STOUFFER, SAMUEL, *et al. Measurement and Prediction.* Princeton: Princeton University Press, 1950.

33. SUCHMAN, E. A., and McCANDLESS, BOYD. "Who Answers Questionnaires?" *Journal of Applied Psychology,* XXIV (1940), 758–69.

34. TERRIS, FAY. "Are Poll Questions Too Difficult?" *Public Opinion Quarterly,* XIII (1949), 314–19.

35. THURSTONE, L. L., and CHAVE, E. J. *The Measurement of Attitudes.* Chicago: University of Chicago Press, 1929.

36. ———. *A Scale for Measuring Attitudes toward the Church.* Chicago: University of Chicago Press, 1930.

CHAPTER X

The Operational Phase of the Practical
Research Design*

1. Introduction

This chapter is addressed primarily to the student taking his first steps along the tortuous road to a research result and to those professional social scientists who have had little opportunity for conducting research.

This chapter consists largely of a set of opinions. In this respect it does not differ much from other discussions of "how" to conduct research. An attempt will be made, however, to formulate the opinions so that they are capable of being tested as methodological hypotheses. The opinions to be offered will differ in another respect from many that appear in the literature: they will be formulated so as to give them some *directive* value.

For an opinion to be of some directive value, its contradictory should also make some sense. In other words, an opinion of directive value should make one of a set of meaningful, mutually exclusive assertions concerning operations. Opinions of the following type do not have this property and hence are not directive:

(1) Observations should be made as carefully as possible.
(2) Instructions to and reports from observers should be as clear as possible.

Such tautologies as these do not deal with alternatives, and they certainly do not tell the research worker what to do in specific research situations. (Imagine someone asserting the contradictory of these!) Such statements may, however, affect the intellectual climate in which research takes place. There is good reason to believe that the kind of intellectual climate which statements like the above tend to produce is usually an undesirable one.

Consider, for example, the first statement: Observations should be made as carefully as possible. Tremendous waste and inefficiency can occur as a conse-

* This chapter was written jointly with Leon Pritzker of the Bureau of the Census.

quence of the striving for a level of "care" far above the requirements of the research objectives. Also, many of our techniques are so little developed that a word like "care" cannot meaningfully be applied to them. Some aspects of the research process are just plain crude. Therefore, at the present stage of technical development in the social sciences, a "principle" like the above may operate to produce compulsive behavior of a most undesirable sort.

To compensate for crudity in some areas, those aspects of the research for which relatively sophisticated techniques are available are sometimes treated in an overly precise way. For example, there is the use of time-consuming, complex statistical tests when "less powerful" but also less expensive tests are available. There is also the rather common phenomenon of much closer examination and "editing" of the contents of each questionnaire or the report of each observer in a study than the gain thus obtained is worth.

Consider the second statement: Instructions to and reports from observers should be as clear as possible. It is quite possible that the understanding of the observer may, in fact, be clouded or that his morale (and efficiency) may be lowered as a consequence of an insistence on "clarity" which forces him to be on guard for the slightest ambiguity or which completely constrains the exercise of his judgment and (scientific) imagination.

This is not to be construed as an argument for mysticism. For example, Flesch indexes of readability (16) have a place in research design, but only on an experimental basis. There seem to be, however, two objections to the clarity principle as stated above. On the one hand, this principle can come to be associated with a kind of logic-chopping and distinction-making that would drive a Philadelphia lawyer to distraction. On the other hand, it can come to be associated with a fetish for "simplicity" in writing instructions which tends to make the average observer believe he is being treated as a simpleton—and tends to make him act like one.

"Scientific" platitudes which invoke "care," "clarity," "simplicity," etc., make easy reading and invoke little disagreement, but they also evoke no science. The platitude, cliché, and tautology indicate the need for methodological research; progress can take place only when this fact is recognized as such.

Two aspects of the discussion in this chapter should be explained. The orientation of much of the discussion is toward large-scale research. This is due to the fact that the operational phases of large-scale research are more conspicuous than are those of small-scale research. The implication of this remark is *not* that operational planning does not need to be as thorough in small-scale as in large-scale research. This, as a matter of fact, is a danger to be guarded against, because small-scale research is the more frequently underplanned in the operational phases.

The second aspect of the following discussion requiring explanation is the abundant use of illustrations from survey research. This is primarily due to the fact that in this type of research the social scientist has attained a relatively high degree of self-consciousness.

2. The Operational Plan

Up to this point, our concern with the practical design has not required us to descend to the depths of really vulgar detail. At this point, however, there is no retreat. The researcher must eventually face the dismal task of planning the actual conduct of the research—of devising techniques for producing the research result.

It is helpful to use as a prototype for the operational plan of research the productive plan of business and industry. The "operational planning" of research is, in fact, productive planning. Research has a *product* (the results and conclusions, usually as presented in a research report). The product has certain quantitative and qualitative specifications. There are production deadlines to be met. Although only some research is conducted (quite legitimately) for monetary profit, there is general agreement that input should in some sense be commensurate with output.

The operational plan takes as its starting point the specifications set forth in the sampling, statistical, and observational phases of the practical design. These specifications constitute a set of proposals for actually conducting the research. The operational designer has the following tasks to perform:

(1) To determine the cost, feasibility, and acceptability of the research specifications (i.e., to evaluate the specifications).

(2) To translate the specifications into operations: into research tasks, research directives, and research instruments.

(3) To provide techniques for determining if the specifications are being followed (i.e., to keep the research in "control").

(4) (In large-scale research) to provide methods for selecting, training, and assigning personnel.

(5) (In large-scale research) to provide administrative procedures.

In the remainder of this chapter we will take up each of these task areas of operational planning in turn. Then we will conclude by considering briefly some additional criteria the operational planner should use in his decision process (i.e., planning). There will be no detailed discussion of an important topic: the personal qualities of the operational planner himself. This omission does not arise from our ignorance of the subject—ignorance has been no obstacle to writing this chapter—but rather from the view that progress in a *science* of method, as distinguished from the *art*, will come from the development of method itself. There is little doubt, however, that most significant social research to date has been performed by people whose intuition, judgment, and artistry were well in advance of their method.

3. Evaluating the Specifications

At the present stage of methodological development the best instrument by which this work of revision and adjustment of competing demands can be accomplished is research itself. That is, past research or new specially planned auxiliary research can best provide a sound basis for evaluation of specifications.

Previous research can very frequently throw light on the planning of current research. In some cases, the current research suggests ways of reanalyzing data obtained in earlier studies so as to provide information useful in the current project. Such analyses cannot automatically be assumed to be pertinent to the current work. That is, the designer must decide how general are the evaluations based on past projects. The lack of social and methodological theory makes it difficult in many cases to infer from one project to another. This point will be considered below in the discussion of theory.

Previous research will seldom provide a sufficient basis for evaluating all the specifications of the present research. Hence, among the most effective design-evaluation tools are the *pilot study*, the *pretest*, and the *trial run*.

These are "offspring" researches designed to facilitate any design phase, but in particular the operational planning of the over-all or "parent" research. There are no precise or generally accepted meanings for these types of research; the terms are frequently used interchangeably. To facilitate this discussion of their function, however, the following usages are proposed:

1. *Pilot study.*—An "offspring" inquiry directed toward determining what are the alternative situations by which the researcher may be confronted in the actual conduct of the research. The alternatives involved are the ones which his operational procedures should be designed to handle. Hence, the pilot study is designed to indicate what *are* the possible alternative operational procedures. Such studies are essentially *descriptive* in character.

2. *Pretest.*—An "offspring" inquiry directed toward evaluating one or more explicitly formulated operational procedures. Hence, the pretest is designed to indicate which operational procedures *should* be used. Such studies are essentially *evaluative* in character.

3. *Trial run.*—An "offspring" inquiry which provides a final check on the exhaustiveness of the alternative operations considered and the efficiency of the

operations selected. Hence this study is designed to evaluate the operational plan as a whole before the final run.

3.1. The Pilot Study

In any situation requiring action one has to take into account "the facts-of-the-case," that is, the "pertinent information." To take a prosaic example, a salesman who wants to sell his product must locate potential buyers, determine their characteristics, find out when they are in, how to reach them, etc. Others may be able to provide him with such information, but, if not, he must dig it out for himself before he can make the sales effort. Similarly in research, before the designer can execute the research, he must determine what are the facts of the case. Has he taken into account all the possible reactions of the subjects, the possible environments into which he may have to go, the difficulty that might arise in arranging to observe or interview a subject, etc.? These and many other similar questions have been raised throughout this book.

Furthermore, once the researcher has identified the alternatives, he may have to learn more about their characteristics. For example, relative to a given operational procedure or (preferably) to a set of alternative procedures, how many refusals should he anticipate or how many call-backs? How much will a call-back cost? What is the average number of people he will find in a cluster of households? How many of the subjects can he reach by phone? That is, the operational planner may want to determine what values to put into his thinking in preparing the operational procedure.

Pilot studies can therefore be divided into two classes: one class includes studies designed to expose (i.e., to itemize) alternatives, *exploratory* studies; the other includes studies designed to determine the pertinent characteristics of (i.e., to assign descriptive values to) alternatives, *estimative* studies.

3.1.1. Exploratory Pilot Studies

Exploratory studies can be of a *probing* sort; that is, they can be directed to finding out what happens if such-and-such is done. For example, if a researcher wants to know what types of responses he is likely to get to certain types of stimuli, he can select a subsample of the sample eventually to be studied, or another sample from the same population, and try the stimuli on those selected to see what responses are actually obtained. This would enable him to develop a classification of possible responses and enable him to prepare himself operationally for each of these classes.

On the other hand, the researcher may want to know what alternative ways

there are of stimulating a certain response. In such a case it may be more difficult to determine where to look to find sources. In the probing type of study the
source is known, but not so in this *searching* type of exploration. For example,
suppose the researcher wants to make sure that he has taken into account all
the ways of relieving racial tension in a community. Part of his problem is
"Where to look?" as well as "What will be found?" Consequently, he must
examine alternative sources, and therefore, first, he has the task of determining
where to look. He may be able to get assistance from those who have been concerned with similar problems in the past, or he may have to analyze the process
involved in order to determine where possible relief of the tension could come
from.

An example of research exploration is to be found in the work of Terman and
Merrill (33), who have reported on the large amount of preparatory activity
which preceded the 1937 revision of the Stanford-Binet intelligence test.

General preliminary researches on particular types of tests and special problems
of method were undertaken by qualified graduate students under our direction in the
laboratory. . . . Bailey's study of the ability of children to make comparisons from
memory and Rulon's study of the verbal absurdities test yielded information that
was of value concerning two important types of tests. Deal's experiment on weight discrimination to determine the effect of differences in instructions and of different series
of weights demonstrated that, at the age levels where the test was applicable, geo-
metrically equal increments in the weight series did not produce equal sense distances
nor make the series equally difficult at every point. On the basis of this study, we selected the optimal weight series and directions only to discard the test finally because of
its poor showing in the statistical analysis of the standardization data [33:7–8].

Whether exploration is of a probing or of a searching character, it should be
systematized so as to assure its exhaustiveness and its nonrepetitiveness. That
is, a probing or search plan should be developed which assures the completeness
and nonrepetitiveness of exploration. Everyone has experienced the frustration
of looking for a pin or coin which has been dropped on the floor. In most un-
organized searches the same places are examined several times, and the place in
which the pin or coin is located has been missed. Only planning can prevent the
analogue from occurring in research.

3.1.2. Estimative Pilot Studies

The best operational decisions in many cases require estimates of various
properties of the population, environment, and/or stimuli relative to one or
more operational procedures. How many people will refuse to answer a certain
question? How much will a call-back cost for various field plans? How many of
the sample will be away on vacation during the interview period? How many

parents will resent their children being used as "guinea pigs"? To answer such questions as these a small subsample of the final sample or a separate sample drawn from the same population can be studied to obtain an estimate of the variable in question, thereby making possible more efficient planning of the subsequent research operations. The researcher sometimes hesitates to engage in such "double research" because he suspects that the preliminary research will only confirm his guess of the value of the property in question. Such an effort, however, need not waste time, money, and effort. To the contrary, if the estimative study is designed with an eye to the parent-project, the results obtained in the pilot study can frequently be incorporated into the results obtained from the final run. This point has already been made in the discussion of double sampling.

Suppose, for example, a researcher wants to obtain an estimate of the variance of a certain property of the population so that he can determine what sample size is required. By the use of a small subsample he can obtain such an estimate, and, if there are no large-scale subsequent revisions in the procedure, the data obtained from the subsample can be incorporated into the results obtained from the second and larger sample. As a matter of fact, he may find in some cases that the first subsample is sufficient to yield the desired level of precision.

3.2. Pretests

The pretest can be used to evaluate one or more alternative operational procedures. For example, in the design of a questionnaire it is generally desirable to know beforehand how efficient an instrument it is: How accurate and reliable are the responses it evokes? In general, one efficient way to answer this question is to test it on a subsample of the (final) sample to which it is to be given or on another (matched) sample from the population to be studied. The use of judges in test design (as described in chap. ix) is a type of pretest.

Pretests which are intended to evaluate an operational design decision should be so conducted as to yield *measures of effectiveness* and not mere data which can only be intuitively evaluated. This means that the pretest should be methodologically designed; all that has been said about the design of research in this book should be applied to the pretest. In particular, the criterion of effectiveness with respect to which the evaluation is to be made should be made explicit *beforehand*, and the conditions under which an alternative will be accepted as "good enough" should be made explicit.

The pretest is truly an "experimental" vehicle. The term "pretest" rather than the term "experiment" is used because, at our present stage of development, pretests must be carried out under essentially the same conditions as the final research itself rather than under laboratory conditions. (More about this point later in this section.) The pretest is a controlled study of alternative research specifications, instruments, or plans in order to determine which alternative is the most efficient.

As was mentioned earlier, a pretest can—and often should—use up a considerable portion of the total funds available for the research. It may be possible, however (as in the case of the estimative pilot study), to use a subsample of the sample to be included in the main research in a manner such that the data of the pretest can be combined with those of the parent-research.

Below are listed some examples, hypothetical and otherwise, of pretests:

a) A decision is required as to whether data for a particular study should be collected by mail or by direct interview. If the criteria of cost, quality, timing, etc., can themselves be explicitly formulated, then a pretest can be useful in reaching an efficient decision.

b) Bancroft and Welch (3) have reported on the use of a pretest to determine if a proposed revised schedule for the Census Bureau's monthly labor-force survey provided better employment statistics than the schedule in use. Their criterion was a higher aggregate employment as a consequence of higher totals for part-time and "unpaid family" employment. Note that their account clearly indicates that they were testing alternatives:

> The new schedule was pretested in April, 1945, in all . . . sample areas throughout the country. The pretest was based on a sample of approximately 2,000 households selected at random from the total . . . sample. The sample households were enumerated with the old schedule as a part of the regular April enumeration. The following week the sample households were enumerated a second time, using the new schedule. The information recorded on the new schedule applied to the same census week as the old schedule. The . . . information . . . was . . . tabulated so as to provide a direct comparison of the employment status information obtained by use of the two schedules [3:307].

Clearly, the research designer would be faced with an impossible task if he had to undertake a pretest for each alternative procedure which he or anyone else could think of, or, for that matter, if he had to run a pilot study for all questions he had concerning alternatives. How does the designer determine where to conduct such studies and where not? One can answer by muttering something about research planning being an art and about the need for experienced researchers with great intelligence, sound judgment, profound intuition, and upright consciences. One should add in an even louder voice that these qualities may not be enough. Here is an example.

Marks and Mauldin (25) have reported on a pretest undertaken in preparation for the Seventeenth Decennial Census of the United States. The pretest was concerned with the evaluation of alternative enumeration techniques. One of the questions raised for the pretest was that of the relative efficiency of self-enumeration (respondent fills out the questionnaire). Two schedule formats were designed to aid in answering this question:

Schedule D: One side of this schedule . . . contained 10 columns of questions for various members of the household—two columns of questions for each individual repeated five times. To complete this side of the schedule, the respondent had to spread it out to its full size (18" × 24"), a rather formidable expanse of paper almost completely covered with fairly fine print. When it came out of the printing press its own parents called it an atrocity. Very few of us expected it to survive its early childhood. However, the schedule had substantial advantages in processing, and, therefore, it seemed worth testing.

Schedule A–I: The A form was a 4 page booklet, the page size being 9" × 11". [It was designed for general household information.] . . . For each member of the household, one of the Individual Enumeration Forms (I) was used. This was a sheet of paper 9" × 11". The questions were printed front and back in two columns. Although the print on the individual form was smaller than is desirable, the schedule arrangement was reasonably "open" and did not appear to be nearly as crowded as did the questions on the D schedule [25:427–28].

Marks and Mauldin continue by pointing out how their (implicit) expectation and the evidence did not exactly agree: "Most of the people concerned with the design of the schedules considered the A and I combination superior to the D schedule in appearance and convenience for the respondent" (24:428). But consider what their results and, more important, what their general conclusions were:

About the same number of respondents (approximately ½) filled out both forms, and the error rates on the two forms also were approximately the same. Furthermore, the total enumerator time per household for D is almost exactly the same as for A. Since only one county was used with each of the forms, the results cannot be conclusive. *However, the lesson we have learned is that it is not safe to rely heavily upon your own judgment in these matters* [25:428].

There seems to be a single important reason why past experience and educated judgment are far from being adequate guides for making design decisions. *It is the absence of theory.* For most aspects of the research design, we do not know when, how, or to what extent to generalize from one study to another. This is why pretests have to be conducted under essentially the same conditions as the parent-research. Also, this is why those who try to conduct methodological experiments in the social sciences are compelled to make somewhat less than sweeping generalizations from them. Consider the following examples:

a) Weilbacher and Walsh (34) have described a study which was designed to deal with the general question: "Do personalized greeting and genuine signature affect returns to mail questionnaires positively?" The study was rather rigorously designed. Yet note how the authors conclude:

Do the results of this experiment apply generally? If we wish to be conservative, then we must say that the results obtained apply only to the alumni members of a professional fraternity located at Columbia University. . . . The general conclusion which we reach is that further investigation with a larger sample and a less specialized population might well be advised [34:336].

b) Durbin and Stuart (12) have reported an elaborately (and rigorously) conducted piece of research directed toward determining what differences, if any, exist in the response rates of experienced as against inexperienced interviewers. The experiment marks a big step forward in survey methodology. As an appendix to the research report, there are comments by various discussants of the paper. Some of the comments attributed to Louis Moss (director of the English Social Survey) are very pertinent to this discussion:

Some of the conclusions should . . . be used in an extremely tentative way. Because of the conditions of the experiment it seemed highly likely that they were not firm indications of what was to be expected in the general run of such work.

For example, it was said that there was no evidence of marked heterogeneity amongst individual investigators. It had, however, been found as a result of experimental work at the Social Survey that differences between investigators, certainly in some fields of work, did exist. . . .

In the same way it appeared from the present results that age of investigator had little effect on the results obtained. At least one Social Survey inquiry had demonstrated that the age of the investigator was related to the results achieved.

No doubt such differences in results of experiments were to be expected until we knew more about standardizing our method of inquiry.

But so far as the present paper was concerned, there was . . . a rather more serious point to be made. Some reference was made to the need for compromise between the methods of the different organizations concerned* in order to reach an effective design for the inquiry. Owing to these compromises the results, on the one hand, were not those to be expected when these organizations were using their normal methods of work and, as the paper pointed out, because of this the results probably underestimated the difference between experienced and inexperienced investigators. On the other hand, it was not possible for the design of the experiment to take into account many known differences in approach and method, and the results reflected these differences in an uncontrolled way. This meant . . . that we must be even more cautious about generalizing from the data given [12:198].

The difficulties arising from lack of theory in methodological experimentation are illustrated in another way by Durbin and Stuart:

Though the inquiry has demonstrated the inferiority of the students in obtaining interviews when compared with professional interviewers, it tells us nothing of the causes of the differences and whether they can be easily remedied [12:184].

* Durbin and Stuart's interviewers came from the London School of Economics, the Social Survey, and the British Institute of Public Opinion.

The need for pretesting operational decisions is inversely proportional to the amount of theory which is available. The amount of theory available, in turn, depends on the extent to which the operations have been studied methodologically, and hence in a way that yields results which are *accumulative.* A pretest can be used to show that interviewers of type A are better than interviewers of type B when using a certain questionnaire under a specific set of conditions. But this is not enough. What happens if the questionnaire or the conditions are changed? Unless the pretest is designed to determine the producers of differences in interviewers, this question cannot be answered. In so far as a pretest fails to expose these producers, its results are not likely to be applicable to any other research design. Consequently, pretests should be designed not only to yield an evaluation of a difference in operations or operators but to yield an *understanding* of the difference; that is, an *explanation* of the difference.

The knowledge gained by explanatory pretests when combined with generalized conceptualization of the operations involved eventually yields a theoretical basis for making operational decisions. This has been the case, for example, in sampling design where there is an extensive theory which in many cases enables efficient operational decisions to be made without the use of pretests. As the discussion in chapter iv has indicated, probability sampling theory has advanced to the stage where choices among alternative designs can be based on theoretical grounds and where generalization beyond the specific results of the research is feasible.

The ideal of "design evaluation" apparent in the development of probability sampling theory has been extended by the sampling theorists to cover certain aspects of the operational design. For example, to the extent that randomization can be introduced into the design, mathematical models are available to aid the operational planner in evaluating the specifications in the following ways:

(1) To aid in determining the number of observers required for a given level of precision and, thus, to determine if the funds are sufficient to conduct the research as specified. See (20).

(2) To aid in determining whether the errors in the processing of data are acceptable. Here the acceptance sampling theory of quality control can be used. See (8:viii).

(3) Where field work is involved, to aid in estimating travel costs. This can be done by computing expected travel distances among a set of randomly selected points.

It is also worth noting that the methods of *linear programming* ([6] and [11]) can be used with considerable effectiveness in determining where field offices should be located so as to minimize travel costs. The applicability of this method to research design is just beginning to be considered; it should prove to be a powerful design tool.

The point that we have tried to emphasize in this discussion is that the pretest is a methodological proving ground which is capable of yielding basic and fundamental knowledge of design operations. When this method is fully exploited, it removes the need for repetition of similar testing in subsequent research. The redundancy of pretesting in current social research is an appalling waste of research effort due to the lack of adequate design.

3.3. The Trial Run

There is a point in the research design where much of the planning has been completed and the questions are raised: "Will the procedure work?" "Will I (or the personnel I have or can get for the job) be able to follow the procedure?" One way to find out is to "give it a try." When the tryout is taken to be tentative, the result is a *trial run*. A trial run (or *preview*, as it is sometimes called) can be used as (1) a basis for deciding whether or not to conduct the research as planned and/or as (2) a device for making "final adjustments" in the research procedures. The trial run is not directed toward comparative evaluations, as is the pretest; it is directed toward the evaluation of one over-all operational plan. Such an over-all evaluation was made by Terman and Merrill in the development of their intelligence test. Their study appears to be deficient with regard to sampling, but it does illustrate the design use of the trial run.

The preliminary tryout provided the necessary data for the selection of tests for the provisional scales. As we have already stated, the retention or rejection of items was based on several criteria. In order of importance these were: (1) validity, (2) ease and objectivity of scoring, and (3) various practical considerations such as time, economy, interest to the subject, the need for variety, etc.

Validity in turn was judged by two criteria: (1) increase in the percents passing from one age (or mental age) to the next, and (2) a weight based on the ratio of difference to the standard error of the difference between the mean age (or mental age) of subjects passing the test and of subjects failing it [33:9].

A trial run permits an over-all evaluation of the research design before the full-scale research procedure is put under way. If there is reason to believe that only minor revisions will be required after the trial run, a subsample of the sample to be studied can be used. In this way the data obtained from the trial run may be capable of being incorporated with the data obtained from the final run. If, however, there is reason to believe that extensive changes may be required, a separate nonoverlapping sample from the pertinent population should be selected. Then none of the final sample of subjects is "used up." At the present time, since so little theory is available which can enable inferences from one population to another, it is important that the trial run be conducted on a sample from the pertinent population. Only by so doing can the applicability of the results to the final run be assured.

The trial run has another important function: it can be used to provide training for the personnel to be involved in the final run. Observers, editors, coders, computers, supervisors, etc., can get realistic experience with the tools they are to use. The operational designer, in turn, can evaluate his staff and make necessary changes in it before he is committed to it.

A good illustration of the use of a trial run is to be found in the *Annual Report of the Secretary of Commerce, 1940:*

A special census of St. Joseph and Marchall Counties, Ind., was authorized by the Secretary of Commerce to be taken as of August 14, 1939. This census, a preview of the decennial census of population, proved to be very helpful in providing a testing ground for the schedules, auxiliary forms, instructions, and procedures planned for the decennial census and indicated some necessary changes in the schedules and procedures. Two innovations of the trial census were the use of objective tests as a means of testing and selecting the enumerators after a period of census training and the employment of squad leaders as supervisors of from 10 to 20 enumerators. Both of these innovations were adopted by the Sixteenth Decennial Census.

This trial census also provided real data for training office employees before the population schedules from the regular census were received. Preliminary editing and coding instructions, card forms, tabulations, and even table forms for the final census reports for 1940 were developed well in advance of any previous census on the basis of the substantial "census preview" [2:42].

Finally, it should be noted that the trial run provides not only an efficient way of training personnel but also a basis for evaluating personnel selected to determine whether they will do a good enough job.

4. The Budget and Time Schedule

The operational planner is in the peculiar position of being better able to see the forest than the trees. Consequently, he must use instruments to magnify the details of the operational plan. Two instruments available to him for this purpose are the *budget* and the *time schedule*. The inability to complete these in precise ways brings about the need for theory and for pilot studies, pretests, and trial runs. Budgeting and scheduling are activities which should commend themselves to graduate students as well as to research directors.

Budgeting and scheduling can usually be combined into a single activity. They should start at the very beginning of the research design, since the design phase itself should be budgeted and scheduled. The value of an early start is that it permits the designer to determine how much *planning* the research needs and can afford. The overexpenditure of resources at the planning stage (happily, not yet a common occurrence) can throw the entire project out of balance. To be sure, the first budget-time schedule prepared will have to be revised.

The preparation of the budget-time schedule (see Fig. 34) requires taking each design specification, translating it into a set of operations, appraising how much the operations will cost in *man-hours* as well as money, and estimating how long the operations will take to accomplish.

It should be stressed that Figure 34 is a *summary* form. The real planning comes in the detailed examination of each phase of the planning itself, the sampling model, the statistical model, and the operational model. It should be noted also that there is nothing in the illustration which contradicts the notion of overlapping activities in time or of suspending activities and then resuming them. The marked human tendency toward "closure" as defined by the Gestalt psychologists has to be overcome at times. It becomes an experimental question whether or not, for example, to delay the processing of data until after all the data have been collected or to conduct a survey "in series" or "in parallel" from geographical area to area.

The matter of estimating research costs is no more and no less understood than the matter of estimating the costs of conducting a business. There has been no consistent theory of cost estimating or of cost accounting developed yet. The most common distinction made in accounting methods is that between a *fixed* cost and a *variable* cost. Yet it is easy to show that even so-called "fixed" costs are only relatively fixed. As a matter of fact, a great deal of economy can come from questioning the apparent "fixity" of a fixed cost. For example, printing costs of research forms are generally taken to contain a fixed element (the layout and plate or stencil preparation) and a variable element (the number of copies, the type of paper, etc.). Yet the fixed element can turn out to be quite variable under examination. The federal government has published a rather instructive bulletin on this subject (14).

To demonstrate the type of detail required for efficient and realistic budgeting, an example (adapted from work done by the design staff at the Bureau of the Census) is given. The problem set is that of determining the field supervision costs of an area sample survey covering the United States:

Definitions of Symbols:

M = total number of areas or primary units (counties or groups of counties) into which the United States may be divided for the purpose of selecting a set of sample areas in which the survey will actually be conducted.
A = average area of a primary unit.
I = total number of interviewers to be employed.
K = average number of days to be worked by all interviewers.
C_1 = daily salary to be paid a supervisor.

Activity	Total	Week Ending	Week Ending	Week Ending	. . .
1. Total *a*) Man-hours *b*) Cost ($) *c*) % of total completed					
2. Planning *a*) Man-hours *b*) Cost *c*) % completed					
3. Pilot Study and Pretests *a*) Man-hours *b*) Cost *c*) % completed					
4. Drawing Sample *a*) Man-hours *b*) Cost *c*) % completed					
5. Preparing Observational Materials *a*) Man-hours *b*) Cost *c*) % completed					
6. Selection and Training *a*) Man-hours *b*) Cost *c*) % completed					
7. Trial Run *a*) Man-hours *b*) Cost *c*) % completed					
8. Revising Plans *a*) Man-hours *b*) Cost *c*) % completed					
9. Collecting Data *a*) Man-hours *b*) Cost *c*) % completed					
10. Processing Data *a*) Man-hours *b*) Cost *c*) % completed					
11. Preparing Final Report *a*) Man-hours *b*) Cost *c*) % completed					

FIG. 34.—Suggested form for budget-time schedule summary. (There is nothing necessary or sufficient about this listing of activities, nor is the order absolute in any sense.)

Definitions of Symbols (Continued):

C_2 = payment per mile to be paid a supervisor for travel.

C_3 = "per diem" payment to a supervisor when he is working outside the sample area in which he lives.

Assumptions:

(1) There will be 1 supervisor per 10 interviewers or $I/10$ supervisors.

(2) There will be a two week (10 day) training session for supervisors. The training will be held at a point roughly equi-distant from the homes of the supervisors.

(3) In addition to the two week training session, supervisors will be needed for 3 weeks longer (15 days) than the interviewers. Thus each supervisor will work $[K/I + 10 + 15]$ days.

(4) Travel to and from sample areas and to and from training centers will not take place during working hours.

(5) It will be necessary to make "per diem" payments to supervisors throughout the period of training, and for half the time they are supervising interviewers.

(6) The distance to be traveled to the training center by the supervisors is on the average equal to the square root of the area of the United States, which is equal to $\overline{AM}$. The average distance to be travelled by a supervisor while working with his interviewers is equal to the square root of that part of the area of the United States in which the sample areas to be covered by the interviewers assigned to him are located. This average distance is assumed to be equal to

$$\sqrt{\frac{10\,AM}{I}}$$

Equation for Training Costs of Supervisors: Based on the above assumptions, the total training costs are equal to

$$\frac{I}{10}\left(10C_1 + \sqrt{AM}\,C_2 + 14C_3\right).$$

Equation for Costs of Supervising Interviews: Based on the above assumptions, the total training costs are equal to

$$\frac{I}{10}\left[(K+15)\left(C_1 + \frac{C_3}{2}\right) + C_2\sqrt{\frac{10\,AM}{I}}\right].$$

Equation for Total Costs of Supervision: Based on the above assumptions, the total costs of supervision are equal to

$$\frac{I}{10}\left[(K+25)C_1 + \left(\sqrt{AM} + \sqrt{\frac{10\,AM}{I}}\right)C_2 + \left(\frac{K}{2} + 21.5\right)C_3\right].$$

The example given is meant to be illustrative. The applicability of the approach, as opposed to the details, is quite general; small-scale as well as large-scale research is subject to such budget analysis. The validity of the cost equations is not being considered here. As with every other phase of the research design, validity is an experimental question.

The budget-time schedule has to be continually re-examined as the research moves forward. This problem and the techniques for dealing with it will be discussed in Section 6 below.

5. Translating the Specifications into Operations

As pointed out above, evaluating the specifications requires that they be translated, conceptually at least, into the operations that have to be performed in order to complete the research as specified. A device that is recommended is the writing of a *working guide*. The architectural equivalent of this *working guide* is the *working drawings* in which the minutest construction details are specified. In the working guide, the various design decisions should be translated into (painstakingly) detailed specifications for specific tasks and materials that are required for the conduct of the research. The preparation of this guide never turns out to be a *mere* breakdown of design decisions. It always involves a recasting of at least some of the decisions. This detailed set of specifications should reflect all the practical considerations involved in conducting the research. It makes possible a final practical translation of the idealized model.

Together with the preparation of the budget-time schedule, the writing of this working guide should provide the chief point of contact between the sampling, statistical, and observational plans, on the one hand, and the research-in-process, on the other. It is at this stage that the intentions of the research designer can be rigorously clarified (and qualified).

The working guide should cover every aspect of every phase of the actual conduct of the research. It should include (subject to modifications due to the nature of the research) detailed specifications of the following operational processes:

1. Drawing the sample
2. Preparing forms and other instruments necessary for taking and controlling observations
3. Selection and training of personnel
4. Taking, recording, and transmitting the observations
5. Editing the data transmitted
6. Putting the data into usable form (e.g., coding and punching on cards)
7. Tabulating the data
8. Analyzing the data
9. Preparing and publishing the final report
10. Controlling each of the above operational phases of the research

To give an idea of the type of detail that should be of concern in preparing the working guide, consider the following list of situations (as set down by Parten) which a survey interviewer might encounter in trying to locate a subject.

1. No one answers the door.
    a) The occupant is not at home.
        (1) He is away for the day—working, visiting, shopping, etc. The interviewer should try to ascertain (probably from neighbors) when the occupant is expected or likely to be home.
        (2) The family is out of the city on vacation or business.
    b) The occupant is at home but does not wish to answer the door. It may be necessary to telephone or write for an appointment, or maybe a call in the evening when the husband returns from work may bring an answer.
    c) There is no occupant—the house is vacant, according to neighbors.
2. The address assigned is or appears to be nonexistent.
    a) The building has been demolished.
    b) The house number has been changed.
    c) The original assignment is in error
        (1) Because of an error in the source list.
        (2) Because of clerical error in the office.
        (3) Because the street name was changed after the source list was compiled.
    d) The interviewer is on the wrong street and so cannot find the correct house number.
3. The dwelling unit assigned is vacant.
    a) Shall the sample case assigned be traced to his new address? If so, what if he has moved out of the city?
4. The original building has been demolished and a new, different type of structure replaces the old.
5. The person or family assigned by the office has moved and a new occupant has moved in.
6. The dwelling unit assigned is not that of the householder but of a roomer.
7. The address assigned contains no dwelling units, only a place of business.
8. The address assigned is both a dwelling unit and a place of business.
9. The building is divided differently from that indicated by the source list; e.g., according to the source this is a one-family house, but since the source was compiled the house has been altered to accommodate three families. Which one or ones shall be scheduled? What shall be done about the others?
10. The address assigned is a rooming house. Shall some or all the lodgers or only the householder's family be scheduled?
11. The address assigned is a social agency, hotel, hospital, or other institution. What information shall be obtained regarding transients, permanent residents, employees, inmates, etc.?
12. The individual assigned is now deceased, has moved out of the city, has moved within the city.
13. The address assigned is not inside the city boundaries.
14. The family assigned sublets light-housekeeping rooms to another family. Shall the subtenant be scheduled on the same or on a separate form?
15. The address assigned is a business structure, but a janitor lives on the premises.
16. The interviewer discovers that the janitor's quarters were not listed on the original source, and so did not have a chance to be included in the sample.
17. The occupants of the dwelling are living in the country during the summer months.

a) They have subleased their quarters for a short time during the summer. The original family may or may not come back to the address in the fall.

b) They have merely closed their homes during the summer, leaving their furniture in the home [27:343–44].

The working guide should cover each of these and any other pertinent possibilities. A corresponding degree of detailed consideration is required for each aspect of the research operations.

The working guide is required whether or not the operational planner carries out the actual research operations himself. The working guide should *not* be regarded as the observers' instructions or as the "manual" of directives for the research; rather (where additional personnel are required) it should be viewed as an intermediate *source document* from which research directives are prepared and the research materials ordered.

5.1. Research Directives

Everyone who has had a hand in the design of research and has had an opportunity to watch others collect observations or conduct interviews on *his* project. knows the frustration of trying to get the observer or interviewer to do what he (the designer) wants. We have not come near solving this problem, though we have made numerous efforts to do so. Research directives are designed to get research personnel to do what the designer wants them to do. These directives consist of instructions, memoranda, orders, etc., issued to the persons engaged in carrying out the various research operations. One can write a series of rules for research directives which call for "clarity," "simplicity," "brevity," etc. We will not, since such rules have been recorded in profusion. Rather, we should like to call attention to an important difference in types of research directives.*

Current efforts to provide operational directives can be classified into the "closed" and "open" types. The closed-directive approach holds as its ideal the construction of a machine or a machine-like observer or interviewer who will provide physically identical auditory or visual stimulation to all subjects or respondents and who will make an exact physical reproduction of the responses to this stimulation. This approach suffers from a major deficiency: it fails to recognize that two physically identical stimuli or responses may have different *meanings* under different circumstances. The word "Yes," for example, does not always signify agreement; under some circumstances it may signify that the respondent wants only to satisfy the interviewer or get rid of him quickly. It takes an interviewer who is sensitive to nonphysical differences in interview situations to modify stimuli or to interpret responses to get at their meaning.

* The remainder of this section consists of a slightly modified portion of an earlier article of the authors (1:330–34).

This "closed" approach may result in a high degree of precision, but in some cases it produces a considerable loss of accuracy.* The use of the closed approach may result in a tremendous bias if interviewers uniformly fail to understand an instruction.

On the other hand, if the observer is given considerable freedom to get information as he sees fit (the "open" approach), there may be a considerable loss in precision, although in some cases this approach will achieve a high degree of accuracy. The open-ended observational or interview procedure, in which the observer or interviewer supplies his own criteria of efficiency to any procedure he adopts, may introduce a variance within and between observers which frequently is reflected in the results.

One way of formulating the dilemma is in terms of the mean square error (MSE): $MSE = b^2 + s^2$, where b^2 (the bias) expresses the deviation of the attained result from the "true" value, and s^2 is the estimate of the variance of the obtained result. In our view, a closed mechanistic set of directives tends to increase the bias and decrease the variance; an open-ended approach will have just the contrary effect.

In most cases, an increase in the efficiency of the research procedures and reduction of the mean square error are approximately equivalent if the cost is fixed. (This is not always the case, however.) Consequently, the problem of providing adequate operational directives can be reformulated for most research situations in terms of providing those instructions to the observer or interviewer which will minimize the mean square error.

So much for a statement of the problem. Now what can we do about it? The job of providing adequate operational directives has received little controlled study. As a result, most principles of design in this area are trivial and nondirective. Consequently, evaluation of operational directives must depend, in most cases, on the use of the pretest.

Assertions concerning the efficiency of alternative operational directives can be formulated as hypotheses which can be tested. This means that the alternatives should be set up in advance and the criterion of efficiency should be made explicit. Such a procedure can reduce the necessity for additions to and revision of operational procedures while the survey is in process. Few things are more destructive of observer and interviewer morale than repeated revisions in instructions.

In the design of operational directives, as in other phases of research design, the criteria of adequacy of decisions stem from the purposes for which the research is being conducted. We can illustrate this point by outlining a procedure for breaking down a definition into an observational directive. Let us return to

* For the distinction between "precision" and "accuracy" see chap. iv.

an earlier example: a survey of chairs in living-rooms. Suppose the survey is studying actual living conditions and involves many other items besides chairs. As we have already indicated, a chair is an object to be defined primarily in terms of its use, not its structure. Suppose, for illustrative purposes, we adopt the following definition of a chair: "an object which is intended to be used and can be used by one and only one person for sitting and for providing a back rest while sitting." We need not go into details of the definition here; it is sufficient to point out that sofas, benches, stools, etc., are excluded by this definition.

The breakdown of the definition into operational directives should proceed as follows:

a) Determine which concepts in the definition are clear for the interviewers. (This may require some testing.) We might find out, for example, that "object," "one person," "sitting," and "providing back rest" are clear; that is, they have the same and correct meaning for all interviewers and hence can produce uniformly accurate responses in them. The validity of this decision should, wherever possible, be checked in a pretest. We will take this up in (*c*) below.

b) Next we should translate the complex concepts in the definition (e.g., "intended," "can be used") into simple operations for determining whether these conditions are satisfied. Consider "can be used for sitting." Should the observer count an object which would ordinarily be called a chair but one of whose legs is missing? Such decisions can be made only by referring to research objectives; where the objectives are clear, the decision is easy. If, for example, the research objective is such as to require information relative to the time of the observation, then chairs in disrepair should be excluded. Such considerations enable the designer to begin to formulate a rule for counting chairs: "Consider that an object can be used for sitting, if *at the time of observation* it can be used for sitting, etc."

c) Once the designer has translated the definition into procedural rules, he should attempt to test their adequacy. As a preliminary check, the definition can be presented to a number of people with experience in the area to be studied to see if they can think of any critical cases which the definition does not cover. Such a procedure can lead to a "tightening up" and clarification of the definition. During this process the designers themselves will think of difficult cases of applying the rules; others will be suggested to them. In the pretest such critical cases can be used in testing the efficiency of the directives finally evolved; that is, different observers or interviewers can be given the directives and these critical problems. Their consistency and accuracy can be observed and analyzed, and revisions can be made accordingly. During the training as well as during the pretest field work, the observers and interviewers should be encouraged to find loopholes in procedures. *That is, those who will follow the directives should be given design responsibilities in preparing the directives.*

It has been our experience that the failure of operational directives is much more likely to be a product of faulty design than of inadequacies of observers and interviewers. The latter can frequently spot inadequacies in the directives. They have an uncañny ability for spotting places where the research designers are not clear as to what they (the designers) want and how to get it. The designer is likely to be sensitive about these aspects of the directives, but pride is not necessarily compatible with operational efficiency.

The allocation of design responsibility to observers, interviewers, etc., can be disruptive if the nature of the criticism desired by the design staff is not made explicit. Observers, interviewers, etc., may tend to pick on minor details pertinent only to a very small percentage of border-line cases rather than major points pertinent to the vast majority of the cases. In many instances border-line cases cannot be taken care of without seriously complicating instructions and training. A great deal of time should not be devoted to the "one-in-a-million" case unless the case is really critical to the research results. In fact, it may be better not to instruct all observers, interviewers, etc., in ways of handling rare cases if only a small percentage of them will have to face such a case. They can be instructed to refer all such cases to their supervisors. The resultant simplification of instructions and training will leave their minds uncluttered with the details of handling special cases and may therefore increase their ability to grasp the meaning of the "majority rules." At any rate, the increased cost of having the supervisor handle the rare case should be compared (where possible) with (1) the cost of additional training to regular personnel if they are to be instructed to handle such cases and (2) the cost of the error that is likely to result if such instruction is not given to these nondesign personnel and if they are required to handle the rare case anyhow.

5.2. Research Materials

Here we have reference to the questionnaires, tests, schedules, control forms, manuals, etc.—the paper requirements. Also, we refer to the machines, gaily colored pencils (without which it seems the work of "coding and editing" cannot go forward), rubber stamps, and other devices for mutilating and otherwise modifying the paper. Finally, we refer to the material components of the physical environment in which the paper is modified—the space, the tables and chairs, the lighting, etc. It would be unfeasible (and also fruitless) to make up any list of research materials either necessary or sufficient for social research.

We would, however, like to make three comments concerning the research materials, which may have some general applicability.

1. The statistical tables and charts ultimately to be constructed out of the data—as well as the punch cards, if any—should be described at an early stage of planning. Making explicit just how the results are to be presented—the cell co-ordinates (row and column descriptions) of each table and the axes of each chart—can prevent a great deal of waste both in the collection and in the processing of data. It can be a frustrating experience indeed to collect the data and discover that a pertinent characteristic of the persons or groups being investigated has been omitted (e.g., race or sex or marital status). It *should be* an equally irritating experience to discover that unnecessary data have been collected. Unfortunately, the former seems to cause a disproportionate amount of anguish as compared to the latter. The early design of the punch cards, if any are to be used, can help in a similar fashion: It can be frustrating to learn that one has a fourteen-category code designed for a card whose columns only provide for entering twelve categories. The resultant complexity can be avoided by forethought.

2. Cataloguing the research materials can aid in the maintenance of cost control as well as facilitate communication between people working on the research.

3. Listing the materials that each person will require may appear to be an obvious requirement. It has one advantage, however, that may not be too apparent: Such a listing may detect unnecessary duplication of *activity* as well as duplication of materials.

6. Maintaining Control

The operational planner should strive to design a process which can be kept *in control*. He has before him the research objectives and the research specifications. His job is to maximize the operational efficiency. This means that, unless (as sometimes happens) he discovers the specifications themselves not to be efficient relative to the research objectives, his job is to minimize, in some overall sense, the deviations from the specifications. There are three questions to be raised in connection with this matter of control:

1. Are the specifications in accord with the objectives?
2. Are the operations that are proposed in accord with the specifications?
3. Are the operations-as-carried-out in accord with the operations-as-proposed?

The first two of these questions have already received attention. It is the last of these questions to which attention is directed here.

In the above paragraphs there are two phrases whose meaning holds the key to the problem of control. The meaning of the first phrase, "minimize, *in some over-all sense,* the deviations . . . ," we must, unhappily, leave to the intuition of the reader. The meaning of the second phrase, ". . . efficient relative to the research objectives," should become apparent as we indicate the measures that can be taken to maintain control.

The efficient answering of the question, "Are the operations-as-carried-out in accord with the operations-as-proposed?" depends on both logical analysis and validation experiments. There are available, however, some techniques which can assist in controlling operations, the *progress record* and *quality control (inspection* and *verification).*

6.1. The Progress Record

For the purpose of maintaining control, the cost of an operation and the time required to complete it are to be regarded as measurable dimensions of the operation. The budget-time schedule shows the operations-as-proposed. The progress record shows the operations-as-carried-out with respect to the dimensions of cost and time. The progress record can be used for the following purposes:

(1) To determine if the budget-time schedule and/or the specifications require revision.

(2) To determine if personnel need additional training or "encouragement" or need to be replaced.

(3) To aid in planning future research.

The progress record should be an exceedingly important part of the social scientist's "notebook." It should be stressed that the progress record's utility increases in proportion to its "up-to-dateness." To wait until after the research is completed and then to reconstruct what happens is a dubious enterprise.

The format of the progress record can be quite similar to that of the budget-time schedule shown in Figure 34. For each activity additional lines are needed to show the "percent of budget" for "man-hours," "cost," and "percent of the total job completed." It is the last point that presents the greatest difficulty. It is no trick at all to use up man-hours or dollars at or below the budgeted rate; either a trick or good control is required in most cases to get the job done at the budgeted rate. This raises the question of *work measurement,* of defining *units* of work for each research activity. Except for tasks that depend on the number of questionnaires or some such obvious item, there are no answers *as yet* available except "judgment and intuition." For example, we have no notion as yet as to what is a "unit of planning." This point will be discussed in Section 6.3 below.

6.2. Quality Control

Operational directives frequently take the following forms:

(1) If the respondent answers "Yes" to question 1, the interviewer is to place an "X" in Code Box A.

(2) If the respondent did any work last week, he is supposed to answer "Yes" to question 7.

(3) If the punch operator sees 56 in Code Box Z, she is supposed to punch 5 in column 23 and 6 in column 24.

Proposed operations such as these can be subjected to a quality-control process. Quality control consists of two phases: (1) *inspection*—the determination of the extent to which operations performed conform with operational specifications, and (2) *verification*—the reduction of errors produced by lack of conformity between operations-as-specified and operations-as-performed.

There is much that sampling theory can contribute to these processes. For an example of its application to the "processing" of data see the article by Deming and Goeffrey (9). For a discussion of reinterview techniques for checking on observer and respondent error in surveys see the article by Eckler and Pritzker (13).

With respect to these techniques of maintaining control, the following points should be emphasized: Control requires an expenditure of time and money. From the standpoint of designed research, then, control itself has to be evaluated.

Even after the quality-control procedure as described is performed, some operationally produced error will remain. Not even all the errors disclosed by inspection procedures can be corrected unless the operation is performed over again; that is, its results are rejected as not satisfying the quality of results required. Furthermore, it may not be feasible to inspect each operation performed or piece of data collected—it may be too lengthy or costly a job. Thus the problems of imposing control can be put in the following form:

(1) What quality of research operations is the minimum that can be tolerated relative to the research objectives?

(2) How can this minimum quality be translated into a set of specifications of measurable characteristics of the operations performed or the results produced?

(3) How can inspection of operations or results be conducted on a sample

basis so as to determine (with acceptable risks) whether or not the operations or results satisfy the minimum specifications (i.e., tolerance
limits)? When should the operations-as-performed be accepted and
when rejected?

As soon as the problem is cast in this form, it becomes clear that it is analogous to the problem of controlling a manufacturing process. In the manufacture
of a product the three questions listed above are applicable. In this area techniques have been developed which make possible the answering of question (3),
where questions (1) and (2) can be answered by other means. These techniques
are referred to as those of *industrial quality control*. It is quite natural, then, that
one should ask if it is possible to apply the methods of industrial quality control
to research operations as well as to manufacturing operations. The idea of so
doing is not new; in fact, it has already been used with considerable success in
some survey work performed in South Africa. The main obstacle to the extensive use of quality-control methods in social research is the difficulty and costli-
ness of repeating observations or other research operations. This obstacle is not
universal, however, and it is worth the social scientist's while to become familiar
with quality-control methods. There are a number of good introductory texts
available which deal with these methods (e.g., [18], [29], and [30]).

The methodology outlined in this book has been intended, among other
things, to make possible the answering of questions (1) and (2) above. The
qualities of research operations which are of concern are their cost, the time
consumed, and the accuracy and precision (bias and variability) of their
product (data). We have attempted to indicate ways of quantifying each of
these and ways of determining the requirements on each imposed by the research objectives. The implication of these remarks is not that it should now be
easy to apply quality-control methods to research operations; rather it is that
the possibility of efforts in this direction can be enhanced by the type of
methodological approach to design advocated in this work. At least the prospect
of using quality-control methods on research operations is one that social science
cannot long afford to leave unexplored.

7. Selection and Training of Research Personnel

A considerable literature has grown up in the last few decades on personnel
problems in general, and an increasing amount has become available on research
personnel problems. Many psychologists have devoted their efforts to the development of criteria of selection and the preparation of tests to determine the
degree to which individuals satisfy these criteria (see [21]). No attempt will be

made here to summarize or review this literature. Rather our purpose is to raise some general design problems with regard to research personnel—problems the solution of which is independent of specific auxiliary devices which may be used in selecting and training personnel. First we will consider the selection of research personnel.

7.1. Selection

A selection procedure may have one of two orientations: (1) to obtain those who are most capable of performing the job (i.e., to select the cream of the crop) and (2) to eliminate those who are least capable of performing the job to be filled. At first glance these two orientations may appear to be equivalent, but further examination indicates that they correspond to the two types of statistical errors which may be obtained. The first orientation is directed toward a reduction of what might be called the *Type I personnel error*, that is, failing to hire a person who is qualified to perform the job. The second orientation is directed toward minimizing the *Type II personnel error:* hiring a person who is not qualified to perform the job. Hence the second approach consists of specifying *minimum* job requirements and devising means for assuring that no personnel are employed who do not meet these minimum conditions. The first is devoted to specifying optimum requirements and devising means for assuring that personnel who meet these conditions are hired.

·It should be made clear that the individuals referred to are such auxiliary research personnel as interviewers, coders, editors, etc., and not the design staff itself. Presumably such a staff would have been selected before the design itself had begun.

The conditions under which the first type of orientation would generally be adopted are the following: (1) a special skill is required for performing the job and/or (2) there is a scarcity of available persons who have the required skill. For example, an interview method requiring some special training and experience, such as the use of nondirective or projective methods (17), imposes the need for specially trained personnel of whom there may be a shortage. In such a case it may be critical to hire all those who seem to have the required skill even at the cost of including some who do not have the required skill. Here the principal mistake to be avoided is that of letting a good person go rather than that of including an unqualified person. If an unqualified person "sneaks through" the selection procedure, it is generally possible in such cases to single him out shortly thereafter and remove him. That is, if the job is a skilled one, the chance of failing to recognize and relieving an unqualified person is negligible, and hence the cost associated with hiring such a person is relatively low. For example, the training period and the trial run can be used as very effective auxiliary selection or screening devices (i.e., to catch the misfits).

The conditions under which the second type of orientation—the minimum requirements approach—would generally be adopted are the following: (1) no special skill is required to perform the job and (2) there is an abundance of available personnel. Here it may be important only to weed out those who are completely or partially illiterate, have physical defects (e.g., poor eyesight or hearing), or are not trustworthy. In such a case, where skill is not important, the cost associated with rejecting a skilled person is low relative to hiring a person who cannot meet minimum requirements.

These two orientations are by no means exclusive. As a matter of fact, an optimum selection policy is one in which an optimum balance between these two types of error is obtained, in much the same way that such a balance can be obtained between Type I and Type II errors in the statistical design of research.

The principal design problems in connection with selection, then, are (1) to specify the optimum or minimum job requirements; (2) to devise means for determining whether an individual meets these requirements; (3) to determine the costs associated with any selection procedure; and (4) to devise means for evaluating the procedure in use so as to provide a better basis for designing subsequent selection procedures.

7.1.1. Specifying Optimum or Minimum Job Requirements

In the field of personnel psychology there has been a rather interesting divergence of emphasis on the type of properties to look for in prospective research personnel. On the one hand, *ability* has been stressed, and the resultant selection procedures have consisted primarily of cognitive tests; for example, reading ability, mathematical ability, etc. On the other hand, *personality* has been stressed, and the resultant selection procedures have consisted primarily of attempts to analyze applicants' attitudes, opinions, beliefs, etc. The personality approach is concerned with biases produced by political, racial, ideological, and other types of prejudices and with such personal qualities of interviewers as "empathy," "sympathy," and "insight." The orientation of psychoanalysis and cultural anthropology is thereby stressed. Hence requirements are made— in this orientation—for "pleasing, outgoing, objective types who can establish rapport with the subject."

The personality orientation has, as yet, been subjected to little experimental evaluation. Unfortunately, "personality requirements" are too often used merely as a justification for inferior research design. The personality approach can too easily be used to divert attention from shortcomings of the research designer. Errors can be blamed on lack of observers' personality rather than on lack of research planning. Furthermore, personality-oriented designs tend to emphasize the number of responses rather than their accuracy. The opposite emphasis, of course, is equally harmful.

In general, an analysis of the job in developing job requirements is seldom made, for intuition is usually permitted to run wild. Any research job can be conceptualized as a process, and ideally we would like to develop an equation which expresses the outcome of the process (the job performance in terms of cost, time, and errors) as a function of a specified set of variables. Our present level of knowledge does not permit such formulations. But even crude efforts in this direction would result in the accumulation of knowledge required. Each such equation becomes a hypothesis to be tested and is a challenge to the research designer. Generally, he can at least test part of the hypothesis without any additional cost and with little additional effort.

The selection-procedure designer can well benefit by taking the machine designer's procedure as a model. The machine designer determines (1) what properties of the final product are desired; (2) what raw materials will be used; (3) what transformations must be made in the raw material to obtain the desired final product; and (4) what operations must be performed efficiently to accomplish this transformation. In this way the machine requirements are derived. This type of process or systems analysis is applicable to the job of observing, coding, computing, editing, etc. The analysis applied to such processes may not yield "sound" results at first, but it did not do so originally for the machine designer. This type of analytical approach helped produce the knowledge necessary for making the results sound—the mechanical engineers did not wait for the knowledge before using such an approach. In short, such an approach has tremendous heuristic value. Even the social scientist is likely to be surprised by the amount of knowledge which is already available and usable in designing the requirements of the operation if he bothers to analyze the process in which the operation is to be involved.

7.1.2. Testing Personnel Relative to Requirements

Ideally the designer would like to observe the applicant or candidate perform the job under research conditions and evaluate his suitability relative to the job requirements. This obviously would be an expensive and time-consuming operation. Hence the designer wants practical means for inferring what the applicant will do under research conditions, and all this before training if possible. It becomes clear that here is a problem to which social research should be able to supply answers. If previous efforts along these lines have failed to do so, it is because such research has been intuitively conceived, executed, and evaluated. If methodologically designed research procedures were applied to the personnel-selection problem, more usable results could not help but be derived. Such "basic" or "auxiliary" research is badly needed—a need which no amount of armchair psychologizing and intuitive experiencing, as opposed to designed experimenting, can satisfy.

7.1.3. Costs Associated with the Selection Procedure

The objective of designing a selection procedure is to produce an optimum balance between quality and cost of the work to be performed. It has become increasingly apparent that the attainment of an optimum selection policy can be approached by making the policy an aspect of the sampling model of the research. That is, a model of the selection process itself can be constructed. Let us consider such a model relative to observers; the applicability of the succeeding remarks to other types of personnel will be apparent. The variables of the model would be:

(1) The costs associated with selecting, training, and retaining observers.

(2) The number and location of the observations to be made.

(3) The magnitudes and likelihood of the errors produced by the observer.

(4) The losses (expressed as costs) associated with these errors.

Some attention has been given of late to the third variable—observer-produced error—particularly in the survey field (see [4], [7], [12], [15], [20], [23], [25], [28], [31], and [35]). The National Opinion Research Center, the Bureau of the Census, and the Bureau of Labor Statistics have been very active in this area, as have been Mahalanobis (22) and Stock and Hochstim (32).

The selection design problem consists in devising a selection (and training and control) procedure for which the cost of selection (and training and control) plus the expected costs associated with the errors produced by the personnel selected is minimized relative to a given operational procedure. The designer should self-consciously attempt to accomplish such minimization even if at present he can only "guesstimate" the values of the variables involved. By so doing, he will force the acquisition of better information on which to base the design of the selection procedure. This will be accomplished by making explicit the basis of the design decisions and thereby exposing them to experimental evaluation.

7.1.4. Evaluating Selection Procedures

The point has been made in this discussion of selection procedures that the procedure should be so designed that it can be tested and evaluated in the course of the research. For example, if estimates are made of the costs of selection, training, etc., accounting methods can be used during the research which will check these estimates and correct them for future use. The effectiveness of a selection procedure can be determined in light of data obtained on the actual performance of those selected. At present it may be easier to compare alternative selection procedures than to evaluate one particular procedure in any absolute sense. It is relatively easy to devise several alternative selection procedures and to conduct the parent-research so that the alternative procedures can be comparatively evaluated. The procedure which can be used will be discussed below in connection with similar comparative evaluation of alternative training procedures.*

7.2. Training

The current status of the design of training programs for research personnel is much the same as that of selection. No general theory and little specific knowledge has been accumulated concerning the effectiveness of various training techniques for specific types of research operations. This leaves the training designer in a position in which he usually relies on common sense and on his own experience and that of others. Many simple training experiments (such as pretests) can be conducted which would yield information that could be accumulated and organized into a firm methodological basis for training design. It is true that shortage of time and funds frequently prevents such efforts, but such experiments consume less time and funds than current practice indicates. For example, here is one type of training experiment that can be conducted in many instances with little additional expenditure of time and effort. Where the number of individuals to be trained for a job is too large to be trained in one class, the individuals to be trained can be randomly assigned to different classes. Different training methods can be used on each group. The trainees can subsequently be randomly assigned to various work loads (e.g., to various interviewing districts). The bias and variability of the results obtained within the training groups can be compared with the bias and variability obtained between the groups. If the between-group variability is significantly larger than the within-group variability, it can be inferred that the training programs affect the performance differently (with respect to variability), and an indication is provided as to which is the better. Similarly, a comparison of the biases produced by each group can be made and used to evaluate the training programs. Such a test was conducted by the United States Bureau of the Census to com-

---

* For a brief outline of one approach to a similar problem see Marks's discussion (23:92) of the problem as to whether college-entrance examinations weed out poorer rather than better students.

pare their standard 1950 census training program with a special television training program. Such experiments as these begin to build up a scientific base on which training programs could be methodologically designed. (The description of the evaluation given here is oversimplified.)

It is worth noting that the same type of process analysis discussed in the last section is applicable to the selection procedure. Here the personnel selected are the "raw materials" whose properties are presumably determined by the selection procedure. The end result can be specified in terms of costs enumerated in the selection model. The training itself can then be analyzed as a transformation process. If each training design decision is explicitly related to a specific transformation (e.g., a given exercise is designed to produce a given level of accuracy in filling out a certain form), the possibility of controlled evaluation becomes apparent and hence encourages the making of such evaluations.

Here again conceptualization and process analysis should not be delayed pending the availability of "sound information." Such conceptualization and analysis performed at present can be the greatest stimulus to the accumulation of the needed information and the resultant theory.

8. Administration

The term "administration" is currently used in two different senses; a distinction between these senses is important in this discussion. On the one hand, administration of research has been taken to be the direction of the actual field or laboratory research operations. On the other hand, it has been taken to refer to only those auxiliary service functions which are necessary in any large-scale operation (i.e., processing job applications, preparation of payrolls, supply and distribution of equipment, forms, etc.).

"Administration" in the first sense refers to the process of directing research operations. Even when used in this way, "administration" is sometimes distinguished from "operational planning"; that is, there has been an inclination to separate the functions of operational planning and directing operations. Hence a so-called "administrative expert" has been created. This separation has raised all kinds of questions as to how much the so-called administrative expert must know of the technical aspects of the research and as to how much the operational planner must know about the actual field or laboratory work. The futility of this discussion itself is good indication of the invidiousness of the distinction. It should be (but is not) obvious that planning an operation and operating a plan cannot be separated in fact. In the first place, the two phases are not so distinct temporally as many suppose. Planning should not stop when operations begin but should be continually modified in light of data obtained on actual operations. In the second place, the determination of the adequacy with which an operational plan is being conducted requires a complete understanding of the motivation and thinking that goes into the actual planning. The indication then is that it is not efficient to separate these two functions. This is not to say that a single individual must both plan the operation and operate the plan; it may of course be done by different members of the research staff. There can be a division of labor among the group. But it is to say that there is no fundamental difference in the knowledge required to plan operations successfully and to operate a plan successfully. In actual practice the separation of functions and skills has produced two types of undesirable results. The research planner who does not feel responsible for the actual performance of the operations in accordance with his specifications tends to design operations which overlook aspects of the actual operations which should be taken into account. He may, for example, require observers to be away from home for a month at a time. When the difficulty of so doing is brought to his attention, he may (and has been known to) dismiss it by saying that that is the administrator's worry, not his. "Let the administrator get people who will stay away for a month at a time." That is, the planner who is disassociated with the actual operations tends to become unrealistic and inefficient in his preparation of the research operations.

On the other hand, the administrator who is not familiar with the planning stages in complete detail tends to modify the operational specifications if there is difficulty in carrying them out. He does not feel any responsibility for the design and can see no harm in modifying a procedure which "the ivory-tower boys back in the home office have cooked up." Such modification, which may appear trivial, can, however, be very serious. For example, in one case (despite instructions to the contrary) a supervisor assigned her interviewers to areas other than those designated by the research agency in order to make the areas assigned to interviewers closer to their homes. The result was that much of the experiment which depended on random assignment of interviewers was made valueless.

The point, then, is that the operating staff and the design staff should not be distinct. The point can be illustrated by referring again to the architectural analogy. Once the working drawings for a building are prepared, the contractor is given the job of actually constructing the building in accordance with the specifications. But the architect's job is not complete at this point. He, as well as the contractor, is held responsible for the building's meeting the design specifications. The contractor may be considered to be an administrator and contributes a good deal to the final outcome, but he does not have final responsibility for interpreting the specifications and controlling the construction;

the architect has. The contractor has responsibility for hiring and firing needed personnel, paying them, getting the materials to the right place at the right time, etc. But he cannot do even this much without understanding the architect's working drawings. The architect must see to it that he does understand, not merely verbally, but in the actual operations performed.

Thus, in large-scale research the research designer himself may not have to direct personally the hiring of personnel, the preparation of payrolls, the supply of materials, etc. He may require administrative assistance; but he should be responsible in an over-all sense for seeing to it (a) that his specifications are met and (b) that, where they are not, changes in the specifications or the operations are made.

The problem of administration in the general sense, then, is simply that of control of the actual research operations (observing, recording data, transmitting data, etc.). This control cannot be automatic and mechanical. The methods for obtaining control have already been discussed; the question raised here is, "*Who* does the controlling?" and the answer is that it should be the research designer(s). The allocation of parts of the job to others should not relieve him of responsibility for over-all direction.

These remarks are not intended to minimize the importance of the administrator in the second and restricted sense—one who provides auxiliary administrative services. Research personnel who are not paid on time, are not provided with necessary equipment *when* they need it, etc., are not going to operate efficiently, if at all. Planning and directing these aspects of the operations is no menial task. But here, too, these details should be a part of the operational plan. At this point of the operational design co-operation is required between the operational planner and those who will provide the administrative services. Too often an operational plan minus the service details is submitted to the administrator as a completed fact, and the administrator is asked to develop an administrative supplement. Experience has repeatedly shown the inadequacy of this procedure. Surveys, for example, have been seriously damaged because the method of personnel payment was incompatible with the type of operations performed. In one case a piece rate was developed to cover all interviewers. Some interviewers worked in sparsely settled areas with poor roads. They balked very quickly, and an operational crisis was created. The operational designer is in a position to prevent such incidents; he should not dispose of the responsibility for them.

9. Consumer and Producer Criteria

In the discussion of the operational design up to this point we have used three criteria for the adequacy of design decisions and operations performed: (1) the cost associated with the operation (the budget); (2) the time expended (the time schedule); and (3) the quality of the results. These criteria, of course, are not distinct. It should be noted that all these criteria are oriented toward the objectives of the immediate consumers in particular. This is to be expected, since the research is, in effect, a product or service purchased by this consumer; and these criteria are designed to assure him a "fair return" for his investment. But the research producers (as well as the consumers) also invest a good deal in the research, and hence they, too, should receive a "fair return." This is where the objectives of the research staff come into play, and it is an important role that they take. In many cases, the consumers' objectives are in fact, if not in principle, completely subordinated to those of the research staff.

We would expect, then, that in addition to the above consumer-criteria there will and should be operative a set of producer-criteria. These criteria will vary in generality depending on the generality of the research staff's objectives which are involved.

First there are the *immediate* or *working* objectives of the research staff. These include the need for sustenance, reasonable working conditions, etc. That is, basically the research staff are workers and, as such, are entitled to payment for their services and satisfactory conditions under which to work. The failure of researchers to recognize this fundamental labor aspect of their activity has led to the exploitation of the research scientist by the research-consumer, although the situation is now changing for the better. Scientific research is one of the most underpaid professions, second perhaps only to teaching. Technical assistants are in general underpaid even "more" than scientists. There is little wonder that so many projects fall down in the operational phases. The implication of these remarks is that the research budget should be constructed so that it assures just compensation for research effort. This is true whether the research is contracted for, is conducted by researchers paid salaries by the research-consumer, or is conducted by scientists on academic payrolls. With respect to the latter, too few universities allow compensatory time off or adjust salaries for those engaged in research—this, despite the fact that the universities benefit by gains in prestige and status resulting from research conducted under their wings.

The quality of any work is in some sense a function of the compensation awarded for it. Inadequate monetary compensation is frequently rationalized on the basis of peripheral benefits such as "self-education," "acquisition of prestige," "importance of the work," etc. All these are familiar to the scientist, since he uses these excuses to rationalize his being exploited and his exploitation of research assistants, particularly graduate students. He fails to raise the question: What is the effect of these practices on the quality of personnel who will enter the profession? These immediate interests of the *scientist-as-worker* have a considerable effect on the status of science in general; that is, to more general research staff objectives.

The *intermediate* or *organizational* objectives of the research staff are those which affect the capacity of that staff for conducting research (other than the project in question) concurrently or in the future; that is, the research staff has ongoing interests. It does not want to consume all its personnel and equipment on one project. The exclusive allocation of time, effort, equipment, and personnel to one project may seriously impair the effectiveness of the staff on other projects. Hence the research staff should rationally allocate its resources to various projects on the basis of a self-conscious weighting of the importance of these projects.

How should available resources be allocated to various research projects? How much of the resources should be used up on any specific project? Such questions as these can only be answered rationally if the alternatives are evaluated. Such questions may raise a host of internal and subsidiary questions. For example, the following situations are typical. Some research personnel may have little value on a specific project, but, if they are let go, they will not be available for subsequent projects to which they can contribute. Should they be "carried" by the current project? Some personnel have little direct "research value" but contribute considerably to the morale of the research organization and hence appear to increase the efficiency of others. Should they be retained? Some personnel have "outlived" their usefulness; they are "too old." Should they be retained? Use of (say, computing) machines at more than a certain rate will produce deterioration and more frequent breakdowns than would occur at a slower rate. The present project is "urgent." Should the machine be overworked? Or, for that matter, should personnel be overworked? Such questions as these can only be answered relative to other research work, and they can only be answered efficiently to the extent that the criteria are made and used explicitly. Hence, the intermediate as well as the immediate research staff interests should be made explicit, evaluated, and used self-consciously in the operational design of a specific research project.

The *ultimate* or *scientific* research objectives involve the interests of the researcher in contributing to the development of science. In so far as the researcher fails to take the objectives of science into account in designing a specific project, he becomes a mere technician. As was pointed out in the Introduction, research is scientific to the extent that it increases the efficiency of subsequent research; that is, to the extent that it contributes to the content and methods of scientific research. Throughout this book the emphasis has been on conducting research in such a way as to produce results which are capable of being accumulated; that is, that will contribute to subsequent research. There have been many instances in which scientists have refused to conduct research because they have seen no way of obtaining anything of scientific value from so doing.

The failure of research to contribute to science may be due to one or more of several factors: (1) The subject matter may be such that use of the research results would be detrimental to the continued development of science. (2) The funds and time available may not allow any evaluation of methods or results in such a way as to permit them to be made usable in subsequent research. (3) The research staff may not be capable of designing research under any circumstances which can significantly contribute to science.

The remark on subject matter is not meant to deprecate applied research; to the contrary, most developments in basic research have arisen out of applied problems. Basic and applied research continually interact. The point is that at any time certain types of knowledge are more likely to be used in a way that is detrimental to science's interests than otherwise. This is not a proclamation of the principle of suppression of knowledge but a statement of the principle that it is important to evaluate an area of proposed research and determine whether the effort it would require might not be better spent somewhere else. The researcher should at least consider the way in which the research results will be used relative to the interests of science.

The limitations on the research as imposed by its sponsor may prevent the research staff from designing the research or from doing any evaluation of the results or methods from a scientific point of view. "Quicky" and "emergency" research may take on this character, as may research conducted under a very restricted budget. This kind of research prevents the researcher from learning anything from the investigation. Such projects are sometimes considered to be necessary evils—necessary in order to make subsequent research possible. It is one thing to conduct research as a practical necessity; it is another to pretend that research so conducted has anything to do with science. The research designer should explicitly state what scientific values he intends a research design to serve, and he should use these objectives as part of the criteria for evaluating his research design.

10. Summary

More has been written but less is known about the operational phase of research design than any other phase. The reason for the abundant literature is apparent. These are aspects of research design which the researcher is forced to face self-consciously, though not necessarily with methodological self-consciousness. The need for methodological principles in this area is so well recognized that any pretense of providing them is likely to be given attention. Finally, since so little is known and the need is so great, a statement of even the obvious is frequently hailed as wisdom. Hence, to a large extent the literature does little more than tantalize with tautologies.

A methodology of operational design has not been provided in this chapter, but an attempt has been made to suggest how a methodology can be developed in each phase of operational planning. In the first place, methods were suggested for evaluating the operational specifications. Attention was called to the pilot study (inquiries directed toward indicating alternatives that might be encountered in research), the pretest (inquiry directed toward evaluating possible alternative design decisions), and the trial run (inquiry designed to evaluate the operational plan as a whole). The necessity for conducting such studies under actual research conditions is due to the lack of theory which would make possible inferences from one situation to another. The pretest and trial run have particular value as methodological proving grounds on which general and specific methodological principles can be tested. Furthermore, these methods assure that a desired quality of result can be obtained at the desired cost within the desired time.

The desired time should be specified in a time schedule; the desired cost, in a research budget. These can be combined in a budget-time schedule which can be used as a basis for design evaluation and operational control.

The research specifications as developed in the sampling, statistical, and observational design must be translated into specific research operations. This can be effectively accomplished by preparing a *working guide*. This guide should cover each and every phase of the research operations and hence can be used as a source for preparing any directives which may be required. These directives themselves may be of the closed (mechanical) or open (functional) type. The first tends to sacrifice accuracy for precision; the second tends to do the converse. To balance optimally between these two is the designer's objective; at present he must resort to the pretest to determine how successful he has been.

The research designer should design into the operations a method for seeing to it that his operational specifications are met, that is, are under control. The principal devices for accomplishing these objectives are the progress record and quality-control procedures. The progress record should provide a constant and current check to determine whether the budget-time schedule is being met. The inspection and verification aspects of quality control are designed to determine whether the quality of the operations specified in the working guide and operational directives is being met and, if not, to correct them.

In the design of research-personnel-selection procedures, two types of error are possible: the failure to select qualified personnel and the selection of un-qualified personnel. Efforts to minimize the former depend on specification of maximum job requirements, whereas the latter depends on specification of minimum requirements. These are not exclusive approaches. A process analysis of the job to be performed can begin to provide a rational basis for personnel specification. Such analysis and resultant selection procedures can be subjected to experimental tests which can be made to yield accumulative knowledge. At present there are no proved methods for determining whether personnel speci-fications are being met; controlled research is needed here also. Beginnings can be made in estimating costs associated with certain selection and training procedures, and accounting and other control methods can be used to evaluate the estimates made. In addition, experiments can and should be made to yield methods of reducing bias and variability of research operations and, hence, the associated costs. The same experimental and evaluative approach to the design of training methods is possible and is badly needed.

In the discussion of administrative planning it was pointed out that planning operations and operating a plan should not be treated as distinct processes. If they are, planning of operations is likely to become unrealistic, and operation of the plan is likely to become loose relative to the specifications. Even the plan-ning and the administration of detailed auxiliary services require integration for efficient procedures to result.

Finally, it was pointed out that the operational planning decisions should be evaluated relative to the research staff's objectives as well as to those of the consumer. Specifically, the following should be taken into account:

(1) The immediate or working objectives which center about the role of the researcher as worker.

(2) The intermediate or organizational objectives which are related to the ongoing aspects of the research organization.

(3) The ultimate or scientific objectives which relate to progressive ac-cumulation of content and methods which facilitate the development of science.

All three types of producers' objectives should be explicitly formulated and used together with the various consumers' objectives as a basis for evaluating all design decisions.

DISCUSSION TOPICS

1. In what respects is the preparation of an operational plan for research similar to or different from planning a manufacturing process?

2. Consider a research project known to all the discussants. Relative to this project, how could a pilot study be (or have been) used? A pretest? A trial run?

3. How does the lack of theory affect the design of pretests?

4. How are the budget-time schedule and the progress record related?

5. In what respect will the *style* of the working guide and operational directives differ?

6. How would you design a control system for selection of a multistage random sample of names from a city directory?

7. Is I.Q. a satisfactory basis for selecting interviewers? Why? If the study consists of a simple election poll, what minimum requirements should be established for the interviewers? How could personnel be trained to conduct such interviews?

8. In what respects are administration and operational design similar? Different?

9. What should be the researcher's objectives for operational design if the researcher is a doctoral candidate and his research is to serve as his thesis? Distinguish between the consumer and producer objectives. How should these be used as a basis for making operational design decisions?

10. The following is a quotation from a recent work by the eminent physicist, Max Born. What design criterion is he discussing? Do you agree with his opinion? Why?

"When the question of a new edition of this book arose I felt a considerable embarrassment. To bring it up-to-date I had to write an account of the scientific development since 1935. But although this period is as full of fascinating discoveries, ideas, theories, as any previous epoch, I could not possibly describe them in the same tone in which the book was written; namely, in the belief that a deep insight of the workshop of nature was the first step towards a rational philosophy and to worldly wisdom. It seems to me that the scientists who led the way to the atomic bomb were extremely skillful and ingenious, but not wise men. They delivered the fruits of their discoveries unconditionally into the hands of politicians and soldiers; thus they lost their moral innocence and their intellectual freedom" (5:280).

EXERCISES

1. Prepare a complete operational plan for your course project.

2. Design a pretest to determine which of two forms of a questionnaire will receive the greatest response rate in a study of a graduate student body of a university.

3. List all the situations which might be encountered by an observer who is sent out to determine how many people are employed in, say, drugstores. Classify these situations in a convenient way. Indicate how each class of situations can be treated.

4. What would be the minimum personal qualifications for a census enumerator? Optimum requirements?

SUGGESTED READINGS

For some detailed discussion of the various types of operations involved in social research see Parten (27).

The literature on interviewer-produced error is abundant and has been referred to in the body of the chapter. For discussion of errors in other operational phases see Deming and Goeffrey (9) and Deming, Tepping, and Goeffrey (10).

An examination of the various directives prepared in connection with the 1950 Decennial Census should prove valuable for all social scientists.

REFERENCES AND BIBLIOGRAPHY

1. ACKOFF, R. L., and PRITZKER, LEON. "The Methodology of Survey Research," *International Journal of Opinion and Attitude Research*, V (1951), 313–34.
2. *Annual Report of the Secretary of Commerce, 1940.* Washington, D.C., 1941.
3. BANCROFT, GERTRUDE, and WELCH, E. H. "Recent Experience with Problems of Labor Force Measurement," *Journal of the American Statistical Association*, XLI (1946), 303–12.
4. BLANKENSHIP, A. B. "A Source of Interviewer Bias," *International Journal of Opinion and Attitude Research*, III (1949), 95–98.
5. BORN, MAX. *The Restless Universe.* 2d rev. ed. New York: Dover Publications, Inc., 1951.
6. CHARNES, ABRAHAM; COOPER, W. W.; and MELLON, B. "Blending Aviation Gasolines: A Study in Programming Interdependent Activities in an Integrated Oil Company," *Econometrica*, XX (1952), 135–70.
7. CLARKSON, E. P. "The Problem of Honesty," *International Journal of Opinion and Attitude Research*, IV (1950), 84–90.
8. DEMING, W. E. *Some Theory of Sampling.* New York: John Wiley & Sons, Inc., 1950.
9. DEMING, W. E., and GOEFFREY, LEON. "On Sample Inspection in the Processing of Census Returns," *Journal of the American Statistical Association*, XXXVI (1941), 351–61.
10. DEMING, W. E.; TEPPING, B. J.; and GOEFFREY, LEON. "Errors in Card Punching," *Journal of the American Statistical Association*, XXXVII (1942), 525–36.
11. DORFMAN, ROBERT. *Applications of Linear Programming to the Theory of the Firm.* Berkeley: University of California Press, 1951.
12. DURBIN, J., and STUART, A. "Differences in Response Rates of Experienced and Inexperienced Interviewers," *Journal of the Royal Statistical Society*, CXIV (1951), 163–206.
13. ECKLER, A. R., and PRITZKER, LEON. "Measuring the Accuracy of Enumerative Surveys" *Proceedings of the International Statistical Conferences* (New Delhi, India). (In press.)
14. EXECUTIVE OFFICE OF THE PRESIDENT, BUREAU OF THE BUDGET. *Appraisal and Control of Duplicating Service.* Washington, D.C.: Superintendent of Documents, 1949.
15. FISHER, HERBERT. "Interviewer Bias in the Recording Operation," *International Journal of Opinion and Attitude Research*, IV (1950), 391–411.
16. FLESCH, RUDOLF. *How To Test Readability.* New York: Harper & Bros., 1949.
17. FRANK, L. K. *Projective Methods.* Springfield, Ill.: Chas. C. Thomas, 1948.
18. GRANT, E. L. *Statistical Quality Control.* New York: McGraw-Hill Book Co., 1946.
19. GUEST, LESTER, and NUCKOLS, ROBERT. "A Laboratory Experiment in Recording

in Public Opinion Interviewing," *International Journal of Opinion and Attitude Research*, IV (1950), 336–52.

20. HANSEN, M. H.; HURWITZ, W. N.; MARKS, E. S.; and MAULDIN, W. P. "Response Errors in Surveys," *Journal of the American Statistical Association*, XLVI (1951), 147–90.

21. HERTZ, D. B., and RUBINSTEIN, A. H. (eds.). *Selection, Training and Use of Personnel in Industrial Research: Proceedings of the Second Annual Conference on Industrial Research, June 1951.* New York: King's Crown Press, 1952.

22. MAHALANOBIS, P. E. "Recent Experiments in Statistical Sampling in the Indian Statistical Institute," *Journal of the Royal Statistical Society*, CIX (1946), 325–70.

23. MANHEIMER, DEAN, and HYMAN, HERBERT. "Interviewer Performance in Area Sampling," *Public Opinion Quarterly*, XIII (1949), 83–92.

24. MARKS, E. S., "Some Sampling Problems in Educational Research," *Journal of Educational Psychology*, XLII (1951), 85–96.

25. MARKS, E. S., and MAULDIN, W. P. "Response Errors in Census Research," *Journal of the American Statistical Association*, XLV (1950), 424–38.

26. METZNER, C. A. "Three Tests for Errors of Report in a Sample Interview Survey," *International Journal of Opinion and Attitude Research*, III (1950), 547–54.

27. PARTEN, MILDRED. *Surveys, Polls, and Samples.* New York: Harper & Bros., 1950.

28. SHEATSLEY, P. B. "The Influence of Sub-questions on Interviewer Performance," *Public Opinion Quarterly*, XIII (1949), 310–13.

29. SHEWHART, W. A. *Economic Control of Quality of Manufactured Product.* New York: D. Van Nostrand Co., 1930.

30. ———. *Statistical Method from the Viewpoint of Quality Control.* Graduate School, Department of Agriculture, 1939.

31. SMITH, H. L., and HYMAN, HERBERT. "The Biasing Effect of Interviewer Expectations on Survey Results," *Public Opinion Quarterly*, XIV (1950), 491–506.

32. STOCK, J. S., and HOCHSTIM, J. R., "A Method of Measuring Interviewer Variability," *Public Opinion Quarterly*, XV (1951), 322–34.

33. TERMAN, L. M., and MERRILL, M. A. *Measuring Intelligence.* Boston: Houghton Mifflin Co., 1937.

34. WEILBACHER, W. M., and WALSH, H. R. "Mail Questionnaires and the Personalized Letter of Transmittal," *Journal of Marketing*, XVII (1952), 331–36.

35. WYATT, D. F., and CAMPBELL, D. T. "A Study of Interviewer Bias as Related to Interviewers' Expectations and Own Opinions," *International Journal of Opinion and Attitude Research*, IV (1950), 77–83.

Method of Weighting a Large
Number of Objectives

(1) Rank the entire set of objectives in terms of preference without assigning quantitative values. This and step (6) need not be carried out if the method is used primarily to simplify the procedure when there is a large number of objectives. The inclusion of this and step (6) gives a measure of the reliability of the procedure.

(2) By random assignment subdivide the set of objectives into groups of no more than six and preferably (though not necessarily) into groups of approximately equal size. Each objective should be included in one and only one group.

(3) Select at random one objective from each group formed in step (2), noting the group from which it was drawn.

(4) Use steps (1)–(5) of the procedure described on pages 24–25 to obtain unstandardized values for the objectives in the group formed in step (3) of this procedure.

(5) Replace the objectives in the groups from which they were drawn. Use steps (1)–(5) of the procedure described on pages 24–25 to obtain unstandardized values for the objectives in the groups formed in step (2) of this procedure. In this process do *not* change the values assigned to the objectives evaluated in step (4) of this procedure. All required adjustments should be made on the values of the other objectives in the groups.

(6) Compare the rankings obtained from steps (2)–(5) of this procedure with those obtained in step (1). If the rank orders differ, reconsider the ranking and if necessary proceed again from steps (2)–(6) of this procedure.

(7) Standardize the values obtained in step (5) of this procedure by dividing the value assigned to each objective by the sum of the values assigned to *all* the objectives.

The procedure just described may be illustrated by the following example. Suppose there are twelve objectives.

(1) Assume these to have been ranked as follows: $O_1, O_2, \ldots, O_{12}$.

(2) The objectives may be assigned at random to three groups as follows:

(a)	(b)	(c)
O_4	O_7	O_9
O_{12}	O_{11}	O_6
O_5	O_8	O_1
O_{10}	O_2	O_3

(3) Three objectives, one from each group, are selected at random; for example, O_4, O_8, and O_3.

(4) Suppose the following unstandardized values to be obtained:

$$O_3 = 1.00$$
$$O_4 = 0.60$$
$$O_8 = 0.30$$

(5) Now each of the groups in step (2) are evaluated holding fixed the values assigned in step (4). Suppose the results are as follows:

(a)	(b)	(c)
$O_4 = 0.60$	$O_2 = 0.90$	$O_1 = 1.20$
$O_5 = 0.50$	$O_7 = 0.35$	$O_3 = 1.00$
$O_{10} = 0.20$	$O_8 = 0.30$	$O_6 = 0.45$
$O_{12} = 0.15$	$O_{11} = 0.10$	$O_9 = 0.25$

(6) A comparison with step (1) shows that O_2 and O_3 and O_{11} and O_{12} have been reversed. If the original ranking were still judged correct, then the values of O_2 and/or O_3 and O_{11} and/or O_{12} should be readjusted in their respective groups. The steps are then carried through as before. Suppose, however, that it is decided that the computed ranking is correct; that is, that the ranking obtained in step (5) is correct. Then the values in step (5) are standardized to obtain the following values:

(7) $O_1 = 0.200$ $O_5 = 0.083$ $O_9 = 0.042$
     $O_2 = 0.150$ $O_6 = 0.075$ $O_{10} = 0.033$
     $O_3 = 0.167$ $O_7 = 0.058$ $O_{11} = 0.017$
     $O_4 = 0.100$ $O_8 = 0.050$ $O_{12} = 0.025$

Analysis of the Concept "Social Group"

The purpose of this appendix is to illustrate briefly how a conceptual analysis can be conducted in conformity with the principles set down in chapter iii. Of importance here is the method of approach rather than the content. The illustration is deliberately made brief, since a complete analysis would require more space than is available in a work of this kind. For complete (and slightly divergent) analysis of the same concept, reference is made to the work of Eubank (5:116–68).

The concept "social group" has only become basic to social science in the last few decades. Prior to that, "society" was taken to be the basic social concept, and "social group" received practically no attention. Social scientists came to realize, however, that there are important social configurations which are not societies. In effect, it was realized that, though all societies are social groups, not all social groups are societies.

Since we are dealing with contemporary rather than historic usage, we have to look for the trend or intention in the defining efforts of contemporary social scientists. Our procedure will be to start with the simplest formulations, note their shortcomings, and see what revisions are necessary and how they are made by others. The definition that this analysis will finally yield will not be identical with any in the literature, but all its components are to be found there, as we shall try to show. Our effort is to produce a definition which expresses better than any alternative the meaning (of "social group") intended by the community of social scientists.

The term "group" ordinarily is taken to mean "a collection of persons or things." It is apparent that, as soon as we append "social" to "group," we limit our interests to collections of persons. But not all collections of persons are social groups. Consequently, one of the first distinctions made by the social scientist in his development of this concept was the distinction between mere "aggregates" of persons and "social groups." The earliest definitions based the distinction on either an "interaction" or "social relationship" holding among the members of a social group. The following definitions given by MacIver, Kulp, Bogardus, and Dawson and Gettys are typical:

> By a group itself we mean any collection of social beings who enter into distinctive social relationship with one another [11:3].

> A group is two or more people interacting [10:226].

> A group is any number of living beings in interaction [1:18].

> The group comes into existence at the moment when there is interaction between two or more persons, whether they are near or remote in space [4:731].

A fusion of the notion of "interaction" and "social relationship" was required, for interaction by itself was not sufficient to differentiate social groups from nonsocial groups. Suppose we have two individuals thrown from an automobile in a collision, and these two persons themselves collide in their "flight"; they interact but do not form a social group. It seems natural to say that such interaction is not social and to require for a social group not mere "interaction" but "social interaction." This additional requirement is seen in the following definition of "social group" given by the Gillins:

> A group is any collection of two or more individuals who are in social interaction, that is, who have social relations with each other [6:19].

In this last definition we can see how "social relationship" and "social interaction" are equated to one another. The problem, of course, is to make clear what "social interaction" is. Two types of answers have been offered. In the first, social interaction is defined (by Good and Eubank) in mentalistic or psychic terms:

> Social group may be defined as a number of individuals whose psychic activities along a certain phase of life have a common relation to one another [7:48].

> [A group is] the *association* which results from the mental interactivity of sentient beings. . . . The one relationship without which the group cannot exist is that of psychic interaction [5:160].

The second type of answer offered by (Katz and Schanck) replaced the causal notion of "interaction" by the functional notions of "stimulus" and "response."

> Social interaction is the term applied to the behavior of two or more people who mutually stimulate and respond to one another [8:10].

Both these attempts to redefine "social interaction" converge on the notion that the type of action of concern is not mere mechanical action but *purposive* behavior. To have social interaction, the individuals must be affecting each other's purposive behavior by means of their own purposive behavior. We have a special name for purposive stimulation and response; it is "communication." Hence, Krueger and Reckless note:

The first significant fact to note about a social group is that it is composed of communicating individuals [9:77–78].

But communication may be only one-directional, though it usually involves more than one person. That is, one person, A, can communicate to another person, B, without B communicating to A. The notion of "mutual" stimulation has to be brought into the definition, and it is in such definitions as the following given by Cuber:

[A social group is] any number of human beings in reciprocal communication [2:265].

This is not yet the end of the matter, for it now appears that two or more individuals must be in constant communication with each other in order for the group to persist. According to this last definition, the group ceases to exist when the reciprocal communication stops. The definition also requires that in large social groups each individual be intercommunicating with each other individual. Now this is obviously not the intention behind the use of the term. We do not require a social group to have its members in constant intercommunication. Eubank says:

A group may be regarded as an entity, of two or more persons, in *active* or *suspended* interaction [5:163; italics mine].

All we seem to require is that reciprocal communication be possible. But this seems to put us in the peculiar position of asserting that any collection of individuals is a social group, since in this day and age intercommunication among almost any collection of individuals is possible. Our answer is that we require more than *mere* possibility of reciprocal communication; we require a certain likelihood or "potentiality" for such intercommunication. By this we mean that, relative to our purposes of inquiry, we can set up a "probability of reciprocal communication" such that only those individuals having at least that probability of intercommunicating will be considered a social group. This means that what we take a group to be depends in part on our research purposes. This relativity of the concept was recognized as early as 1905 by A. W. Small but was subsequently forgotten. Small defined a social group as a number of people whose relations to each other are *sufficiently impressive to demand attention* [13:495].

This relativistic flavor does not put the concept "social group" into any special category, for, to define an object such as "chair," we have to do the same thing. To define a chair, we have to resort to "potentially usable for sitting." An object does not have to be "sat in" to be a chair. It must have a capacity (greater than some specified amount) for being "sat in." Similarly, a "social group" must have a possibility (greater than some specified amount) for reciprocal communication.

Then, by way of concluding this brief analysis, we can formulate a definition of "social group" as follows:

Two or more psychological individuals who are in potential or actual reciprocal communication.

REFERENCES

1. Bogardus, E. S. *Sociology.* New York: Macmillan Co., 1947.
2. Cuber, J. F. *Sociology.* New York: D. Appleton–Century Co., 1947.
3. Davis, Jerome, and Barnes, H. E. *An Introduction to Sociology.* Boston: D. C. Heath & Co., 1927.
4. Dawson, C. A., and Gettys, W. E. *An Introduction to Sociology.* 3d ed. New York: Ronald Press Co., 1948.
5. Eubank, E. E. *The Concepts of Sociology.* Boston: D. C. Heath & Co., 1932.
6. Gillin, J. L. and J. P. *An Introduction to Sociology.* New York: Macmillan Co., 1943.
7. Good, Alvin, *Sociology and Education.* New York: Harper & Bros., 1926.
8. Katz, Daniel, and Schanck, R. L. *Social Psychology.* New York: John Wiley & Sons, 1938.
9. Krueger, E. T., and Reckless, W. C. *Social Psychology.* New York: Longmans, Green & Co., 1933.
10. Kulp, D. H., II. *Introductory Sociology for Students of Nursing.* New York: Macmillan Co., 1930.
11. MacIver, R. M. *Society: A Textbook of Sociology.* New York: Farrar & Rinehart, 1937.
12. Sapir, Edward. "Group," in *Encyclopedia of the Social Sciences,* VII, 178–82. New York: Macmillan Co., 1932.
13. Small, A. W. *General Sociology.* Chicago: University of Chicago Press, 1905.
14. Young, Kimball. *Sociology: A Study of Society and Culture.* New York: American Book Co., 1942.

Some Frequently Used Symbols

a (alpha) = significance level (i.e., Type I error)

B = true regression coefficient

b = estimated (i.e., sample) regression coefficient

χ^2 (chi square) = $\mathrm{DF}s^2/\sigma^2$

DF = degrees of freedom

$F = s_1^2/s_2^2$

F_i = theoretical frequency

f_i = observed frequency

$f(x)$ = function of x

i = any individual member of a class

j = any individual member of a class

k = number of samples

$\ln$ = natural logarithm

m = true median of a population (also used to represent the number of observations in a cell)

m' = estimated (i.e., sample) median

μ (mu) = true mean of a population

N = number of elements in a population

n = number of elements in a sample

OC = Operating Characteristic Curve

p = true proportion of a population having a specified characteristic

$\bar{p}$ = estimated (i.e., sample) proportion

pc = true percentage of a population having a specified characteristic

$\overline{pc}$ = estimated (i.e., sample) percentage

R = range (i.e., difference between greatest and least value in a sample)

ρ (rho) = true correlation coefficient

r (mu) = estimated (i.e., sample) correlation coefficient

σ (sigma) = true standard deviation

s = estimated (i.e., sample) standard deviation

σ^2 = true variance

s^2 = estimated (i.e., sample) variance

Σ = sum of (e.g., $\displaystyle\sum_{}^{n} x_i$ = sum of individual x's from first to nth)

T = total of column or row

$t = |x_i - \mu|/s_{x_i}$

$t' = |x_i - \mu|/R$

u = unit deviation

V = a variable

X = a class of observations

x_i = individual observations

$\bar{x}$ = estimated (i.e., sample) mean

Y = a class of observations

y_i = individual observations

$z = |x - \mu|/\sigma$

$>$ = is greater than

$<$ = is less than

$\geq$ = is greater than or equal to

$\leq$ = is less than or equal to

$|x - y|$ = the absolute difference between x and y (i.e., independent of sign)

Illustration of Method of Selecting Optimum Sample Size

Assume that the problem consists of estimating the mean (μ) of a population characteristic. Let μ_e represent an estimated value of μ. Then, if $\mu_e > \mu$, there is an error of overestimation, and, if $\mu_e < \mu$, there is an error of underestimation. Let k_1 represent the cost of an error of underestimation and k_2 represent the cost of an error of overestimation. The values of k_1 and k_2 will generally depend on the size of the error. That is, k_1 is generally a function (g) of ($\mu - \mu_e$), where $\mu > \mu_e$:

$$k_1 = g(\mu - \mu_e), \qquad \mu > \mu_e. \tag{1}$$

Similarly,

$$k_2 = h(\mu_e - \mu), \qquad \mu_e > \mu. \tag{2}$$

Consider a specific error of overestimation ($\mu_{e_i} - \mu$). On any one specific application of the estimation procedure this particular error either is or is not made, and, hence, the cost due to it either is or is not incurred. In the long run however, this error will occur a certain proportion of the time (p). Thus, $p(\mu_{e_i})$ is the probability that μ_{e_i} will be obtained as an estimate. The value $p(\mu_{e_i})$ will vary for different values of μ_e. A complete description of these variations constitutes the probability density function of μ_e.

The expected cost ($\bar{k}$) per estimate for a particular error ($\mu_{e_i} - \mu$) is equal to the probability of the error's occurrence times the cost resulting from its occurrence:

$$\bar{k}_{2_i} = p(\mu_{e_i}) k_{2_i}. \tag{3}$$

But this is only one of the possible errors of overestimation. To obtain the total expected cost of overestimation, it is necessary to sum over all the possible values of μ_e which are greater than μ. That is,

$$\Sigma k_{2_i} p(\mu_{e_i}) = \Sigma h(\mu_{e_i} - \mu) p(\mu_{e_i}), \tag{4}$$

where all

$$\mu_{e_i} > \mu.$$

If there is an infinite number of possible values of μ_{e_i} greater than μ, and if the μ_{e_i} scale is a continuous one (e.g., height and weight), this summation can be accomplished by integration:

$$\int_{\mu}^{\infty} h\,(\mu_{e_i} - \mu)\, p\,(\mu_{e_i})\, d\mu_{e_i}\,. \tag{5}$$

The total expected cost of underestimation would be similarly obtained:

$$\int_{-\infty}^{\mu} g\,(\mu - \mu_{e_i})\, p\,(\mu_{e_i})\, d\mu_{e_i}\,. \tag{6}$$

Then the sum of these two totals, (5) and (6), would be the total expected cost of the error of the estimate.

This cost, however, is not the only one associated with making an estimate. There is also the cost of taking the observations. Let C represent the cost of making a single observation and n represent the number of observations. Then, if the cost per observation is independent of n, nC would represent the cost of taking n observations. But the cost per observation may not be independent of n. Therefore, let C_n represent the cost of taking n observations. Then C_n is a function (θ) of n and C:

$$C_n = \theta(n, C)\,. \tag{7}$$

C_n would contain any costs of overhead as well as actual field costs. If there is a fixed cost of overhead (C_0), then C_n may be represented as follows:

$$C_n = C_0 + \theta(n, C)\,. \tag{8}$$

The total expected cost of the estimate (K) can be given by

$$K = C_n + \int_{-\infty}^{\mu} g\,(\mu - \mu_e)\, p\,(\mu_e)\, d\mu_e + \int_{\mu}^{\infty} h\,(\mu_e - \mu)\, p\,(\mu_e)\, d\mu_e\,, \tag{9}$$

where μ_e can take on any value from minus infinity to plus infinity.

Now one way of formulating the problem of determining what sample size to use is to select a sample size (n) which will minimize the total expected cost (TC). However, this is not the only way of formulating the problem. For example, the researcher may want to minimize the "maximum cost" that he might encounter. If he does, an equation other than (9) would be used, but the logic of the approach would be similar.

To see how equation (9) can be used to select a sample size which will minimize the expected total cost, consider the case specified by the following conditions:

a) A simple random sample is taken, and $\bar{x}$ (the average of the sampled values) is used as an estimate of μ (i.e., $\bar{x} = \mu_e$). The possible estimates $(\bar{x}_i)$ are normally distributed. This can be represented mathematically as follows:

$$p(\bar{x}) = \frac{\sqrt{n}}{\sqrt{2\pi}\sigma} e^{-n(\bar{x}-\mu)^2/2\sigma^2}. \tag{10}$$

b) The cost of underestimation and overestimation is a linear function of the size of the error. For example, if $\bar{x}$ deviates from μ by one unit, the cost will be 1 cost unit; if $\bar{x}$ deviates from μ by two units, the cost will be 2 cost units. That is,

$$k_{(\mu-\bar{x})} = g(\mu - \bar{x}) = k_1(\mu - \bar{x}), \tag{11}$$

where

$$\mu > \bar{x} ;$$

and

$$k_{(\bar{x}-\mu)} = h(\bar{x} - \mu) = k_2(\bar{x} - \mu), \tag{12}$$

where

$$\bar{x} > \mu .$$

c) The total cost of taking the observations is a linear function of the number of observations. That is,

$$C_n = nC . \tag{13}$$

Equation (9) can now be rewritten on the basis of these conditions.

$$K = nC + \int_{-\infty}^{\mu} (k_1)(\mu - \bar{x}) \frac{\sqrt{n}}{\sqrt{2\pi}\sigma} e^{-n(\bar{x}-\mu)^2/2\sigma^2} d\bar{x}$$
$$+ \int_{\mu}^{\infty} (k_2)(\bar{x} - \mu) \frac{\sqrt{n}}{\sqrt{2\pi}\sigma} e^{-n(\bar{x}-\mu)^2/2\sigma^2} d\bar{x} . \tag{14}$$

Equation (14) can be simplified by integration as follows:

$$K = nC + k_1 \frac{1}{\sqrt{2\pi}} \sigma_{\bar{x}} + k_2 \frac{1}{\sqrt{2\pi}} \sigma_{\bar{x}} = nC + \frac{0.4 k_1 \sigma}{\sqrt{n}} + \frac{0.4 k_2 \sigma}{\sqrt{n}}$$
$$= nC + \frac{0.4\sigma(k_1 + k_2)}{\sqrt{n}} . \tag{15}$$

Now the problem is to find the value of n which minimizes K. This can be done by obtaining the derivative of K with respect to n, setting the result equal to zero, and, if this result is a minimum point in the distribution of K, solving for n.

$$\frac{dK}{dn} = C - \frac{0.2\sigma(k_1 + k_2)}{\sqrt{n^3}} = 0 . \tag{16}$$

This value is a minimum because

$$\frac{d^2K}{dn^2} > 0, \qquad \text{for } n = 1.$$

Then,

$$n^3 = \frac{0.04\,\sigma^2(k_1 + k_2)^2}{C^2}$$

and

$$n = \left[\frac{0.04\,\sigma^2(k_1 + k_2)^2}{C^2}\right]^{1/3}. \tag{17}$$

This value of n minimizes K.

Consider the following numerical example. Let

k_1 = cost per unit of underestimation = 0.50 dollars.
k_2 = cost per unit of overestimation = 0.25 dollars.
σ = 4,100.
C = cost per observation of taking random sample = 0.50 dollars.

Substituting these values in equation (17), we obtain

$$n^3 = \frac{(0.04)(4,100)^2(0.50 + 0.25)^2}{(0.50)^2} = 1,512,900;$$

$$n = 115.$$

APPENDIX V

Tables I–XII and Figures I–VI

TABLE I

PROPORTION OF AREA UNDER NORMAL CURVE LYING ABOVE AND
BELOW CERTAIN VALUES OF z

z*	P†	Q‡	z	P	Q	z	P	Q
.00	.5000	.5000	1.25	.8944	.1056	2.50	.9938	.0062
.05	.5199	.4801	1.30	.9032	.0968	2.55	.9946	.0054
.10	.5398	.4602	1.35	.9115	.0885	2.60	.9953	.0047
.15	.5596	.4404	1.40	.9192	.0808	2.65	.9960	.0040
.20	.5793	.4207	1.45	.9265	.0735	2.70	.9965	.0035
.25	.5987	.4013	1.50	.9332	.0668	2.75	.9970	.0030
.30	.6179	.3821	1.55	.9394	.0606	2.80	.9974	.0026
.35	.6368	.3632	1.60	.9452	.0548	2.85	.9978	.0022
.40	.6554	.3446	1.65	.9505	.0495	2.90	.9981	.0019
.45	.6736	.3264	1.70	.9554	.0446	2.95	.9984	.0016
.50	.6915	.3085	1.75	.9599	.0401	3.00	.9987	.0013
.55	.7088	.2912	1.80	.9641	.0359	3.05	.9989	.0011
.60	.7257	.2743	1.85	.9678	.0322	3.10	.9990	.0010
.65	.7422	.2578	1.90	.9713	.0287	3.15	.9992	.0008
.70	.7580	.2420	1.95	.9744	.0256	3.20	.9993	.0007
.75	.7734	.2266	2.00	.9772	.0228	3.25	.9994	.0006
.80	.7881	.2119	2.05	.9798	.0202	3.30	.9995	.0005
.85	.8023	.1977	2.10	.9821	.0179	3.35	.9996	.0004
.90	.8159	.1841	2.15	.9842	.0158	3.40	.9997	.0003
.95	.8289	.1711	2.20	.9861	.0139	3.45	.9997	.0003
1.00	.8413	.1587	2.25	.9878	.0122	3.50	.9998	.0002
1.05	.8531	.1469	2.30	.9893	.0107	3.55	.9998	.0002
1.10	.8643	.1357	2.35	.9906	.0094	3.60	.9998	.0002
1.15	.8749	.1251	2.40	.9918	.0082	3.65	.9999	.0001
1.20	.8849	.1151	2.45	.9929	.0071	3.70	.9999	.0001

* $z = |x - \mu|/\sigma$.

† P = Proportion of area (1) above x where $x < \mu$, or (2) below x if $x > \mu$.

‡ Q = Proportion of area (1) below x where $x < \mu$, or (2) above x if $x > \mu$.

TABLE II

z Values for Various Significance Levels

(Two-tailed Test)

Significance Level (α)	z_α	Significance Level (α)	z_α
.01.........	2.576	.50.........	.674
.02.........	2.326	.60.........	.524
.05.........	1.960	.70.........	.385
.10.........	1.645	.80.........	.253
.20.........	1.282	.90.........	.126
.30.........	1.036	1.00.........	0
.40.........	.842		

TABLE III*

t Values

DF	SIGNIFICANCE LEVELS: α						
	.50	.25	.10	.05	.025	.01	.005
1.....	1.00000	2.4142	6.3138	12.706	25.452	63.657	127.32
2.....	.81650	1.6036	2.9200	4.3027	6.2053	9.9248	14.089
3.....	.76489	1.4226	2.3534	3.1825	4.1765	5.8409	7.4533
4.....	.74070	1.3444	2.1318	2.7764	3.4954	4.6041	5.5976
5.....	.72669	1.3009	2.0150	2.5706	3.1634	4.0321	4.7733
6.....	.71756	1.2733	1.9432	2.4469	2.9687	3.7074	4.3168
7.....	.71114	1.2543	1.8946	2.3646	2.8412	3.4995	4.0293
8.....	.70639	1.2403	1.8595	2.3060	2.7515	3.3554	3.8325
9.....	.70272	1.2297	1.8331	2.2622	2.6850	3.2498	3.6897
10.....	.69981	1.2213	1.8125	2.2281	2.6338	3.1693	3.5814
11.....	.69745	1.2145	1.7959	2.2010	2.5931	3.1058	3.4966
12.....	.69548	1.2089	1.7823	2.1788	2.5600	3.0545	3.4284
13.....	.69384	1.2041	1.7709	2.1604	2.5326	3.0123	3.3725
14.....	.69242	1.2001	1.7613	2.1448	2.5096	2.9768	3.3257
15.....	.69120	1.1967	1.7530	2.1315	2.4899	2.9467	3.2860
16.....	.69013	1.1937	1.7459	2.1199	2.4729	2.9208	3.2520
17.....	.68919	1.1910	1.7396	2.1098	2.4581	2.8982	3.2225
18.....	.68837	1.1887	1.7341	2.1009	2.4450	2.8784	3.1966
19.....	.68763	1.1866	1.7291	2.0930	2.4334	2.8609	3.1737
20.....	.68696	1.1848	1.7247	2.0860	2.4231	2.8453	3.1534
21.....	.68635	1.1831	1.7207	2.0796	2.4138	2.8314	3.1352
22.....	.68580	1.1816	1.7171	2.0739	2.4055	2.8188	3.1188
23.....	.68531	1.1802	1.7139	2.0687	2.3979	2.8073	3.1040
24.....	.68485	1.1789	1.7109	2.0639	2.3910	2.7969	3.0905
25.....	.68443	1.1777	1.7081	2.0595	2.3846	2.7874	3.0782
26.....	.68405	1.1766	1.7056	2.0555	2.3788	2.7787	3.0669
27.....	.68370	1.1757	1.7033	2.0518	2.3734	2.7707	3.0565
28.....	.68335	1.1748	1.7011	2.0484	2.3685	2.7633	3.0469
29.....	.68304	1.1739	1.6991	2.0452	2.3638	2.7564	3.0380
30.....	.68276	1.1731	1.6973	2.0423	2.3596	2.7500	3.0298
40.....	.68066	1.1673	1.6839	2.0211	2.3289	2.7045	2.9712
60.....	.67862	1.1616	1.6707	2.0003	2.2991	2.6603	2.9146
120.....	.67656	1.1559	1.6577	1.9799	2.2699	2.6174	2.8599
∞	.67449	1.1503	1.6449	1.9600	2.2414	2.5758	2.8070

* Reproduced by special permission of the editors of *Biometrika* from XXXII (1945), 300, "Table of Percentage Points of the *t*-Distribution," by Maxine Merrington.

TABLE IV*

t' VALUES

TEST OF SIGNIFICANCE OF MEAN USING RANGE (R)

n	TEST OF H_0: $\mu = a$ AGAINST H_1: $\mu \neq a$ Significance Level: α			TEST OF H_0: $\mu_1 = \mu_2$ AGAINST H_1: $\mu \neq_1 \mu_2$ Significance Level: α		
	.05	.01	.001	.05	.01	.001
2	6.353	31.828	318.31	3.427	7.916	25.23
3	1.304	3.008	9.58	1.272	2.093	4.18
4	.717	1.316	2.85+	.813	1.237	1.99
5	.507	.843	1.58	.613	.896	1.35
6	.399	.628	1.07	.499	.714	1.03
7	.333	.507	.82	.426	.600	.85
8	.288	.429	.67	.373	.521	.73
9	.255	.374	.57	.334	.464	.64
10	.230	.333	.50	.304	.419	.58
11	.210	.302	.44	.280	.384	.52
12	.194	.277	.40	.260	.355	.48
13	.181	.256	.37	.243	.331	.45−
14	.170	.239	.34	.228	.311	.42
15	.160	.224	.32	.216	.293	.39
16	.151	.212	.30	.205	.278	.37
17	.144	.201	.28	.195+	.264	.35
18	.137	.191	.26	.187	.252	.34
19	.131	.182	.25+	.179	.242	.32
20	.126	.175	.24	.172	.232	.31

* This table is abridged from Tables 9 and 10 in "The Use of Range in Place of Standard Deviation in the t-Test," by E. Lord, *Biometrika*, XXXIV (1947), 64–67, by kind permission of the editor and the author.

TABLE V*
CHI SQUARE (χ^2)

SIGNIFICANCE LEVEL: α

DF†	.99	.98	.95	.90	.80	.70	.50	.30	.20	.10	.05	.02	.01
1	.000157	.000628	.00393	.0158	.0642	.148	.455	1.074	1.642	2.706	3.841	5.412	6.635
2	.0201	.0404	.103	.211	.446	.713	1.386	2.408	3.219	4.605	5.991	7.824	9.210
3	.115	.185	.352	.584	1.005	1.424	2.366	3.665	4.642	6.251	7.815	9.837	11.345
4	.297	.429	.711	1.064	1.649	2.195	3.357	4.878	5.989	7.779	9.488	11.668	13.277
5	.554	.752	1.145	1.610	2.343	3.000	4.351	6.064	7.289	9.236	11.070	13.388	15.086
6	.872	1.134	1.635	2.204	3.070	3.828	5.348	7.231	8.558	10.645	12.592	15.033	16.812
7	1.239	1.564	2.167	2.833	3.822	4.671	6.346	8.383	9.803	12.017	14.067	16.622	18.475
8	1.646	2.032	2.733	3.490	4.594	5.527	7.344	9.524	11.030	13.362	15.507	18.168	20.090
9	2.088	2.532	3.325	4.168	5.380	6.393	8.343	10.656	12.242	14.684	16.919	19.679	21.666
10	2.558	3.059	3.940	4.865	6.179	7.267	9.342	11.781	13.442	15.987	18.307	21.161	23.209
11	3.053	3.609	4.575	5.578	6.989	8.148	10.341	12.899	14.631	17.275	19.675	22.618	24.725
12	3.571	4.178	5.226	6.304	7.807	9.034	11.340	14.011	15.812	18.549	21.026	24.054	26.217
13	4.107	4.765	5.892	7.042	8.634	9.926	12.340	15.119	16.985	19.812	22.362	25.472	27.688
14	4.660	5.368	6.571	7.790	9.467	10.821	13.339	16.222	18.151	21.064	23.685	26.873	29.141
15	5.229	5.985	7.261	8.547	10.307	11.721	14.339	17.322	19.311	22.307	24.996	28.259	30.578
16	5.812	6.614	7.962	9.312	11.152	12.624	15.338	18.418	20.465	23.542	26.296	29.633	32.000
17	6.408	7.255	8.672	10.085	12.002	13.531	16.338	19.511	21.615	24.769	27.587	30.995	33.409
18	7.015	7.906	9.390	10.865	12.857	14.440	17.338	20.601	22.760	25.989	28.869	32.346	34.805
19	7.633	8.567	10.117	11.651	13.716	15.352	18.338	21.689	23.900	27.204	30.144	33.687	36.191
20	8.260	9.237	10.851	12.443	14.578	16.266	19.337	22.775	25.038	28.412	31.410	35.020	37.566
21	8.897	9.915	11.591	13.240	15.445	17.182	20.337	23.858	26.171	29.615	32.671	36.343	38.932
22	9.542	10.600	12.338	14.041	16.314	18.101	21.337	24.939	27.301	30.813	33.924	37.659	40.289
23	10.196	11.293	13.091	14.848	17.187	19.021	22.337	26.018	28.429	32.007	35.172	38.968	41.638
24	10.856	11.992	13.848	15.659	18.062	19.943	23.337	27.096	29.553	33.196	36.415	40.270	42.980
25	11.524	12.697	14.611	16.473	18.940	20.867	24.337	28.172	30.675	34.382	37.652	41.566	44.314
26	12.198	13.409	15.379	17.292	19.820	21.792	25.336	29.246	31.795	35.563	38.885	42.856	45.642
27	12.879	14.125	16.151	18.114	20.703	22.719	26.336	30.319	32.912	36.741	40.113	44.140	46.963
28	13.565	14.847	16.928	18.939	21.588	23.647	27.336	31.391	34.027	37.916	41.337	45.419	48.278
29	14.256	15.574	17.708	19.768	22.475	24.577	28.336	32.461	35.139	39.087	42.557	46.693	49.588
30	14.953	16.306	18.493	20.599	23.364	25.508	29.336	33.530	36.250	40.256	43.773	47.962	50.892

* Reprinted from R. A. Fisher, *Statistical Methods for Research Workers* (London: Oliver & Boyd, Ltd., 1941), Table III, by permission of the author and publisher.

† For degrees of freedom greater than 30, the expression $\sqrt{2\chi^2} - \sqrt{2n'-1}$ may be used as a normal deviate with unit variance, where n' is the number of degrees of freedom.

TABLE VI

F Distribution
(.50 Significance Level)

DF_1

DF_2	1	2	3	4	5	6	7	8	9	10	12	15	20	24	30	40	60	120	∞
1	1.0000	1.5000	1.7092	1.8227	1.8937	1.9422	1.9774	2.0041	2.0250	2.0419	2.0674	2.0931	2.1190	2.1321	2.1452	2.1584	2.1716	2.1848	2.1981
2	0.66667	1.0000	1.1349	1.2071	1.2519	1.2824	1.3045	1.3213	1.3344	1.3450	1.3610	1.3771	1.3933	1.4014	1.4096	1.4178	1.4261	1.4344	1.4427
3	0.58506	0.88110	1.0000	1.0632	1.1024	1.1289	1.1482	1.1627	1.1741	1.1833	1.1972	1.2111	1.2252	1.2322	1.2393	1.2464	1.2536	1.2608	1.2680
4	0.54863	0.82843	0.94054	1.0000	1.0367	1.0617	1.0797	1.0933	1.1040	1.1126	1.1255	1.1386	1.1517	1.1583	1.1649	1.1716	1.1782	1.1849	1.1916
5	0.52807	0.79877	0.90715	0.96456	1.0000	1.0240	1.0414	1.0545	1.0648	1.0730	1.0855	1.0980	1.1106	1.1170	1.1234	1.1297	1.1361	1.1426	1.1490
6	0.51489	0.77976	0.88578	0.94191	0.97654	1.0000	1.0169	1.0298	1.0398	1.0478	1.0600	1.0722	1.0845	1.0907	1.0969	1.1031	1.1093	1.1156	1.1219
7	0.50572	0.76655	0.87095	0.92619	0.96026	0.98334	1.0000	1.0126	1.0224	1.0304	1.0423	1.0543	1.0664	1.0724	1.0785	1.0846	1.0908	1.0969	1.1031
8	0.49898	0.75683	0.86004	0.91464	0.94831	0.97111	0.98757	1.0000	1.0097	1.0175	1.0293	1.0412	1.0531	1.0591	1.0651	1.0711	1.0771	1.0832	1.0893
9	0.49382	0.74938	0.85168	0.90580	0.93916	0.96175	0.97805	0.99037	1.0000	1.0077	1.0194	1.0311	1.0429	1.0489	1.0548	1.0608	1.0667	1.0727	1.0788
10	0.48973	0.74349	0.84508	0.89882	0.93193	0.95436	0.97054	0.98276	0.99232	1.0000	1.0116	1.0232	1.0349	1.0408	1.0467	1.0526	1.0585	1.0645	1.0705
11	0.48644	0.73872	0.83973	0.89316	0.92608	0.94837	0.96445	0.97661	0.98610	0.99373	1.0052	1.0168	1.0284	1.0343	1.0401	1.0460	1.0519	1.0578	1.0637
12	0.48369	0.73477	0.83530	0.88848	0.92124	0.94342	0.95943	0.97152	0.98097	0.98856	1.0000	1.0115	1.0231	1.0289	1.0347	1.0405	1.0464	1.0523	1.0582
13	0.48141	0.73145	0.83159	0.88454	0.91718	0.93926	0.95520	0.96724	0.97665	0.98421	0.99560	1.0071	1.0186	1.0243	1.0301	1.0360	1.0418	1.0476	1.0535
14	0.47944	0.72862	0.82842	0.88119	0.91371	0.93573	0.95161	0.96360	0.97298	0.98051	0.99186	1.0033	1.0147	1.0205	1.0263	1.0321	1.0379	1.0437	1.0495
15	0.47775	0.72619	0.82569	0.87830	0.91073	0.93267	0.94850	0.96046	0.96981	0.97732	0.98863	1.0000	1.0114	1.0172	1.0229	1.0287	1.0345	1.0403	1.0461
16	0.47628	0.72406	0.82330	0.87578	0.90812	0.93001	0.94580	0.95773	0.96705	0.97454	0.98582	0.99716	1.0086	1.0143	1.0200	1.0258	1.0315	1.0373	1.0431
17	0.47499	0.72219	0.82121	0.87357	0.90584	0.92767	0.94342	0.95532	0.96462	0.97209	0.98334	0.99466	1.0060	1.0117	1.0174	1.0232	1.0289	1.0347	1.0405
18	0.47385	0.72053	0.81936	0.87161	0.90381	0.92560	0.94132	0.95319	0.96247	0.96993	0.98116	0.99245	1.0038	1.0095	1.0152	1.0209	1.0267	1.0324	1.0382
19	0.47284	0.71906	0.81771	0.86987	0.90200	0.92375	0.93944	0.95129	0.96056	0.96800	0.97920	0.99047	1.0018	1.0075	1.0132	1.0189	1.0246	1.0304	1.0361
20	0.47192	0.71773	0.81621	0.86830	0.90038	0.92210	0.93776	0.94959	0.95884	0.96626	0.97746	0.98870	1.0000	1.0057	1.0114	1.0171	1.0228	1.0285	1.0343
21	0.47108	0.71653	0.81487	0.86688	0.89891	0.92060	0.93624	0.94805	0.95728	0.96470	0.97587	0.98710	0.99838	1.0040	1.0097	1.0154	1.0211	1.0268	1.0326
22	0.47033	0.71545	0.81365	0.86559	0.89759	0.91924	0.93486	0.94665	0.95588	0.96328	0.97444	0.98565	0.99692	1.0026	1.0082	1.0139	1.0196	1.0253	1.0311
23	0.46965	0.71446	0.81255	0.86442	0.89638	0.91800	0.93360	0.94538	0.95459	0.96199	0.97313	0.98433	0.99558	1.0012	1.0069	1.0126	1.0183	1.0240	1.0297
24	0.46902	0.71356	0.81153	0.86335	0.89527	0.91687	0.93245	0.94422	0.95342	0.96081	0.97194	0.98312	0.99436	1.0000	1.0057	1.0113	1.0170	1.0227	1.0284
25	0.46844	0.71272	0.81061	0.86236	0.89425	0.91583	0.93140	0.94315	0.95234	0.95972	0.97084	0.98201	0.99324	0.99887	1.0045	1.0102	1.0159	1.0215	1.0273
26	0.46793	0.71195	0.80975	0.86145	0.89331	0.91487	0.93042	0.94217	0.95135	0.95872	0.96983	0.98099	0.99220	0.99783	1.0035	1.0091	1.0148	1.0205	1.0262
27	0.46744	0.71124	0.80894	0.86061	0.89244	0.91399	0.92952	0.94126	0.95044	0.95779	0.96889	0.98004	0.99125	0.99687	1.0025	1.0082	1.0138	1.0195	1.0252
28	0.46697	0.71059	0.80820	0.85983	0.89164	0.91317	0.92869	0.94041	0.94958	0.95694	0.96802	0.97917	0.99036	0.99598	1.0016	1.0073	1.0129	1.0186	1.0243
29	0.46654	0.70999	0.80753	0.85911	0.89089	0.91241	0.92791	0.93963	0.94879	0.95614	0.96722	0.97835	0.98954	0.99515	1.0008	1.0064	1.0121	1.0177	1.0234
30	0.46616	0.70941	0.80689	0.85844	0.89019	0.91169	0.92719	0.93839	0.94805	0.95540	0.96647	0.97759	0.98877	0.99438	1.0000	1.0056	1.0113	1.0170	1.0226
40	0.46330	0.70531	0.80228	0.85357	0.88516	0.90654	0.92197	0.93351	0.94272	0.95003	0.96104	0.97211	0.98323	0.98880	0.99440	1.0000	1.0056	1.0113	1.0169
60	0.46053	0.70122	0.79770	0.84873	0.88017	0.90144	0.91679	0.92838	0.93743	0.94471	0.95566	0.96667	0.97773	0.98328	0.98884	0.99441	1.0000	1.0056	1.0112
120	0.45774	0.69717	0.79314	0.84392	0.87521	0.89637	0.91164	0.92318	0.93218	0.93943	0.95032	0.96128	0.97228	0.97780	0.98333	0.98887	0.99443	1.0000	1.0056
∞	0.45494	0.69315	0.78866	0.83918	0.87029	0.89135	0.90654	0.91802	0.92698	0.93418	0.94503	0.95593	0.96687	0.97236	0.97787	0.98339	0.98891	0.99445	1.0000

* Reproduced by special permission of the editors of *Biometrika*, from XXXIII (1943–46), 78–87, "Tables of Percentage Points of the Inverted Beta (F) Distribution," by Maxine Merrington and C. M. Thompson.

TABLE VI—Continued

F DISTRIBUTION
(.25 SIGNIFICANCE LEVEL)

DF_1

DF_2	1	2	3	4	5	6	7	8	9	10	12	15	20	24	30	40	60	120	∞
1	5.8285	7.5000	8.1999	8.5810	8.8198	8.9833	9.1021	9.1922	9.2631	9.3202	9.4064	9.4934	9.5813	9.6255	9.6698	9.7144	9.7591	9.8041	9.8492
2	2.5714	3.0000	3.1534	3.2320	3.2799	3.3121	3.3352	3.3526	3.3661	3.3770	3.3934	3.4098	3.4263	3.4345	3.4428	3.4511	3.4594	3.4677	3.4761
3	2.0239	2.2798	2.3555	2.3901	2.4095	2.4218	2.4302	2.4364	2.4410	2.4447	2.4500	2.4552	2.4602	2.4626	2.4650	2.4674	2.4697	2.4720	2.4742
4	1.8074	2.0000	2.0467	2.0642	2.0723	2.0766	2.0790	2.0805	2.0814	2.0820	2.0826	2.0829	2.0828	2.0827	2.0825	2.0821	2.0817	2.0812	2.0806
5	1.6925	1.8528	1.8843	1.8927	1.8947	1.8945	1.8935	1.8923	1.8911	1.8899	1.8877	1.8851	1.8820	1.8802	1.8784	1.8763	1.8742	1.8719	1.8694
6	1.6214	1.7622	1.7844	1.7872	1.7852	1.7821	1.7789	1.7760	1.7733	1.7708	1.7668	1.7621	1.7569	1.7540	1.7510	1.7477	1.7443	1.7407	1.7368
7	1.5732	1.7010	1.7169	1.7157	1.7111	1.7059	1.7011	1.6969	1.6931	1.6898	1.6843	1.6781	1.6712	1.6675	1.6635	1.6593	1.6548	1.6502	1.6452
8	1.5384	1.6569	1.6683	1.6642	1.6575	1.6508	1.6448	1.6396	1.6350	1.6310	1.6244	1.6170	1.6088	1.6043	1.5996	1.5945	1.5892	1.5836	1.5777
9	1.5121	1.6236	1.6315	1.6253	1.6170	1.6091	1.6022	1.5961	1.5909	1.5863	1.5788	1.5705	1.5611	1.5560	1.5506	1.5450	1.5389	1.5325	1.5257
10	1.4915	1.5975	1.6028	1.5940	1.5853	1.5765	1.5688	1.5621	1.5563	1.5513	1.5430	1.5338	1.5235	1.5179	1.5119	1.5056	1.4990	1.4919	1.4843
11	1.4749	1.5767	1.5798	1.5704	1.5598	1.5502	1.5418	1.5346	1.5284	1.5230	1.5140	1.5041	1.4930	1.4869	1.4805	1.4737	1.4664	1.4587	1.4504
12	1.4613	1.5595	1.5609	1.5503	1.5389	1.5286	1.5197	1.5120	1.5054	1.4996	1.4902	1.4796	1.4678	1.4613	1.4544	1.4471	1.4393	1.4310	1.4221
13	1.4500	1.5452	1.5451	1.5336	1.5214	1.5105	1.5011	1.4931	1.4861	1.4801	1.4701	1.4590	1.4465	1.4397	1.4324	1.4247	1.4164	1.4075	1.3980
14	1.4403	1.5331	1.5317	1.5194	1.5066	1.4952	1.4854	1.4770	1.4697	1.4634	1.4530	1.4414	1.4284	1.4212	1.4136	1.4055	1.3967	1.3874	1.3772
15	1.4321	1.5227	1.5202	1.5071	1.4938	1.4820	1.4718	1.4631	1.4556	1.4491	1.4383	1.4263	1.4127	1.4052	1.3973	1.3888	1.3796	1.3698	1.3591
16	1.4249	1.5137	1.5103	1.4965	1.4827	1.4706	1.4601	1.4511	1.4433	1.4366	1.4255	1.4130	1.3990	1.3913	1.3830	1.3742	1.3646	1.3543	1.3432
17	1.4186	1.5057	1.5015	1.4873	1.4730	1.4605	1.4497	1.4405	1.4325	1.4256	1.4142	1.4014	1.3869	1.3790	1.3704	1.3613	1.3514	1.3406	1.3290
18	1.4130	1.4988	1.4938	1.4790	1.4644	1.4516	1.4406	1.4312	1.4230	1.4159	1.4042	1.3911	1.3762	1.3680	1.3592	1.3497	1.3395	1.3284	1.3162
19	1.4081	1.4925	1.4870	1.4717	1.4568	1.4437	1.4325	1.4228	1.4145	1.4073	1.3953	1.3819	1.3666	1.3582	1.3492	1.3394	1.3289	1.3174	1.3048
20	1.4037	1.4870	1.4808	1.4652	1.4500	1.4366	1.4252	1.4153	1.4069	1.3995	1.3873	1.3736	1.3580	1.3494	1.3401	1.3301	1.3193	1.3074	1.2943
21	1.3997	1.4820	1.4753	1.4593	1.4438	1.4302	1.4186	1.4086	1.4000	1.3925	1.3801	1.3661	1.3502	1.3414	1.3319	1.3217	1.3105	1.2983	1.2848
22	1.3961	1.4774	1.4703	1.4540	1.4382	1.4244	1.4126	1.4025	1.3937	1.3861	1.3735	1.3593	1.3431	1.3341	1.3245	1.3140	1.3025	1.2900	1.2761
23	1.3928	1.4733	1.4657	1.4491	1.4331	1.4191	1.4072	1.3969	1.3880	1.3803	1.3675	1.3531	1.3366	1.3275	1.3176	1.3069	1.2952	1.2824	1.2681
24	1.3898	1.4695	1.4615	1.4447	1.4285	1.4143	1.4022	1.3918	1.3828	1.3750	1.3621	1.3474	1.3307	1.3214	1.3113	1.3004	1.2885	1.2754	1.2607
25	1.3870	1.4661	1.4577	1.4406	1.4242	1.4099	1.3976	1.3871	1.3780	1.3701	1.3570	1.3422	1.3252	1.3158	1.3056	1.2945	1.2823	1.2689	1.2538
26	1.3845	1.4629	1.4542	1.4368	1.4203	1.4058	1.3935	1.3828	1.3737	1.3656	1.3524	1.3374	1.3202	1.3106	1.3002	1.2889	1.2765	1.2628	1.2474
27	1.3822	1.4600	1.4510	1.4334	1.4166	1.4021	1.3896	1.3788	1.3696	1.3615	1.3481	1.3329	1.3155	1.3058	1.2953	1.2838	1.2712	1.2572	1.2414
28	1.3800	1.4572	1.4480	1.4302	1.4133	1.3986	1.3860	1.3752	1.3658	1.3576	1.3441	1.3288	1.3112	1.3013	1.2906	1.2790	1.2662	1.2519	1.2358
29	1.3780	1.4547	1.4452	1.4272	1.4102	1.3953	1.3826	1.3717	1.3623	1.3541	1.3404	1.3249	1.3071	1.2971	1.2863	1.2745	1.2615	1.2470	1.2306
30	1.3761	1.4524	1.4426	1.4244	1.4073	1.3923	1.3795	1.3685	1.3590	1.3507	1.3369	1.3213	1.3033	1.2933	1.2823	1.2703	1.2571	1.2424	1.2256
40	1.3626	1.4355	1.4239	1.4045	1.3863	1.3706	1.3571	1.3455	1.3354	1.3266	1.3119	1.2952	1.2758	1.2649	1.2529	1.2397	1.2249	1.2080	1.1883
60	1.3493	1.4188	1.4055	1.3848	1.3657	1.3491	1.3349	1.3226	1.3119	1.3026	1.2870	1.2691	1.2481	1.2361	1.2229	1.2081	1.1912	1.1715	1.1474
120	1.3362	1.4024	1.3873	1.3654	1.3453	1.3278	1.3128	1.2999	1.2886	1.2787	1.2621	1.2428	1.2200	1.2068	1.1921	1.1752	1.1555	1.1314	1.0987
∞	1.3233	1.3863	1.3694	1.3463	1.3251	1.3068	1.2910	1.2774	1.2654	1.2549	1.2371	1.2163	1.1914	1.1767	1.1600	1.1404	1.1164	1.0838	1.0000

TABLE VI—*Continued*

F DISTRIBUTION
(.10 SIGNIFICANCE LEVEL)

DF₁

DF₂	1	2	3	4	5	6	7	8	9	10	12	15	20	24	30	40	60	120	∞
1	39.864	49.500	53.593	55.833	57.241	58.204	58.906	59.439	59.858	60.195	60.705	61.220	61.740	62.002	62.265	62.529	62.794	63.061	63.328
2	8.5263	9.0000	9.1618	9.2434	9.2926	9.3255	9.3491	9.3668	9.3805	9.3916	9.4081	9.4247	9.4413	9.4496	9.4579	9.4663	9.4746	9.4829	9.4913
3	5.5383	5.4624	5.3908	5.3427	5.3092	5.2847	5.2662	5.2517	5.2400	5.2304	5.2156	5.2003	5.1845	5.1764	5.1681	5.1597	5.1512	5.1425	5.1337
4	4.5448	4.3246	4.1908	4.1073	4.0506	4.0098	3.9790	3.9549	3.9357	3.9109	3.8955	3.8689	3.8443	3.8310	3.8174	3.8036	3.7896	3.7753	3.7607
5	4.0604	3.7797	3.6195	3.5202	3.4530	3.4045	3.3679	3.3393	3.3163	3.2974	3.2682	3.2380	3.2067	3.1905	3.1741	3.1573	3.1402	3.1228	3.1050
6	3.7760	3.4633	3.2888	3.1808	3.1075	3.0546	3.0145	2.9830	2.9577	2.9369	2.9047	2.8712	2.8363	2.8183	2.8000	2.7812	2.7620	2.7423	2.7222
7	3.5894	3.2574	3.0741	2.9605	2.8833	2.8274	2.7849	2.7516	2.7247	2.7025	2.6681	2.6322	2.5947	2.5753	2.5555	2.5351	2.5142	2.4928	2.4708
8	3.4579	3.1131	2.9238	2.8064	2.7265	2.6663	2.6241	2.5893	2.5612	2.5380	2.5020	2.4642	2.4246	2.4041	2.3830	2.3614	2.3391	2.3162	2.2926
9	3.3603	3.0065	2.8129	2.6927	2.6106	2.5509	2.5053	2.4694	2.4403	2.4163	2.3789	2.3396	2.2983	2.2768	2.2547	2.2320	2.2085	2.1843	2.1592
10	3.2850	2.9245	2.7277	2.6053	2.5216	2.4606	2.4140	2.3772	2.3473	2.3226	2.2841	2.2435	2.2007	2.1784	2.1554	2.1317	2.1072	2.0818	2.0554
11	3.2252	2.8595	2.6602	2.5362	2.4512	2.3891	2.3416	2.3040	2.2735	2.2482	2.2087	2.1671	2.1230	2.1000	2.0762	2.0516	2.0261	1.9997	1.9721
12	3.1765	2.8068	2.6055	2.4801	2.3940	2.3310	2.2828	2.2446	2.2135	2.1878	2.1474	2.1049	2.0597	2.0360	2.0115	1.9861	1.9597	1.9323	1.9036
13	3.1362	2.7632	2.5603	2.4337	2.3467	2.2830	2.2341	2.1953	2.1638	2.1376	2.0966	2.0532	2.0070	1.9827	1.9576	1.9315	1.9043	1.8759	1.8462
14	3.1022	2.7265	2.5222	2.3947	2.3069	2.2426	2.1931	2.1539	2.1220	2.0954	2.0537	2.0095	1.9625	1.9377	1.9119	1.8852	1.8572	1.8280	1.7973
15	3.0732	2.6952	2.4898	2.3614	2.2730	2.2081	2.1582	2.1185	2.0862	2.0593	2.0171	1.9722	1.9243	1.8990	1.8728	1.8454	1.8168	1.7867	1.7551
16	3.0481	2.6682	2.4618	2.3327	2.2438	2.1783	2.1280	2.0880	2.0553	2.0281	1.9854	1.9399	1.8913	1.8656	1.8388	1.8108	1.7816	1.7507	1.7182
17	3.0262	2.6446	2.4374	2.3077	2.2183	2.1524	2.1017	2.0613	2.0284	2.0009	1.9577	1.9117	1.8624	1.8362	1.8090	1.7805	1.7506	1.7191	1.6856
18	3.0070	2.6239	2.4160	2.2858	2.1958	2.1296	2.0785	2.0379	2.0047	1.9770	1.9333	1.8868	1.8368	1.8103	1.7827	1.7537	1.7232	1.6910	1.6567
19	2.9899	2.6056	2.3970	2.2663	2.1760	2.1094	2.0580	2.0171	1.9836	1.9557	1.9117	1.8647	1.8142	1.7873	1.7592	1.7298	1.6988	1.6659	1.6308
20	2.9747	2.5893	2.3801	2.2489	2.1582	2.0913	2.0397	1.9985	1.9649	1.9367	1.8924	1.8449	1.7938	1.7667	1.7382	1.7083	1.6768	1.6433	1.6074
21	2.9609	2.5746	2.3649	2.2333	2.1423	2.0751	2.0232	1.9819	1.9480	1.9197	1.8750	1.8272	1.7756	1.7481	1.7193	1.6890	1.6569	1.6228	1.5862
22	2.9486	2.5613	2.3512	2.2193	2.1279	2.0605	2.0084	1.9668	1.9327	1.9043	1.8593	1.8111	1.7590	1.7312	1.7021	1.6714	1.6389	1.6042	1.5656
23	2.9374	2.5493	2.3387	2.2065	2.1149	2.0472	1.9949	1.9531	1.9189	1.8903	1.8450	1.7964	1.7439	1.7159	1.6864	1.6554	1.6224	1.5871	1.5490
24	2.9271	2.5383	2.3274	2.1949	2.1030	2.0351	1.9826	1.9407	1.9063	1.8775	1.8319	1.7831	1.7302	1.7019	1.6721	1.6407	1.6073	1.5715	1.5327
25	2.9177	2.5283	2.3170	2.1843	2.0922	2.0241	1.9714	1.9292	1.8947	1.8658	1.8200	1.7708	1.7175	1.6890	1.6589	1.6272	1.5934	1.5570	1.5176
26	2.9091	2.5191	2.3075	2.1745	2.0822	2.0139	1.9610	1.9188	1.8841	1.8550	1.8090	1.7596	1.7059	1.6771	1.6468	1.6147	1.5805	1.5437	1.5036
27	2.9012	2.5106	2.2987	2.1655	2.0730	2.0045	1.9515	1.9091	1.8743	1.8451	1.7989	1.7492	1.6951	1.6662	1.6356	1.6032	1.5686	1.5313	1.4906
28	2.8939	2.5028	2.2906	2.1571	2.0645	1.9959	1.9427	1.9001	1.8652	1.8359	1.7895	1.7395	1.6852	1.6560	1.6252	1.5925	1.5575	1.5198	1.4784
29	2.8871	2.4955	2.2831	2.1494	2.0566	1.9878	1.9345	1.8918	1.8568	1.8274	1.7808	1.7306	1.6759	1.6465	1.6155	1.5825	1.5472	1.5090	1.4670
30	2.8807	2.4887	2.2761	2.1422	2.0492	1.9803	1.9269	1.8841	1.8490	1.8195	1.7727	1.7223	1.6673	1.6377	1.6065	1.5732	1.5376	1.4989	1.4564
40	2.8354	2.4404	2.2261	2.0909	1.9968	1.9269	1.8725	1.8289	1.7929	1.7627	1.7146	1.6624	1.6052	1.5741	1.5411	1.5056	1.4672	1.4248	1.3769
60	2.7914	2.3932	2.1774	2.0410	1.9457	1.8747	1.8194	1.7748	1.7380	1.7070	1.6574	1.6034	1.5435	1.5107	1.4755	1.4373	1.3952	1.3476	1.2915
120	2.7478	2.3473	2.1300	1.9923	1.8959	1.8238	1.7675	1.7220	1.6843	1.6524	1.6012	1.5450	1.4821	1.4472	1.4094	1.3676	1.3203	1.2646	1.1926
∞	2.7055	2.3026	2.0838	1.9449	1.8473	1.7741	1.7167	1.6702	1.6315	1.5987	1.5458	1.4871	1.4206	1.3832	1.3419	1.2951	1.2400	1.1686	1.0000

TABLE VI—Continued

F Distribution

(.05 SIGNIFICANCE LEVEL)

DF₂										DF₁									
	1	2	3	4	5	6	7	8	9	10	12	15	20	24	30	40	60	120	∞
1	161.45	199.50	215.71	224.58	230.16	233.99	236.77	238.88	240.54	241.88	243.91	245.95	248.01	249.05	250.09	251.14	252.20	253.25	254.32
2	18.513	19.000	19.164	19.247	19.296	19.330	19.353	19.371	19.385	19.396	19.413	19.429	19.446	19.454	19.462	19.471	19.479	19.487	19.496
3	10.128	9.5521	9.2766	9.1172	9.0135	8.9406	8.8868	8.8452	8.8123	8.7855	8.7446	8.7029	8.6602	8.6385	8.6166	8.5944	8.5720	8.5494	8.5265
4	7.7086	6.9443	6.5914	6.3883	6.2560	6.1631	6.0942	6.0410	5.9988	5.9644	5.9117	5.8578	5.8025	5.7744	5.7459	5.7170	5.6878	5.6581	5.6281
5	6.6079	5.7861	5.4095	5.1922	5.0503	4.9503	4.8759	4.8183	4.7725	4.7351	4.6777	4.6188	4.5581	4.5272	4.4957	4.4638	4.4314	4.3984	4.3650
6	5.9874	5.1433	4.7571	4.5337	4.3874	4.2839	4.2066	4.1468	4.0990	4.0600	3.9999	3.9381	3.8742	3.8415	3.8082	3.7743	3.7398	3.7047	3.6688
7	5.5914	4.7374	4.3468	4.1203	3.9715	3.8660	3.7870	3.7257	3.6767	3.6365	3.5747	3.5108	3.4445	3.4105	3.3758	3.3404	3.3043	3.2674	3.2298
8	5.3177	4.4590	4.0662	3.8378	3.6875	3.5806	3.5005	3.4381	3.3881	3.3472	3.2840	3.2184	3.1503	3.1152	3.0794	3.0428	3.0053	2.9669	2.9276
9	5.1174	4.2565	3.8626	3.6331	3.4817	3.3738	3.2927	3.2296	3.1789	3.1373	3.0729	3.0061	2.9365	2.9005	2.8637	2.8259	2.7872	2.7475	2.7067
10	4.9646	4.1028	3.7083	3.4780	3.3258	3.2172	3.1355	3.0717	3.0204	2.9782	2.9130	2.8450	2.7740	2.7372	2.6996	2.6609	2.6211	2.5801	2.5379
11	4.8443	3.9823	3.5874	3.3567	3.2039	3.0946	3.0123	2.9480	2.8962	2.8536	2.7876	2.7186	2.6464	2.6090	2.5705	2.5309	2.4901	2.4480	2.4045
12	4.7472	3.8853	3.4903	3.2592	3.1059	2.9961	2.9134	2.8486	2.7964	2.7534	2.6866	2.6169	2.5436	2.5055	2.4663	2.4259	2.3842	2.3410	2.2962
13	4.6672	3.8056	3.4105	3.1791	3.0254	2.9153	2.8321	2.7669	2.7144	2.6710	2.6037	2.5331	2.4589	2.4202	2.3803	2.3392	2.2966	2.2524	2.2064
14	4.6001	3.7389	3.3439	3.1122	2.9582	2.8477	2.7642	2.6987	2.6458	2.6021	2.5342	2.4630	2.3879	2.3487	2.3082	2.2664	2.2230	2.1778	2.1307
15	4.5431	3.6823	3.2874	3.0556	2.9013	2.7905	2.7066	2.6408	2.5876	2.5437	2.4753	2.4035	2.3275	2.2878	2.2468	2.2043	2.1601	2.1141	2.0658
16	4.4940	3.6337	3.2389	3.0069	2.8524	2.7413	2.6572	2.5911	2.5377	2.4935	2.4247	2.3522	2.2756	2.2354	2.1938	2.1507	2.1058	2.0589	2.0096
17	4.4513	3.5915	3.1968	2.9647	2.8100	2.6987	2.6143	2.5480	2.4943	2.4499	2.3807	2.3077	2.2304	2.1898	2.1477	2.1040	2.0584	2.0107	1.9604
18	4.4139	3.5546	3.1599	2.9277	2.7729	2.6613	2.5767	2.5102	2.4563	2.4117	2.3421	2.2686	2.1906	2.1497	2.1071	2.0629	2.0166	1.9681	1.9168
19	4.3808	3.5219	3.1274	2.8951	2.7401	2.6283	2.5435	2.4768	2.4227	2.3779	2.3080	2.2341	2.1555	2.1141	2.0712	2.0264	1.9796	1.9302	1.8780
20	4.3513	3.4928	3.0984	2.8661	2.7109	2.5990	2.5140	2.4471	2.3928	2.3479	2.2776	2.2033	2.1242	2.0825	2.0391	1.9938	1.9464	1.8963	1.8432
21	4.3248	3.4668	3.0725	2.8401	2.6848	2.5727	2.4876	2.4205	2.3661	2.3210	2.2504	2.1757	2.0960	2.0540	2.0102	1.9645	1.9165	1.8657	1.8117
22	4.3009	3.4434	3.0491	2.8167	2.6613	2.5491	2.4638	2.3965	2.3419	2.2967	2.2258	2.1508	2.0707	2.0283	1.9842	1.9380	1.8895	1.8380	1.7831
23	4.2793	3.4221	3.0280	2.7955	2.6400	2.5277	2.4422	2.3748	2.3201	2.2747	2.2036	2.1282	2.0476	2.0050	1.9605	1.9139	1.8649	1.8128	1.7570
24	4.2597	3.4028	3.0088	2.7763	2.6207	2.5082	2.4226	2.3551	2.3002	2.2547	2.1834	2.1077	2.0267	1.9838	1.9390	1.8920	1.8424	1.7897	1.7331
25	4.2417	3.3852	2.9912	2.7587	2.6030	2.4904	2.4047	2.3371	2.2821	2.2365	2.1649	2.0889	2.0075	1.9643	1.9192	1.8718	1.8217	1.7684	1.7110
26	4.2252	3.3690	2.9751	2.7426	2.5868	2.4741	2.3883	2.3205	2.2655	2.2197	2.1479	2.0716	1.9898	1.9464	1.9010	1.8533	1.8027	1.7488	1.6906
27	4.2100	3.3541	2.9604	2.7278	2.5719	2.4591	2.3732	2.3053	2.2501	2.2043	2.1323	2.0558	1.9736	1.9299	1.8842	1.8361	1.7851	1.7307	1.6717
28	4.1960	3.3404	2.9467	2.7141	2.5581	2.4453	2.3593	2.2913	2.2360	2.1900	2.1179	2.0411	1.9586	1.9147	1.8687	1.8203	1.7689	1.7138	1.6541
29	4.1830	3.3277	2.9340	2.7014	2.5454	2.4324	2.3463	2.2782	2.2229	2.1768	2.1045	2.0275	1.9446	1.9005	1.8543	1.8055	1.7537	1.6981	1.6377
30	4.1709	3.3158	2.9223	2.6896	2.5336	2.4205	2.3343	2.2662	2.2107	2.1646	2.0921	2.0148	1.9317	1.8874	1.8409	1.7918	1.7396	1.6835	1.6223
40	4.0848	3.2317	2.8387	2.6060	2.4495	2.3359	2.2490	2.1802	2.1240	2.0772	2.0035	1.9245	1.8389	1.7929	1.7444	1.6928	1.6373	1.5766	1.5089
60	4.0012	3.1504	2.7581	2.5252	2.3683	2.2540	2.1665	2.0970	2.0401	1.9926	1.9174	1.8364	1.7480	1.7001	1.6491	1.5943	1.5343	1.4673	1.3893
120	3.9201	3.0718	2.6802	2.4472	2.2900	2.1750	2.0867	2.0164	1.9588	1.9105	1.8337	1.7505	1.6587	1.6084	1.5543	1.4952	1.4290	1.3519	1.2539
∞	3.8415	2.9957	2.6049	2.3719	2.2141	2.0986	2.0096	1.9384	1.8799	1.8307	1.7522	1.6664	1.5705	1.5173	1.4591	1.3940	1.3180	1.2214	1.0000

TABLE VI—*Continued*

F DISTRIBUTION

(.025 SIGNIFICANCE LEVEL)

DF_1

DF_2	1	2	3	4	5	6	7	8	9	10	12	15	20	24	30	40	60	120	∞
1	647.79	799.50	864.16	899.58	921.85	937.11	948.22	956.66	963.28	968.63	976.71	984.87	993.10	997.25	1001.4	1005.6	1009.8	1014.0	1018.3
2	38.506	39.000	39.165	39.248	39.298	39.331	39.355	39.373	39.387	39.398	39.415	39.431	39.448	39.456	39.465	39.473	39.481	39.490	39.498
3	17.443	16.044	15.439	15.101	14.885	14.735	14.624	14.540	14.473	14.419	14.337	14.253	14.167	14.124	14.081	14.037	13.992	13.947	13.902
4	12.218	10.649	9.9792	9.6045	9.3645	9.1973	9.0741	8.9796	8.9047	8.8439	8.7512	8.6565	8.5599	8.5109	8.4613	8.4111	8.3604	8.3092	8.2573
5	10.007	8.4336	7.7636	7.3879	7.1464	6.9777	6.8531	6.7572	6.6810	6.6192	6.5246	6.4277	6.3285	6.2780	6.2269	6.1751	6.1225	6.0693	6.0153
6	8.8131	7.2598	6.5988	6.2272	5.9876	5.8197	5.6955	5.5996	5.5234	5.4613	5.3662	5.2687	5.1684	5.1172	5.0652	5.0125	4.9589	4.9045	4.8491
7	8.0727	6.5415	5.8898	5.5226	5.2852	5.1186	4.9949	4.8994	4.8232	4.7611	4.6658	4.5678	4.4667	4.4150	4.3624	4.3089	4.2544	4.1989	4.1423
8	7.5709	6.0595	5.4160	5.0526	4.8173	4.6517	4.5286	4.4332	4.3572	4.2951	4.1997	4.1012	3.9995	3.9472	3.8940	3.8398	3.7844	3.7279	3.6702
9	7.2093	5.7147	5.0781	4.7181	4.4844	4.3197	4.1971	4.1020	4.0260	3.9639	3.8682	3.7694	3.6669	3.6142	3.5604	3.5055	3.4493	3.3918	3.3329
10	6.9367	5.4564	4.8256	4.4683	4.2361	4.0721	3.9498	3.8549	3.7790	3.7168	3.6209	3.5217	3.4186	3.3654	3.3110	3.2554	3.1984	3.1399	3.0798
11	6.7241	5.2559	4.6300	4.2751	4.0440	3.8807	3.7586	3.6638	3.5879	3.5257	3.4296	3.3299	3.2261	3.1725	3.1176	3.0613	3.0035	2.9441	2.8828
12	6.5538	5.0959	4.4742	4.1212	3.8911	3.7283	3.6065	3.5118	3.4358	3.3736	3.2773	3.1772	3.0728	3.0187	2.9633	2.9063	2.8478	2.7874	2.7249
13	6.4143	4.9653	4.3472	3.9959	3.7667	3.6043	3.4827	3.3880	3.3120	3.2497	3.1532	3.0527	2.9477	2.8932	2.8373	2.7797	2.7204	2.6590	2.5955
14	6.2979	4.8567	4.2417	3.8919	3.6634	3.5014	3.3799	3.2853	3.2093	3.1469	3.0501	2.9493	2.8437	2.7888	2.7324	2.6742	2.6142	2.5519	2.4872
15	6.1995	4.7650	4.1528	3.8043	3.5764	3.4147	3.2934	3.1987	3.1227	3.0602	2.9633	2.8621	2.7559	2.7006	2.6437	2.5850	2.5242	2.4611	2.3953
16	6.1151	4.6867	4.0768	3.7294	3.5021	3.3406	3.2194	3.1248	3.0488	2.9862	2.8890	2.7875	2.6808	2.6252	2.5678	2.5085	2.4471	2.3831	2.3163
17	6.0420	4.6189	4.0112	3.6648	3.4379	3.2767	3.1556	3.0610	2.9849	2.9222	2.8249	2.7230	2.6158	2.5598	2.5021	2.4422	2.3801	2.3153	2.2474
18	5.9781	4.5597	3.9539	3.6083	3.3820	3.2209	3.0999	3.0053	2.9291	2.8664	2.7689	2.6667	2.5590	2.5027	2.4445	2.3842	2.3214	2.2558	2.1869
19	5.9216	4.5075	3.9034	3.5587	3.3327	3.1718	3.0509	2.9563	2.8800	2.8173	2.7196	2.6171	2.5089	2.4523	2.3937	2.3329	2.2695	2.2032	2.1333
20	5.8715	4.4613	3.8587	3.5147	3.2891	3.1283	3.0074	2.9128	2.8365	2.7737	2.6758	2.5731	2.4645	2.4076	2.3486	2.2873	2.2234	2.1562	2.0853
21	5.8266	4.4199	3.8188	3.4754	3.2501	3.0895	2.9686	2.8740	2.7977	2.7348	2.6368	2.5338	2.4247	2.3675	2.3082	2.2465	2.1819	2.1141	2.0422
22	5.7863	4.3828	3.7829	3.4401	3.2151	3.0546	2.9338	2.8392	2.7628	2.6998	2.6017	2.4984	2.3890	2.3315	2.2718	2.2097	2.1446	2.0760	2.0032
23	5.7498	4.3492	3.7505	3.4083	3.1835	3.0232	2.9024	2.8077	2.7313	2.6682	2.5699	2.4665	2.3567	2.2989	2.2389	2.1763	2.1107	2.0415	1.9677
24	5.7167	4.3187	3.7211	3.3794	3.1548	2.9946	2.8738	2.7791	2.7027	2.6396	2.5412	2.4374	2.3273	2.2693	2.2090	2.1460	2.0799	2.0099	1.9353
25	5.6864	4.2909	3.6943	3.3530	3.1287	2.9685	2.8478	2.7531	2.6766	2.6135	2.5149	2.4110	2.3005	2.2422	2.1816	2.1183	2.0517	1.9811	1.9055
26	5.6586	4.2655	3.6697	3.3289	3.1048	2.9447	2.8240	2.7293	2.6528	2.5895	2.4909	2.3867	2.2759	2.2174	2.1565	2.0928	2.0257	1.9545	1.8781
27	5.6331	4.2421	3.6472	3.3067	3.0828	2.9228	2.8021	2.7074	2.6309	2.5676	2.4688	2.3644	2.2533	2.1946	2.1334	2.0693	2.0018	1.9299	1.8527
28	5.6096	4.2205	3.6264	3.2863	3.0625	2.9027	2.7820	2.6872	2.6106	2.5473	2.4484	2.3438	2.2324	2.1735	2.1121	2.0477	1.9796	1.9072	1.8291
29	5.5878	4.2006	3.6072	3.2674	3.0438	2.8840	2.7633	2.6686	2.5919	2.5286	2.4295	2.3248	2.2131	2.1540	2.0923	2.0276	1.9591	1.8861	1.8072
30	5.5675	4.1821	3.5894	3.2499	3.0265	2.8667	2.7460	2.6513	2.5746	2.5112	2.4120	2.3072	2.1952	2.1359	2.0739	2.0089	1.9400	1.8664	1.7867
40	5.4239	4.0510	3.4633	3.1261	2.9037	2.7444	2.6238	2.5289	2.4519	2.3882	2.2882	2.1819	2.0677	2.0069	1.9429	1.8752	1.8028	1.7242	1.6371
60	5.2857	3.9253	3.3425	3.0077	2.7863	2.6274	2.5068	2.4117	2.3344	2.2702	2.1692	2.0613	1.9445	1.8817	1.8152	1.7440	1.6668	1.5810	1.4822
120	5.1524	3.8046	3.2270	2.8943	2.6740	2.5154	2.3948	2.2994	2.2217	2.1570	2.0548	1.9450	1.8249	1.7597	1.6899	1.6141	1.5299	1.4327	1.3104
∞	5.0239	3.6889	3.1161	2.7858	2.5665	2.4082	2.2875	2.1918	2.1136	2.0483	1.9447	1.8326	1.7085	1.6402	1.5660	1.4835	1.3883	1.2684	1.0000

TABLE VI—*Continued*

F DISTRIBUTION
(.01 SIGNIFICANCE LEVEL)

	DF_1																		
DF_2	1	2	3	4	5	6	7	8	9	10	12	15	20	24	30	40	60	120	∞
1	4052.2	4999.5	5403.3	5624.6	5763.7	5859.0	5928.3	5981.6	6022.5	6055.8	6106.3	6157.3	6208.7	6234.6	6260.7	6286.8	6313.0	6339.4	6366.0
2	98.503	99.000	99.166	99.249	99.299	99.332	99.356	99.374	99.388	99.399	99.416	99.432	99.449	99.458	99.466	99.474	99.483	99.491	99.501
3	34.116	30.817	29.457	28.710	28.237	27.911	27.672	27.489	27.345	27.229	27.052	26.872	26.690	26.598	26.505	26.411	26.316	26.221	26.125
4	21.198	18.000	16.694	15.977	15.522	15.207	14.976	14.799	14.659	14.546	14.374	14.198	14.020	13.929	13.838	13.745	13.652	13.558	13.463
5	16.258	13.274	12.060	11.392	10.967	10.672	10.456	10.289	10.158	10.051	9.8883	9.7222	9.5527	9.4665	9.3793	9.2912	9.2020	9.1118	9.0204
6	13.745	10.925	9.7795	9.1483	8.7459	8.4661	8.2600	8.1016	7.9761	7.8741	7.7183	7.5590	7.3958	7.3127	7.2285	7.1432	7.0568	6.9690	6.8801
7	12.246	9.5466	8.4513	7.8467	7.4604	7.1914	6.9928	6.8401	6.7188	6.6201	6.4691	6.3143	6.1554	6.0743	5.9921	5.9084	5.8236	5.7372	5.6495
8	11.259	8.6491	7.5910	7.0060	6.6318	6.3707	6.1776	6.0289	5.9106	5.8143	5.6668	5.5151	5.3591	5.2793	5.1981	5.1156	5.0316	4.9460	4.8588
9	10.561	8.0215	6.9919	6.4221	6.0569	5.8018	5.6129	5.4671	5.3511	5.2565	5.1114	4.9621	4.8080	4.7290	4.6486	4.5667	4.4831	4.3978	4.3105
10	10.044	7.5594	6.5523	5.9943	5.6363	5.3858	5.2001	5.0567	4.9424	4.8492	4.7059	4.5582	4.4054	4.3269	4.2469	4.1653	4.0819	3.9965	3.9090
11	9.6460	7.2057	6.2167	5.6683	5.3160	5.0692	4.8861	4.7445	4.6315	4.5393	4.3974	4.2509	4.0990	4.0209	3.9411	3.8596	3.7761	3.6904	3.6025
12	9.3302	6.9266	5.9526	5.4119	5.0643	4.8206	4.6395	4.4994	4.3875	4.2961	4.1553	4.0096	3.8584	3.7805	3.7008	3.6192	3.5355	3.4494	3.3608
13	9.0738	6.7010	5.7394	5.2053	4.8616	4.6204	4.4410	4.3021	4.1911	4.1003	3.9603	3.8154	3.6646	3.5868	3.5070	3.4253	3.3413	3.2548	3.1654
14	8.8616	6.5149	5.5639	5.0354	4.6950	4.4558	4.2779	4.1399	4.0297	3.9394	3.8001	3.6557	3.5052	3.4274	3.3476	3.2656	3.1813	3.0942	3.0040
15	8.6831	6.3589	5.4170	4.8932	4.5556	4.3183	4.1415	4.0045	3.8948	3.8049	3.6662	3.5222	3.3719	3.2940	3.2141	3.1319	3.0471	2.9595	2.8684
16	8.5310	6.2262	5.2922	4.7726	4.4374	4.2016	4.0259	3.8896	3.7804	3.6909	3.5527	3.4089	3.2588	3.1808	3.1007	3.0182	2.9330	2.8447	2.7528
17	8.3997	6.1121	5.1850	4.6690	4.3359	4.1015	3.9267	3.7910	3.6822	3.5931	3.4552	3.3117	3.1615	3.0835	3.0032	2.9205	2.8348	2.7459	2.6530
18	8.2854	6.0129	5.0919	4.5790	4.2479	4.0146	3.8406	3.7054	3.5971	3.5082	3.3706	3.2273	3.0771	2.9990	2.9185	2.8354	2.7493	2.6597	2.5660
19	8.1850	5.9259	5.0103	4.5003	4.1708	3.9386	3.7653	3.6305	3.5225	3.4338	3.2965	3.1533	3.0031	2.9249	2.8442	2.7608	2.6742	2.5839	2.4893
20	8.0960	5.8489	4.9382	4.4307	4.1027	3.8714	3.6987	3.5644	3.4567	3.3682	3.2311	3.0880	2.9377	2.8594	2.7785	2.6947	2.6077	2.5168	2.4212
21	8.0166	5.7804	4.8740	4.3688	4.0421	3.8117	3.6396	3.5056	3.3981	3.3098	3.1729	3.0299	2.8796	2.8011	2.7200	2.6359	2.5484	2.4568	2.3603
22	7.9454	5.7190	4.8166	4.3134	3.9880	3.7583	3.5867	3.4530	3.3458	3.2576	3.1209	2.9780	2.8274	2.7488	2.6675	2.5831	2.4951	2.4029	2.3055
23	7.8811	5.6637	4.7649	4.2635	3.9392	3.7102	3.5390	3.4057	3.2986	3.2106	3.0740	2.9311	2.7805	2.7017	2.6202	2.5355	2.4471	2.3542	2.2559
24	7.8229	5.6136	4.7181	4.2184	3.8951	3.6667	3.4959	3.3629	3.2560	3.1681	3.0316	2.8887	2.7380	2.6591	2.5773	2.4923	2.4035	2.3099	2.2107
25	7.7698	5.5680	4.6755	4.1774	3.8550	3.6272	3.4568	3.3239	3.2172	3.1294	2.9931	2.8502	2.6993	2.6203	2.5383	2.4530	2.3637	2.2695	2.1694
26	7.7213	5.5263	4.6366	4.1400	3.8183	3.5911	3.4210	3.2884	3.1818	3.0941	2.9579	2.8150	2.6640	2.5848	2.5026	2.4170	2.3273	2.2325	2.1315
27	7.6767	5.4881	4.6009	4.1056	3.7848	3.5580	3.3882	3.2558	3.1494	3.0618	2.9256	2.7827	2.6316	2.5522	2.4699	2.3840	2.2938	2.1984	2.0965
28	7.6356	5.4529	4.5681	4.0740	3.7539	3.5276	3.3581	3.2259	3.1195	3.0320	2.8959	2.7530	2.6017	2.5223	2.4397	2.3535	2.2629	2.1670	2.0642
29	7.5976	5.4205	4.5378	4.0449	3.7254	3.4995	3.3302	3.1982	3.0920	3.0045	2.8685	2.7256	2.5742	2.4946	2.4118	2.3253	2.2344	2.1378	2.0342
30	7.5625	5.3904	4.5097	4.0179	3.6990	3.4735	3.3045	3.1726	3.0665	2.9791	2.8431	2.7002	2.5487	2.4689	2.3860	2.2992	2.2079	2.1107	2.0062
40	7.3141	5.1785	4.3126	3.8283	3.5138	3.2910	3.1238	2.9930	2.8876	2.8005	2.6648	2.5216	2.3689	2.2880	2.2035	2.1142	2.0194	1.9172	1.8047
60	7.0771	4.9774	4.1259	3.6491	3.3389	3.1187	2.9530	2.8233	2.7185	2.6318	2.4961	2.3523	2.1978	2.1154	2.0285	1.9360	1.8363	1.7263	1.6006
120	6.8510	4.7865	3.9493	3.4796	3.1735	2.9559	2.7918	2.6629	2.5586	2.4721	2.3363	2.1915	2.0346	1.9500	1.8600	1.7628	1.6557	1.5330	1.3805
∞	6.6349	4.6052	3.7816	3.3192	3.0173	2.8020	2.6393	2.5113	2.4073	2.3209	2.1848	2.0385	1.8783	1.7908	1.6964	1.5923	1.4730	1.3246	1.0000

TABLE VI—Continued

F DISTRIBUTION

(.005 SIGNIFICANCE LEVEL)

DF₁

DF₂	1	2	3	4	5	6	7	8	9	10	12	15	20	24	30	40	60	120	∞
1	16211	20000	21615	22500	23056	23437	23715	23925	24091	24224	24426	24630	24836	24940	25044	25148	25253	25359	25465
2	198.50	199.00	199.17	199.25	199.30	199.33	199.36	199.37	199.39	199.40	199.42	199.43	199.45	199.46	199.47	199.47	199.48	199.49	199.51
3	55.552	49.799	47.467	46.195	45.392	44.838	44.434	44.126	43.882	43.686	43.387	43.085	42.778	42.622	42.466	42.308	42.149	41.989	41.829
4	31.333	26.284	24.259	23.155	22.456	21.975	21.622	21.352	21.139	20.967	20.705	20.438	20.167	20.030	19.892	19.752	19.611	19.468	19.325
5	22.785	18.314	16.530	15.556	14.940	14.513	14.200	13.961	13.772	13.618	13.384	13.146	12.903	12.780	12.656	12.530	12.402	12.274	12.144
6	18.635	14.544	12.917	12.028	11.464	11.073	10.786	10.566	10.391	10.250	10.034	9.8140	9.5888	9.4741	9.3583	9.2408	9.1219	9.0015	8.8793
7	16.236	12.404	10.882	10.050	9.5221	9.1554	8.8854	8.6781	8.5138	8.3803	8.1764	7.9678	7.7540	7.6450	7.5345	7.4225	7.3088	7.1933	7.0760
8	14.688	11.042	9.5965	8.8051	8.3018	7.9520	7.6942	7.4960	7.3386	7.2107	7.0149	6.8143	6.6082	6.5029	6.3961	6.2875	6.1772	6.0649	5.9505
9	13.614	10.107	8.7171	7.9559	7.4711	7.1338	6.8849	6.6933	6.5411	6.4171	6.2274	6.0325	5.8318	5.7292	5.6248	5.5186	5.4104	5.3001	5.1875
10	12.826	9.4270	8.0807	7.3428	6.8723	6.5446	6.3025	6.1159	5.9676	5.8467	5.6613	5.4707	5.2740	5.1732	5.0705	4.9659	4.8592	4.7501	4.6385
11	12.226	8.9122	7.6004	6.8809	6.4217	6.1015	5.8648	5.6821	5.5368	5.4182	5.2363	5.0489	4.8552	4.7557	4.6543	4.5508	4.4450	4.3367	4.2256
12	11.754	8.5096	7.2258	6.5211	6.0711	5.7570	5.5245	5.3451	5.2021	5.0855	4.9063	4.7214	4.5299	4.4315	4.3309	4.2282	4.1229	4.0149	3.9039
13	11.374	8.1865	6.9257	6.2335	5.7910	5.4819	5.2529	5.0761	4.9351	4.8199	4.6429	4.4600	4.2703	4.1726	4.0727	3.9704	3.8655	3.7577	3.6465
14	11.060	7.9217	6.6803	5.9984	5.5623	5.2574	5.0313	4.8566	4.7173	4.6034	4.4281	4.2468	4.0585	3.9614	3.8619	3.7600	3.6553	3.5473	3.4359
15	10.798	7.7008	6.4760	5.8029	5.3721	5.0708	4.8473	4.6743	4.5364	4.4236	4.2498	4.0698	3.8826	3.7859	3.6867	3.5850	3.4803	3.3722	3.2602
16	10.575	7.5138	6.3034	5.6378	5.2117	4.9134	4.6920	4.5207	4.3838	4.2719	4.0994	3.9205	3.7342	3.6378	3.5388	3.4372	3.3324	3.2240	3.1115
17	10.384	7.3536	6.1556	5.4967	5.0746	4.7789	4.5594	4.3893	4.2535	4.1423	3.9709	3.7929	3.6073	3.5112	3.4124	3.3107	3.2058	3.0971	2.9839
18	10.218	7.2148	6.0277	5.3746	4.9560	4.6627	4.4448	4.2759	4.1410	4.0305	3.8599	3.6827	3.4977	3.4017	3.3030	3.2014	3.0962	2.9871	2.8732
19	10.073	7.0935	5.9161	5.2681	4.8526	4.5614	4.3448	4.1770	4.0428	3.9329	3.7631	3.5866	3.4020	3.3062	3.2075	3.1058	3.0004	2.8908	2.7762
20	9.9439	6.9865	5.8177	5.1743	4.7616	4.4721	4.2569	4.0900	3.9564	3.8470	3.6779	3.5020	3.3178	3.2220	3.1234	3.0215	2.9159	2.8058	2.6604
21	9.8295	6.8914	5.7304	5.0911	4.6808	4.3931	4.1789	4.0128	3.8799	3.7709	3.6024	3.4270	3.2431	3.1474	3.0488	2.9467	2.8408	2.7302	2.6140
22	9.7271	6.8064	5.6524	5.0168	4.6088	4.3225	4.1094	3.9440	3.8116	3.7030	3.5350	3.3600	3.1764	3.0807	2.9821	2.8799	2.7736	2.6625	2.5455
23	9.6348	6.7300	5.5823	4.9500	4.5441	4.2591	4.0469	3.8822	3.7502	3.6420	3.4745	3.2999	3.1165	3.0208	2.9221	2.8198	2.7132	2.6016	2.4837
24	9.5513	6.6610	5.5190	4.8898	4.4857	4.2019	3.9905	3.8264	3.6949	3.5870	3.4199	3.2456	3.0624	2.9667	2.8679	2.7654	2.6585	2.5463	2.4276
25	9.4753	6.5982	5.4615	4.8351	4.4327	4.1500	3.9394	3.7758	3.6447	3.5370	3.3704	3.1963	3.0133	2.9176	2.8187	2.7160	2.6088	2.4960	2.3765
26	9.4059	6.5409	5.4091	4.7852	4.3844	4.1027	3.8928	3.7297	3.5989	3.4916	3.3252	3.1515	2.9685	2.8728	2.7738	2.6709	2.5633	2.4501	2.3297
27	9.3423	6.4885	5.3611	4.7396	4.3402	4.0594	3.8501	3.6875	3.5571	3.4499	3.2839	3.1104	2.9275	2.8318	2.7327	2.6296	2.5217	2.4078	2.2867
28	9.2838	6.4403	5.3170	4.6977	4.2996	4.0197	3.8110	3.6487	3.5186	3.4117	3.2460	3.0727	2.8899	2.7941	2.6949	2.5916	2.4834	2.3689	2.2469
29	9.2297	6.3958	5.2764	4.6591	4.2622	3.9830	3.7749	3.6130	3.4832	3.3765	3.2111	3.0379	2.8551	2.7594	2.6601	2.5565	2.4479	2.3330	2.2102
30	9.1797	6.3547	5.2388	4.6233	4.2276	3.9492	3.7416	3.5801	3.4505	3.3440	3.1787	3.0057	2.8230	2.7272	2.6278	2.5241	2.4151	2.2997	2.1760
40	8.8278	6.0664	4.9759	4.3738	3.9860	3.7129	3.5088	3.3498	3.2220	3.1167	2.9531	2.7811	2.5984	2.5020	2.4015	2.2958	2.1838	2.0635	1.9318
60	8.4946	5.7950	4.7290	4.1399	3.7600	3.4918	3.2911	3.1344	3.0083	2.9042	2.7419	2.5705	2.3872	2.2898	2.1874	2.0789	1.9622	1.8341	1.5885
120	8.1790	5.5393	4.4973	3.9207	3.5482	3.2849	3.0874	2.9330	2.8083	2.7052	2.5439	2.3727	2.1881	2.0890	1.9839	1.8709	1.7469	1.6055	1.4311
∞	7.8794	5.2983	4.2794	3.7151	3.3499	3.0913	2.8968	2.7444	2.6210	2.5188	2.3583	2.1868	1.9998	1.8983	1.7891	1.6691	1.5325	1.3637	1.0000

TABLE VII*

TABLE FOR TESTING HOMOGENEITY OF VARIANCES
(.05 SIGNIFICANCE LEVEL)

k	0.0	0.5	1.0	1.5	2.0	2.5	3.0	3.5	4.0	4.5	5.0	6.0	7.0	8.0	9.0	10.0	12.0
3	5.99	6.47	6.89	7.20	7.38	7.39	7.22										
4	7.81	8.24	8.63	8.96	9.21	9.38	9.43	9.37	9.18								
5	9.49	9.88	10.24	10.57	10.86	11.08	11.24	11.32	11.31	11.21	11.02						
6	11.07	11.43	11.78	12.11	12.40	12.65	12.86	13.01	13.11	13.14	13.10	12.78					
7	12.59	12.94	13.27	13.59	13.88	14.15	14.38	14.58	14.73	14.83	14.88	14.81	14.49				
8	14.07	14.40	14.72	15.03	15.32	15.60	15.84	16.06	16.25	16.40	16.51	16.60	16.49	16.16			
9	15.51	15.83	16.14	16.44	16.73	17.01	17.26	17.49	17.70	17.88	18.03	18.22	18.26	18.12	17.79		
10	16.92	17.23	17.54	17.83	18.12	18.39	18.65	18.89	19.11	19.31	19.48	19.75	19.89	19.89	19.73	19.40	
11	18.31	18.61	18.91	19.20	19.48	19.76	20.02	20.26	20.49	20.70	20.89	21.21	21.42	21.52	21.49	21.32	
12	19.68	19.97	20.26	20.55	20.83	21.10	21.36	21.61	21.84	22.06	22.27	22.62	22.88	23.06	23.12	23.07	22.56
13	21.03	21.32	21.60	21.89	22.16	22.43	22.69	22.94	23.18	23.40	23.62	23.99	24.30	24.53	24.66	24.70	24.44
14	22.36	22.65	22.93	23.21	23.48	23.75	24.01	24.26	24.50	24.73	24.95	25.34	25.68	25.95	26.14	26.25	26.17
15	23.68	23.97	24.24	24.52	24.79	25.05	25.31	25.56	25.80	26.04	26.26	26.67	27.03	27.33	27.56	27.73	27.80

c_1

* Abridged from Tables 1 and 2 in "Tables for Testing the Homogeneity of a Set of Estimated Variances," by C. M. Thompson and Maxine Merrington, *Biometrika*, XXXIII (1946), 295–304, by kind permission of the editor and the authors.

TABLE VII—*Continued*

TABLE FOR TESTING HOMOGENEITY OF VARIANCES

(.01 SIGNIFICANCE LEVEL)

C_1

k	0.0	0.5	1.0	1.5	2.0	2.5	3.0	3.5	4.0	4.5	5.0	6.0	7.0	8.0	9.0	10.0	12.0
3	9.21	9.92	10.47	10.78	10.81	10.50	9.83										
4	11.34	11.95	12.46	12.86	13.11	13.18	13.03	12.65	12.03								
5	13.28	13.81	14.30	14.71	15.03	15.25	15.34	15.28	15.06	14.66	14.07						
6	15.09	15.58	16.03	16.44	16.79	17.07	17.27	17.37	17.37	17.24	16.98	16.03					
7	16.81	17.27	17.70	18.10	18.46	18.77	19.02	19.21	19.32	19.35	19.28	18.84	17.92				
8	18.48	18.91	19.32	19.71	20.07	20.39	20.67	20.90	21.08	21.20	21.25	21.13	20.64	19.76			
9	20.09	20.50	20.90	21.28	21.64	21.97	22.26	22.52	22.74	22.91	23.03	23.10	22.91	22.41	21.56		
10	21.67	22.06	22.45	22.82	23.17	23.50	23.80	24.08	24.32	24.52	24.69	24.90	24.90	24.61	24.15	23.33	
11	23.21	23.59	23.97	24.33	24.67	25.00	25.31	25.59	25.85	26.08	26.28	26.57	26.70	26.65	26.38	25.86	
12	24.72	25.10	25.46	25.81	26.15	26.48	26.79	27.08	27.35	27.59	27.81	28.16	28.39	28.46	28.37	28.07	26.79
13	26.22	26.58	26.93	27.28	27.62	27.94	28.25	28.54	28.81	29.07	29.30	29.70	29.99	30.16	30.19	30.06	29.22
14	27.69	28.04	28.39	28.73	29.06	29.38	29.69	29.98	30.26	30.52	30.77	31.19	31.53	31.77	31.89	31.88	31.39
15	29.14	29.49	29.83	30.16	30.49	30.80	30.11	31.40	31.68	31.95	32.20	32.66	33.03	33.32	33.51	33.59	33.37

TABLE VIII*

VALUES OF THE CORRELATION COEFFICIENT FOR DIFFERENT LEVELS OF SIGNIFICANCE

DF	SIGNIFICANCE LEVEL: a			
	.10	.05	.02	.01
1.....	.98769	.996917	.9995066	.9998766
2.....	.90000	.95000	.98000	.990000
3.....	.8054	.8783	.93433	.95873
4.....	.7293	.8114	.8822	.91720
5.....	.6694	.7545	.8329	.8745
6.....	.6215	.7067	.7887	.8343
7.....	.5822	.6664	.7498	.7977
8.....	.5494	.6319	.7155	.7646
9.....	.5214	.6021	.6851	.7348
10.....	.4973	.5760	.6581	.7079
11.....	.4762	.5529	.6339	.6835
12.....	.4575	.5324	.6120	.6614
13.....	.4409	.5139	.5923	.6411
14.....	.4259	.4973	.5742	.6226
15.....	.4124	.4821	.5577	.6055
16.....	.4000	.4683	.5425	.5897
17.....	.3887	.4555	.5285	.5751
18.....	.3783	.4438	.5155	.5614
19.....	.3687	.4329	.5034	.5487
20.....	.3598	.4227	.4921	.5368
25.....	.3233	.3809	.4451	.4869
30.....	.2960	.3494	.4093	.4487
35.....	.2746	.3246	.3810	.4182
40.....	.2573	.3044	.3578	.3932
45.....	.2428	.2875	.3384	.3721
50.....	.2306	.2732	.3218	.3541
60.....	.2108	.2500	.2948	.3248
70.....	.1954	.2319	.2737	.3017
80.....	.1829	.2172	.2565	.2830
90.....	.1726	.2050	.2422	.2673
100.....	.1638	.1946	.2301	.2540

* Reprinted from R. A. Fisher, *Statistical Methods for Research Workers* (London: Oliver & Boyd, Ltd., 1948), p. 209, by kind permission of the author and publishers.

TABLE IX*

PROBABILITY THAT S ATTAINS OR EXCEEDS A SPECIFIED VALUE

(Shown Only for Positive Values; Negative Values Obtained by Symmetry)

S	n				S	n		
	4	5	8	9		6	8	10
0	.625	.592	.548	.540	1	.500	.500	.500
2	.375	.408	.452	.460	3	.360	.386	.431
4	.167	.242	.360	.381	5	.235	.281	.364
6	.042	.117	.274	.306	7	.136	.191	.300
8		.042	.199	.238	9	.068	.119	.242
10		.0083	.138	.179	11	.028	.068	.190
12			.089	.130	13	.0083	.035	.146
14			.054	.090	15	.0014	.015	.108
16			.031	.060	17		.0054	.078
18			.016	.038	19		.0014	.054
20			.0071	.022	21		.00020	.036
22			.0028	.012	23			.023
24			.00087	.0063	25			.014
26			.00019	.0029	27			.0083
28			.000025	.0012	29			.0046
30				.00043	31			.0023
32				.00012	33			.0011
34				.000025	35			.00047
36				.0000028	37			.00018
					39			.000058
					41			.000015
					43			.0000028
					45			.00000028

* Reprinted from M. G. Kendall, *The Advanced Theory of Statistics* (London: Chas. Griffin & Co., Ltd., 1947), I, 405, by kind permission of the author and the publisher.

TABLE X*

z' VALUES FOR r

r	z'	r	z'	r	z'	r	z'	r	z'
.000	.000	.200	.203	.400	.424	.600	.693	.800	1.099
.005	.005	.205	.208	.405	.430	.605	.701	.805	1.113
.010	.010	.210	.213	.410	.436	.610	.709	.810	1.127
.015	.015	.215	.218	.415	.442	.615	.717	.815	1.142
.020	.020	.220	.224	.420	.448	.620	.725	.820	1.157
.025	.025	.225	.229	.425	.454	.625	.733	.825	1.172
.030	.030	.230	.234	.430	.460	.630	.741	.830	1.188
.035	.035	.235	.239	.435	.466	.635	.750	.835	1.204
.040	.040	.240	.245	.440	.472	.640	.758	.840	1.221
.045	.045	.245	.250	.445	.478	.645	.767	.845	1.238
.050	.050	.250	.255	.450	.485	.650	.775	.850	1.256
.055	.055	.255	.261	.455	.491	.655	.784	.855	1.274
.060	.060	.260	.266	.460	.497	.660	.793	.860	1.293
.065	.065	.265	.271	.465	.504	.665	.802	.865	1.313
.070	.070	.270	.277	.470	.510	.670	.811	.870	1.333
.075	.075	.275	.282	.475	.517	.675	.820	.875	1.354
.080	.080	.280	.288	.480	.523	.680	.829	.880	1.376
.085	.085	.285	.293	.485	.530	.685	.838	.885	1.398
.090	.090	.290	.299	.490	.536	.690	.848	.890	1.422
.095	.095	.295	.304	.495	.543	.695	.858	.895	1.447
.100	.100	.300	.310	.500	.549	.700	.867	.900	1.472
.105	.105	.305	.315	.505	.556	.705	.877	.905	1.499
.110	.110	.310	.321	.510	.563	.710	.887	.910	1.528
.115	.116	.315	.326	.515	.570	.715	.897	.915	1.557
.120	.121	.320	.332	.520	.576	.720	.908	.920	1.589
.125	.126	.325	.337	.525	.583	.725	.918	.925	1.623
.130	.131	.330	.343	.530	.590	.730	.929	.930	1.658
.135	.136	.335	.348	.535	.597	.735	.940	.935	1.697
.140	.141	.340	.354	.540	.604	.740	.950	.940	1.738
.145	.146	.345	.360	.545	.611	.745	.962	.945	1.783
.150	.151	.350	.365	.550	.618	.750	.973	.950	1.832
.155	.156	.355	.371	.555	.626	.755	.984	.955	1.886
.160	.161	.360	.377	.560	.633	.760	.996	.960	1.946
.165	.167	.365	.383	.565	.640	.765	1.008	.965	2.014
.170	.172	.370	.388	.570	.648	.770	1.020	.970	2.092
.175	.177	.375	.394	.575	.655	.775	1.033	.975	2.185
.180	.182	.380	.400	.580	.662	.780	1.045	.980	2.298
.185	.187	.385	.406	.585	.670	.785	1.058	.985	2.443
.190	.192	.390	.412	.590	.678	.790	1.071	.990	2.647
.195	.198	.395	.418	.595	.685	.795	1.085	.995	2.994

* Reprinted from A. L. Edwards, *Experimental Design in Psychological Research* (New York: Rinehart & Co., 1950), p. 409, by kind permission of the author and the publisher.

TABLE XI*

CRITICAL VALUES OF r_s FOR THE SIGN TEST

n		a			n		a		
	.01	.05	.10	.25		.01	.05	.10	.25
1......					46......	13	15	16	18
2......					47......	14	16	17	19
3......				0	48......	14	16	17	19
4......				0	49......	15	17	18	19
5......			0	0	50......	15	17	18	20
6......		0	0	1	51......	15	18	19	20
7......		0	0	1	52......	16	18	19	21
8......	0	0	1	1	53......	16	18	20	21
9......	0	1	1	2	54......	17	19	20	22
10......	0	1	1	2	55......	17	19	20	22
11......	0	1	2	3	56......	17	20	21	23
12......	1	2	2	3	57......	18	20	21	23
13......	1	2	3	3	58......	18	21	22	24
14......	1	2	3	4	59......	19	21	22	24
15......	2	3	3	4	60......	19	21	23	25
16......	2	3	4	5	61......	20	22	23	25
17......	2	4	4	5	62......	20	22	24	25
18......	3	4	5	6	63......	20	23	24	26
19......	3	4	5	6	64......	21	23	24	26
20......	3	5	5	6	65......	21	24	25	27
21......	4	5	6	7	66......	22	24	25	27
22......	4	5	6	7	67......	22	25	26	28
23......	4	6	7	8	68......	22	25	26	28
24......	5	6	7	8	69......	23	25	27	29
25......	5	7	7	9	70......	23	26	27	29
26......	6	7	8	9	71......	24	26	28	30
27......	6	7	8	10	72......	24	27	28	30
28......	6	8	9	10	73......	25	27	28	31
29......	7	8	9	10	74......	25	28	29	31
30......	7	9	10	11	75......	25	28	29	32
31......	7	9	10	11	76......	26	28	30	32
32......	8	9	10	12	77......	26	29	30	32
33......	8	10	11	12	78......	27	29	31	33
34......	9	10	11	13	79......	27	30	31	33
35......	9	11	12	13	80......	28	30	32	34
36......	9	11	12	14	81......	28	31	32	34
37......	10	12	13	14	82......	28	31	33	35
38......	10	12	13	14	83......	29	32	33	35
39......	11	12	13	15	84......	29	32	33	36
40......	11	13	14	15	85......	30	32	34	36
41......	11	13	14	16	86......	30	33	34	37
42......	12	14	15	16	87......	31	33	35	37
43......	12	14	15	17	88......	31	34	35	38
44......	13	15	16	17	89......	31	34	36	38
45......	13	15	16	18	90......	32	35	36	39

* Reprinted from W. J. Dixon and F. J. Massey, Jr., *Introduction to Statistical Analysis* (New York: McGraw-Hill Book Co., 1951), p. 324, by kind permission of the authors and the publisher.

For values of n larger than 90, approximate values of r_s may be found by taking the nearest integer less than $(n - 1)/2 - k\sqrt{n + 1}$, where k is 1.2879, 0.9800, 0.8224, and 0.5752 for the .01, .05, .10, and .25 values, respectively.

TABLE XII*

$u_{.025}$ AND $u_{.975}$ FOR RUNS AMONG ELEMENTS IN SAMPLES OF SIZE n_1 AND n_2

$u_{.025}$

n_2	2	3	4	5	6	7	8	9	10	11	12	13	14	15	16	17	18	19	20
2....																			
3....																			
4....																			
5....			2	2															
6....		2	2	3	3														
7....		2	2	3	3	3													
8....		2	3	3	3	4	4												
9....		2	3	3	4	4	5	5											
10....		2	3	3	4	5	5	5	6										
11....		2	3	4	4	5	5	6	6	7									
12....	2	2	3	4	4	5	6	6	7	7	7								
13....	2	2	3	4	5	5	6	6	7	7	8	8							
14....	2	2	3	4	5	5	6	7	7	8	8	9	9						
15....	2	3	3	4	5	6	6	7	7	8	9	9	10						
16....	2	3	4	4	5	6	6	7	8	8	9	9	10	10	11				
17....	2	3	4	4	5	6	7	7	8	9	9	10	10	11	11	11			
18....	2	3	4	5	5	6	7	7	8	8	9	9	10	10	11	11	12	12	
19....	2	3	4	5	6	6	7	8	8	9	10	10	11	11	12	12	13	13	
20....	2	3	4	5	6	6	7	8	9	9	10	10	11	12	12	13	13	13	14

$u_{.975}$

n_2	2	3	4	5	6	7	8	9	10	11	12	13	14	15	16	17	18	19	20
1....	4																		
2....	5																		
3....	5	6																	
4....	5	7	8																
5....	5	7	8	9															
6....	5	7	8	9	10														
7....	5	7	9	10	11	12													
8....	5	7	9	10	11	12	13												
9....	5	7	9	11	12	13	13	14											
10....	5	7	9	11	12	13	14	15	15										
11....	5	7	9	11	12	13	14	15	16	16									
12....	5	7	9	11	12	13	15	15	16	17	18								
13....	5	7	9	11	13	14	15	16	17	18	18	19							
14....	5	7	9	11	13	14	15	16	17	18	19	19	20						
15....	5	7	9	11	13	14	15	17	17	18	19	20	21	21					
16....	5	7	9	11	13	15	16	17	18	19	20	20	21	22	22				
17....	5	7	9	11	13	15	16	17	18	19	20	21	22	22	23	24			
18....	5	7	9	11	13	15	16	17	18	19	20	21	22	23	24	24	25		
19....	5	7	9	11	13	15	16	17	19	20	21	22	22	23	24	25	25	26	
20....	5	7	9	11	13	15	16	17	19	20	21	22	23	24	24	25	26	26	27

* Reprinted from Churchill Eisenhart and F. S. Swed, "Tables for Testing Randomness of Grouping in a Sequence of Alternatives," *Annals of Mathematical Statistics*, XIV (1943), 66, by kind permission of the authors and the editor.

TABLE XII—*Continued*

$n_1 = n_2$	$u_{.025}$	$u_{.975}$	$n_1 = n_2$	$u_{.025}$	$u_{.975}$
20.........	14	27	40......	31	50
21.........	15	28	42......	33	52
22.........	16	29	44......	35	54
23.........	16	31	46......	37	56
24.........	17	32	48......	38	59
25.........	18	33	50......	40	61
26.........	19	34	55......	45	66
27.........	20	35	60......	49	72
28.........	21	36	65......	54	77
29.........	22	37	70......	58	83
30.........	22	39	75......	63	88
32.........	24	41	80......	68	93
34.........	26	43	85......	72	99
36.........	28	45	90......	77	104
38.........	30	47	95......	82	109
			100......	86	115

The values listed are such that a number less than or equal to the $u_{.025}$ value will occur not more than 2.5 per cent of the time and a number greater than $u_{.975}$ will occur not more than 2.5 per cent of the time.

For values of n_1 and n_2 larger than 20, a normal approximation may be used. The mean is $2n_1n_2/(n_1 + n_2) + 1$, and the variance is $2n_1n_2(2n_1n_2 - n_1 - n_2)/(n_1 + n_2)^2(n_1 + n_2 - 1)$. For example, for $n_1 = n_2 = 20$, the mean is 21 and the variance is 9.74. The .025 and .975 percentiles are $21 + 1.96\sqrt{9.74} = 27.1$ and $21 - 1.96\sqrt{9.74} = 14.9$.

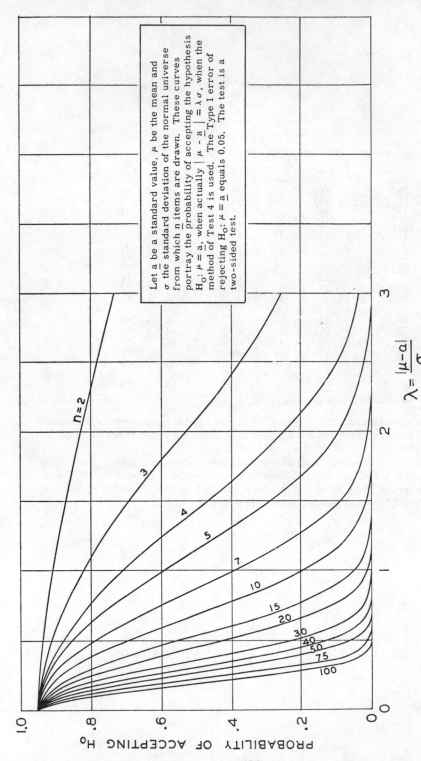

The figure contains the following text within a boxed note:

Let a be a standard value, μ be the mean and σ the standard deviation of the normal universe from which n items are drawn. These curves portray the probability of accepting the hypothesis $H_0: \mu = a$, when actually $|\mu - a| = \lambda \sigma$, when the method of Test 4 is used. The Type I error of rejecting $H_0: \mu = a$ equals 0.05. The test is a two-sided test.

Axis labels:

PROBABILITY OF ACCEPTING H_0

$\lambda = \dfrac{|\mu - a|}{\sigma}$

Curve labels: $n = 2$, 3, 4, 5, 7, 10, 15, 20, 30, 40, 50, 75, 100

FIG. I.—Operating Characteristic Curves of the two-sided t test (applicable to Tests 4 and 16). (Appendix Figs. I–VI are reproduced from C. D. Ferris, F. E. Grubbs, and C. L. Weaver, "Operating Characteristics for the Common Statistical Tests of Significance," *Annals of Mathematical Statistics*, XVII [1946], 178–92, by kind permission of the authors and the editor.)

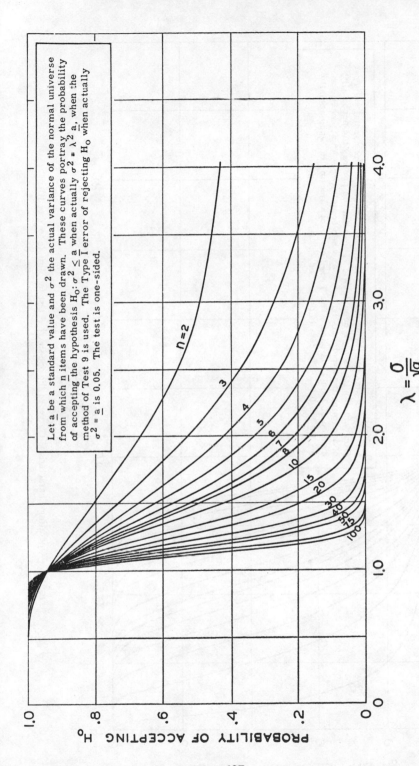

Let a be a standard value and σ^2 the actual variance of the normal universe from which n items have been drawn. These curves portray the probability of accepting the hypothesis H_0: $\sigma^2 \leq a$, when actually $\sigma^2 = \lambda^2 a$, when the method of Test 9 is used. The Type I error of rejecting H_0 when actually $\sigma^2 = a$ is 0.05. The test is one-sided.

$$\lambda = \frac{\sigma}{\sqrt{a}}$$

PROBABILITY OF ACCEPTING H_0

$n=2$

3

4

5

6

7

8

10

15

20

30

40

50

75

100

Fig. II.—Operating Characteristic Curves of the one-sided χ^2 test (applicable to Test 9)

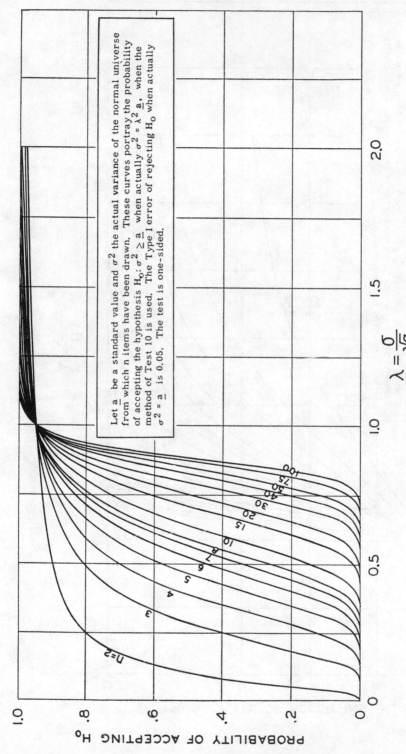

Let $\underline{a}$ be a standard value and σ^2 the actual variance of the normal universe from which n items have been drawn. These curves portray the probability of accepting the hypothesis H_0; $\sigma^2 \geq \underline{a}$, when actually $\sigma^2 = \lambda^2 \underline{a}$, when the method of Test 10 is used. The Type I error of rejecting H_0 when actually $\sigma^2 = \underline{a}$ is 0.05. The test is one-sided.

FIG. III.—Operating Characteristic Curves of the one-sided χ^2 test (applicable to Test 10)

PROBABILITY OF ACCEPTING H_0

$\lambda = \dfrac{\sigma}{\sqrt{a}}$

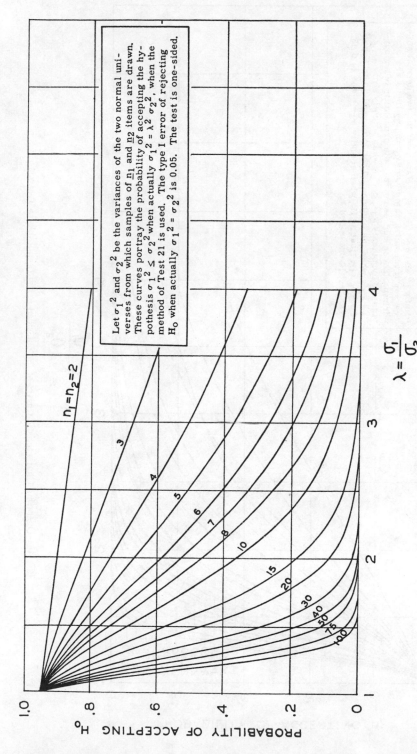

Let $\sigma_1{}^2$ and $\sigma_2{}^2$ be the variances of the two normal universes from which samples of n_1 and n_2 items are drawn. These curves portray the probability of accepting the hypothesis $\sigma_1{}^2 \leq \sigma_2{}^2$ when actually $\sigma_1{}^2 = \lambda^2 \sigma_2{}^2$, when the method of Test 21 is used. The type I error of rejecting H_o when actually $\sigma_1{}^2 = \sigma_2{}^2$ is 0.05. The test is one-sided.

$n_1 = n_2 = 2$

3

4

5

6

7

8

10

15

20

30

40

50

75

100

$\lambda = \dfrac{\sigma_1}{\sigma_2}$

PROBABILITY OF ACCEPTING H_o

1.0

.8

.6

.4

.2

0

1

2

3

4

FIG. IV.—Operating Characteristic Curves of the one-sided F test (applicable to Test 21)

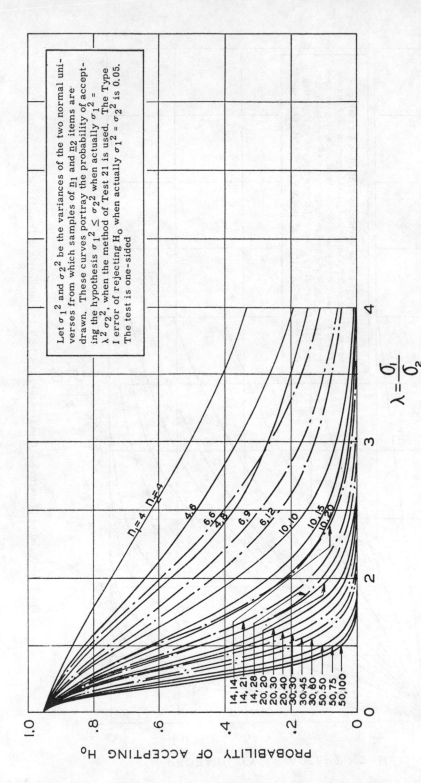

Let $\sigma_1{}^2$ and $\sigma_2{}^2$ be the variances of the two normal universes from which samples of n_1 and n_2 items are drawn. These curves portray the probability of accepting the hypothesis $\sigma_1{}^2 \leq \sigma_2{}^2$ when actually $\sigma_1{}^2 = \lambda^2 \sigma_2{}^2$, when the method of Test 21 is used. The Type I error of rejecting H_0 when actually $\sigma_1{}^2 = \sigma_2{}^2$ is 0.05. The test is one-sided

$\lambda = \dfrac{\sigma_1}{\sigma_2}$

PROBABILITY OF ACCEPTING H_0

$n_1 = 4 \quad n_2 = 4$

4, 6
6, 6
4, 8
6, 9
6, 12
10, 10
10, 20

14, 14
14, 21
14, 28
20, 20
20, 30
20, 40
30, 30
30, 45
30, 60
50, 50
50, 75
50, 100

Fig. V.—Operating Characteristic Curves of the one-sided F test (applicable to Test 21)

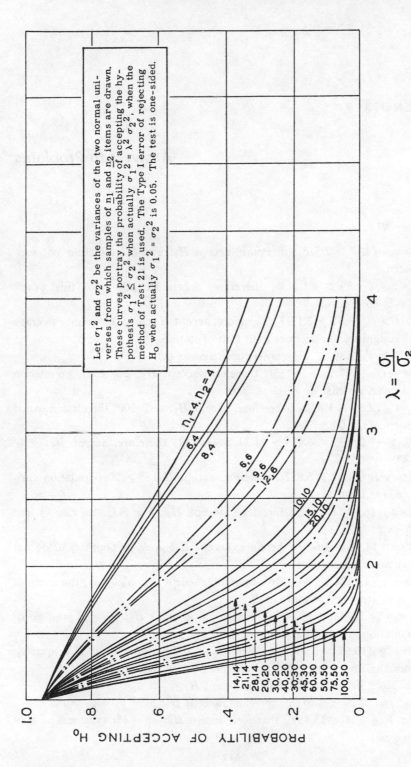

Let $\sigma_1{}^2$ and $\sigma_2{}^2$ be the variances of the two normal universes from which samples of n_1 and $\underline{n_2}$ items are drawn. These curves portray the probability of accepting the hypothesis $\sigma_1{}^2 \leq \sigma_2{}^2$ when actually $\sigma_1{}^2 = \lambda^2 \sigma_2{}^2$, when the method of Test 21 is used. The Type I error of rejecting H_o when actually $\sigma_1{}^2 = \sigma_2{}^2$ is 0.05. The test is one-sided.

$\lambda = \dfrac{\sigma_1}{\sigma_2}$

PROBABILITY OF ACCEPTING H_O

$n_1 = 4, n_2 = 4$
6,4
8,4
6,6
9,6
12,6
15,10
20,10
10,10

14,14
21,14
28,14
20,20
30,20
40,20
30,30
45,30
60,30
50,50
75,50
100,50

Fig. VI.—Operating Characeristic Curves of the one-sided F test (applicable to Test 21)

411

Answers to Problems

Chapter VI

1. $z > z_{.01}$ (4.17 > 2.576); therefore, accept H_1: $\mu \neq 6$; prediction not supported.

2. $z > z_{.10}$ (−.89 > −1.645); therefore, accept H_1: $\mu \geq 1.56$; this year's class is not inferior.

3. (a) $t > t_{.05}$ (3.51 > 2.1315); therefore, accept H_1: $\mu \neq 32$; county average is significantly different from that of state.
   (b) $t' > t'_{.05}$ (.39 > .151); same conclusion as (a).

4. $t > -t_{.01}$ (1.47 > −2.8453); therefore, accept H_0: $\mu \geq 20.0$; population has mean at least as great as 20.0.

5. $t > t_{.10}$ (2.56 > 1.8946); therefore, accept H_1: $\mu \neq 100$; the class mean is not equal to 100.

6. $\chi^2_{.05} > \chi^2 > \chi^2_{.95}$ (36.415 > 23.34 > 13.848); therefore, accept H_0: $\sigma^2 = 1,300$.

7. $\chi^2 > \chi^2_{.99}$ (14.00 > 5.812); therefore, accept H_0: $\sigma^2 \geq 20$; population variance is at least 20.

8. $z > z_{.20}$ (6.30 > 1.282); therefore, accept H_1: $p \neq .43$; the city is not typical.

9. $z > z_{.10}$ (4.14 > 1.645); therefore, accept H_1: $\mu_1 \neq \mu_2$; populations do not have same mean.

10. $t > -t_{.10}$ (−.74 > −1.8946); therefore, accept H_0: $\mu_A \geq \mu_B$; the mean of A is as great as the mean of B.

11. $\chi^2 < \chi^2_{.01}$ (3.17 < 11.345); therefore, accept H_0: $\mu_1 = \mu_2 = \mu_3 = \mu_4$; population means are equal.

12. $t > t_{.005}$ (10.89 > 2.90 approximately); therefore, accept H_1: $\mu_1 \neq \mu_2$; graduates and undergraduates are not equally proficient.

13. $t' > t'_{.05}$ (.373 > .216); therefore, accept H_1: $\mu_1 \neq \mu_2$.

14. $F < F_{.01}$ (2.29 < 4.3126); therefore, accept H_0: $\mu_1 = \mu_2 = \mu_3 = \mu_4$.

15. $F < F_{.025}$ (8.3 < 15.439); therefore, accept H_0: $\sigma_1^2 = \sigma_2^2$; variances of sales are equal.

16. $F > F_{.20}$ (1.375 > 1.2249); therefore, accept H_1: $\sigma_e^2 > \sigma_a^2$; variance of incomes of engineers is greater than that of architects.

17. $z < z_{.05}$ (.85 < 1.96); therefore, accept H_0: $p_A = p_B$; neighborhoods have equal percentages in favor of rent control.

18. $z > z_{.01}$ (3.47 > 2.576); therefore, accept H_1: $p \neq .58$; sample not random.

19. $b_{yx} = .7659$, $t < t_{.05}$ (.7356 < 2.4469); therefore, accept H_0: $B_{yx} = 0$; regression coefficient not significant.

20. $r > r_{.01}$ (.93 > .7646); therefore, accept H_1: $\rho \neq 0$; correlation coefficient is significant.

21. $z < z_{.05}$ (.86 < 1.96); therefore, accept H_0: $\rho_1 = \rho_2$; correlation coefficients are equal.

22. $z < z_{.01}$ (.425 < 2.576); therefore, accept H_0: $\rho = .40$; belief substantiated.

23. Table value of S (.117) > .5 (.10); therefore, accept H_0: $\rho = 0$; correlation coefficient not significant.

Chapter VII

1. $F_I < F_{.10}$ (2.25 < 9.00); no significant difference between columns (i.e., training periods).
   $F_i < F_{.10}$ (4.00 < 8.5263); no significant difference between rows (i.e., training conditions).

2. $F_I > F_{.01}$ (107.65 > 6.9266); significant difference between columns.
   $F_i > F_{.01}$ (20.60 > 5.9526); significant difference between rows.
   $F_{in} > F_{.01}$ (5.80 > 4.8206); significant interaction.

3. $F_I > F_{.10}$ (43.22 > 3.2888); significant difference between individuals.
   $F_i < F_{.10}$ (2.12 < 3.2888); no significant difference between tests.
   $F_j > F_{.10}$ (16.65 > 3.2888); significant difference between order of tests.

4. $F_i > F_{.05}$ (7.29 > 3.9823); significant difference between adjusted number of mistakes; that is, noise level produces a significant effect.

Chapter VIII

1. $\chi^2 < \chi^2_{.10}$ (.75 < 2.706); therefore, accept H_0: the variables are independent.

2. $\chi^2 > \chi^2_{.20}$ (20.32 > 9.803); therefore, accept H_1: the variables are not independent.

5. $r_s > r_{s(.05)}$ (4 > 1); therefore, accept H_0: there is no difference between stores.

6. $r_s > r_{s(.05)}$ (4 > 1); therefore, accept H_0: $m_x = m_y$; no difference between stores.

7. $r_s > r_{s(.01)}$ $(4 > 0)$; therefore, accept H_0: $m_A = m_B + \$1,000$.

8. $u_{.025} < u < u_{.975}$ $(6 < 9 < 15)$; therefore, accept H_0: $m = 40$.

9. $u_{.025} < u < u_{.975}$ $(3 < 6 < 10)$; therefore, accept H_0: observations are drawn at random from a single population.

10. $110.7 \leq \mu \leq 123.3$.

11. $25.77 \leq \mu \leq 29.23$.

12. $599.1 \leq \sigma^2 \leq 2,184.4$.

13. $.54 \leq p \leq .84$.

14. $-6.88 \leq (\mu_1 - \mu_2) \leq -5.52$.

15. $-2.258 \leq B \leq 13.678$.

16. $.32 \leq \rho \leq .93$.